THE ARCHAEOLOGY OF
LARGE-SCALE MANIPULATION OF PREY

The Archaeology *of* Large-Scale Manipulation *of* Prey

THE ECONOMIC AND SOCIAL DYNAMICS OF MASS HUNTING

EDITED BY

Kristen Carlson *and* Leland C. Bement

UNIVERSITY PRESS OF COLORADO
Louisville

Published by University Press of Colorado
245 Century Circle, Suite 202
Louisville, Colorado 80027

The University Press of Colorado is a proud member of
the Association of University Presses.

The University Press of Colorado is a cooperative publishing enterprise supported, in part, by Adams State University, Colorado State University, Fort Lewis College, Metropolitan State University of Denver, Regis University, University of Colorado, University of Northern Colorado, Utah State University, and Western State Colorado University.

∞ This paper meets the requirements of the ANSI/NISO Z39.48-1992 (Permanence of Paper).

ISBN: 978-1-60732-681-6 (cloth)
EISBN: 978-1-60732-682-3 (ebook)
https://doi.org/10.5876/9781607326823

Library of Congress Cataloging-in-Publication Data

Names: Carlson, Kristen, 1980– editor. | Bement, Leland C., editor.
Title: Archaeology of large-scale manipulation of prey : the economic and social dynamics of mass hunting / edited by Kristen Carlson and Leland Bement C.
Description: Boulder : University Press of Colorado, [2018] | Includes bibliographical references and index.
Identifiers: LCCN 2017037724| ISBN 9781607326816 (cloth) | ISBN 9781607326823 (ebook)
Subjects: LCSH: Hunting, Prehistoric—Social aspects. | Hunting, Prehistoric—Economic aspects. | Hunting and gathering societies—Food. | American bison hunting.
Classification: LCC GN799.H84 A73 2018 | DDC 306.3/64—dc23
LC record available at https://lccn.loc.gov/2017037724

Cover illustrations: Jens Kreutzmann watercolor (ca. mid-1800s) courtesy of the National Museum and Archive of Greenland (*top*); © 2011 by Kristen Carlson (*bottom, left and right*); courtesy of Ulla Odgaard (*bottom, middle*).

Contents

THE ARCHAEOLOGY OF
LARGE-SCALE MANIPULATION OF PREY

An Introduction to Large-Scale Manipulation of Prey

An Economic and Social Discussion

Leland C. Bement

The various studies assembled in this book investigate the prehistoric development of large-scale prey manipulation and cooperative hunting adaptations. Stemming from two symposia offered at the Society for American Archaeology conferences in 2012 and 2013, the topic of large-scale prey manipulation and cooperative hunting continues as an important research topic through time and across regions. The archaeological signature of large-scale hunting adaptations worldwide shares certain characteristics, yet displays a wide diversity of forms. At their core, these various adaptations require the presence of a large number of animals in a predictable location. After meeting this basic requirement, human groups developed a plethora of cooperative hunting technologies to manipulate, trap, and kill this resource. Once developed, these adaptations often become more than simply means to acquire sustenance. In fact, the large-scale manipulation of game often includes complex social and even political attributes. The how and why large-scale hunting evolved in various settings are the core questions of this book.

A cursory review of the literature on large-scale hunting adaptations worldwide reveals a diversity of hunting scenarios and prey animals sought, and covers quite a time depth. These hunting adaptations share a number of characteristics developed to overcome the challenges of large-scale hunting, which, by definition, requires the production of a surplus of resources to provision a large group of people for a short period

DOI: 10.5876/9781607326823.c001

of time. Key problems addressed include scheduling, ensuring the presence of a sufficiently large animal resource, presence of an adequate trap/kill facility (pound, cliff, arroyo, weir, net), a sufficiently large labor force to carry out the kill and processing, and a location with adequate additional resources to support a large gathering. Often accompanying or incorporated into these hunting adaptations are rituals, feasting, and hierarchal divisions of labor either by age, gender, experience, or proven leadership. Ethnographic accounts indicate large-scale hunting scenarios require the cooperation of all members of an extended group or groups, including women and children in the tasks of moving animals toward a containment/kill facility and in the processing of the considerable surplus of animal resource after the successful kill event (Balme, chapter 3 and Odgaard, chapter 4 in this volume; Satterthwait 1987; Verbicky-Todd 1984).

Projecting the attributes of the ethnographic systems back in time and the identification of archaeological signatures for the various components of large-scale cooperative hunts present significant challenges for archaeologists as illustrated by the hunting structure inundated by Lake Huron (O'Shea et al. 2014) or lack of open-air sites in the case of Australia (Balme, chapter 3). As indicated by the scope of subjects covered by the chapters of this book, researchers rely on studies from both archaeological and nonarchaeological sources to draw insight into the organization of large-scale hunting adaptations. To better understand the role of animal behavior, Maxwell and Driver (chapter 5) study the migration patterns of wildebeest in Africa. Although no known prehistoric large-scale hunting ever targeted wildebeest (Speth 2010; Speth et al. 2013), study of the movement of these large grassland grazers provides analogues for other prehistoric species such as the North American bison and European bison. In particular, the assessment of the conditions that lead to the development of migration within ungulate species as well as the nature of such migrations is key for making migrating animals a predictable and reliable resource susceptible to large-scale manipulation and hunting. The studies of Graves (chapter 6) and Carlson and Bement (chapter 7) show how trace element analysis of bison tooth enamel and stable carbon and nitrogen isotopes of bison bone can indicate the extent and character of *Bison antiquus* migrations during the Folsom period. The identification of the bison migration pattern led to the conclusion that Folsom hunters intercepted bison as they migrated through the Beaver River region of northwestern Oklahoma. The concentration of late summer large-scale arroyo traps along a 700 m stretch of the Beaver River provides convincing evidence that the migrating bison provided a large animal resource in a predictable location that was tapped first by Clovis and then repeatedly by Folsom hunters. These studies transform the structure of large-scale bison hunting adaptations from one of following herds across the landscape to one of intercepting migrating herds as they move in predictable patterns across the region. The increased logistics associated with the latter scenario gets to the heart of the development of large-scale hunting adaptations (Speth, chapter 8).

Bryan Hockett and colleagues (2013) studied the manpower required to create the facilities employed in concentrating and trapping animals in the Great Basin (United States). Balme (chapter 3) also provides estimates of the time and effort required to construct nets and fishing embayments. Both of these studies conclude that a communal level of organization was indicated. The construction and maintenance of labor-intensive facilities have profound ramifications in the social development of large-scale hunting adaptations. The social aspects reflected in these facilities can include aspects of ownership, suggest the extent that all members of a group participated in their construction, and provide insight into the amount of manpower required for their construction (Balme, chapter 3; Zedeño, Ballenger, and Murray 2014). Zedeño (chapter 2) argues that group investment in kill facilities eventually led to political agency that identified hunting group territories where core areas and passes were guarded and protected from outside groups. Prehistoric use of structures ranges from the construction of extensive drive lines and pound systems for bison hunting in North America (Carlson and Bement 2013), to construction of winged containment structures or kites in the Near East (Zeder et al. 2013), to manufacture of large game nets in Australia and North America (Balme chapter 3).

The future of large-scale hunting research faces several hurdles, including the development of research tools to aid in the archaeological identification of aggregation sites, social aspects of hunt organization, and the ecological ramifications of these hunts. Graves (chapter 6) and Carlson and Bement (chapter 7) suggest the number of disparate lithic sources represented in the projectile point assemblage indicates the participation of aggregated hunters during Folsom times. Leland C. Bement (2003) suggests the very presence of large-scale kills juxtaposed with small-scale kills is evidence that human aggregations occurred to conduct the large-scale events. It follows that if small kills are the product of dispersed hunters, then large-scale kills are the product of coalesced hunting groups. The proximity of bison jumps, large encampments, and ritual sites during protohistoric times on the northern Plains links various aspects of large-scale bison hunting with group aggregations, ritual behavior, and establishment of territories (Zedeño, chapter 2).

Little archaeological evidence currently exists to identify the hierarchical organization of prehistoric large-scale hunts. Ethnographic studies suggest the presence of spiritual leaders, hunt leaders, and so on, in carrying out the hunt (Verbicky-Todd 1984). As hunt sizes increase, so does the requirement for a larger workforce (Balme, chapter 3). To accommodate the need for more participants, it may be necessary for all members of a group to participate in the hunt. This includes men, women, children, and the aged. How can these various groups be identified archaeologically? If these groups cannot be identified archaeologically, then researchers should err on the side of caution and assume the presence of all able-bodied members of a group rather than just assume the presence of men as some researchers have, including interpretations at the Folsom type-site (Meltzer 2006).

Problems of distributing information and maintaining social order increase as more people are attracted to a large-scale hunting venue, leading to the formation of at least temporary hierarchies as scalar stresses increase (Johnson 1982). Ethnographic accounts describe the formation of such hierarchies to distribute information and maintain control (Kelly 2013; Zedeño, chapter 2). Taboos against individual hunting often accompany large-scale hunting adaptations. Such taboos serve a practical function of not scaring away or dispersing the concentrated animal resource being targeted (Verbicky-Todd 1984).

The ecological ramifications of large-scale hunting adaptations are also hard to detect archaeologically. The effect of large-scale cooperative hunting on prey populations is undoubtedly related to the periodicity of kill events, size of kill events, and the natural carrying capacity of the environment. While repeated large-scale kills have the potential to decimate the prey population in an area, this situation can, in the short term, be averted by staggering the occurrence of such events. In the long term, however, if the intensity of large-scale kills overtakes the ability of the prey species to reproduce and maintain a viable population, then population decline could lead to the extirpation of a species from the region. A case in point is provided by the large-scale hunting of gazelle and possibly onager in the Levant about 6,000 years ago (Zeder et al. 2013). Today in this region all three species of gazelle are endangered and live in small remnant populations. However, 6,000 years ago these animals were the subject of organized, large-scale hunts where migrating herds were diverted to follow stone-lined drive lanes into enclosures today called kites. Melinda Zeder et al. (2013) suggest the 2,000 to 3,000 kites principally employed during the fourth and third millennia BC decimated the steppe animal populations, extirpating them from the Levant. The decline in game animals is accompanied by a decline in kite use. The decline of steppe animals is recorded in the faunal assemblages from the habitation sites of the time. By the end of this era, gazelle and onager bones represent less than 5 percent of the total faunal assemblage (Zeder et al. 2013:121). The massive slaughter of gazelle as they moved between breeding and calving grounds eventually reduced the population below the level of rebound. Zeder et al. credit the social aspect of these kill events with the destruction of these wild animals. The kills targeted wild populations that were no longer needed to provide the bulk of animal products during this time since domesticates functioned in that role. Because the domestic animals were deemed too important, wild animals were sought to provision social events; hence the development of massive kills using drive lanes and containment structures targeting wild animals.

Currently, there is little evidence that hunters were concerned about conserving animal resources by restricting the number of animals taken. This situation is seen in the Levantine example and in North American large-scale bison kill sites. Evidence from the bison jumps on the northwestern Plains and from Folsom-age kills on the southern Plains suggests that an excess of animals were killed. At the Beaver River complex Folsom kill sites, the extent of underused resources at these kills is indicated by the butchering pattern that targeted only the hump and rib meat, leaving over 50 percent of each carcass untouched (Bement 2003, 2010; Johnson and Bement 2009).

Even less archaeological evidence exists that prehistoric hunters altered the landscape to enhance ungulate forage quality, thereby luring them to particular pastures. The use of fire to burn off patches to enhance the growth of new grasses and to attract bison has been proposed for the Late Prehistoric hunting complexes of the North American northwestern Plains (Zedeño, Ballenger, and Murray 2014). The difficulty lies in distinguishing between natural fires and deliberately set fires.

Many of the above-mentioned issues or attributes of large-scale cooperative hunting adaptations are designed to ensure the highest-possible success rates: availability of large numbers of animals; knowledge of prey animal behavior (Carlson and Bement 2013); matching that behavior to available traps/kill locations; availability of a large workforce to carry out all aspects of the hunt, including processing the kill; and availability of knowledgeable leaders. In addition to these aspects, many large-scale cooperative hunting adaptations incorporate rituals designed to ensure a successful outcome (Bement 1999; Kehoe 1999; Verbicky-Todd 1984). Ethnographic accounts of hunting rituals associated with large-scale hunts include the use of buffalo calling stones, painted rocks, and painted bison skulls placed at the entrance to pounds (Verbicky-Todd 1984). Archaeological evidence of rituals associated with large-scale bison hunting includes a painted bison skull in the second kill episode at the Folsom-age Cooper site in Oklahoma (Bement 1999; Bement et al. 1997), a possible bison skull on pedestal at Lake Theo in Texas (Harrison and Killen 1978; Harrison and Smith 1975), a possible shaman pole with offerings at Jones Miller in Colorado (Stanford 1978), and the shaman hut at the Ruby site in Wyoming (Frison 1971). The ritual use of a circular stone structure associated with the Laidlaw antelope trap in southeastern Alberta, Canada, is another example (Brumley 1984:125). Pictographic representations of large-scale bison kills during the Upper Paleolithic in France have been interpreted as ritual representations of several hunts combined into composite scenes, or distilled into basic components such as a massive bison bull charging into a corral (Kehoe 1999). Given what is at stake if the large-scale kill is unsuccessful, it is not surprising that supernatural intervention is sought on behalf of the hunters.

Less tangible aspects of large-scale cooperative hunting ventures occur at the intersection of cooperation and competition. On the one hand, large-scale kills require the cooperation of all participants to follow a set plan (Driver 1990). At the same time, competition exists between participants to advance to filling key roles, including hunt director, spiritual leader, runner (in the case of bison jumps), and net attendants (in the case of net hunters). This competition is present at the highest level. If a cooperative kill is unsuccessful, the leaders risk losing face and the confidence of the followers, who may then seek another venue with other hosts or leaders at a later time (Fawcett 1987).

Discriminating between instances where large-scale hunts move to a new location because of recent failure (host incompetency) and the shift in hunt location because of herd movement or scheduled host reciprocity is currently beyond the capabilities of archaeological techniques. Changes in participant groups may be signaled archaeologically by shifts in the lithic sources represented in the kill assemblages, if each source material is indicative of a separate social unit attending the aggregation (Wilmsen and Roberts 1978).

The spatial requirements of hunting programs have a direct corollary to the number of participants. More animals = more hunters and more organization: not just 1 animal, 1 hunter/killer/butcher, but multiple animals = multiple drivers, spearers (dispatchers), butchers, etc. (Balme, chapter 3). An increase in scale of hunt equates to an increase in participant differentiation and specialization, and the concomitant creation of hierarchies and leadership roles (i.e., scalar stress; Johnson 1982). How these changes in scale manifest archaeologically is one of the major challenges facing future large-scale hunting research. Differentiation and specialization included prekill activities, including scouting, signaling, and directing hunting groups. In addition, studying the tension between cooperation and competition (the requirement for cooperation between participants and the competition to occupy leadership roles) offers an even greater challenge for large-scale hunting research.

CYCLICAL NUCLEATION AT SURPLUS FOOD SOURCES

A central issue to be considered by the future study of large-scale cooperative hunting is to address the question: Why did large-scale cooperative hunting develop in a particular place at a particular time? I personally believe that the why is found in the human need for social gatherings (see Speth, chapter 8 for further discussion). If there is an innate requirement for social interaction, then large social gatherings (termed *aggregations*, *rendezvous*, or *nucleations*; Schaedel 1995) must be provisioned with an adequate food supply to support a larger-than-normal number of people for a specific period of time. Prior to the development of agriculture, the requisite food supply relied on the natural bounty provided by seasonal surpluses of nuts, wild grains, schooling/migrating fish, migrating birds, and so on. Large social gatherings were scheduled to take advantage of periods of food surplus. Large-scale cooperative hunting was only one of several adaptations that were developed by people following patterns of cyclical nucleation at a surplus food source (Carlson and Bement 2013; Zedeño, chapter 2). In areas where surplus nuts or acorns were seasonally available, social aggregations were linked to those resources. In areas where large game was available, large-scale cooperative hunting programs developed. In both scenarios, the technology to acquire and process the various foodstuffs (acorns, bison, rabbits, wild rice, fish) was already developed at the individual level. All that remained was the exponential amplification of resource use at a higher scale.

At some point, the resource changed from one of immediate consumption to one of delayed consumption. This change follows in step with an increase in scale where stored foods are required to provision groups aggregated into extended-stay situations (Zedeño chapter 2; Zedeño, Ballenger, and Murray 2014).

The answer to why cooperative hunting developed can also vary according to scale. At one end of the continuum are the communal gatherings of short duration that rely on a food surplus to provision those gathered over the course of a short period of time, perhaps a couple of weeks. At the other end are communal gatherings that occurred in areas of high resource density that lasted for several months. An example of the former is the single large-scale bison kill of the Folsom-age Beaver River Complex where it is hypothesized that a single large kill provisioned several groups for a period of a week or two. An example of the latter is the multimonth aggregation of several groups in bison wintering grounds by the Blackfeet tribes where multiple large-scale kills were sequentially conducted to provision the group over the course of the winter (Zedeño, Ballenger, and Murray 2014). The variation in scale is reflected in the number of animals killed over the course of the period of aggregation (less than 100 for Folsom times to over 1,000 for Protohistoric times), the extent of butchery (gourmet style of only hump and shoulder for Folsom times to the complete butchering and bone grease rendering for pemmican production as seen for Proto-historic times), and number of people in the aggregation (less than 200 for Folsom period to more than 2,000 for Protohistoric times). When viewed from the perspective of scale, the adaptation exemplifies the hierarchal structure and development outlined by Gregory Johnson (1982) as a response to scalar stress. An increase in scale leads to greater development of hierarchies, leading to greater complexity in social structure. Stress is seen in population pressure, resource pressure, and social pressure, which all contain an element of duration. The longer the period of stress, the more structured the societal response.

Perhaps a closer look is in order at what is meant by social gathering provisioned by a resource surplus. Surplus does not mean the windfall discovery of a beached whale, followed by an impromptu hoedown. Nor is it necessarily a state dinner followed by a royal ball. The social gatherings are planned events. The planning in many instances requires months, if not years, of preparation, including building or maintaining nets, drive lanes, or traps. In many cases the surplus foodstuff may be generated by an exponential increase in local resource exploitation as in the case of rabbit and deer netting. Or it could be the targeting of seasonally specific migrant animals, including caribou/reindeer in northern latitudes (Odgaard, chapter 4; O'Shea et al. 2014), waterfowl in Australia (Satterthwait 1987), gazelle in the Levant (Zeder et al. 2013), and bison on the southern Plains of North America as suggested by trace element and stable isotope analyses (Graves 2010, chapter 6; Carlson and Bement 2013, chapter 7),

The corollary question is: Why did large-scale cooperative hunting cease in areas and after times in the areas where it had developed? The answer to this question probably lies in the realm of ecology. The telltale signs that large-scale hunting waxed and waned is found in the shifts in seasonality of kill sites by time period; the shift in projectile point styles; the hiatus in kill site use over time as seen at Head Smashed In and Vore (Brink 2008; Reher and Frison 1980); the shift in stone tool source; and the composition of trash middens as seen in the Levantine kites (Zeder et al. 2013). It is doubtful that the need to provision a social aggregation ceased to exist, but rather that an alternative surplus foodstuff was required when climatic or ecological conditions removed the existing foodstuff (whether it be plant or animal) from exploitation. It has been argued for large-scale bison hunting on the northwestern Plains of North America that large-scale bison hunting could only occur when bison populations were above a certain threshold and that the threshold was controlled by environmental factors related to bison-carrying capacity (Reher and Frison 1980). When bison numbers were down, large-scale bison hunting ceased. I would offer that research needs to shift to answer the question: What foodstuff surplus replaced bison when bison numbers fell below the threshold required to successfully conduct large-scale cooperative hunts? I doubt that social aggregations ceased. The shift in resource surplus may require altering aggregation schedules to coincide with the seasonal availability of another food source to meet the subsistence requirements for those aggregations.

Is it purely a coincidence that the amount of meat from the Clovis age bison kills at Murray Springs and Blackwater Locality 1, and Jake Bluff are equivalent to or surpass the amount of meat from Clovis-age mammoth kills in these same regions (Bement and Carter 2015:273)? Did Clovis hunters shift to large-scale cooperative bison hunting as a response to fulfill the requirement of a certain level of meat after the extirpation of mammoths? A similar line of inquiry may shed light on the penecontemporaneous occurrence in the Lower Pecos region of Texas (United States) of large-scale resource exploitation of desert succulents (as evidenced by large burned rock middens), communal rabbit hunts and deer netting (as depicted in pictographs), and the bison jump at Bonfire shelter (Turpin 1982, 2004). Did these shifts occur sequentially with the waxing and waning of resources? Or were shifts in the use of these various forms of producing food surpluses predicated on the ecological limitations of each resource to meet the need of provisioning planned social aggregations? And finally, could the recurrence of the use of large-scale cooperative kills belie a shift in the availability of prey densities to the levels required for successful communal kills as in the case of the resurgence of bison kills after hiatuses of over 1,000 years on the North American Plains (Bement and Buehler 1997; Brink 2008; Frison 2004)?

We have come full circle. From the contributions to this volume and other recent publications it is clear that large-scale hunting is as much a social activity as it is a subsistence activity. The social aspect is archaeologically manifest as a line of piled rocks leading to a cliff, or a concentration of bones in arroyo deposits, or a large net stored in a dry cave, or the constructed rock diversions leading to an enclosure. These mundane features are infused with societal complexity. As such, communal hunting at all scales should be relegated to the realm of social organization and integrated with other social activities, particularly those associated with ritual observances and feasting.

The chapters of this book are highly varied in topics covered, time period contexts, and world regions. The eclectic nature of this volume reflects the highly complex social issues that come into play when large-scale hunting adaptations are viewed through a social lens. The contributions to this book, then, find commonality in the organization of large-scale hunting, ranging from understanding how large-scale hunting defines group identity and territories (Zedeño, chapter 2), the ethnographic definition of large-scale hunting organization in Australia (Balme, chapter 3), ethnographic views of caribou hunting in Greenland (Odgaard, chapter 4), developing models of prehistoric prey populations and behavior from modern wildebeest behavior (Maxwell and Driver, chapter 5), determining bison mobility patterns during the Paleoindian period (Graves, chapter 6), and characterizing mobility structure of bison through stable isotopic analysis (Carlson and Bement, chapter 7). Chapter 8 (Speth) presents a retrospective of the social aspects of large-scale hunting adaptations worldwide and discusses the intriguing prospect that projectile point styles go beyond what is functionally necessary to kill large animals and probably developed as a means of signaling group identity and social connectedness. Not only should earlier concepts of large-scale hunting adaptations be brought under the lens, but also, too, should our basic ideas forming the foundations to our understanding of social identities, hunter-gatherer mobility, and technology (Speth, chapter 8). The eclecticism of this volume ensures that all readers will find something useful to their research into large-scale prey manipulation and hunting adaptations worldwide.

REFERENCES CITED

Bement, Leland C. 1999. *Bison Hunting at Cooper Site: Where Lightning Bolts Drew Thundering Herds*. Norman: University of Oklahoma Press.

Bement, Leland C. 2003. "Constructing the Cooper Model of Folsom Bison Kills on the Southern Plains." *Great Plains Research* 13(1):27–41.

Bement, Leland C. 2010. "Replicating Bone Tools and Other Fauno Technologies." In *Designing Experimental Research in Archaeology, Examining Technology through Production and Use*, ed. Jeffrey R. Ferguson, 225–40. Boulder: University Press of Colorado.

Bement, Leland C., and Kent J. Buehler, eds. 1997. "Southern Plains Bison Procurement and Utilization from Paleoindian to Historic." Plains Anthropologist Memoir 29.

Bement, Leland C., and Brian J. Carter. 2015. "From Mammoth to Bison: Changing Clovis Prey Availability at the End of the Pleistocene." In *Clovis: On the Edge of a New Understanding*, ed. Ashley Smallwood and Thomas Jennings, 263–75. College Station: Texas A&M Press.

Bement, Leland C., Marian Hyman, Michael E. Zolensky, and Brian J. Carter. 1997. "A Painted Skull from the Cooper Site: A Folsom Bison Kill in NW Oklahoma." *Current Research in the Pleistocene* 14:6–8.

Brink, Jack. 2008. *Imagining Head Smashed In*. Edmonton, AB: Alberta University Press.

Brumley, John H. 1984. "The Laidlaw Site: An Aboriginal Antelope Trap from Southeastern Alberta." In *Archaeology in Alberta 1983*, ed. David Burley, 96–127. Occasional Paper No. 23. Edmonton, AB: Archaeological Survey of Alberta.

Carlson, Kristen, and Leland Bement. 2013. "Organization of Bison Hunting at the Pleistocene/Holocene Transition on the Plains of North America." *Quaternary International* 297:93–99. https://doi.org/10.1016/j.quaint.2012.12.026.

Driver, Jonathan C. 1990. "Meat in Due Season: The Timing of Communal Hunts." In *Hunters of the Recent Past*, ed. Leslie B. Davis and Brian O. K. Reeves, 11–33. London: Unwin Hyman.

Fawcett, William B. 1987. "Communal Hunts, Human Aggregations, Social Variation, and Climatic Change: Bison Utilization by Prehistoric Inhabitants of the Great Plains." PhD dissertation, Department of Anthropology, University of Massachusetts, Amherst.

Frison, George. 1971. "The Buffalo Pound in North-Western Plains Prehistory: Site 48 CA 302." *American Antiquity* 36 (1): 77–91. https://doi.org/10.2307/278024.

Frison, George. 2004. *Survival by Hunting: Prehistoric Human Predators and Animals Prey*. Berkeley: University of California Press. https://doi.org/10.1525/california /9780520231900.001.0001.

Graves, Adam C. 2010. "Investigating Resource Structure and Human Mobility: An Example from Folsom-age Bison Kill Sites on the U.S. Southern Great Plains." PhD diss., Department of Anthropology, University of Oklahoma, Norman.

Harrison, Billy R., and Kay L. Killen. 1978. *Lake Theo: A Stratified, Early Man Bison Butchering and Camp Site, Briscoe County, Texas*. Special Archeological Report 1. Canyon, TX: Panhandle-Plains Historical Museum.

Harrison, Billy R., and H. C. Smith. 1975. "Excavations at the Lake Theo Site, PPHM-A917." *Panhandle-Plains Historical Review* (Briscoe County, TX) 48:70–106.

Hockett, Bryan, Cliff Creger, Beth Smith, Craig Young, James Carter, Eric Dillingham, Rachel Crews, and Evan Pellegrini. 2013. "Large-Scale Trapping Features from the Great Basin, USA: The Significance of Leadership and Communal Gatherings in Ancient Foraging Societies." *Quaternary International* 297:64–78. https://doi.org/10.1016/j.quaint.2012.12.027.

Johnson, Eileen, and Leland C. Bement. 2009. "Bison Butchery at Cooper: A Folsom Site on the Southern Plains." *Journal of Archaeological Science* 36 (7): 1430–46. https://doi.org/10.1016/j.jas.2009.02.007.

Johnson, Gregory A. 1982. "Organizational Structure and Scalar Stress." In *Theory and Explanation in Archaeology*, ed. C. Renfrew, M. Rowlands, and B. A. Segravees-Whallon, 389–421. New York: Academic Press.

Kehoe, Thomas F. 1999. "Subsistence and Beyond in Upper Paleolithic Bison Economy." In *Le Bison: Gibier et moyen de subsistance des homes du Paléolithique aux Paléoindiens des Grandes Plaines*, ed. J.-Ph. Brugal, F. David, J. G. Enloe, and J. Jaubert, 249–60. Antibes, France: Association Pour La Promotion et la Diffusion des Connaissances Archéologiques.

Kelly, Robert L. 2013. *The Lifeways of Hunter-Gatherers: The Foraging Spectrum*. Cambridge: Cambridge University Press. https://doi.org/10.1017/CBO9781 139176132.

Meltzer, David J. 2006. *Folsom: New Archaeological Investigations of a Classic Paleoindian Bison Kill*. Berkeley: University of California Press.

O'Shea, John M., Ashley K. Lemke, Elizabeth P. Sonnenburg, Robert G. Reynolds, and Brian D. Abbott. 2014. "A 9,000-y-Old Caribou Hunting Structure Beneath Lake Huron." *Proceedings of the National Academy of Sciences*. Early Edition. https://doi.org/10.1073/pnas.1404404111.

Reher, Charles A., and George C. Frison. 1980. "The Vore Site, 48CK302: A Stratified Buffalo Jump in the Wyoming Black Hills." Plains Anthropologist Memoir 16.

Satterthwait, Leonn. 1987. "Socioeconomic Implications of Australian Aboriginal Net Hunting." *Man* 22 (4): 613–36. https://doi.org/10.2307/2803355.

Schaedel, Richard P. 1995. "The Temporal Variants of Proto-State Societies." In *Alternative Pathways to Early States*, ed. Nikolay N. Kradin and Valeri A. Lynsha, 47–53. Vladivostok: Dal'nauka.

Speth, John D. 2010. *The Paleoanthropology and Archaeology of Big-Game Hunting*. New York: Springer. https://doi.org/10.1007/978-1-4419-6733-6.

Speth, John D., Khori Newlander, Andrew A. White, Ashley K. Lemke, and Lars E. Anderson. 2013. "Early Paleoindian Big-Game Hunting in North America: Provisioning or Politics?" *Quaternary International*. https://doi.org/10.1016/j.quaint .2010.10.027.

Stanford, Dennis J. 1978. "The Jones-Miller site: An Example of Hell Gap Bison Procurement Strategy." In *Bison Procurement and Utilization: A Symposium*, ed. L. B. Davis and M. Wilson, 90–97. Plains Anthropologist Memoir 14.

Turpin, Solveig A. 1982. "Seminole Canyon: The Art and the Archeology, Val Verde County, Texas." *Texas Archeological Survey Research Report No. 83*. Austin: University of Texas.

Turpin, Solveig A. 2004. "Cyclical Nucleation and Sacred Space: Rock Art at the Center." In *New Perspectives on Prehistoric Art*, ed. Gunter Berghaus, 51–64. Westport, CT: Praeger.

Wilmsen, Edwin N., and Frank H. H. Roberts, Jr. 1978. *Lindenmeier, 1934–1974: Concluding Report on Investigations*. Contributions to Anthropology 24. Washington, DC: Smithsonian Institution. https://doi.org/10.5479/si.00810223.24.1.

Verbicky-Todd, Eleanor. 1984. "Communal Buffalo Hunting among the Plains Indians." Occasional Paper No. 24. Edmonton, AB: Archaeological Survey of Alberta.

Zedeño, Maria Nieves, Jesse A. M. Ballenger, and John R. Murray. 2014. "Landscape Engineering and Organizational Complexity among Late Prehistoric Bison Hunters of the Northwestern Plains." *Current Anthropology* 55 (1): 23–58. https://doi.org/10.1086/674535.

Zeder, Melinda A., Guy Bar-Oz, Scott J. Rufolo, and Frank Hole. 2013. "New Perspectives on the Use of Kites in Mass-kills of Lavantine Gazelle: A View from Northeastern Syria." *Quaternary International* 297:110–25. https://doi.org/10.1016/j.quaint.2012.12.045.

2

Territory Formation among Ancestral Blackfoot Bison Hunters of the Northwestern Plains

María Nieves Zedeño

In this chapter I discuss processes of territory formation among mobile big-game hunters, in this case the late prehistoric or Old Women's phase (AD 1000–1750) bison hunters of the northwestern Plains, who are in turn considered ancestral to the Blackfoot speakers (Peck 2011:403–8). Territory and territoriality are tackled from a perspective of political agency, which assumes that each action that involves land potentially has political consequences for humans as actors and transformers of the landscape (Zedeño and Anderson 2010). The premise of political agency is that decision-making processes and solutions to problems of land and resource access by hunter communities may in time lead to territory formation.

Essentialist approaches of land and resource use generally view mobility as the antithesis of territoriality. Classic socioevolutionary typologies of the 1960s, which to a greater or lesser extent continue to influence anthropology, categorize big-game hunters as having few, if any, geopolitical concerns; territories are understood as stable, explicit perimeters around a fixed parcel of land—something that people who make a living from the pursuit of mobile prey can rarely afford. Implementation of territorial strategies to protect the homeland is seen as a consequence of intra- and/or intergroup competition and differentiation, which is a characteristic of sedentary groups.[1]

Yet, geopolitics constitute an enduring dilemma among big-game hunters, who must have the flexibility

DOI: 10.5876/9781607326823.c002

to move about the landscape while keeping control over their prime hunting grounds, winter camps, access routes, and sacred sites. The hunters' territorial dilemma is generally resolved through culturally specific strategies ranging from the adoption of defense mechanisms to the development of rights and obligations within and between groups. I argue that northwestern Plains bison hunters structured group territories through the construction of large hunting facilities, effigies, vision quest sites, and monuments, and the reuse of encampments in protected wintering areas. This engineered landscape was permanent and thus visible to friend and foe.

Elsewhere, I have argued for a material definition of territory as the aggregate of places, objects, and resources (Zedeño 1997, 2008); this definition, together with Zedeño and Anderson's developmental approach to hunter-gatherer land tenure (Zedeño and Anderson 2010), is deployed here to develop a model of ancestral Blackfoot territory and territoriality that focuses on mobility and its geopolitical consequences. Taking the communal bison-hunting landscape of the Two Medicine River Valley, Montana, as the focal point, I discuss the relationship between the construction of permanent stone architecture and the formation of territorial identity as recorded in early historical accounts, as well as its implications for the emergence of well-defined aboriginal territories. This perspective contrasts sharply with earlier models of pedestrian big-game hunters (bison hunters in particular) that emphasize high mobility, fluid social structures, and lack of permanent territorial attachments due to the migratory nature of their prey. Not all the pieces of information are in place to demonstrate how and why territorial organization developed among ancestral Blackfoot hunters, or what shape it took before it was recorded in a map. Nevertheless, I attempt to piece together what information is available at various temporal and spatial scales to outline a framework for territory formation.

FRAMEWORK FOR A DISCUSSION OF TERRITORY FORMATION

The traditional, ecological view of pedestrian bison hunters as highly mobile folks with fluid social structures and no territorial attachments to impede their ability to follow migrating bison herds (Frison 1978; Kehoe 1993; Oliver 1962:17; Wheat 1972), dominated Plains archaeology for the better part of the twentieth century. With few notable exceptions (e.g., Bamforth 1988; Kehoe 1960, 1967, 1978; Reher and Frison 1980), updated models of the behavioral and evolutionary ecology of big-game hunters, mostly published in the 1960s through the 1980s (see reviews by Binford 2001 and Kelly 2007) have not had a significant impact on the study of bison hunter society and culture, at least not in the northwestern Plains, where the perplexities of culture history have dominated archaeological practice. Two large-scale studies of bison hunter cultural ecology (Bamforth 1988) and social organization (Fawcett 1987) stood alone until very recently, when Trevor Peck (2004) and Judith Cooper (2008) reevaluated them in light of new paleoenvironmental and archaeological data for the Plains region (also Bamforth 2011).

A phenomenological model of Blackfoot landscape values and territorial attachments has been proposed in the past eight years by Gerry Oetelaar and colleagues (Oetelaar 2006, 2014; Oetelaar and Meyer 2006; Oetelaar and Oetelaar 2011). Their characterization of ancestral Blackfoot land tenure is strongly grounded in historic and ethnographic information pertaining to sacred geography and cultural landscape formation. They argue that repeated movement across the landscape and use of staple resources created attachments to named places that were, in turn, linked by paths and acknowledged in narratives. The Gerald and Joy Oetelaar use this standpoint to explain reuse of a deeply stratified site in the Cypress Hills of southeastern Alberta not simply as the result of localized resource availability, but also of the cultural investment, spiritual energy, and historical memory embodied in this and other sites (Oetelaar and Oetelaar 2006).

Gerald Oetelaar's most recent model (2014) of a territory structured around assiduous movement through time, is novel for the northwestern Plains and a good fit to the character of bison hunters' archaeological record. Yet, phenomenology alone tends to overemphasize homogeneity and long-term continuity in land- and resource-use strategies while downplaying the dynamic and often opportunistic political agency derived from them, thus promoting a view of ancestral Blackfoot conservatism and a sense of timelessness. What this chapter does instead is firmly set foot on the inescapable economic imperative of the hunt and link it to a broader, political and ideological model that incorporates frameworks developed for complex-hunter-gatherer research. As well, the argument integrates elements of Oetelaar's phenomenological approach as these are not only complementary but speak about distinctive components of bison hunter trajectories. Geography, architecture, site layout, resource-use patterns, and portable material culture as well as site reuse and connectivity will be discussed here as appropriate.

Finally, the discussion of a territorial footprint as vast as that of the ancestral Blackfoot necessitates a multiscalar perspective, one that not only looks at the largest spatial distribution of "diagnostic" elements of land use and material culture (e.g., Vickers and Peck 2009), but also focuses on the diversity of focal or core developments in particular areas within the territorial footprint. This chapter presents a brief study of one such development—The Two Medicine River—that I consider to be representative of the majority (if not all) territorial cores of the Blackfoot.

TERRITORY AND TERRITORIALITY

For archaeological purposes it is useful to decouple the concept of territory as the aggregate of land, natural resources, and human modifications, from that of territoriality as the sum of actions and emotions toward a specific space, with emphasis toward influence, regulation, control, and differential access (Zedeño 1997:69; 2008:211; Zedeño and Anderson 2010:11). Both operational definitions, when scrutinized individually, are integral to a discussion of hunter-gatherer organization: the former treats land, resources, and facilities as discrete but interwoven components to which mobile hunters may attach in peculiar ways at different points in time, while the later identifies key connections between land tenure and group identity, values, and sovereignty. That intimate connection among hunter, prey, and hunting ground is not simply economic but also a political tool and a worldview that informs all aspects of hunting culture and society.

Land tenure among terrestrial big-game hunters is defined by mobility; as Bob Kelly (2007) notes, mobility is central to the hunter ethos, both as an ideological value and a survival strategy. Thus, from exploration of new land to naturalization of territorial identity, land tenure may be thought of as reflective of the evolving hunter ethos. This ethos informs exploration and insinuates itself in strategies of colonization and expansion into new or uninhabited landscapes (Rockman 2003; Tolan-Smith 2003:118). This ethos may eventually generate a distinctive land tenure footprint that represents economic and political behaviors and choices as well as worldviews and that may be identified materially across vast areas, as is the case of the Old Women's phase architectural footprint that spread across the northwestern Plains.

At some point in this trajectory, it may become necessary to assert rights over the entrenched landscape by controlling access to cores and movement through pathways. Such thresholds may be internal to the hunting community or the ethnic group, for example, stresses caused by an imbalance between demographic growth and resource availability; or external, such as threats from, and conflict with, unrelated people. If resources are abundant or at least partially predictable, hunters may invest heavily on the landscape. Social investments that promote economic intensification and allow hunters to plan for the future, such as the construction of massive drive-line complexes connected to large gathering basins and bison migration routes, may warrant defense. If the group has the social means and the population mass to assert rights, then territorial identities emerge and defensible perimeters become apparent (Aldenderfer 2010; Fitzhugh 2003).

In a process akin to what R. A. Joyce, J. A. Hendon, and J. Lopiparo call "emplacement"—that is, the deliberate construction of domestic, extractive, and ceremonial facilities (Joyce, Hendon, and Lopiparo 2009)—landscape engineering around valuable places and resources becomes formalized, ritualistic, and strategic, both to express a clear, overarching sense of identity and to optimize land and resource use (Zedeño, Ballenger, and Murray 2014). Likewise, pathways become the focus of control of the movement of people and prey. Political oversight by stable and authoritarian leadership (certain esoteric societies and individual leaders, among the Blackfoot) may be required to organize the group around the defense of valuable cores and pathways.

Eventually, the territory is "naturalized," that is, justified as a god-given right, and specific investments are explained as the products of god's creation (Zedeño and Anderson 2010:21; Zedeño, Hollenback, and Grinnell 2009;). The aboriginal territory of the Blackfoot is naturalized materially and orally; for instance, anthropomorphic effigies characteristic of the Old Women's phase are thought to have been built by the Creator Napi in his own likeness (Vickers and Peck 2009:489) (figure 2.1). Virtually all of the major rivers where massive bison-hunting facilities are located have origin stories associated with them, particularly in relation to the acquisition of the Beaver Bundle in ancient times, and have one or more Napi effigies, zoomorphic effigies, and memorial monuments.

Why are cores so significant in understanding broad territorial organization? I propose that the development of densely engineered landscapes composed of monumental hunting facilities that Old Women's phase hunters planned, built, used repeatedly and maintained, along with large campsites and nondomestic features, represent the solution to political dilemmas these hunters faced in the last millennium before European contact and thus should be considered material evidence of the ancestral Blackfoot's territorial identity. In the remainder of this chapter, I explore the possibility that this process of territorialization of the hunting ground was complete by the time of first European contact.

HISTORIC PEOPLE AND TERRITORIES

According to oral tradition, the ancestral Blackfoot had a stronghold on the sheltered valleys and prairies of Rocky Mountain Front, where they spent the

FIGURE 2.1. *Carol Murray (Piikani Blackfoot) stands by the Old Man Napi Effigy, Madison River Valley, Montana*

colder and most productive hunting months of the year. They, too, blocked mountain passes to impede access to bison herds. However, in the summer they moved east toward the open plain where the large bison herds were to be found. It was during these warmer months that their western neighbors could venture into the foothills in search of straggler herds (Allan Pard, personal communication 2014; Mike Durglo Sr., personal communication, 2014). Such arrangements were only possible during peacetime and likely before the rise of the fur trade in the late eighteenth century. Importantly, recent geographical analysis of more than 1,500 Old Women's phase sites in Alberta, Saskatchewan, and Montana (Bethke 2016) support the traditional history of intensive foothills occupation, coupled with the development of territorial cores on the farther eastern prairie before European contact.

Historic Blackfoot speakers were well known for their aggression toward outsiders. Nestled against the foothills of the Rocky Mountain Front, the rich and remote hunting and wintering grounds of the Blackfoot were dangerous places to neighboring ethnic groups as well as European fur traders (Ewers 1958; Jackson 2000). Early records of the fur trade indicate that the Blackfoot kept traders and trappers at bay by encouraging them to build posts along the northern edge of the confederacy's territory (North Saskatchewan River) rather than inside their core area (Moore 2012; Smyth 2001). Not surprisingly, there is little eyewitness information of this core area before Prince Maximilian of Wied visited the Blackfoot in 1833 (Witte and Gallagher 2008).

Nevertheless, documents dating to the mid-eighteenth century strongly suggest that the Blackfoot were not only populous but also wealthy; they had elaborate social and ritual institutions, means to incorporate captives into society, manage labor and hunting output, and maintain ties and obligations between bands and between divisions of the Blackfoot Confederacy (Ewers 1955; Jackson 2000; Tyrrell 1916). From early accounts it is clear that the Blackfoot territory extended as far south as the Missouri River headwaters; in fact, the "Muddy Indians" were the Piikani division of the confederacy.

Traditional historians regard the presence of the Blackfoot to the south of the Old Man River in southern Alberta as a result of their adoption of the horse. Since the nineteenth century, historians collected conflicting oral traditions and concluded that the Blackfoot did not arrive at the foothills south of the Bow River until after 1730, when they displaced various other groups in their quest for bison and control of the gun and horse trade. For example, Hugh Dempsey cites an oral account of likely Sarsi (Athaphaskan) origin (Dempsey 1994, cited in Peck 2011:373; also Dempsey 2001) to insinuate that in the Protohistoric period the Shoshone controlled the area known historically as the Piikani Blackfoot territory. Paul Raczka (2016), on the other hand, suggests that the Shoshone or Snake Indians ventured north only in the late seventeenth century—a diaspora caused by virgin soil epidemics raging across the Basin-Plateau region of the United States.

The Crow, too, have traditions that point to a stint on the Alberta plains during their migration from the Middle Missouri River to the Yellowstone River basin and adjacent mountain ranges (Graetz and Graetz 2000). The Kootenai and Salish speakers, for their part, have traditions that point to the existence of a Plains band among them that was pushed west into the Rockies by the aggressive Blackfoot, who curtailed the Plateau tribes' access to bison herds through violence or by requesting that they negotiate passage (Teit 1930). Some of these traditions have historical documentation; however, the archaeological record does not necessarily support all of them, as I explain in the sections below.

A piece of evidence for the existence of an ancient Blackfoot territory is the map that Hudson's Bay Company trader Peter Fidler collected in 1801 from a Blackfoot chief known as Ac ko mok ki (Haig 1991; Moodie and Kaye 1977). In his map, Ac ko mok ki clearly showed familiarity with the geography of what may be considered to be the marjority of the Blackfoot territory, extending from the South Saskatchewan River to the Three Forks of the Missouri River.

Oetelaar's (2014; Oetelaar and Oetelaar 2011) model of Blackfoot land use strategies and territorial organization explicitly integrates this map with information on sacred places and cultural resources known through oral tradition, historic records, and archaeology. Using specific named locations in the same map as point of departure, Paul Raczka (2016) examines winter counts and narratives of travel describing intertribal interactions to distinguish between areas controlled by the Blackfoot and areas jointly used by more than one tribe. The resulting territorial map closely matches not only Ac ko mok ki's map (Raczka 2016:19–23) but also the distribution of Old Women's phase material culture as mapped by Roderick Vickers and Trevor Peck (Vickers and Peck 2009) and by Brandi Bethke (2016) (figure 2.2).

Oetelaar, Raczka, and Bethke each take mobility into account to develop their reconstructions of political agency and territoriality among the Blackfoot. Raczka's approach is fundamentally historic and ethnographic, while Oetelaar projects oral tradition and historical accounts into the prehistoric past. While incredibly valuable, these reconstructions do not address the rise of territorial organization, but only its consequences, namely, the existence of a clear Blackfoot territorial identity that has been naturalized through stories of emergence and divine intervention. Bethke's model, on the other hand, explicitly models access to water and wood as well as landscape complexity (pasture in particular) to ascertain the location of residential and extractive cores within the distribution of Old Women's phase sites before and after the adoption of the horse. Significantly, these three models conform closely to the aboriginal view of what constituted Blackfoot territory in the past 1,000 years, until the establishment of Indian reservations in Canada and the United States.

THE PEOPLE WITHIN: OLD WOMEN'S PHASE

In the northwestern Plains, the onset of communal bison kills that extensively utilize a driving technology dates to the Middle Prehistoric period (ca. 5,000 years ago, though some may argue that communal hunting began much earlier on the basis of findings at Head-Smashed-In), flourishing among groups known for their Besant dart points and effective kills (ca. 1,500–2,000 years ago) (Frison 1991:199; Peck 2011:241). It has been suggested that, with the addition of the Avonlea bow and arrow technology around AD 1200, mass killing success may have improved dramatically (Kornfeld, Frison, and Larson 2010:260, 268; Kehoe 1978; Reeves 1990:168). The distinctive Avonlea horizon, known for its exquisitely made arrow points, spread from east to west across the northern Plains. The bow and arrow technology is thought to have been

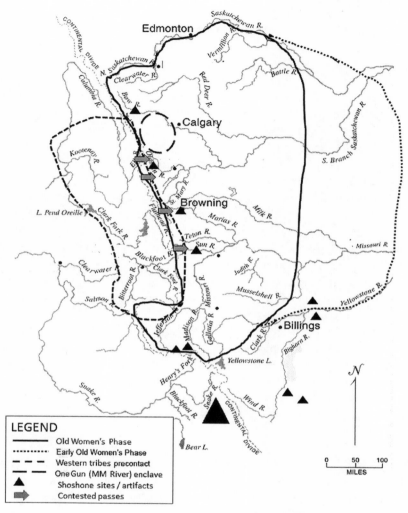

FIGURE 2.2. *Composite map showing the distribution of Old Women's phase, One Gun and Shoshone artifacts*

initially restricted to certain individuals or groups, eventually becoming more widely available through transfer of technological knowledge, purchase of bows and arrows, or emulation (Brink and Dawe 1989; Walde 2006a).

Organizational change among bison hunters is associated with the Avonlea horizon. Brian Reeves (1983; 1990:185–89) suggests that the combination of

driving technology, storage technology, and the bow and arrow was the cata-
lyzing factor for economic intensification and internal differentiation beginning as early as 2,000 years ago; however, the full impact of this catalysis is not
visible archaeologically until after AD 1000 (Brink and Dawe 1989:296). While
Avonlea shows an increasing preference for bison hunting supplemented by
other animal foods in some areas, specialized intensive bison hunting is characteristic of the subsequent Old Women's phase and complex (AD 1000–1750)
(Peck 2011:373). This phase is currently considered to be an amalgamation of
local and nonlocal people (or of cultural knowledge) associated with Middle
Prehistoric period game-driving systems and Avonlea weapon technologies
(Peck 2011:455).

Communal kills predating AD 1000 differed from subsequent kills in
important ways, and may thus hold the key to unpacking Blackfoot territory
formation. First, earlier kills most commonly involved luring a few animals
into pounds or traps rather than cliff jumps, though these were used, notably
at Calderwood, Alberta (Brink 2008; Peck, personal communication, 2012).
Second, the classic jump with its extensive cairn-lined driving systems pre-
dominated in the Late Prehistoric period. Second, the ability to process large
quantities of transportable and storable dry meat and pemmican made it possible to take full advantage of large bison harvests, but its effect on surplus
production and trading power is not visible until the Late Prehistoric period,
when the expansion of rock-ring encampments and construction of multiple
drive-line systems and jumps in given areas suggest an increase in group size
(Bethke et al. 2016).

And third, the few known Middle Prehistoric processing sites show moderate to low carcass-processing intensity, which points to preference for meat
retrieval (Peck 2011:322). In contrast, transitional sites and Late Prehistoric
occupations in multicomponent sites such as Head-smashed-In (Brink 2008)
generally exhibit extensive deposits filled with crushed bone, fat-rendering
features, and berry-smashing stones and other tools associated with pemmican production and hide processing (Brink and Dawe 1989; Brink 2008).
Importantly, such intensification is also coeval with the establishment of the
vast Middle Missouri trade network (Mitchell 2013) and with the presence of
enclaves or colonies from the Middle Missouri area in the midst of Blackfoot
territory (Zarrillo and Kooyman 2006).

Taken together, all these changes strongly suggest that ecological, demographic, and cultural conditions were ripe for economic intensification that
required substantial investment in landscape engineering, as well as development of mechanisms of social and geopolitical control. Unfortunately,

anyone who tackles this line of research faces some limitations. Surface stone architecture that characterizes bison hunter landscapes is difficult to date and even more difficult to integrate with excavated sites without determining appropriate temporal and spatial scales in the first place. There is a dearth of systematic surveys and excavations that focus on scales commensurate with the expanse of land that bison and their human predators actually had to traverse in pursuit of survival. These limitations, coupled with outdated models of terrestrial big-game hunters territories (or lack thereof) have relegated bison hunters to the backseat of critical theoretical advances in hunter-gatherer studies.

Enter recent, broad-scale research on the distribution of sites with diagnostic material culture by Vickers and Peck (Vickers and Peck 2009; Peck 2011), Bethke (2016), Dale Walde (2004; Walde et al. 1995), and Cody Newton (2011) on the distribution of Old Women's, One Gun or Middle Missouri, and protohistoric Shoshone material culture, respectively, which together help lay a foundation for estimating the geographical extent of ancestral Blackfoot territory. Vickers and Peck mapped material culture diagnostic of the Old Women's phase, focusing on the occurrence of massive hunting complexes, side-notched projectile point varieties, ceramics, anthropomorphic effigies, "death lodge" medicine wheels, and ammonite fossils. They convincingly delineate what could be interpreted as a territory used largely, or perhaps exclusively, by Old Women's phase hunters, which extends from the upper Saskatchewan River to the Three Forks of the Missouri River (Raczka 2016:19). Although it does not include a sufficient number of Late Prehistoric sites in Montana, theirs is the first explicit and archaeologically founded acknowledgment of a culturally distinctive, late prehistoric/protohistoric spatial unit that roughly matches the boundaries of the Blackfoot aboriginal territory, as defined historically.[2]

To counteract various arguments that the Montana portion of the Blackfoot territory was in the hands of others in the centuries leading to the arrival of the horse in this area, I have overlaid Cody Newton's distribution of Shoshone material culture (see figure 2.2). Interestingly, published instances of diagnostic Shoshone materials stop at the boundary of the Old Women's phase distribution, with few exceptions—for instance, sites where Shoshone projectile points have been found overlaying an Old Women's phase site (Peck, personal communication, 2017). In contrast, Walde's (2004) distribution map for the One Gun phase sites, thought to represent short-lived enclaves of Middle Missouri Hidatsa people, indicates that these were established within the heartland of the Siksika or Blackfoot proper. This isn't surprising, given the prehistoric and historic evidence of interaction between the Blackfoot hunters and the Mandan and Hidatsa farmers, which involved trade in bison products and agricultural products (Brink and Dawe 1989; Binnema 2004; Smyth 2001; Zedeño 2017) as well as exchange or transfer of ritual knowledge and objects, in particular bird feathers (Zedeño 2017), black pipes, and bundles (Toupal and Hollenback 2008). Thus, while it many have been possible for other ethnic groups to enter Blackfoot territory in precontact times, it must be acknowledged that the ancestral Blackfoot were present in Montana before members of these groups (e.g., hunters, war parties) ventured into it.

Finally, James Teit's description of Kootenai and mountain Salish hunting territories includes the northern Rocky Mountain Front (Teit 1930:303–5). However, according to Claude Schaeffer's (1934) study of Kootenai society and culture, as well as more recent archaeological work by Reeves (2006), neither archaeological nor ethnographic data demonstrate a distinctive or exclusive Kootenai presence east of the Continental Divide, at least for the period of interest. Simply put, if Old Women's phase sites (particularly drive lines, campsites, and effigies) in Alberta and Saskatchewan are generally assigned a Blackfoot affiliation, then so should those found in Montana as far south as the Three Forks region, as their distinctive layout and architectural details are the same in all these provinces. The distribution of diagnostic material culture supports Dale's contention that the geopolitical organization of Late Prehistoric bison hunters in the northwestern Plains involved roughly bounded territories, probably with joint use areas along the boundaries (Walde 2006b). The earliest observation of a defended boundary comes in fact from Hudson's Bay Company trader Henry Kelsey, who in 1691 witnessed a conflict along the eastern boundary of the Blackfoot territory (Bell 1928). Territorial circumscription is visible on this boundary, as competing groups (Atsina, Cree, and Assiniboine) moved into west-central Saskatchewan.

TWO MEDICINE RIVER: A CASE FOR TERRITORIAL ORGANIZATION

Located within the Old Women's phase culture area, the Two Medicine River Valley is one of at least a dozen permanent streams that run from the Rocky Mountain Front on the west to the open prairie on the east, emptying into a major tributary of the Missouri River. The prehistoric landscape was reticulated by a combination of streams and coulees on the foothills and adjacent that created pathways of movement for people and bison. Between streams, huge gathering basins sprinkled with springs and kettle lakes attracted substantial herds during the fall and winter, making this an ideal landscape for the development of specialized communal bison hunting and population aggregation (Reher 1983).

The Two Medicine River basin was traversed sporadically by hunters beginning in the Paleoindian–Early Middle Prehistoric transition (Kehoe 2001), but very little information exists about the timing of colonization of the entire valley by communal bison hunters. A few indicators of Late Middle Prehistoric and transitional exploration by groups carrying Besant or Avonlea technology weaponry have been found in Upper Two Medicine River and in Badger Creek 10 km to the south (Davis 1972). Archaeologists characterize Besant and Avonlea as representing small groups of wide-ranging, highly mobile hunters who pursued bison and other migratory big game (Walde 2006a); they are certainly represented in small hunting and fishing camps in the St. Mary River and upper Two Medicine River (Kehoe 2001; Zedeño et al. 2016). In contrast, Late Prehistoric hunter groups appear to have dwelled in place for longer periods of time, leaving more permanent remains of their presence, as Kehoe's initial surveys of the Blackfeet Indian Reservation indicate (Kehoe 1960, 1967; Lewis 1947).

Because Avonlea hunters were ancestral to Old Women's, it is likely that the earlier hunter groups may have left a path of exploration that succeeding generations of hunters used as guidelines for colonization. The Upper Kutoyis ritual area has one Besant projectile point as well as Avonlea's and early Old Womens' age structures (Feathers 2012; Feathers et al. 2015; Zedeño, Ballenger, and Murray 2014:table 2), but no Avonlea projectile points have been found on its surface. Classic Avonlea sites are more common downriver, along the Marias basin.

However tenuous, these remains suggest that hunting groups colonized the valley at the onset of climatic conditions that were ideal for specialization and intensification. Judith Cooper's (2008) research indicates that beginning in AD 600, or during Avonlea times, climatic conditions fostered the expansion of rich pastures in the northwestern Plains, a trend that continued until the historic period. I suggest that the foothills irrigated by the Two Medicine River were colonized during this period, with entrenchment taking root after AD 980, which is the earliest date obtained for a hunting complex. Between AD 1350 and 1650, the valley was emplaced through the decisive construction of massive hunting complexes organized in five clusters evenly spaced along the valley (Zedeño, Ballenger, and Murray 2014). The Two Medicine chronology shows that these sites were used consistently throughout the early Equestrian period (ca. 1730–1800) and perhaps later.

Systematic GPS mapping of surface architecture and exposed bison bone beds along the Two Medicine River was undertaken in 2009–12 by the Kutoyis Archaeological Project (Zedeño, Ballenger, and Murray 2014). The survey was designed to relocate and record sites originally mapped by Thomas Kehoe (1960, 1967) and utilize resulting data to identify other topographically similar localities with potential for unreported containing remains of bison hunting. The surveyed area comprised the central portion of the river valley and adjacent uplands, from the mouth of the South Fork of Two Medicine to the mouth of Badger Creek (48 km in length). The ridges of the upper valley are too high and perilous to drive bison efficiently, while the lower valley is a narrow, steep canyon. Both upper and lower valleys were explored but deemed of low potential for site recovery because of topographic constraints and extensive plowing of the uplands toward the river mouth. The survey resulted in the documentation of seven bison drive-line systems and four hunting complexes (Zedeño, Ballenger, and Murray 2014). Only one site at the river mouth was integrated in this study (Thirty Knot, Ferguson 2007). In addition, a large campsite located on Mission Lake, 8 km to the north of Kutoyis, was also mapped in its entirety. Relevant to reconstructing territory formation are the following results from the survey:

Indicators of Emplacement

All sites are located on both sides of the river and near the mouth of its major tributaries. Pairs of drive-line systems face each other across the river. These pairs seem to be spaced evenly along the middle valley (figure 2.3). Thirty Knot originally was one of a pair of facing sites (Kehoe 1967), but the second site was destroyed by plowing. Remnant segments of drive-line may be found between Kutoyis and Thirty Knot but these are not sufficient to reconstruct funnel patterns. The mapped sites, nonetheless, represent 30 percent of the entire length of the river. Notably, the geography is best suited for bison driving and jumping on the central valley, where the large sites have been preserved. This is true for neighboring drainages, notably Cut Bank Creek (Kehoe 1967; Zedeño et al. 2017).

Indicators of High Investment and Shared Practice

Architecture along the river is remarkably homogeneous, with substantial investment in double-course rock rings as large as 8–10 m in diameter (lodge infrastructures) as well as drive-line systems made of aligned rock piles. The number of cairns built for marking each driving funnel ranges from the low

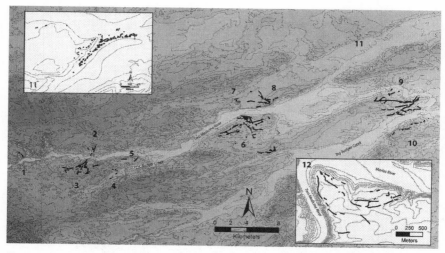

FIGURE 2.3 *Distribution of communal bison kill sites along the Two Medicine River: (1) South Fork, (2) Magee, (3) Stranglewolf, (4) Racine, (5) Runningfisher, (6) Mission, (7) Spring Coulee, (8) Two Medicine/Schultz, (9) Kutoyis, (10) Lower Badger, (11) Mission Lake, (12) 30 Knot/Lower Enclosure (from Zedeño, Ballenger, and Murray 2014:32)*

hundreds to over 8,000. Within campsites, size variation in domestic structures and clustering was observed, suggesting differential distribution of large lodges as well as the existence of multilodge households toward the center of encampments. More than 1,000 rock rings have been thus far recorded but many more remain unmapped. The same is true for ancillary features.

Indicators of Ritualization of the Hunting Ground

In addition to memorial monuments built within the domestic space and oversized, possible lodges for esoteric society rituals, there are three types of dedicated ritual spaces in close association to drive-line systems: at least one dead lodge medicine wheel, effigies, and vision quest sites. These have not been recorded in their entirety. Yet, tipi rings located in close proximity to the terminus of the driving funnels were recorded in several sites, conforming to oral traditions that speak of ceremonies being carried out shortly in advance of the pedestrian bison drive (Raczka 2016:89–93).

Evidence of Broadly Shared Temporality

Artifacts are scarce on site surfaces, but a few projectile points and abundant split-cobble tools may be dated to the Late Prehistoric period. Confirming this age are OSL and C14 dates from the Kutoyis Complex as well single C14 dates from four of the largest drive-line systems with exposed stratified bone beds dating between AD 980 and AD 1690, with two OSL dates around AD 1400–1700, and another two in the early AD 1800s. C14 dates recovered from hearths in the processing camp generally fall between AD 1350–1650 (Bethke et al. 2016; Feathers et al. 2015; Zedeño, Ballenger, and Murray 2014). Thus, the vast majority of the chronological assays available for the valley support intensive use of the valley in the three centuries preceding European contact. It is possible that, sometime between AD 1650 and 1730, Shoshone hunting parties utilized some of these jumps when the Blackfoot were in other areas of the territory; however, there are not enough archaeological indicators to ascertain this possibility.

Indicators of Valley-Scale Intensification

Kutoyis and four other sites contain evidence of multiple, stratified bone beds, many of which were burned. Two of these sites also have evidence of grassland burning apparently associated with the period of intensive bison hunting. As part of the Kutoyis Archaeological Project, Christopher Roos and colleagues (2014) systematically sampled on- and off-site soil columns and conducted a series of analyses involving stratigraphic radiocarbon dating, magnetic susceptibility, and measurements of charcoal and phosphorous concentrations in alluvial and colluvial deposits (Roos, Zedeño, Hollenback 2014). This research indicates that peak fire and postfire erosion activity occurred during the use of landscape-scale archaeological features such as drive-line systems for intensive, communal bison hunting (ca. AD 1350–1650). In other words, the intensity of grassland management during the period of intense bison hunting in the valley actually contributed to landscape change.

At a smaller scale, the encampment immediately below the Kutoyis kill site contains dozens of hearth features identified with a magnetometer. Excavation and comparative analysis of bone remains recovered from the bone beds and the processing camp showed that these hearth features are associated with intensive processing of bone for marrow extraction for the manufacture of pemmican (Bethke et al. 2016); the presence of macrofloral berry remains and berry mashers confirms this interpretation. Other activities associated with these features include stone tool repair, bead working, and red paint preparation (Zedeño, Ballenger, and Murray 2014).

Evidence Suggestive of Demographic Growth

The surveyed area is 288 sq. km. The average number of domestic structures per surveyed campsite is 240. Even accounting for accretional construction over a period of time, this average, which is characteristic of the upper Missouri Basin, far exceeds the oft-used maximum of forty structures per encampment elsewhere (Deaver et al. 1999; Oetelaar 2003).[3] If the size of Late Prehistoric bison hunter groups approached that of the historic Blackfoot bands that wintered on the central Two Medicine River (average of 300 souls per band, Schaeffer and Schaeffer 1934), then population pressure during the harsh northern winters, combined with six-month wintering seasons, would have been enough stimulus for competition and concomitant boundary-making around valuable cores and access pathways.

There is no evidence of resource diversification during this time period, at least not from excavated deposits. It is possible that the sites in the valley were not reused every year or even every decade, but the valley at large was assiduously occupied during the Late Prehistoric period, and sites were intensively used whenever hunters settled in their vicinity.

CONCLUSION

Old Women's phase sites recorded by the KAP represent a territorial core so productive and so invested that it was likely worth defending from intruders; in fact, the Two Medicine River is the scenario of the 1806 gunfight between the Piikani Blackfoot and the Meriwether Lewis party of the Corps of Discovery (Ewers 1958). Territorial cores such as this had large gathering basins on the uplands connected by stone drive lines with localities suited for pushing bison herds off the cliff or for impounding, and ample space for processing and other domestic activities near a source of firewood and water. Variables such as direction of prevailing winds, exposure, and aspect of the kill location were also important hunters' considerations.

Significantly, the highest density of Late Prehistoric bison kill sites and large campsites coincide with bison winter grounds. This settlement pattern, along with fetal bones recovered from excavations at the Kutoyis site, supports Arthur's 1975 original proposal and supporting data presented by Michael Quigg (1978) and Vickers (1991), among others, that pedestrian mass kills orchestrated by large groups of people, probably entire bands and even band aggregations, were primarily conducted during the coldest months of the year, when large quantities of meat could be safely stored on ice until needed or until processed into pemmican. A cursory visit to what became the aboriginal Blackfoot territory in Montana is sufficient to impress upon the visitor that these hunters had access to immense gathering basins with plentiful water, shelter, wood, and edible plants (especially berries needed to process and store bison meat as pemmican). Equally important, the topography of the foothills lent itself to the siting of highly efficient kill sites, many of which were repeatedly used until the historic period. Similar cores may be found to the north, in Alberta and Saskatchewan (Bethke et al. 2016; Peck 2011).

Was this incredibly rich hunting ground coveted by more than one ethnic group? There are fifteen passes connecting both sides of the Rocky Mountains and providing access to the eastern streams; oral histories recorded in the nineteenth century indicate that many such passes (e.g., the Marias Pass) near Two Medicine were scenarios of endemic warfare between the Blackfeet and the western tribes (Jackson 2000). Other passes (e.g., the Sun River Pass near one of the most heavily occupied basins in prehistoric and historic times [Fawcett 1987]) were negotiated with those who wanted access to summer bison hunting grounds in the open prairie. And lest we forget, there is the Missouri River as the most significant pathway of movement from the Rockies to the Mississippi River. Thus the potential for resource competition, circumscription, and territorialization of hunting grounds was considerable for the centuries prior to European contact. The attachment of the Blackfoot to their territory became clear once the first European traders and their native companions attempted unsuccessfully to penetrate beyond the confines of its boundaries (Moore 2012).

Yet another facet of land tenure and territorial circumscription that has yet to be explored systematically is that ancestral Blackfoot bands were attached to specific drainages within the Old Women's phase culture area. From historic records, it is known that the middle Two Medicine River Valley was the wintering ground of two large (100–300 members each) Piikani Blackfoot bands: Grease Melters and Lone Eaters (Schaeffer and Schaeffer 1934), who owned the sites we have been investigating and used them interchangeably depending on the hunting conditions and location of the herds. A third, unnamed band wintered near the confluence of Two Medicine and the Marias River. Each of these bands had their own hunting complexes. A similar pattern of band associations to certain winter hunting grounds was reported for Piikani bands along the Milk River, Cut Bank Creek, Teton River, Sun River, and Three Forks of the Missouri. The same may be said for North Peigan, Blood, and Siksika bands to the north, each of whom had preferences in the choice of camping and hunting locations (Allan Pard and Jerry Potts, personal communication, 2016).

We suggest that territory formation during the Old Women's phase was multiscalar: territories were likely formed both around regional wintering areas as well within them. Geopolitical boundaries between ethnic groups perhaps characterized the outermost perimeters, whereas social boundaries and "permissible accommodations" were likely established between divisions of the same ethnic group, and even between bands of the same division. In the 1890s, Walter McClintock (1999:438) was told by the valley's bison hunters that, depending on the location of the herds, the Two Medicine bands required access to specific drive-line systems on either side of the river to achieve a successful hunt. Thus, negotiation of access to other bands' sites, as well as interband cooperation during very large drives, was essential to sustain intensive harvesting for subsistence and trade. If valuable cores and pathways connecting them needed to be defended against intruders, then the bands would need to come together under common leadership.

In conclusion, the results of recent research on the Two Medicine River Valley strongly suggest that processes beyond episodic bison hunting and low-input, long-term architectural accretion are responsible for the archaeological record preserved there. It is currently not possible to fully characterize demography and trace the trajectory of territory formation without first refining the Old Women's phase chronology and outlining what constitutes "social time" on the valley. Concerted effort among northern Plains archaeologists must be undertaken to fill in knowledge gaps so blaringly pointed out in Vickers and Peck's (2009) maps of the Old Women's phase culture area and in Bethke's (2016) evaluation of site records available for Montana. Site records, land owner surveys, interviews with emeritus archaeologists, and pedestrian reconnaissance are needed to create a working database that will illuminate patterns of land tenure and territorial organization far beyond that is currently possible, as suggested in this chapter.

Finally, it is necessary to begin an archival and field investigation regarding defensive strategies that may have been in place among ancestral Blackfoot hunters; the historic record is sparse but clear about the construction of defensive "forts" but the prehistoric record remains silent in this regard.

NOTES

1. The archaeological and anthropological literature of territory and territoriality has been reviewed in detail by Zedeño (1997, 2008; Zedeño and Anderson 2010; Zedeño, Hollenback, and C. Grinnell 2009) and thus is not recounted in this chapter.

2. It is useful to check the letter of the Fort Laramie Treaty of 1851, as this is the official acknowledgment of aboriginal Blackfoot territorial boundaries. http://digital
.library.okstate.edu/kappler/vol2/treaties/sio0594.htm#mn9

3. This disparity may be a function of gross underestimation of the number of domestic features due to sampling bias and right-of-way surveys.

REFERENCES CITED

Aldenderfer, Mark. 2010. "Gimme that Old Time Religion: Rethinking the Role of Religion in the Emergence of Social Inequality." In *Pathways to Power: New Perspectives on the Emergence of Social Inequality*, ed. T. D. Price and G. Feinman, 77–94. Lincoln: University of Nebraska Press. https://doi.org/10.1007/978-1-4419-6300-0_4.

Arthur, G. A. 1975. "An Introduction to the Ecology of Early Historic Communal Bison Hunting among the Northern Plains Tribes." Archaeological Survey of Canada Paper 37. Ottawa: National Museums of Canada.

Bamforth, Douglas B. 1988. *Ecology and Human Organization on the Great Plains*. New York: Plenum. https://doi.org/10.1007/978-1-4899-2061-4.

Bamforth, Douglas B. 2011. "Origin Stories, Archaeological Evidence, and Postclovis Paleoindian Bison Hunting on the Great Plains." *American Antiquity* 76 (01): 24–40. https://doi.org/10.7183/0002-7316.76.1.24.

Bell, Charles N. 1928. *The Journal of Henry Kelsey, 1691–1692*. Manitoba Historical Society Transactions Series 2 (4). Winnepeg: Manitoba Historical Society.

Bethke, Brandi. 2016. "Dog Days to Horse Days: Evaluating the Rise of Nomadic Pastoralism among the Blackfoot." PhD dissertation, School of Anthropology, University of Arizona, Tucson.

Bethke, Brandi, María Nieves Zedeño, Geoffrey Jones, and Matthew Pailes. 2016. "Complementary Approaches to the Identification of Bison Processing for Storage at the Kutoyis Complex, Montana." *Journal of Archaeological Science: Reports*. Online corrected proof, May 24. https://doi.org/10.1016/j.jasrep.2016.05.028.

Binford, Lewis R. 2001. *Constructing Frames of Reference: An Analytical Method for Archaeological Theory Building Using Hunter-gatherer and Environmental Data Sets*. Berkeley: University of California Press.

Binnema, Theodore. 2004. *Common and Contested Ground*. Norman: University of Oklahoma Press.

Brink, Jack W. 2008. *Imagining Head-Smashed-In*. Edmonton, AB: Athabasca University Press.

Brink, Jack W., and Robert Dawe. 1989. *Final Report of the 1985 and 1986 Field Season at Head-Smashed-In Buffalo Jump, Alberta*. Edmonton, AB: Archaeological Survey of Alberta.

Cooper, Judith. 2008. "Bison Hunting and Late Prehistoric Subsistence Economies in the Great Plains." PhD dissertation, Southern Methodist University, Dallas.

Davis, Leslie B. 1972. "The Prehistoric Use of Obsidian in the Northwestern Plains." PhD dissertation, University of Calgary, Calgary.

Deaver, Ken, Lynelle Peterson, and Timothy E. Roberts. 1999. *Class I Investigations of Shallow Stone Feature Sites in Central Montana*. Vol. 8. Cultural Investigations along the Montana Segment of the Express Pipeline. Billings, MT: Ethnoscience.

Dempsey, Hugh A. 1994. *The Amazing Life of Calf Shirt and Other Blackfoot Stories*. Saskatoon: Fifth House Publishers.

Dempsey, Hugh A. 2001. "Blackfoot." In *Handbook of North American Indians*. Vol. 13, Plains, ed. R. DeMallie, 604–28. Washington, DC: Smithsonian Institution Press.

Ewers, John C. 1955. "The Horse in Blackfeet Indian Culture: With Comparative Material from Other Western Tribes." Smithsonian Institution Bureau of American Ethnology, Bulletin 159. Washington, DC: Government Printing Office.

Ewers, John C. 1958. *The Blackfeet: Raiders of the Northwestern Plains*. Norman: University of Oklahoma Press.

Fawcett, William Bloys, Jr. 1987. "Communal Hunts, Human Aggregations, Social Variation, and Climatic Change: Bison Utilization by Prehistoric Inhabitants of the Great Plains." PhD dissertation, University of Massachusetts, Amherst.

Feathers, James. 2012. "Luminescence Dating of Anthropogenic Rock Structures in the Northern Rockies and Adjacent High Plains, North America: A Progress Report." *Quaternary Geochronology* 10 (July):399–405. https://doi.org/10.1016/j.quageo.2011.11.006.

Feathers, James, María Nieves Zedeño, Lawrence Todd, and Stephen Aaberg. 2015. "Dating Stone Alignments by Luminescence." *Advances in Archaeological Practice* 3 (04): 378–96. https://doi.org/10.7183/2326-3768.3.4.378.

Ferguson, David. 2007. "A Class III Cultural Resource Inventory of the Montana-Alberta TIE Ltd., Proposed Transmission Line: Preferred Route, Glacier, Pondera, Teton, Chouteau and Cascade Counties, Montana." Report prepared for AMEC Earth and Environmental, Helena, Montana, and Montana-Alberta TIE, Ltd., Calgary. Butte, MT: GCM Services.

Fitzhugh, Ben. 2003. *The Evolution of Complex Hunter-gatherers: Archaeological Evidence from the North Pacific*. New York: Plenum. https://doi.org/10.1007/978-1-4615-0137-4.

Frison, George. 1978. "Animal Population Studies and Cultural Interference." *Plains Anthropologist* 23 (82, pt.2): 44–52.

Frison, George. 1991. *Prehistoric Hunters of the Great Plains*. San Diego, CA: Academic Press.

Graetz, Rick, and Susie Graetz. 2000. *Crow Country: Montana's Crow Tribe of Indians*. Billings. Northern Rockies Publishing Company.

Haig, Brian. 1991. *Journal of a Journey Overland from Buckingham House to the Rocky Mountains in 1792 and 93*. Lethbridge, AB: Historical Research Centre.

Jackson, John C. 2000. *The Piikani Blackfeet.* Missoula, MT: Mountain Press Publishing Company.

Joyce, R. A., J. A. Hendon, and J. Lopiparo. 2009. "Being in Place: Intersections of Identity and Experience on the Honduran Landscape." In *Archaeology of Meaningful Places,* ed. B. Bowser and M. N. Zedeño, 53–72. Salt Lake City: University of Utah Press.

Kehoe, Alice. 1993. "How the Ancient Peigans Lived." *Research in Economic Anthropology* 14:85–107.

Kehoe, Thomas F. 1960. "Stone Tipi Rings in North-Central Montana and the Adjacent Portion of Alberta, Canada." *Bureau of American Ethnology Bulletin* 173:421–73.

Kehoe, Thomas F. 1967. "The Boarding School Bison Drive Site." *Plains Anthropologist* 12 (35): 1–165.

Kehoe, Thomas F. 1978. "Paleo-Indian Bison Drives: Feasibility Studies." *Plains Anthropologist* 23 (82, pt. 2): 79–83.

Kehoe, Thomas F. 2001. "The Billy Big Spring Site, Montana." *Archaeology in Montana* 42 (2): 27–40.

Kelly, Robert L. 2007. *The Foraging Spectrum: Diversity in Hunter-Gatherer Lifeways.* Washington, DC: Smithsonian Institution Press.

Kornfeld, Marcel, George Frison, and Mary Lou Larson. 2010. *Prehistoric Hunter-Gatherers of the High Plains and Rockies.* Walnut Creek, CA: Left Coast Press.

Lewis, H. P. 1947. "Buffalo Kills of Montana." Manuscript on file at National Park Service, Midwestern Archaeological Center, Lincoln.

McClintock, Walter. 1999. *The Old North Trail: Life, Legends and Religion of the Blackfeet Indians.* Lincoln: University of Nebraska Press.

Mitchell, Mark. 2013. *Crafting History in the Northern Plains.* Tucson: University of Arizona Press.

Moodie, D. W., and Barry Kaye. 1977. "The Ac ko mok ki Map." *The Beaver* (Spring):4–15.

Moore, Kaytlin. 2012. "Negotiating the Middle Ground in a World System: The Niitsitapi (Blackfoot) and Ktunaxa´ (Kootenai) in the Rocky Mountain Fur Trade." MA thesis. School of Anthropology, University of Arizona, Tucson.

Newton, Cody. 2011. "Towards a Context for Late Precontact Culture Change: Comanche Movement Prior to Eighteenth-Century Spanish Documentation." *Plains Anthropologist* 56 (217): 53–69. https://doi.org/10.1179/pan.2011.006.

Oetelaar, Gerald A. 2003. "Tipi Rings and Alberta Archaeology: A Brief Overview." In *Archaeology in Alberta: A View from the New Millennium,* ed. J. W. Brink and J. F. Dormaar, 104–30. Medicine Hat: Archaeological Society of Alberta.

Oetelaar, Gerald A. 2006. "Mobility and Territoriality on the Northwestern Plains of Alberta, Canada." In *Notions de territoire et de mobilité*, ed. C. Bressy, A. Burke, P. Challard, and H. Martin, 137–49. ERAUL 116. Liège, Belgium: Université de Liège.

Oetelaar, Gerald A. 2011. "The Structured World of the Niitsitapi: The Landscape as Historical Archive among Hunter-Gatherers of the Northern Plains." In *Structured Worlds: The Archaeology of Hunter-Gatherers Thought and Action*, ed. Aubrey Cannon, 69–94. Cambridge: Cambridge University Press.

Oetelaar, Gerald A. 2014. "Better Homes and Pastures: Human Agency and the Construction of Place in Communal Bison Hunting on the Northwestern Plains." *Plains Anthropologist* 59 (229): 9–37. https://doi.org/10.1179/2052546X13Y.0000000004.

Oetelaar, Gerald A., and David Meyer. 2006. "Movement and Native American Landscapes: A Comparative Approach." *Plains Anthropologist* 51 (199): 355–74. https://doi.org/10.1179/pan.2006.030.

Oetelaar, Gerald A., and D. Joy Oetelaar. 2006. "People, Places, and Paths: The Cypress Hills and the Niitsitapi Landscape of Southern Alberta." *Plains Anthropologist* 51 (199): 375–97. https://doi.org/10.1179/pan.2006.031.

Oetelaar, Gerald A., and D. Joy Oetelaar. 2011. "The Structured World of the *Nitsitapii*: The Landscape as Historical Archive among Hunter-Gatherers of the Northern Plains." In *Structured Worlds: The Archaeology of Hunter-Gatherer Thought and Action*, ed. Aubrey Cannon, 69–94. Cambridge: Cambridge University Press.

Oliver, Symmes C. 1962. "Ecological and Cultural Continuity as Contributing Factors in the Social Organization of the Plains Indians." *University of California Publications in American Archaeology and Ethnology* 48 (1): 1–90.

Peck, Trevor R. 2004. *Bison Ethnology and Native Settlement Patterns during the Old Women's Phase on the Northwestern Plains. BAR International Series 1278*. Oxford: Archaeopress.

Peck, Trevor R. 2011. *Light from Ancient Campfires*. Edmonton, AB: Athabasca University Press.

Quigg, J. Michael. 1978. "Winter Bison Procurement in Southwestern Alberta." *Plains Anthropologist* 23 (82, pt. 2): 53–57.

Raczka, Paul. 2016. *Sikiaitapi Itsinniiki: Telling the Old Stories (A Blackfoot History— The Winter Counts)*. Altona, Manitoba: Blackfoot Books (Paul Raczka, publisher).

Reeves, Brian O. K. 1983. "Culture Change in the Northern Plains: 1000 BC–AD 1000." Occasional Paper No. 20. Edmonton: Archaeological Survey of Alberta.

Reeves, Brian O. K. 1990. "Communal Bison Hunters of the Northern Plains." In *Hunters of the Recent Past*, ed. L. B. Davis and B. O. K. Reeves, 168–94. London: Unwin Hyman.

Reeves, Brian O. K. 2006. *Mistakis: Final Report, Archaeology, Glacier-Waterton International Peace Park*. Ed. Leslie Davis. Bozeman: Montana State University.

Reher, Charles A. 1983. "Analysis of Spatial Structure in Stone Circle Sites." *Plains Anthropologist* 28 (102, pt. 2): 193–222.

Reher, Charles A., and George C. Frison. 1980. "The Vore Site, 48CK302, a Stratified Buffalo Jump in the Wyoming Black Hills." *Plains Anthropologist* 25 (88, pt. 2).

Rockman, M. 2003. "Knowledge and Learning in the Archaeology of Colonization." In *Colonization of Unfamiliar Landscapes*, ed. M. Rockman and J. Steele, 3–24. London: Routledge. https://doi.org/10.4324/9780203422908.

Roos, C., M. N. Zedeño, and K. L. Hollenback. 2014. "Alluvial and Colluvial Records of Multi–Centennial Fire Histories from Blackfoot Country." Paper presented at the Annual Conference of the Plains Anthropological Society, Fayetteville, AK.

Schaeffer, Claude E. 1934. "Kootenai Papers." On file at the Glenbow Museum, Calgary, AB.

Schaeffer, Claude E., and Mrs. Schaeffer. 1934. "Field Work among Blackfeet Indians, Montana." Correspondence and Field Notes. On file at the Glenbow Museum, Calgary, AB.

Smyth, David. 2001. *Niitsitapi Trade: Euroamericans and the Blackfoot-Speaking People until 1830*. PhD dissertation, Department of History, Carleton University, Ottawa. Ann Arbor: University of Michigan Microfilm.

Teit, James. 1930. *The Salishan Tribes of the Western Plateaus. 45th Annual Report of the Bureau of American Ethnology*. Washington, DC: Smithsonian Institution.

Tolan-Smith, C. 2003. "The Social Context of Landscape Learning and the Glacial-Early Postglacial Recolonization of the British Isles." In *Colonization of Unfamiliar Landscapes*, ed. M. Rockman and J. Steele, 116–29. London: Routledge.

Toupal, Rebecca, and Kacy Hollenback. 2008. *Native American Oral Histories of Fort Union Trading Post National Historic Site. Tucson: Bureau of Applied Research in Anthropology, University of Arizona*. Lincoln: National Park Service Midwest Regional Office.

Tyrrell, Joseph Burr, ed. 1916. *David Thompson's Narrative of his Explorations in Western America, 1784–1812*. Toronto: Champlain Society.

Vickers, Roderick. 1991. "Seasonal Round Problems on the Alberta Plains." *Canadian Journal of Archaeology* 15:55–72.

Vickers, Roderick, and Trevor Peck. 2009. "Identifying the Prehistoric Blackfoot: Approaches to Nitsitapii (Blackfoot) Culture History." In *Painting the Past with a Broad Brush: Papers in Honour of James Valliere Wright*, ed. D. Keenlyside and J.-L. Pilon, 473–97. Gatineau: Canadian Museum of Civilization.

Walde, Dale. 2004. "Morlatch and One Gun: Phase to Phase." In *Archaeology on the Edge*, ed. Brian Kooyman and Jane Kelley, 31–59. Calgary: University of Calgary Press.

Walde, Dale. 2006a. "Avonlea and Athabaskan Migrations, a Reconsideration." *Plains Anthropologist*:185–97.

Walde, Dale. 2006b. "Sedentism and Pre-contact Tribal Organization on the Northern Plains: Colonial Imposition or Indigenous Development?" *World Archaeology* 38 (2): 291–310. https://doi.org/10.1080/00438240600694032.

Walde, Dale, David Meyer, and Wendy Unfreed. 1995. "The Late Period on the Canadian and Adjacent Plains." *Revista de Arqueología Americana* 9:7–66.

Wheat, Joe Ben. 1972. "The Olsen-Chubbuck Site: A Paleo-Indian Bison Kill." Memoir No. 26. Washington, DC: Society for American Archaeology.

Witte, Stephen S., and Marsha V. Gallagher. 2008. *April–September 1833*. Vol. 2. The North American Journals of Prince Maximilian of Wied. Norman: University of Oklahoma Press.

Zarrillo, S., and B. P. Kooyman. 2006. "Evidence for Berry and Maize Processing on the Canadian Plains from Starch Grain Analysis." *American Antiquity* 71 (3): 473–99. https://doi.org/10.2307/40035361.

Zedeño, María Nieves. 1997. "Landscape, Land Use, and the History of Territory Formation: An Example from the Puebloan Southwest." *Journal of Archaeological Method and Theory* 4 (1): 67–103. https://doi.org/10.1007/BF02428059.

Zedeño, María Nieves. 2008. "The Archaeology of Territory and Territoriality." In *Handbook of Landscape Archaeology*, ed. B. David and J. Thomas, 210–17. Walnut Creek, CA: Left Coast Press.

Zedeño, María Nieves. 2017. "Rethinking the Impact of Abundance on the Rhythm of Bison Hunter Societies." In *The Archaeology of Plenitude*, ed. Monica Smith, 23–44. Boulder: University Press of Colorado. https://doi.org/10.5876/9781607325949.c002.

Zedeño, María Nieves, and Derek Anderson. 2010. "Agency and Politics in Hunter-Gatherer Territory Formation." *Revista de Arqueología de Brasil* 23 (1): 10–30. https://doi.org/10.24885/sab.v23il.285.

Zedeño, María Nieves, Jesse A. Ballenger, and John R. Murray. 2014. "Landscape Engineering and Organizational Complexity among Late Prehistoric Bison Hunters of the Northwestern Plains." *Current Anthropology* 55 (1): 23–58. https://doi.org/10.1086/674535.

Zedeño, M. N., K. Hollenback, and C. Grinnell. 2009. "From Path to Myth: Journeys and the Naturalization of Territorial Identity along the Missouri River." In *Landscapes of Movement: The Anthropology of Paths, Trails, and Roads*, ed. J. Snead, C. Ericson, and A. Darling, 106–32. Philadelphia: University of Pennsylvania Press.

Zedeño, M. N., M. Pailes, J. Ballenger, and C. Francois, Lanoe Daughtrey, B. Bethke, and W. A. White. 2016. "Archaeological Investigations at the St. Mary River Bridge Site, Glacier National Park, Montana." Final report prepared for the National Park Service, Rocky Mountain Region. Tucson: Bureau of Applied Research in Anthropology, School of Anthropology, University of Arizona.

Zedeño, María Nieves, William A. White, and Virgil Edwards. 2017. "Class III Survey of the Boarding School Bison Jump Site, Blackfeet Indian Reservation, Montana." Final report prepared for the Blackfeet Tribal Historic Preservation Office and the Montana Bureau of Indian Affairs. Tucson: Bureau of Applied Research in Anthropology, School of Anthropology, University of Arizona.

3

Communal Hunting by Aboriginal Australians

Archaeological and Ethnographic Evidence

JANE BALME

DOI: 10.5876/9781607326823.c003

There is some debate about precisely when Sahul, consisting of modern-day Australia, New Guinea, and the Aru Islands (figure 3.1) was first occupied by people. However, most archaeologists agree that it was at least by 45,000 years ago (Allen and O'Connell 2014), and some have suggested that it was as early as 65,000 years BP (Clarkson et al. 2017). Rising seas separated Australia from the northern parts of Sahul some 8,000 years ago, and subsequently, the two main landmasses, Australia and Papua New Guinea, had very different histories. Papua New Guinea experienced frequent interaction with other cultures and, to different extents in different places, depended on domesticated plants and animals. The southern landmass, Australia, was a "continent of hunter-gatherers" (Lourandos 1997) until European settlers began usurping Aboriginal hunting grounds from the late eighteenth century.

The Australian environment is very diverse, with tropical rainforests in the northeast, a monsoonal north, an arid desert center, temperate forests, and cool Tasmania. All of these environmental zones were occupied by at least 40,000 years ago (Allen and O'Connell 2014) ago. Apart from ground axes in northern Australia, the rapid expansion throughout these diverse environments was associated with a non-specialized stone tool kit. Organic materials, including string, are suggested to have had an important role in Aboriginal technology from the earliest times

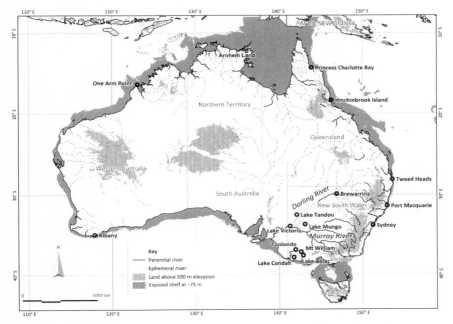

FIGURE 3.1. *Australia showing the outline of Sahul during the Last Glacial Maximum and places mentioned in the text.*

(Balme and O'Connor 2014). More specialized stone tools were included over time, particularly from the mid Holocene (Hiscock 2008:148–54), but organic technologies continued to be important.

Apart from rats and mice of the Muridae family, bats and the dingo (*Canis familiaris dingo*), the last of which was introduced in the late Holocene (Gollan 1984:924), there were no indigenous placental mammals in Australia before Europeans arrived; instead Australia is a land of marsupials. When the first Australians arrived, there were probably many more species of large (defined here as over 45 kg) animals in the landscape than there are today. The late Pleistocene fauna included twenty-three genera of "megafauna," including one bird genus, reptiles, and mammals that are now extinct (Roberts et al. 2001). Whether people or changing environment caused these extinctions is a subject of continuing debate (e.g., Field and Wroe 2012; Sandom et al. 2014). While none of the extant species reach the size of the largest megafauna (see Flannery 1990:47), several species of the extant kangaroo family can also weigh over 45 kg. These include the red kangaroo (*Macropus rufus*) an arid land species with males weighing up to 85 kg, *M. giganteus* in the east, *M. fuliginosus* in the south, and *M. antilopinus* in the north (Strahan 1983). All of the extant large species have been recovered from archaeological deposits; however, remains of any of the extinct species are rare and none of these large mammals have been found in site contexts that meet the criteria that can be interpreted as "mass kill." This is true even using P. M. Lubinski's (2013:169) liberal criterion for such an event that the number of animals can be as few as five as long as it can be shown that their death was caused by humans in a single mortality.

Nevertheless there is some ethnohistorical evidence that large game were communally caught in large numbers. For example, J. Dawson, an early European settler in southwestern Victoria who recorded details of nineteenth-century Aboriginal life in the region, describes communal drives of kangaroos and emus associated with gatherings of groups of people in southwestern Victoria (Dawson 1881). As elderly people, women, and children moved to a central gathering point they formed a human circle 25–30 km in diameter closing in on a central point. Close to the final destination, the men joined them and the animals were frightened with yells until they were sufficiently concentrated in a small area to be dispatched with clubs and spears (Dawson 1881:79). It is not altogether clear how many animals might have been caught in this way, but as marsupials are not migratory, and as they had no natural predators before people arrived and they are not herding animals, the numbers are not likely to have been large.

There are many reasons why evidence of such hunts might not be found in the archaeological record. The techniques described by Dawson require much organization and are unlikely to be a common occurrence, so the chances of finding the refuse from such events are small. In addition, archaeology is a relatively small discipline in Australia and unlike North America and Europe where mass kill sites of large animals have been identified, in Australia, there are fewer excavations. Most sites with good bone preservation are in cave and rock shelter deposits rather than open situations where such events might have occurred and where the animals might have been eaten. The evidence of mass kills of large animals is less likely to have been transported into caves and rock shelters than to be processed and eaten in open sites. Finally, there is the technology. Apart from the wooden clubs and spears that were used to kill the animals, the form of hunting described by Dawson is not associated with inorganic material technologies that usually survive in the archaeological record. Hafted stone points that might have been used as part of hunting spears do not occur in the archaeological record until relatively recently and are not widespread until the mid-Holocene (Hiscock 2008:156).

However, there is good historic and ethnographic evidence that Aboriginal people did use a variety of organic technologies to capture animals communally, at least in the recent past. While these technologies were used to capture large species, they were much more commonly used to capture smaller animals, including fish. Here I review the evidence for and contexts in which communal hunting occurred to catch large numbers of animals in Australia during the European contact period and discuss the implications of archaeological evidence for such hunting. I then briefly consider some of the implications for mass kill sites elsewhere.

COMMUNAL MASS HUNTING TECHNOLOGIES IN THE HISTORIC RECORD

Historic and ethnographic accounts cite two main technologies used by Aboriginal people to capture large numbers of animals: traps and nets. Traps were used to capture large numbers of fish and, in some places, eels, and nets were used to capture a wide variety of animals including mammals, bats, birds, and fish.

Traps

Fish traps were constructed along ocean coastlines and in rivers and streams. Those along the coasts and estuaries depended on tidal movement to capture fish. Pools were constructed out of stone or wood, sometimes also taking advantage of natural rock pools, in the tidal zone near the shore. As the tide came in, fish swam over the walled pools, where they became trapped as the tide receded. The fish could then be gathered from the pools. Some of these traps are complex. For example, J. Campbell (1982) describes tidal fish traps at Hinchinbrook Island, in northeastern Australia, as covering an area of about 21,600 square meters, though it is clear that not all parts of the system are the same age.

In northwestern Australia, Bardi people traditionally caught fish with traps, spears, poisons, and fishing boomerangs. However, they reported that stone fish traps were the most efficient and reliable methods as "it is the only one where you don't have to stand around and herd the fish. . . . you just pick them up" (Smith 1983:31). It is also possible to collect greater numbers of fish from traps. While there is not a lot of information on how many fish could be collected in a single episode from tidal traps, M. Smith (1983:53) observed Bardi people collecting sixty trevally, each weighing at least 500 grams, from a tidal trap (figure 3.2) in the "rubbish fishing time of the year." This last comment by

FIGURE 3.2. *Remains of tidal fish trap used by Bardi people in northwest Australia. (Photo courtesy of Moya Smith, Western Australian Museum.)*

a Bardi traditional owner suggests that, at other times of the year, quantities of fish collected could be expected to be much larger.

The suggestion that quantities of fish caught in tidal traps varies seasonally is supported by the ethnohistoric literature. This same literature also consistently refers to the periods of especially great abundance being used to supply large social gatherings. For example, near Albany in southwest Australia, there are extensive estuarine tidal stone fish traps. C. E. Dortch's (1999) review of the historic references to these traps identifies the social importance of seasonal winter abundance of fish that allowed ceremonial gatherings of people. For example, one description (Neill 1845:426), describes the use of a trap about 65 km west of Albany that "abounds in the winter months; and the different tribes, from all parts of the coast, assemble there, by invitation of the proprietors of the ground, who make great feasts on the occasion." Another example from the northeast coast of New South Wales where stone tidal fish traps dot the coast, especially between about 100 km south of Port Macquarie and Tweed Heads, reports similar use of the traps. These traps were commonly observed to have been associated with gatherings of up to 1,000 people, particularly during fish migrations in July to September (see Coleman 1982:4), and these gatherings were reportedly associated with feasting and ceremonies.

In rivers, fish traps relied on the water flow to capture fish. Most were reported to have been made of sticks and brush with apertures in which collection baskets were placed. Very few of these still survive, but Dortch and Gardner (1976) describe a wooden structure interpreted as a fish trap in a freshwater stream at Broke Inlet near Albany. In Arnhem Land, Northern Australia, J. C. Altman (1983) provides a description of similar traps that were being used and repaired during his fieldwork in 1980. Fish were particularly plentiful in the early dry season (midyear), which is the time in which gatherings for ceremony occurs in this region. While the trap has lost importance recently with changes in Aboriginal economy, Altman (1983:70) reports that it is clear that large quantities of fish could be obtained from these devices and cites the reported sale of 400 kilograms (presumably surplus to the fishers' requirement) of barramundi being sold to the local progress association in 1977.

A very well-known surviving river fish trap is made of stone in the Darling River at Brewarrina in New South Wales. Fish were caught in the stone pools as they made their way downstream. R. H. Mathews (1903) reports that individual pens were owned by different groups of people. These traps too provided communal foods for gatherings of people at times when fish were abundant. The nature of this abundance is indicated by a report about the Brewarrina traps in the *South Australian Register* newspaper on April 18, 1859: "When the river is low the several tribes suspend their hostilities, and assembling at a point about eight miles above the Falls, they come down the stream in a body, causing a great commotion in the water, and making very loud and peculiar noises, which have the effect of driving the fish towards the cellular contrivances, where they are speared in some of the numerous cells by a succession of dexterous assailants. Drayloads of fish are thus taken, and a season of festivity of gluttony supervenes" (Anon 1859).

Traps were also used to catch large numbers of eels in western Victoria, which, Dawson (1881:94) reported, were especially prized by Aboriginal people in the region. Stone or wooden structures were built across streams to catch the eels when they migrated to the sea to spawn. For example, near Lake Bolac, George Augustus Robinson (many of whose journals have been presented in volumes edited by Presland) observed a large weir at least "100 yards" long and was told by his Aboriginal companions that it was made for catching eels when "the big water came" (Presland 1977:49). The weir was made of "stout sticks, from 2–3 inches thick drove in to the ground and vertically fixed, and other sticks interlaced in an horizontal manner. A hole is left in the centre and a long eel pot made of basket or matting is placed before it and into which the eels gather and are thus taken" (Presland 1977:49).

Other descriptions of such weirs provide more information about season of use and the size of groups that could be provided for when the eels were running. Dawson (1881) describes stone weirs that divert currents into baskets used to collect eels. So abundant were the eels in autumn that, for a month or two, the whole area from Lake Bolac to the sea (about 40 km) "appeared like a village" (Dawson 1881:94). A. S. Kenyon (1928:146), also referring to the area around Lake Bolac, wrote that "during the eeling season, from eight hundred to one thousand natives at one time have been seen." He went on to suggest that this "spot celebrated for its eels and central situation, appears to have been fixed by general consent for the great annual meeting of tribes of the interior" (Kenyon 1928:146).

Dawson (1881:94) also reported that sometimes the traps could involve earth constructions. This was when the streams flooded over the marshes. Clay embankments "two to three feet high" and sometimes "two to three hundred yards" long were built across and the current diverted again into narrow openings in which baskets were placed. Robinson recorded a description of the eel trap systems at Mount William, in Victoria, observed in July 1841:

> ... an immense piece of ground trenched and banked ... for catching
> eels. ... These trenches are hundreds of yards in length. I measured at one place
> in one continuous triple line for the distance of 500 yards. These triple water-
> courses led to other ramified and extensive trenches of a most tortuous form.
> An area of at least 15 acres [6 ha] was thus turned over. ... [These works were
> constructed with a lever, which is] a stick chisel, sharpened at one end, by which
> force they threw up clods of soil and thus formed the trenches, smoothing the
> water channel with their hands. The soil displaced went to form the embank-
> ment. (Presland 1980:91)

The nearby Lake Condah area is rocky, and, as well as trenches, there are stone weirs, channels and races. P. J. Coutts, R. K. Frank, and P. Hughes (Coutts, Frank, and Hughes 1978) and A. Clarke (1991) have produced detailed recordings of seventy-eight stone-walled fish traps. Coutts, D. Witter, and D. Parsons. estimated that hundreds of tonnes of basalt boulders have been moved at Lake Condah (Coutts, Witter, and Parsons 1977:197). Eels, and probably fish, were again caught in baskets placed in gaps in the weirs. In addition, as the flood water subsided after the winter rains filled the rocky hollows, water became trapped in what Coutts, Frank, and Hughes (1978:28) suggest are "eel holding ponds."

At Darlots Creek, outlet from Lake Condah, H. Builth (2004) recorded channels constructed to divert water from the creek into depressions linked through further channels. She hypothesized that these "pens" were used to hold young eels swimming upstream during spring and to provide favorable long-term conditions for growth into adulthood. Following maturation, adult eels would, after their normal seven- to twenty-year terrestrial life cycle, begin their autumn migration downstream, where many were trapped and killed for consumption. Thus she suggests that Aboriginal people in western Victoria were practicing "eel aquaculture" (Builth 2004:168–69).

On the basis of his archaeological work at Toolondo, H. Lourandos (1980, 1987) also suggested large-scale management of eels in western Victoria. At Toolondo, Lourandos recorded 3.75 km of channels cut into the earth, but there is evidence that the system may have been more complex. The main channel is 2.5 m wide and 1m deep, but would have been deeper as there is evidence of erosion infill. The channels connect two swamps, one of which is within the natural range of eels but the second of which is not. According to Lourandos, "the size and construction of these drains points to their operation as more than mere eel harvesting devices." Toolondo worked by taking runoff and seepage down the drains to ensure a fast current into both swamps (Lourandos 1980:253). The drained surface runoff into swamps caused them to overflow, flushing eels and fish into channels where traps were laid.

Nets

Fiber has been argued to be an important part of Aboriginal technology since the first settlement (Balme 2013; Balme and O'Connor 2014) and in ethnographic times was widely used as a binder, to make baskets and to make nets used for hunting. L. D. Satterthwait (1986) summarizes records of the use of hunting nets by Aboriginal people recorded up until the early half of the twentieth century. The records derive from the observations of European explorers, settlers, government officials and some museum specimens, and so the detail of the records varies. Figure 3.3 is based on Satterthwait's (1986:33) Map 1 and shows the distribution of net hunting in Australia. The most obvious thing about this distribution is that there are many more records in the east of Australia than the west, and there are no records in Tasmania. There are good records for Tasmanian material culture and, although people used fiber for a variety of purposes including for woven baskets, no hunting nets have been recorded, suggesting that they were not used in Tasmania, at least in the period immediately before European occupation. For mainland Australia the distribution undoubtedly reflects the greater intensity of European occupation and of exploration in the east. However putting this bias aside, nets have been recorded in a great variety of environments from the tropical north to the

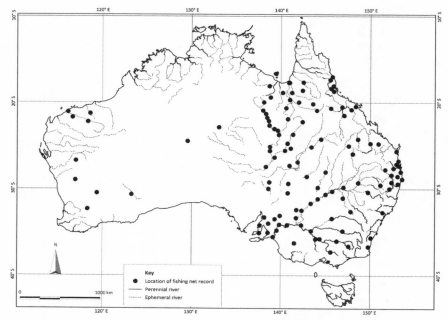

FIGURE 3.3. *Distribution of net hunting in Australia from historic and museum records. (Based on Satterthwait 1986 Map 1 page 33.)*

central deserts and temperate south of the continent but are most common in riverine regions. Satterthwait (1986:33) points out that this may be because, as nets cannot be projected a great distance, they are usually stationary when in use and so are best used to catch stationary or slow-moving prey or prey that travels into the net. This means that nets are most successful where game is plentiful, concentrated, and predictable.

Nets can be used either to capture a few animals, such as by throwing one over an animal drinking at a water hole or by using a handheld net to catch individual fish, or they can be used to capture large numbers of animals. Satterthwait (1987:616) records the use of nets to capture a large variety of animals including kangaroos and wallabies, emus, bats, waterfowl, and other birds. All of these could be captured either by intercepting the animals as they flew down flyways or moved along game trails, by drawing the animals into a net with calls and baits, or by driving the animals into the net, sometimes with fire. Satterthwait does not discuss the use of fishing nets, but there are ample records for net fishing in coastal and inland river regions Australia, particularly for the riverine districts of southeastern Australia.

While net hunting is often associated with "large catches," in the historic record, the observers are seldom specific in the numbers acquired. Indications of some quantities of different kinds of animals caught in single hunting events are provided by a list in Satterthwait (1987:619). In western Queensland, for example, three men caught 100 pigeons in two hours, and six or seven people caught 1,218 pigeons and finches in one morning (on this occasion the hunters were taking advantage of an arid spell so that the birds had all flocked to one of the few remaining waterholes). On the Murray River, five or six individuals took 20–30 ducks daily over several days, and 50–100 ducks were caught in a single drive. A single drive also resulted in twenty wallabies being caught by fifty people in Queensland.

The size of fishing nets, the communal nature of net fishing, and the quantities of fish caught in single netting expeditions are mainly indicated by records along the Murray River that borders New South Wales and Victoria. For example, P. Beveridge (1889:45–46) describes a seine fishing net about '100 yards' long with a 3 in. mesh and that was weighed down at the bottom and floated with reed bundles at the top. This was used in a lagoon known to have many fish. He says that two men could set such a net, but, if the haul is successful, all available muscle, including women and children, was needed. Few people record how many fish were caught in such hauls, but Beveridge (1889:47) goes on to say that he had on many occasions seen—3–4 cwt (about 100–200 kg) drawn from lagoons in a single occasion. Such quantities are also suggested by E. J. Eyre (1845:2:252), who recorded a gathering of about 600 people at Lake Victoria on the Murray River who, he described, were living at the time almost entirely on fish. Eyre makes clear that some of the nets used in the Murray River region were gill nets, particularly when lagoons and swamps were full. These were set in a zigzag fashion away from the shore on the Murray River (Eyre 1845:2:254). Gill nets were also used in the sea, for example, at Princess Charlotte Bay in tropical northeastern Queensland, fish were driven into nets by "beaters" (Hale and Tindale 1933:111).

LABOR INVESTMENT OF MASS CAPTURE TECHNOLOGIES IN AUSTRALIA

Although it is clear that both traps and nets can be and were used to capture large numbers of animals, this came at some cost. Each required a large labor investment to both construct and maintain. Of the three main technologies discussed above—stone fish traps and weirs, earth (and stone) channel systems, and nets—if stone is readily available, stone fish traps probably take the least amount of person hours to create and maintain. Smith (1983:32) reports on the rebuilding of a fish trap that had been disused by Bardi people in the western Kimberley, for about forty years. The foundations of the trap remained, but the walls were not high enough to retain fish. They built a 25 m length of wall 1.3 m high that was 1.3 m wide at base, narrowing to 1 m at top. The effort required 7,500 stones, but only took six person hours (Smith 1983:32). However, in this experiment the stones were readily available (as they reused those from the previous trap) and, when the tide came in and the fish easily leaped over the walls, it was clear that the walls had not been built high enough. In addition, the actual time taken was much longer than the actual building time because construction could be done only at low tide (about four days a months with daylight in July to September).

There are no observations of digging earth eel trap channels, but Lourandos (1980:381) estimated that the Toolondo site involved 7,644 cubic meters of soil movement. By comparison with the labor time associated with ditch digging using wooden tools by people in present-day New Guinea, he suggests that the Toolondo ditches took 12,700 person hours to dig. Of course, all of this may not have been done at once, but there is clear evidence that the site was maintained over time (Lourandos 1980:253).

Although obviously dependent on the net and mesh size, net manufacture is particularly labor intensive. It requires collection of appropriate plant material to make the fiber. The material used varies by region but can be made from rhizome stems, reeds, leaves, and stems of grasses and bark from some species such as kurrajong. Once collected, the plant material has to be processed sometimes by drying and sometimes by soaking beforehand. The twine is made by twisting the prepared plant material, which is then knotted, perhaps with the help of a bone needle (Lamond 1950:169), to form the net. Some nets were then tanned before use (Lamond 1950:169). Satterthwait (1987:615), for example, estimates that a 18.3 × 12.2 meter waterfowl net (Eyre 1845: 2:286) with meshes 5 cm on a side (Mitchell 1839: 2:153) would contain, depending on the configuration of its meshes, between 7,500 and 9,000 meters of cord and some 90,000 netting knots. If cord were produced at a rate of 100 meters per day and knots woven at a rate of seven seconds each (a figure suggested by experiment and by observation of contemporary Aboriginal net-making), then such a net would have taken between 97 and 112 days of individual labor to construct.

This estimate is supported by the ethnohistoric literature, where, for example, the nineteenth-century naturalist Hermann Krefft's 1862–65 observed that *Typha* (bulrush) fiber for nets was obtained at gatherings of "whole tribes" and that net making entailed "astonishing' perseverance" (cited by Satterthwait 1987:615). W. E. Roth's (1901:28) notes that a 7.2 × 4.6 m fiber kangaroo net made from the bark of *Sterculia* sp. (a tropical kurrajong tree) took an entire local camp some three weeks to make, and A. Duncan-Kemp (1933:122) reports that a large duck net took as long as "two to three years" to finish. While this last estimate may seem to overstate the time, it might well be true given the time needed to make the net and the fact that net making would not have been a full-time occupation.

Perhaps because of the labor investment, many of these mass capture technologies appear to have been "owned" by a few people. For example, Dawson (1881:94) recorded that individual social groups built and controlled or owned specific eel stone weirs in Salt Creek linked to Lake Bolac (figure 3.1). A review by Satterthwait (1987:624) concludes that, while small nets were widely owned by individuals, large nets used for communal hunting were less common, and he cites ethnohistorical evidence from southern Queensland, interior New South Wales, and northern Victoria that such nets were owned or controlled by particular men (elders). In contemporary Aboriginal societies, older men are prominent in the management of large-scale hunting and fishing activities and control the equipment, such as fish traps, associated with these activities (Altman 1983:63; Thomson 1949:17–20).

LABOR ORGANIZATION

Not only did these technologies require an investment in labor time to produce, some required a great deal of organization of labor to construct and/or to use in order to reap the rewards of the labor investment. Even the technology-free communal circle drives described at the beginning of this chapter and observed by Dawson (1881) and others, such as Robinson (Presland 1980), required a good deal of preparation to communicate with participants over long distances and to ensure that the closing of the circle was coordinated so that the hunters involved moved in and arrived the central location at one time. Reports of organizers of such hunts in southwestern Victoria are referred to as "band leaders" in the historic literature (Lourandos 1977:216).

To be effective the fish and eel traps of the types described here needed design planning, knowledge of local tides and currents, and organization of labor to complete the different structures within the overall plan. Individuals may have constructed nets, but Satterthwait's (1987:615) review of the ethnohistoric literature suggests that several people were often involved in different aspects of net construction. However, their use in mass animal capture often required coordination of many people. For eels, as I. J. McNiven and Bell (2010:89) point out, with so many groups operating weirs, controlling water flows, and removing eels, considerable coordination and negotiations would be required to ensure that participants downstream had access to eels.

Nets can be operated by one or two people, but, to increase the numbers of large animals captured in a net, people had to be organized to drive animals to guide them into the net with others ready to dispose of the animals (Satterthwait 1986:37). Satterthwait's (1986:39–42) review of historic descriptions of net hunting indicates that large- and medium-sized mammals, such as kangaroos and wallabies, were driven into nets by several hunters. Emus were also driven into nets, and in some places this required the division of the hunting party into several task specific teams to drive, direct, and kill the birds (Satterthwait 1986:40). Communal hunting of waterfowl with set nets strung in watercourses was achieved by coordination of hunters to chase the birds toward the net while other hunters stationed in trees along the expected flight path made sure that the birds continued on path by throwing objects in the air to make sure that they did not fly over it (Satterthwait 1986:39).

SOCIAL CONTEXT OF COMMUNAL HUNTING

The common theme with all of the historic records of communal hunting is their connection to gatherings of people and ceremonies during times of abundance. In the present and recent past in Australia ceremonies were associated with initiations, taking of marriage partners, trade and exchange, death, and other religious events. Because people may attend these from hundreds of kilometers away (e.g., Berndt 1951), they can last up to several months (e.g., Berndt and Berndt 1964:240), and so the food requirements to support the ceremonies must be considerable.

On such occasions the advantage of techniques, such as the game drives, and technologies such as fish traps and nets, is that, though the technologies might take some skill to make and the execution of the hunt may require much organization, participation in drives and the use of nets and traps requires much less skill than individuals hunting with spears or boomerangs, for example. In communal hunting everyone can participate in the hunt.

ANTIQUITY

The antiquity and extent of communal hunting are difficult to ascertain for the reasons identified at the beginning of this chapter. No archaeological deposits have been found that can be interpreted as the result of communal game drives. Because of the transient nature of the technologies associated with communal animal capture, and in some cases their position in water where they are not in dateable contexts, the antiquity of those that do survive is difficult to interpret. Lourandos (1980:253) obtained a date of 210 ± 120 BP for the infilling of the base of the main Toolondo channel, which he interprets as the final stages of the drain's use, but he was not able to estimate the initial use. The initial stages of building the Muldoons Trap Complex at Lake Condah have been estimated by McNiven et al. (2012) to be about 6,600 cal. BP on the basis of AMS dates from charcoal recovered from infill in the one of the two lowest channels of the complex. However, this does not preclude a greater antiquity for such systems elsewhere.

I have previously argued that the use of fiber netting, most probably gill nets, is implied by fish remains in Pleistocene sites at Lake Tandou on the Darling River in western New South Wales (Balme 1995). The evidence for such use is the abundance of fish of uniform size (up to 251 individuals) within middens representing single foraging events that date from 27,000 years BP (~31,500 years cal. BP). K. Kefous (1977) has suggested that the sizes of fish found on the Lake Mungo lunette are also restricted and may also result from net capture, though she does not suggest that the fish in these middens represent single foraging events. While it could be argued that abundances of fish resulting from a single foraging event could be the result of particular environmental circumstances, such as the drying of a lake, and that the narrow size range of the fish can be explained by physiological stress, it is difficult to explain the repeated consistent pattern of the same size range of different fish species over many time periods on the Darling River lakes unless the same technique was used to select and capture the fish (Balme 1995:15). The age of net use in this part of Australia is consistent with the earliest direct evidence for nets in the world, which is in the form of preserved impressions in clay from Moravian Gravettian sites dating to at least 28,000 years ago (e.g., Adovasio et al. 2001; Soffer et al. 1998, 2000; Soffer, Adovasio, and Hyland 2002). O. Soffer (2000) has argued that because of the hypothesized relatively small mesh size of the nets, they were most likely used to hunt small-sized prey.

This evidence suggests that as long ago as 30,000 years, people were taking advantage of periodic abundances to gather and possibly conduct ceremonies that may have been vital to maintain networks over long distances. We have no evidence that ceremonies were associated with these particular fishing events, but there is evidence for burial ceremonies from 40,000 years ago in the Willandra Lakes area, including cremation and fragmentation of the bones of one person and ochre sprinkled on the burial of another (Bowler et al. 1970; Bowler and Thorne 1976; Bowler et al. 2003). There is also much evidence for long-distance networks from about 32,000 years ago (Balme et al. 2009:64). All of this supports an argument that gatherings involving communal hunting have an antiquity of at least 30,000 years.

DISCUSSION AND CONCLUSIONS

Most discussions of mass kill sites associated with hunter-gatherer societies refer to large ungulates suggested to be communally hunted by taking advantage of migration patterns and/or herding behaviors to trap or divert animals so that they could be easily captured. Such activities required a great amount of organization and often made use of natural features such as cliffs and arroyos. While sometimes additional technologies such as artificially made corrals (see papers in Kornfeld, Frison, and Larson 2010 for North American bison hunting) or Kites in the Middle East (e.g., Nadel et al. 2010) were used with these drives, they did not necessarily require specialized technologies beyond those used for hunting of small numbers of animals. The meat obtained from communal mass hunts could then be stored for winter and the hides processed for clothing and other uses. In Australia there are no large migratory or herding animals, and there is little evidence of animal food storage in a continent in which only a few small areas have seasons as marked as the northern latitudes. However, social and ceremonial gatherings that seem to have taken place from at least 30,000 years ago created temporary resource pressure on the hosting groups, and it was for this reason that they were organized to take advantage of seasonal abundance of resources. In some parts of Australia such ceremonies are known to have been associated with plant abundances. For example in southeast Queensland, bunya nuts (*Araucaria bidwillii*) (e.g., Petrie 1904) and in northern Australia cycad (*Cycas* sp.) seeds are an important symbolic food source for gatherings (see Bradley 2006), even though they need to be extensively processed to remove toxins. In this chapter I have discussed the evidence for the use of specialized technologies designed to harvest seasonal abundances of small animal species, particularly fish and eels that were used to supply gatherings of people. While each of these technologies could be used to obtain small numbers of animals, the enormous labor investment associated with their construction would only be of value if they were used to provide communal foods. The technologies are also particularly useful for such occasions as they have the advantage that, while they each take some planning and time to create, they can all be operated by unskilled labor as long as some people organize and coordinate the harvest.

We do not know whether people regularly caught more than could be eaten at one time so it is not possible to determine whether, as J. Speth (2013) has suggested for North America, prestige might be associated with hunting prowess indicated by excessive kills. In Australia, because of the difficulty in hunting large animals (primarily kangaroo) even with firearms and vehicles today, Aboriginal hunters are often unsuccessful (see for e.g., Bird, Bird, and Codding 2009; Bird et al. 2012). Hunters who are lucky enough to catch a large kangaroo acquire much social prestige (e.g., Bliege Bird and Smith 2005) in recognition of their hunting skills and because the meat obtained from a single animal can be shared between several people. However, the prestige associated with a hunt of this kind is for an individual. The prestige is associated with hunting skills, not with ceremonial or law status within the community. Organization of the labor to both construct, use and, in some cases, own the mass capture technologies described here seems to have been associated with status of a few, older individuals who traditionally have these roles. The political and social dimensions of hunting are complex and inferences about them depend on social context, and the reasons for the hunt but they are also very dependent on the technology used.

REFERENCES CITED

Adovasio, J. M., O. Soffer, D. C. Hyland, J. S. Illingworth, B. Klíma, and J. Svoboda. 2001. "Perishable Industries from Dolní Věstonice I: New Insights into the Nature and Origin of the Gravettian." *Archaeology, Ethnology & Anthropology of Eurasia* 2 (6): 48–65.

Allen, J., and J. O'Connell. 2014. "Both Half Right: Updating the Evidence for Dating First Human Arrivals in Sahul." *Australian Archaeology* 79 (1): 86–108. https://doi.org/10.1080/03122417.2014.11682025.

Altman, J. C. 1983. "Eastern Gunwinggu Fish Trapping at Gunbatgarrr." *Beagle* 1 (7): 59–71.

Anon. 1859. "The Murray Navigation." *The South Australian Register*, April 18, p. 4. http://trove.nla.gov.au/newspaper/article/49904221?searchTerm=drayloads%20of%20fish&searchLimits=.

Balme, J. 1995. "30,000 Years of Fishery in Western New South Wales." *Archaeology in Oceania* 30 (1): 1–21. https://doi.org/10.1002/j.1834-4453.1995.tb00324.x.

Balme, J. 2013. "Of Boats and String: The Maritime Colonisation of Australia." *Quaternary International* 285:68–75. https://doi.org/10.1016/j.quaint.2011.02.029.

Balme, J., I. Davidson, J. McDonald, N. Stern, and P. Veth. 2009. "Symbolic Behaviour and the Peopling of the Southern Arc Route to Australia." *Quaternary International* 202 (1–2): 59–68. https://doi.org/10.1016/j.quaint.2008.10.002.

Balme, J., and S. O'Connor. 2014. "Early Modern Humans in Island Southeast Asia and Sahul: Adaptive and Creative Societies with Simple Lithic Industries." In *Southern Asia, Australia and the Search for Human Origins*, ed. R. Dennell and M. Porr, 164–74. Cambridge: Cambridge University Press. https://doi.org/10.1017/CBO9781139084741.013.

Berndt, R. M. 1951. "Ceremonial Exchange in Western Arnhem Land." *Southwestern Journal of Anthropology* 7 (2): 156–76. https://doi.org/10.1086/soutjanth.7.2.3628621.

Berndt, R. M., and C. H. Berndt. 1964. *The World of the First Australians*. Sydney: Ure Smith.

Beveridge, P. 1889. *The Aborigines of Victoria and Riverina*. Melbourne: Hutchinson.

Bird, D. W., R. Bliege Bird, and B. Codding. 2009. "In Pursuit of Mobile Prey: Martu Hunting Strategies and Archaeofaunal Interpretation." *American Antiquity* 74 (1): 3–29. https://doi.org/10.1017/S000273160004748X.

Bird, D. W., B. Codding, R. Bliege Bird, and D. Zeanah. 2012. "Risky Pursuits: Martu Hunting and the Effects of Prey Mobility: Reply to Ugan and Simms." *American Antiquity* 77 (1): 186–94. https://doi.org/10.7183/0002-7316.77.1.186.

Bliege Bird, R., and E. A. Smith. 2005. "Signaling Theory, Strategic Interaction, and Symbolic Capital." *Current Anthropology* 46 (2): 221–48. https://doi.org/10.1086/427115.

Bowler, J., H. Johnston, J. Olley, J. Prescott, R. Roberts, W. Shawcross, and N. Spooner. 2003. "New Ages for Human Occupation and Climatic Change at Lake Mungo, Australia." *Nature* 421 (6925): 837–40. https://doi.org/10.1038/nature01383.

Bowler, J. M., R. Jones, H. Allen, and A. G. Thorne. 1970. "Pleistocene Human Remains from Australia: A Living Site and Human Cremation from Lake Mungo, Western New South Wales." *World Archaeology* 2 (1): 39–60. https://doi.org/10.1080/00438243.1970.9979463.

Bowler, J. M., and A. Thorne. 1976. "Human Remains from Lake Mungo: Discovery and Excavation of Lake Mungo III." In *The Origin of the Australians*, ed. R. L. Kirk and A. G. Thorne, 127–38. Canberra: Australian Institute of Aboriginal Studies.

Bradley, J. 2006. "The Social, Economic and Historical Construction of Cycad Palms." In *The Social Archaeology of Australian Indigenous Societies*, ed. B. David, B. Barker, and I. J. McNiven, 161–81. Canberra: Australian Institute of Aboriginal Studies.

Builth, H. 2004. "Mt Eccles Lava Flow and the Gunditjmara Connection: A Landform for all Seasons." *Proceedings of the Royal Society of Victoria* 116 (1): 165–84.

Campbell, J. 1982. "Automatic Seafood Retrieval Systems: The Evidence form Hinchinbrook Island and Its Implications." In *Coastal Archaeology in Eastern Australia*, ed. S. Bowdler, 96–107. Canberra: Australian National University.

Clarke, A. 1991. *Lake Condah Project Aboriginal Archaeology Resource Inventory.* Occasional Report no. 36. Melbourne: Victoria Archaeological Survey, Department of Conservation and Environment.

Clarkson, C., Z. Jacobs, B. Marwick, R. Fullagar, L. Wallis, M. Smith, R. Roberts, E. Hayes, K. Lowe, X. Carah, S. A. Florin, J. McNeil, D. Cox, L. J. Arnold, Q. Hua, J. Huntley, H. E. A. Brand, T. Manne, A. Fairbairn, J. Schulmeister, L. Lyle, M. Salinas, M. Page, K. Connell, G. Park, K. Norman, T. Murphy, and C. Pardoe. 2017. "Human Occupation of Northern Australia by 65,000 Years Ago." *Nature* 547:306–25.

Coleman, J. 1982. "A New Look at the North Coast: Fish Traps and Villages." In *Coastal Archaeology in Eastern Australia*, ed. S. Bowdler, 1–10. Canberra: Australian National University.

Coutts, P. J., R. K. Frank, and P. Hughes. 1978. *Aboriginal Engineers of the Western District, Victoria. Records of the Victorian Archaeological Survey Number 7.* Melbourne: Aboriginal Affairs Victoria.

Coutts, P. J., D. Witter, and D. Parsons. 1977. "Impact of European Settlement on Aboriginal Society in Western Victoria." *Search* 8:194–205.

Dawson, J. 1881. *Australian Aborigines: The Languages and Customs of Several Tribes of Aborigines in the Western District of Victoria.* Melbourne: George Robertson.

Dortch, C. E. 1999. "Archaeological Assessment of Aboriginal Estuarine Fishing on the Southern Ocean Coast of Western Australia." In *Australian Coastal Archaeology*, ed. J. Hall and I. J. McNiven, 25–35. Canberra: ANH Publications, The Australian National University.

Dortch, C. E., and G. Gardner. 1976. "Archaeological Investigations in the Northcliffe District, Western Australia." *Records of the Western Australian Museum* 4 (3): 257–93.

Duncan-Kemp, A. 1933. *Our Sandhill Country: Nature and Man in South-Western Queensland.* Sydney: Angus and Robertson.

Eyre, E. J. 1845. *Journals of Expeditions of Discovery into Central Australia.* London: Boone.

Field, J., and S. Wroe. 2012. "Aridity, Faunal Adaptations and Australian Late Pleistocene Extinctions." *World Archaeology* 44 (1): 56–74. https://doi.org/10.1080/0 0438243.2012.647572.

Flannery, T. 1990. "Pleistocene Faunal Loss: Implications of the Aftershock for Australia's Past and Future." *Archaeology in Oceania* 25 (2): 45–55. https://doi.org/10 .1002/j.1834-4453.1990.tb00232.x.

Gollan, K. 1984. "The Australian Dingo in the Shadow of Man." In *Vertebrate Zoogeography and Evolution in Australasia*, ed. M. Archer and G. Clayton, 921–27. Perth: Hesperian Press.

Hale, H. M., and N. B. Tindale. 1933. "Aborigines of Princess Charlotte Bay, North Queensland, Pt. I." *Records of the South Australian Museum* 5 (1): 64–116.

Hiscock, P. 2008. *Archaeology of Ancient Australia*. London: Routledge. https://doi .org/10.4324/9780203448359.

Kefous, K. 1977. "We Have a Fish with Ears, and Wonder If It's Valuable." Honours thesis, ANU, Canberra, Australia.

Kenyon, A. S. 1928. "The Aboriginal Protectorate of Port Phillip: Report of an Expedition to the Aboriginal Tribes of the Western Interior by the Chief Protector, George Augustus Robinson." *Victorian Historical Magazine* 12 (47): 134–72.

Kornfeld, M., G. C. Frison, and M. L. Larson, eds. 2010. *Prehistoric Hunter-Gatherers of the High Plains and Rockies*. 3rd ed. Walnut Creek, CA: Left Coast Press.

Lamond, H. G. 1950. "Aboriginal Net Making." *Mankind* 4 (4): 168–69.

Lourandos, H. 1977. "Aboriginal Spatial Organisation and Population: South-Western Victoria Re-considered." *Archaeology & Physical Anthropology in Oceania* 12 (3): 202–25.

Lourandos, H. 1980. "Change or Stability? Hydraulics, Hunter-Gatherers and Population in Temperate Australia." *World Archaeology* 11 (3): 245–64. https://doi .org/10.1080/00438243.1980.9979765.

Lourandos, H. 1987. "Swamp Managers of Southwestern Victoria." In *Australians to 1788*, ed. D. J. Mulvaney and J. P. White, 292–307. Sydney: Fairfax, Syme and Weldon.

Lourandos, H. 1997. *Continent of Hunger-Gatherers: New Perspectives in Australian Prehistory*. Cambridge: Cambridge University Press.

Lubinski, P. M. 2013. "What Is Adequate Evidence for Mass Procurement of Ungulates in Zooarchaeology?" *Quaternary International* 297 (May): 167–75. https://doi.org/10.1016/j.quaint.2012.12.030.

Mathews, R. H. 1903. "The Aboriginal Fisheries at Brewarrina." *Royal Society of New South Wales* 37:146–56.

McNiven, I. J., and D. Bell. 2010. "Fishers and Farmers: Historicising the Gunditjmara Freshwater Fishery, Western Victoria." *La Trobe Journal* 85 (May): 83–105.

McNiven, I. J., J. Crouch, T. Richards, N. Dolby, and G. Jacobsen, and the Gunditj Mirring Traditional Owners Corporation. 2012. "Dating Aboriginal Stone Walled Fish Traps at Lake Condah, Southeast Australia." *Journal of Archaeological Science* 39 (2): 268–86. https://doi.org/10.1016/j.jas.2011.09.007.

Mitchell, T. L. 1839. *Three Expeditions into the Interior of Eastern Australia*. London: Boone.

Nadel, D., G. Bar-Oz, U. Avner, E. Boaretto, and D. Malkinson. 2010. "Walls, Ramps and Pits: The Construction of the Samar Desert Kites, Southern Negev, Israel." *Antiquity* 84 (326): 976–92. https://doi.org/10.1017/S0003598X00067028.

Neill, J. 1845. "Catalogue of Reptiles and Fish, Found at King George's Sound." In *Journals of Discovery into Central Australia, and Overland from Adelaide to King George's Sound, in the Years 1840–1841*, by E. J. Eyre, vol. 1., 412–31. London: T. and W. Boone.

Petrie, C. 1904. *Tom Petrie's Reminiscences of Early Queensland. Brisbane*. Brisbane, Australia: Watson, Ferguson & Co.

Presland, G., ed. 1977. *Journals of G.A. Robinson March 1841–May 1841. Records of the Victorian Archaeological Survey, No. 6*. Melbourne: Ministry for Conservation.

Presland, G., ed. 1980. *Journals of G.A. Robinson May–August 1841. Records of the Victorian Archaeological Survey, No. 11*. Melbourne: Ministry for Conservation.

Roberts, R. G., T. F. Flannery, L. K. Ayliffe, H. Yoshida, J. M. Olley, G. J. Prideaux, G. M. Laslett, A. Baynes, M. A. Smith, R. Jones, et al. 2001. "New Ages for the Last Australian Megafauna: Continent-Wide Extinction about 46,000 Years Ago." *Science* 292 (5523): 1888–92. https://doi.org/10.1126/science.1060264.

Roth, W. E. 1901. "Food: Its Search, Capture, and Preparation." *North Queensland Ethnography Bulletin*, No. 3.

Sandom, C., S. Faurby, B. Sandel, and J.-C. Svenning. 2014. "Global Late Quaternary Megafauna Extinctions Linked to Humans, Not Climate Change." *Proceedings of the Royal Society B* 281 (1787): 20133254. https://doi.org/10.1098/rspb.2013.3254.

Satterthwait, L. D. 1986. "Aboriginal Australian Net Hunting." *Mankind* 16 (1): 31–48.

Satterthwait, L. D. 1987. "Socioeconomic Implications of Aboriginal Net Hunting." *Man* 22 (4): 613–36. https://doi.org/10.2307/2803355.

Smith, M. 1983. "Joules from Pools: Social and Techno-Economic Aspects of Bardi Stone Fish Traps." In *Archaeology at ANZAAS 1983*, ed. M. Smith, 29–45. Perth: Western Australian Museum.

Soffer, O. 2000. "Gravettian Technologies in Social Contexts." In *Hunters of the Golden Age: The Mid Palaeolithic of Eurasia 30,000–20,000 BP*, ed. W. Roebroeks, M. Mussi, J. Svoboda, and K. Fennema, 59–75. Leiden: University of Leiden Press.

Soffer, O., J. M. Adovasio, D. C. Hyland, B. Klíma, and J. Svoboda. 1998. "Perishable Technologies and the Genesis of the Eastern Gravettian." *L'Anthropologie* 36 (1–2): 43–68.

Soffer, O., J. M. Adovasio, J. S. Illingworth, H. A. Amirkhanov, N. D. Praslov, and M. Street. 2000. "Palaeolithic Perishables Made Permanent." *Antiquity* 74 (286): 812–21. https://doi.org/10.1017/S0003598X00060464.

Soffer, O., J. M. Adovasio, and D. C. Hyland. 2002. "Perishable Technologies and Invisible People: Nests, Baskets, and 'Venus' Wear ca 26,000 BP." In *Enduring Records: The Environmental and Cultural Heritage of Wetlands*, ed. B. A. Purdy, 233–45. Oxford: Oxbow Books.

Speth, J. 2013. "Thoughts about Hunting: Some Things We Know and some Things We Don't Know." *Quaternary International* 297 (May): 176–85. https://doi.org/10.1016/j.quaint.2012.12.005.

Strahan, R. 1983. *The Australian Museum Complete Book of Australian Mammals*. Sydney: Angus and Robertson.

Thomson, D. F. 1949. *Economic Structure and the Ceremonial Exchange Cycle in Arnhem Land*. London: Macmillan.

4

According to Greenlandic tradition, an Inuit hunter is expected to demonstrate respect for prey by avoiding overhunting. Today this remains an important self-image constituting the identity of Greenlandic hunters. Archaeologically however, examples of mass-kill sites such as hunting drive systems for caribou, and middens with large heaps of bones indicate high levels of hunting success. This apparent paradox will be discussed through the examination of three drive hunt systems and the interpretations of their use. Further, meat wasting versus nonwasting strategies will be discussed on the basis of prehistoric and contemporary treatment of caribou bones.

Driving the Caribou

Greenlandic Hunting Drive Systems and Ethical Aspects

Ulla Odgaard

OUTRAGEOUS GUESSWORK

In 1958 Jens Rosing, a Greenlandic artist and author—and at that time also participant in an experiment of introducing caribou herding to Greenland—wrote a newspaper article about an ancient drive-hunt system he discovered in the mountains of southwest Greenland during the caribou-herding project. In this article he vividly described the prehistoric slaying of multiple animals by chasing them over the edge of a cliff (Rosing 1958a).

In a following letter to the editor, with the headline "outrageous guesswork!" another Greenlandic citizen, Vittus Mikiassen, wrote: "I honour and revere our ancestors, and I find it outrageous to label them as having hunted with cruelty to animals." He further states that common knowledge passed on through the

DOI: 10.5876/9781607326823.c004

legends indicate that women drove and men shot the animals with bow and arrow from blinds. "But the legends also tell that they would stop when they had caught as many animals as they could process in a day ... We never heard anything about the driving of a large herd of caribou to the cliffs to kill them by chasing them over the edge. Should we accuse our ancestors of being animal torturers? In warm weather it will not take long for an animal, which is not butchered, to decay, and if you kill that many animals at one time, a number of animals must have decayed" (Mikiassen 1958; my translation from Danish).

Archaeological evidence confirms Mikiassen's statement that his ancestors were careful with the animals and did not waste the meat, which seems to be the "normal" pattern. On the other hand archaeology can also confirm the story concerning intensive hunting, where meat was wasted.

THE GEOGRAPHICAL AND CULTURAL SETTING

Most of Greenland is covered by ice, but in West Greenland a strip of land up to 150 km wide along with fjords provide access to the inland landscapes, where caribou prefer to calve and stay during summers. In these areas many archaeological traces of people hunting caribou, have been found (figure 4.1).

Direct ancestors of Vittus Mikiassen and other modern Greenlanders of Inuit decent were the people of the Thule culture. The Thule culture was a hunting culture originating in Alaska (Friesen and Arnold 2008; Mason 2009), where it spread eastward and reached northern Greenland around AD 1200. During the following three centuries this culture made their camps in most of Greenland, which was then occupied only by the Norse in the southwesternmost part of the country (Gulløv 1997:204). Older archaeological traces in Western Greenland derive from the Paleoeskimo cultures: Saqqaq, 2500 BC–800 BC; and Dorset, 800–200 BC. Saqqaq and Dorset were part of the Arctic small tool tradition that was rooted in the Neolithic cultures of northeastern Siberia (Dumond 1984; McGhee 1996; Powers and Jordan 1990; Wright 1995;). They were not directly related to the Inuit culture, and it seems that they had left Greenland except for the Thule-area in Northwest Greenland, when the people of the Thule culture arrived (Gulløv 2004).

DRIVE HUNTING

In the following three examples of different types of prehistoric Greenlandic large-scale, drive hunting systems will be discussed with current interpretations of the hunting processes.

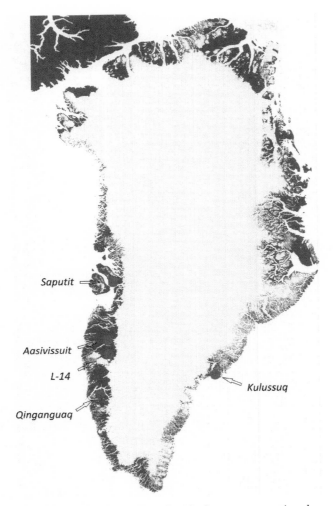

Saputit

Aasivissuit

L-14

Kulussuq

Qinganguaq

FIGURE 4.1. *Map of Greenland with place-names mentioned in the text.*

THE QINGANGUAQ DRIVE

The same year as the previously mentioned newspaper article, Jens Rosing published another article with a careful description of the drive system in the Nuuk Fjord (Rosing 1958b). Here he described the Qinganguaq-mountain (translated as "the small ridge") as an island in the middle of a large sea of mountains. At the north and east side it drops steeply down, while the west

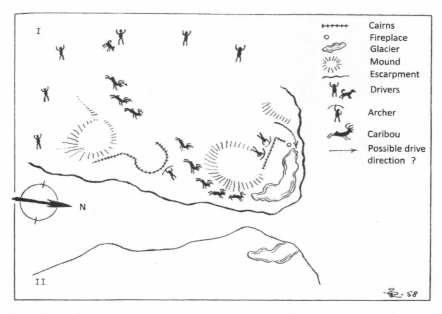

FIGURE 4.2. *Draft of the cairn systems at Qinganguaq with interpretation of the drive hunting (Rosing 1958b).*

and south sides together melt smoothly into a wide, fertile valley. This mountain has the form of two humps, the southern around 700 m above sea level; the northern about 1,000 m above sea level. Here are two drive systems for caribou hunting. On the north side of the southern hump is a large cairn system, and on the north side of the northern hump at 1,000 m level are sixty cairns along a hanging glacier (figure 4.2).

The height of the cairns in the 700 m level varies from 43 to 96 cm with the most common averaging at 70 to 72 cm. This lowest-lying system, located in part around a talus field, includes a shooting blind. The system measures from one end to the other 330 m and consists of thirty-three cairns positioned at intervals from 3 m to 60 m. Despite some missing cairns, the overall impression of the system is similar to a "fold," whose opening faces south-southwest. "It is therefore natural to think that the drivers have frightened the caribou into the corral, where the animals would find themselves captured in the talus field, which functioned as a 'leg-breaker' system" (Rosing 1958b, 386).

At 1,000 m the height of the cairns varies between 35 and 90 cm with the most common height measuring 60–80 cm. This system consists of two rows

FIGURE 4.3. *The northern cairn system (the cairns are outlined in white) at Qinganguaq. The position of the fireplace is at the arrow to the right. (Rosing 1958b.)*

of cairns meeting in a 90 degree angle. The longest row—facing east-west—measures about 82 m and consists of forty-four cairns. The shorter row—facing south-north—consists of sixteen cairns, and has a length of about 30 m, that is, less than 2 m between each cairn (figure 4.3). Twelve m from the northern cairn is a fireplace, 48 × 41 cm, made of fist-sized stones. Cairns are arranged in a sort of staggered double row or zigzag system, where the terrain offers the best escape opportunities for the caribous. The intention was obviously to make a closer barring on vulnerable places.

The 112 m of cairn system form a half frame around a chute sloping from west to east and runs into a hanging glacier covering the mountain slope to the east. Approximately 75–100 m below the system is a gap, described by Jens Rosing to be like scary jaws with teeth of talus rocks covering the foot of Qinganguaq (Rosing 1958b).

In the cairn rows Jens Rosing distinguished and named four types of cairns:

Human cairn—*inussuk* (plural: *inussuit*)—most often three to five stones on top of each other, sometimes with arms and head marked (figure 4.4); column

FIGURE 4.4. *Human cairn—inussuk.*

cairn—a columnar stone, placed upright on a flat stone or rock (figure 4.5); head cairn—a single, more or less round stone, placed on a large stone or rock (figure 4.6); and "scraping board cairn"—a generally flat rectangular stone, upright, leaning on one or two smaller stones, so the shape is reminiscent of a scraping board used during the scraping of seal blubber from the skin (Rosing 1958b:385).

At the foot of each cairn Rosing found large heaps of gray mosses and concluded that the three types of cairns—human, column, and scraping board cairns—had clearly been wrapped in moss and provided with a lump of peat at the top to create the illusion of fur-clad people peering above the rock. The head cairns did not appear wrapped up; instead, they had a single tuft of moss placed on top. He further suggested that for the system to function properly, it would have a smell placed around it, and he assumed that the head cairns were weighing down with old pieces of hide. Oral traditions refers to cairn systems as *aulatsivit* (waving-sites). This suggests that hunters drove caribou toward the mossy cairns by waving bird wings and pieces of hide. Positioned in between the cairns, the archers would meet the animals with a shower of arrows. As the drivers moved in and surrounded the hunting system, the many animals began—as is customary to caribous—to run round and round in the direction against the sun's path. The animals were thus pressed over the slippery shoulder of the glacier and fell into the depths and were mutilated or

FIGURE 4.5. *Column cairn.*

killed among the talus rocks. Here a few heavily weathered animal bones were found, and bones were also melting out of the glacier (Rosing 1958b:387–88).

In the newspaper article from 1958, which Mikiassen reacted strongly against, Jens Rosing interpreted the hunting process to have been as follows: "True hell breaks loose. A rushing horde of caribou pops up on Qinganguaq. Behind them the drivers show up, waving bird wings and skin pieces. The drivers spread out following a particular pattern and gradually take all critical points under control. The caribou herd is confused, scenting and jumps, balks

FIGURE 4.6. *Head cairn.*

at a new smell that strikes the nose heavily like a fist. The animals are jumping back and forth. Everywhere people are popping up. The noise from the yell of the drivers and the agitated dogs' barking grow as they approach the caribou" (Rosing 1958a; my translation from Danish).

It should be noted that dogs assisting in hunting have not been observed in Greenland. Rosing, however, speculates that findings of numerous dog bones at archaeological sites in southern Greenland, where dog sledding is uncommon, suggests a use of dogs for drive hunting (Rosing 1958b). Rosing continues below, partly as seen from the animals' perspectives:

> There is a thunder from the many hooves, and calves, who in the confusion got separated from their mothers, grunts and coughs in fear. Suddenly the herd runs to the east, but then turns back. Their way is obstructed by the escarpment.
>
> Now they continue up over the hill along the escarpment to the north, and from here the animals get out on the glacier and continue towards west and south. The animals in the front stomp their hooves in the glacier so it splutters, and the rear-guard, who have not yet seen the close row of cairns against the sky, run their chest into the rear of the front animals. Everywhere there are noisy people, all routes are blocked, only to the north the way is open; a black gap awaits the caribou, who dare to take the ride. To complete the panic, a fire is lit, and the effect is horrible. Between the moss clad cairns archers are waiting, and a shower of arrows whiz down over the poor animals. The caribou herd is running around against the sun's path, and for each round the glacier gets more slippery. Animals are forced out, and with the tip of their hooves stumped in the ice they tremble for a little while before they plunge into the depths. (Rosing 1958b; my translation from Danish)

Also the final part of the drive hunt is described as being quite dramatic and noisy:

> The roar of joy from the wildly excited hunters rises to a veritable inferno that resonates in the mountains. Finally the last caribou is hit in the heart by a well-aimed arrow and tumbles in a wild death race right out into the air, hits the edge of the glacier and swirls like a brown bundle of antler, bone and fur down into the greedy talus.
>
> The howl of joy persists. The great hunt is over. The hunters walk around among the killed animals and start to slaughter the caribous, which are labeled by their arrows. Parts are awarded to the drivers, and those animals, which without arrow crashed to their death, are divided among the people, who took part in the successful battue. In the evening and late at night there are fires at the hunters' camp, and people are eating the tallow fat meat. Our ancestors must have hunted caribou at Qinganguaq, in this way. (Rosing 1958b; my translation from Danish)

THE SAPUTIT FENCE

Another place where drive hunting is thought to have included "jumps" is found in the Northern Disco Bay at the east side of the small inlet Saputit

FIGURE 4.7. *The Saputit fence. (Photo by Jens Fog Jensen.)*

on the south side of Nuussuaq Peninsula (Nellemann 1969/70, 1970). Here a fence extends from the coast of the fjord over a rocky moraine and through a moist valley down to the foot of a steep mountain—in total approximately 600 m. This fence can stop the animals coming from two valleys extending inland. In its present state, stones of varying size are piled to form a fence up to 1 m in height over long distances (figure 4.7). As large earthbound rocks are part of the fence, it winds its way through the terrain.

According to Nellemann the Saputit fence were used both for driving caribou over precipices and toward hidden hunters; in some places the stony moraine is so uneven and steep as to create places from which animals could be driven to their death (Nellemann 1969/70:140). However in this case the "jumps" are fairly low. On Nellemann's drawing the fence has three openings, the one in the middle around 8 m in width and the two others around 20 m (figure 4.8).

Nellemann does not give an interpretation of hunting technique at this structure. Instead, he refers to a couple of historic, fairly general descriptions of drive hunting from the 1700s, probably made by people who did not witness the hunt themselves. There is only one source, written as a poem in Latin, composed by a priest Ole Lange in 1744, which might describe hunting with a fence: "They drove the terrified animals towards stone fences. When the

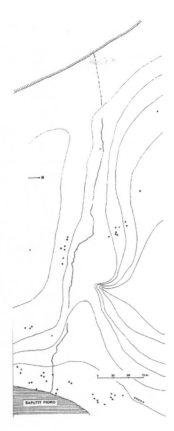

FIGURE 4.8. *Draft of the Saputit fence. Dots are meat caches and traces of shelters (Nellemann 1969/70:136).*

animals in vain crash their chests against these barriers, the hunters will from a close range throw their lances against them and kill them uttering strong roars" (Nellemann 1970:292; my translation from Danish).

The Saputit fence is probably very old as indicated by the slow-growing arctic vegetation seen to cover the fence in several places. At least twenty-seven meat caches and twenty hiding and sleeping places for hunters are found close to the fence. Archaeological excavations have not been carried out, but in the Disko Bay area around Ilulissat Icefjord, which was earlier one of the most densely populated in Greenland, the oral tradition tells that people in ancient times went caribou hunting at Saputit (Nellemann 1970:295).

However, while the cairn/inussuk drive systems like the one at Qinganguaq, described by Rosing, are known from historical sources to have been used by the Inuit/Thule culture, the fence system at Saputit might have been built and used by the Paleoeskimos, prior to being used by the Inuit. Lately it has been observed that in Canada caribou drives fall into two distinct categories (Friesen 2013:20): The first category consists of rows of individual and often quite small inuksuit. They are described in oral history and are believed to have been built by Inuit and Thule culture hunters using bows and arrows. The second category consists of lines that are made up of two continuous walls forming an approximately 90 degree "V" shape with a relatively narrow gap around 8 m in width. These are believed to have been built by the Paleoeskimo Dorset people, who—unlike their Saqqaq predecessors and Thule successors—did not use bows and arrows, but hunted with lances, which made it necessary to get within very short range of the animals. In Canada the hypothesis is that fences deriving from Dorset were built on the presence of Dorset aggregation camps nearby fence systems and, in one instance, because of the presence of diagnostic Dorset artifacts in the drive (Friesen 2013:21).

Despite differences in the arrangement, which might be explained in topographic variation, the Saputit drive system could similarly derive from the Dorset hunters, who were present in the Disko Bay area and had several camps there (Jensen 2006a:105f; Jensen 2006b:199f; Larsen and Meldgaard 1958) prior to use by later Thule and Inuit hunters. This question, however, still remains to be archaeologically investigated.

Only a few other fences have been found in Greenland; Kulussuq is one in the Ammassalik area, Eastern Greenland. The fence is located in a narrow pass between hills and was described in 1912 to be a stone wall or fence, two to three feet wide made of upraised stones connected with a shooting cover for use in reindeer hunting. The stones were comparatively small with no trace of sod between them, and in the middle of the wall was an opening, like a gate. In 1912 elderly men believed they could remember from childhood that it had been taller, so high in fact, that earlier it reached up to the chest of a full-grown man (Thalbitzer 1914:405f). Also this structure has not been fully investigated archaeologically. However, a connection to the Paleoeskimo cultures has been suggested due to the drastic decline in the area's caribou population as well as the overall diminution of the animals themselves leading to a small dwarfish species by AD 1200, a species that then went extinct during the following decades (Møbjerg 1988:92; Meldgaard 1986:40ff).

In Greenland the abovementioned two examples (Qinganguaq and Saputit) together with a third system in the mountains of the Nuuk Fjord area mentioned by George Nellemann (1969/70:141) are the only examples hitherto recorded in which driving over the edge of cliffs took place. This is a practice that Vittus Mikiassen thought could not be connected to his ancestors. According to Nellemann (1970:292–99), the archaeology complements the oral tradition with information that none of the old historical sources provide, namely, that they drove the caribou over the edge of steep mountainsides.

At many other sites, however, drive systems are built for channeling animals toward hunters or into lakes (Grønnow 2009; Grønnow 1986; Grønnow, Meldgaard, and Berglund Nielsen 1983; Nellemann 1970). One of the best documented is the Aasivissuit inussuk system and fence in the "inland" of West Greenland, where excavations in the adjacent midden were also made.

THE AASIVISSUIT SYSTEM

Along two mountain tops, which form a continuous stretch inland from the site Aasivissuit, a complex of structures is found: over 100 single stones and cairns at varying intervals form a row nearly 4 km long along the side of a mountain slope (figure 4.9). This row, which is much more openly spaced than the Qinganguaq rows, consists of a total of 104 recorded inussuit of different construction. Seventy percent are "composite inussuit" and could be described as cairns, being usually constructed of six to ten stones. The height of the cairns is now on average about 50 cm, but the majority have partially collapsed. Thirty percent are "single-stone inussuit" consisting of one prominently placed large stone and including the types elsewhere called "head cairns," "pillar cairns," and "scraping-board stones" (Jens Rosing 1958b). The composite inussuit are in most instances erected on bedrock, whereas the large majority of single-stone inussuit are raised on in situ blocks. They are both easily distinguished from the naturally bedded stones and blocks, often forming conspicuous rows of silhouettes resembling human figures.

The inussuk row can be divided into three sections, 1–3, with different characteristics (figure 4.10). Section 3: On this stretch (A180–A162), the inussuit are placed relatively close together (average distance 39 m). Many caribou trails cross the valley and pass through this section.

Section 2 is more open (average distance in the terrain is 99 m). From the highest point A154 at about 400 m above sea level, this section falls to A139 at about 280 m above sea level. A large number of caribou trails run through the prominent pass between A141 and A139. Section 1 is the stretch between the pass and lake Aasivissuit Tasiat. This part of the row, A139–A72, is characterized by high density (average distance in the terrain 20 m). A110–A107 deviate from the line and form a wing down toward the valley. On the stretch A120–A94, the row is traversed by a few caribou trails (Grønnow et al. 1983).

FIGURE 4.9. *The Aasivissuit drive system. Section I—the stretch between the pass and the lake Aasivissuit Tasiat—of the inussuit row (broken line), looking WSW with Aasivissuit Tasiat in the background. (Grønnow, Meldgaard, and Berglund Nielsen 1983:figure 43.)*

About 150 m west of the campsite is a low fence constructed of stone blocks placed close together, with a present height of 20–60 cm. The fence begins at the talus below the escarpment and runs straight down the slope to the flat area near the lakeshore. The total length is about 70 m. On the west side of the fence are remains of a likely older fence, which finishes just above a bank about 15 m from the lakeshore. The fence crosses around thirty caribou trails on the slope.

Bjarne Grønnow's et al. 1983 interpretation of this inussuk row and fence as structures related to drive hunting is based on the information on battues known from historical sources, and observations on caribou behavior in the catchment area of the camp. When the inussuit are activated, that is to say, the individual structures are linked by means of seal-skin ropes and furnished with turf " heads" or fluttering birds' wings, the row functions as a hunting structure.

It will guide the caribou coming from the east down to the Aasivissuit Lake (see Figure 4.11). The moving caribou will first meet the activated inussuk row

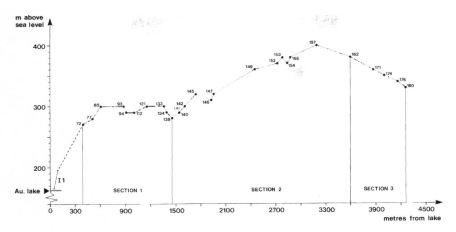

FIGURE 4.10. *The Aasivissuit drive system. Diagram showing elevation and density of the inussuit row. The position of each inussuk is projected onto a vertical section through the mountain ridge. (Grønnow et al. 1983:fig. 42.)*

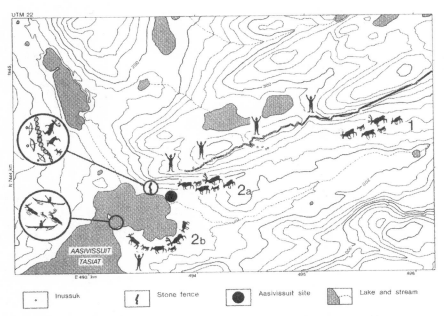

FIGURE 4.11. *Interpretation of the function of the Aasivissuit drive system. (Grønnow et al. 1983:fig. 45.)*

at the most easterly end of the complex (Section III). They will deviate in the direction offering the least resistance to their natural westerly migration course, which means that they will move southwest, parallel to Section III. In this way all the animals are channeled down to follow the system of trails below the relatively steep mountainside toward Section II of the row. Along this stretch only a few inussuit are required to ensure that the animals remain in the valley. Some caribou will constantly enter the WNW passes, but encounter the activated and now denser row of Section I. All the caribou are thus steered in a WSW-oriented route down toward the camp area near the lake. (condensed from Grønnow et al. 1983)

From this point the row of inussuit ends and there are two possible scenarios for the continued hunt:

The final dispatch of the caribou can have been effected in a couple of different ways, since there are natural migration routes both along the slope north of the camp and east of it along the small inlet. If the animals are directed east of the camp, they will pass down over the little river, traverse the flats along the inlet, and finally turn west onto the promontory. Once the caribou are on the promontory, the mere presence of a few beaters will be sufficient to drive them into one body into the water, where they are an easy target for the hunters in kayaks, who shoot forward from their concealment behind the 2 m high southwestern shore to surround the swimming animals and slay them with lances. The dead caribou are then easily towed the short distance across the inlet to the camp. If, on the other hand, it was the intention to turn the caribou along the slope north of the camp, it would be natural to include the fence in the complex. In this case the animals are steered along the increasingly steep slope above the camp, until they are stopped abruptly by a row of bowmen, appearing from behind the fence across their path. (condensed from Grønnow et al. 1983)

The descriptions and interpretations of drive hunting present different scenarios. Jens Rosing (1958a) and Lange (Nellemann 1970) envisioned terrified animals in panic and yelling drivers, while Grønnow et al. 1983 envisioned the driving as a more silent "guiding" process. This less dramatic picture can be confirmed by an eyewitness account, made by Diamond Jenness (1922), of a Canadian Copper Inuit hunter participating in drive hunting with bow and arrow:

Here he lies, face downwards, with his bow and arrows by his side, waiting for the deer to be driven within range. The women and children, in the meantime, have gone to windward, and the deer either catch their scent and move off down the wind, or are set in motion by wolf-howls. If the women are not in sight the caribou usually reach the hunters walking or slowly trotting, at intervals one behind the other, so that often the first is shot before the rest are yet in sight. Sometimes, as they dash back after the first animal is shot, an Eskimo will utter a sudden loud shout, when often they will stop amazed for a moment, and allow him to launch another shaft. Generally, though, the hunter still tries to keep in concealment, and the caribou, meeting the women as they run back, return again. I have seen them driven backwards and for-wards in this way three or four times before the remainder of the herd broke through the lines past the archers and galloped away. Small herds of four or five deer are occasionally exterminated, but usually some of them escape, while not infrequently the deer break past the women at the very begin-ning and never approach the hunters at all. Natives who have only bows and arrows, however, much prefer this method to simple stalking, even in the case of a single caribou, because they are much more certain of securing a shot at close range. (Jenness 1922:149f)

BOWS AND FIRST GUNS

Jenness could witness hunting with bow and arrow in the early 1900s, because in Canada the Copper Inuit did not gain access to firearms until the 1920s (Friesen 2013). In Greenland the flint-lock gun was introduced in the mid-1700s (Grønnow et al. 1983). One watercolor painted by Jens Kreutzmann (1828–99), who was a Greenlandic hunter, shows a large-scale hunting drive, with hunters using bow and arrow (figure 4.12). Even though bow and arrow were more or less replaced after the introduction of the gun in the second half of the 1700s, they enjoyed a revival during the war between Denmark and England (1807–14), and also in the period after the war, when ammunition became difficult to obtain in Greenland (Grønnow et al. 1983). However, at the time of Kreutzmann, large-scale communal hunting was not practiced, and the adherent text to Kreutzmann's watercolor says that it is portraying how the hunt was carried out in earlier times. Small-scale drive hunting, however, continued well into the days of the flint gun. Thus Rosing describes that in the Godthåbsfjord (Nuuk fjord) area there was still a living memory of Anne Johanne, "a fast runner of a girl," and men competed to have her as their driver. From shooting blinds at mountain passes and paths they shot the caribou that Anne Johanne drove up to them. Flint guns were so ineffective that they were hardly worth more than bow and arrow (Rosing 1958b, 388–89).

FIGURE 4.12. *Watercolor by Jens Kreutzmann from the mid-1800s displaying drive hunting with bow and arrow before the introduction of guns. (The National Museum and Archive of Greenland.)*

CRUELTY OR GUIDANCE?

Now let us again return to Vittus Mikiassen, the Greenlandic citizen, who in the newspaper in 1958 strongly reacted against the vivid description recounted by Jens Rosing, which gave him an impression of his ancestors having hunted with cruelty. Jens Rosing was a Greenlandic author and artist with substantial knowledge of the cultural history and wildlife of Greenland. From working on a project introducing caribou herding to Greenland, during import of semi-nomadic reindeer from Norway, he had experience working closely with the animals. This background made it possible for him to give a vivid description of his intuitive vision on the former drive hunting, and additionally as seen from the animals' perspective. His artistic account provides associations of fear and massacre, which is likely the reason behind Mikiassen's reaction to the description as being "cruel."

Some would argue that killing of animals per definition is cruel. Hunter-gatherers, however, do not see animals as a passive resource, or as victims, but rather as active participants in hunting (Schmidt and Dowsley 2010). The hunt is a social relationship, and the animals are sentient beings who can freely decide to give themselves to the hunters (Fienup-Riordan 1994; Nadasdy 2007).

The hunting structures such as cairn lines, fences and shooting blinds, where archers were waiting, made it possible to get very close to the animals. Probably the more silent guiding or channeling process as interpreted by Grønnow et al. (1983) and experienced by Jenness (1922) are better descriptions of the processes that took place. Rosing tells that the Greenlandic name for the cairn systems is: *aulatsiviit* (waving sites), and a picture of people "waving" fits better than "scaring" to define a relationship or even partnership between hunters and animals. The waving was guiding that merely eased the way for a process—the hunt—in which, according to the traditional concept, both hunter and animal had an interest.

But is the idea that the animals were taking a willingly part in the hunt a valid concept at all? Well—not as seen from a Western, Euro-American view. When discussing hunting ethics, however, maybe we should take a more humble attitude as suggested by some. For example, Nadasdy, who conducted research among First Nation hunters in Yukon, Canada, argues that we should at least keep an open mind about the role of animals in the ongoing human-animal relationship of hunting. Also we should be willing to consider the possibility that northern hunters' theories about human-animal relations might be of practical (as well as symbolic and metaphorical) significance. "Much of the time, there is, in fact, no basis on which to evaluate the relative merits of indigenous versus Euro-American theories about animals; each seems to have about the same degree of explanatory power" (Nadasdy 2007:35).

WASTE

Large-scale drive hunting made it possible to kill many animals in a single event. The large midden at the Aasivissuit site has five layers, ranging from a Greenlandic Dorset layer (undated) to a discontinuous Thule culture sequence reaching from circa AD 1200–1950 (Grønnow 1986:59–60). The comprehensive bone collection was well preserved and caribou bones were dominant in all phases, while also arctic hare, arctic fox, and waterfowl were represented. Through all phases animals were killed during the summer and early autumn, and bucks and young animals were hunted more frequently than does. Layer 3 (AD 1700–1750) stood out as different from the other layers, and was characterized as a large bone heap without internal stratification (figure 4.13). Furthermore this layer differed in showing a low degree of bone fragmentation and a high degree of bone articulation, resulting from coarse butchering

FIGURE 4.13. *Excavation at the Aasivissuit midden. Layer 3 is characterized by a low degree of bone fragmentation, which shows clearly in the profile. (Photo by Bjarne Grønnow.)*

(Grønnow 1986:60–61), that is, a low level of utilization. At this time, there was a caribou maximum, followed by a marked decline in the 1750s (Grønnow et al. 1983:83). However, the midden layer 4 (4a—a period around AD 1300, and 4b—a period around AD 1500) from the previous period showed a high level of utilization, though it was also built up during the caribou maxima (Grønnow et al. 1983:73). Consequently, abundance does not necessarily cause a change in the level of utilization. So what did cause this change of strategy from intensive to coarse butchering?

At another ancient camp, L-14, in the area of Angujaartorfiup Nunaa south of the Kangerlussuaq fjord, where concentrated archaeological surveys have been conducted (Odgaard 2007), test excavations revealed thick layers of caribou bones (figure 4.14). In contrast to results from test excavations and surface analyses from other camps in the area, the bones at the site L-14 were mostly complete. Not only were the bones not broken, but complete spinal columns and entire legs in anatomical order were also found (Pasda and Odgaard 2011). This means, as in the layer 3 in Aasivissuit mentioned above, that meat was still on the bones, when thrown in the midden. Two 14C dates from these layers could not be dated with certainty but are younger than AD 1650. However, a glass

FIGURE 4.14. *Test pits in the L-14 midden showed thick layers of mostly whole caribou bones.*

bead in the top layer could be dated to after AD 1730 (Gulløv 1997). Apparently the use of the midden and the site stopped shortly after this period. The many bones in articulated order are interpreted as the remnants of a hunt for many hides (Pasda and Odgaard 2011), which meant that the level of utilization of the animals as additional sources of dried meat and tallow for storing was low, which was also suggested as explanation for the similar layer in the Aasivissuit midden (Grønnow et al. 1983). Arrowheads have been found in the discussed layers at both Aasivissuit and in Angujaartorfiup Nunaa, but no traces of flint from flint guns. So it was not modern hunting implements that caused the change. There was, however, a huge change in the Greenlandic society.

In the 1600s, trading possibilities began with European whalers and, at the beginning of the 1700s, with Danish trade stations (Gulløv 1997:2004). Caribou hides could be traded for foreign articles (Gad 1969), but perhaps became most important in the accelerated internal exchange of raw materials and finished commodities. For example, the price of a small soapstone kettle was 8 to 10 caribou hides and for a lamp, 2, 3, or 4 baleen plates or just as many caribou hides (Egede 1925) as described by Grønnow et al. (1983:86–87).

In the Angujaartorfiup Nunaa area the topography, unlike the topography in the Aasivissuit area, is not well suited for large-scale drive hunting. Nonetheless a number of systems have been estimated to be of a magnitude and complexity that could indicate occasional use of communal drives (Grønnow 2009:204). One of these is close to the camp L-14, and we suspect that the midden should be interpreted as a result of drive hunting (Pasda and Odgaard 2011).

But why did Mikiassen react against the idea of his ancestors having hunted so many animals that the meat would decay? Greenlandic hunters have often been accused of their hunting not being sustainable. In his book *A Farewell to Greenland's Wildlife*, Kjeld Hansen (2002) describes how intensive hunting has decimated the numbers of animals and birds and how great quantities of meat (57% of the catch) are being wasted. Hansen, a Danish journalist and author specializing in environmental and consumer issues, is not the first person to criticize the Greenlandic hunters. In the 1920s, the ethnographer Kai Birket-Smith wrote, "When deer hunting, the West Greenlanders formerly showed the greatest lack of temperance, and in some places conditions may not, even now, be very much improved." He further refers to Karl Ludwig Giesecke, who 100 years earlier wrote: "Gemeinlich nehmen sie von jedem Thiere das Herz, das Bruststück, den Rückgrad, einen Schenkel, das Talg, selten die Geweihe, hauptsächlich aber das Fell mit, welches letztere für sie der Hauptsache und ein Artikel des Luxus für die Weiber ist (Commonly, from every animal they take the heart, the breast, the backbone, a leg, the fat, rarely the antlers, but principally the fur, which for them is the main thing and an item of luxury for women). And he continues: "But now and again, the hunter only took the skin" (Birket-Smith 1924:349).

We—the archaeological team—however, got a totally different impression in the modern hunting camp in Angujaartorfik during our fieldwork in 2003. Here, seventy-three-year-old Agnethe Rosing, who participated in caribou hunting in the inland since her youth, demonstrated the traditional so-called nothing is wasted ideal (Odgaard et al. 2005; Odgaard 2009). To hunt where "nothing is wasted," Agnethe meant that everything from a hunted caribou is used: antler, fur, meat, fat, sinews, bone fat, and bone marrow. At the end of the butchering process, she smashed the richly myelinated bones, which were cooked in a pan to get at the marrow and the bone fat. This practice leaves only clean, splintered bones, and traces of the same pattern of caribou bone treatment have also been observed in many archaeological sites in the area of Angujaartorfiup Nunaa. Caribou bones were scattered on the surface at numerous sites. Some of these surface bones and those from a few test excavations were analyzed. Most of the bones had been smashed into small pieces and had obviously been cooked afterward as Agnethe did in 2003. The same bone treatment has been observed in many other archaeological sites in Greenland, too. Hence it seems the ideal that "nothing is wasted" was shared by some of the prehistoric hunters (Pasda and Odgaard 2011).

PARADOX

Although today few hunters actually use every part of the animal, as shown by Agnethe, the ideal that "nothing is wasted" is strongly cherished. Again and again, during later fieldwork in 2010 and 2012, it was explicitly expressed to us as a hunting ethic by many people—both young and older hunters—who also said that you should "only shoot to eat." On the other hand trophy hunters, hunting either caribou and especially muskox—which were introduced in West Greenland in the 1960s and are today plentiful in the area—are leaving carcasses in the landscape. Why do some hunters today stress that "nothing is wasted," while others waste the majority of the meat? And did the same paradox exist in the past?

The modern caribou hunters in Angujaartorfik don't waste any meat, and they express anger toward some trophy hunters. There are "good" and "bad" trophy hunters. The good ones take all the meat to the butcher, while the bad ones leave the carcasses. The caribou hunters are angry because of the waste of meat, but also because the carcasses are seen as waste that pollutes, if left close to a camp. In the camp a lot of care is taken to keep the site clean of waste. Based on registrations at modern sites and through interviews with the hunters, we know that today the bones are occasionally smashed, but not into such small pieces as in the past, and as done by Agnethe. As a rule, only the marrow cavity is opened to get hold of the marrow but most bones are usually not cooked anymore. The modern treatment of the catch reflects a butchering system that leaves a lot of smelly bone refuse. However, around the modern camp in Angujaartorfik, which is still in use, no bones were visible on the surface. Today, the bones are thrown into the water or onto the riverbank, with the intention that the tidewater will take the bones away. Often the bones are sailed out in a boat and dumped into the fjord. This is done because the animal waste will attract flies that can ruin the drying meat (Pasda and Odgaard 2011).

CACHES

Some modern hunters gave another explanation for taking care of waste. They said that the living caribou could smell the remains and would not come unless they got rid of it by either putting it in water or "under rocks."

At some of the prehistoric sites in the inland, we have observed a pattern of depositing caribou bones "under rocks." Since bones are also found on the surface—some as old as 3,000 years, that is, from the preceding Paleoeskimo period—differing preservation conditions do not create these patterns. In one instance in a camp, there was a cache (figure 4.15) that we at first mistook for a child's grave, located on a small knoll close to another small hilltop with a human grave on top. This grave was so well built that it is not possible to peek into it. The cache had narrow openings between the rocks, which made it possible to discern that inside were bones of caribou. Similar caches with bones have been found; some are "closed" by rocks like the one mentioned, but also many are open at the top. Another variants of deposits found at some of the settlements are deposition of bones in natural cavities under large rocks.

We supposed that, logically, caches built of rocks were used for storing the dried meat, to protect it from foxes. The only possible preservation technique when staying in the inland is to dry the meat. During this process, as demonstrated by Agnethe, all the bones—except for the ribs—must be separated from the meat. Therefore, if the caches were only for storing meat until the end of the season—even if some of the meat was not used or brought out to the coast—the caches would logically be empty, except perhaps for some rib bones. However, there are many other bones in the caches, some of which are full of bones. What is the explanation for this treatment of the bones?

None of the modern hunters knew the meaning of the caches with bones in the inland. During hunting they do build caches for storing a killed animal for a short time, while searching for more animals. But on the way back to the camp, they will take the animal with them and nothing will be left inside.

IDEOLOGY AND ETHICS

From an older questionnaire (Nationalmuseet 1948), we can read that earlier, the bones of caribou were kept separate and isolated from the bones of other animals. Furthermore, the bones were thrown into crevices, which could not be entered from below (questionnaire on file at the National Museum, Copenhagen).

The probable explanation for this bone treatment, which complements some of our observations in the archaeological material, should be sought in ideology

FIGURE 4.15. *Closed cache with content of caribou bones.*

and ethics. Traditionally, hunting by Inuit was connected to strict rules. The rules were principally concerned with fasting and abstinence, but also included certain regulations as to clothing, outdoor life, and daily occupations in general (Rink 1974). Animals were seen as equal to human beings and, in relation to hunting, many ideas and customs, such as bringing gifts to the dead animal and treating it with respect, were known. The general idea was that the number of game animals remained constant if the old rules were observed (Bak 1982). The traditional religious ideas of the historical Greenland Inuit are to a great extent identical to the ideas of the historical Inuit groups in North America, as known from the myths and other information collected during the eighteenth to twentieth centuries. The myths are recorded in several variations but with strong common features (see Sonne 2004). Among Inuit in Alaska (and among other circumpolar people; cf. Brandstrup 1985), the game animals were seen as guests, and failure to host animals properly invited disaster. If people treated an animal's body thoughtlessly, or carelessly wasted or trampled on food, the animals would not return in the future. On the contrary the animals would reward a hunters if they took proper care of the bones of their catch (Fienup-Riordan 1994).

Against this background, the bone-filled caches and crevices at the prehistoric sites can be interpreted as signs of the earlier hunters' conscious care for the remains of the butchered animals. The modern hunters' cleaning up and aversion against the wasting of meat by the trophy hunters possibly also have roots in the traditional ideas about paying respect to the animals. During our interviews with hunters, some said that it is necessary to treat the animals with care, for example, be gentle when cutting the joints.

THE FORAGER'S MODE OF THOUGHT—A MODEL

Considering meat and waste: Did the people of the Thule culture at first share ethics, and did they change this view when they changed their hunting strategy? And what about modern caribou hunters who follow the ethics of "nothing is wasted" and the accusations of Greenlandic hunters' overhunting and waste of meat?

As a way of looking at these contradictions from a wider perspective, Alan Barnard's model, in his article "The Foraging Mode of Thought" (Barnard 2002), can be useful. It has provided a way of discussing and perhaps even of getting closer to a deeper understanding of the dilemmas around Greenlandic hunting.

Barnard's model is built on a long debate within anthropology concerning the relationship between hunter-gatherers and land and resources. One of the most important contributions to this debate is "The Giving Environment" (Bird-David 1990), in which the author describes how hunter-gatherers in South India conceive of their environment as parental. The environment provides food unconditionally for its children—the hunter-gatherers. There is a strong ethic of sharing, and their daily interactions concerning food are like those between siblings, conducted in the idiom of "giving" and "requests to be given." Further, Nurit Bird-David hypothesized that hunter-gatherers elsewhere share the characteristic that their community's views of the environment are centered around metaphors that commonly draw on primary kin relations, though not necessarily just on the "parent" relation (Bird-David 1990).

Barnard has built on this and other arguments and created a simple model that divides all societies into either "foragers" or "nonforagers" (Barnard 2002). According to him, hunter-gatherers are people who see themselves as hunters or gatherers. Foragers, however, belong to a wider category, which includes recent former foragers. These are populations whose older representatives remember the foraging lifestyle or populations that retain values associated with foraging culture.

Nonforaging peoples in the modern world will tend to see people as citizens and the state as a sacred trust. Foragers and recent former foragers, however, see people as free individuals and the state as a constraining authority. This doesn't necessarily have anything to do with colonialism, for in the eyes of hunter-gatherers and other small-scale societies, colonial authority and

TABLE 4.1. Foragers versus nonforagers

	Foragers and recent former foragers	Nonforagers
Economy	Sharing	Accumulation
People	People as free individuals	People as citizens
	State as constraining authority	State as sacred trust
Ideology	The giving Environment	Science—sustainability—conservation
	Reciprocal relationship	Management

Source: Modes of Thought—following Barnard 2002, with my additions

nation-state authority are seen as the same thing. They are both perceived as external to the people.

Barnard finds that foraging populations are more resilient than was previously acknowledged, and that mode of thought is more resilient than mode of production generally, and that the two are interdependent (Barnard 2002:6).

The Greenlandic caribou hunters—both now and earlier—belong to the "foragers." Earlier the economy was fully based on hunting and fishing, but today many have other jobs in order to earn money and much of the food is bought in stores. However, the older representatives remember the foraging lifestyle, and the whole identity of Greenlandic society is still very much defined by the foraging culture. Although our questions to the caribou hunters were about the practices of hunting, their answers often expressed care and respect for the animals. Mark Nuttall—who did research in a North Western Greenlandic hunting and fishing society—also found that in Greenland, successful hunting still depends on right action and respect for animals. "While there may not be colourful and observable rituals to ensure success in hunting, recognition that seals must come to the hunter is implicit in pragmatic behaviour and unspoken attitudes that imply respect and dependence" (Nuttall 1992:137–38).

Greenland today has self-government but it was a Danish colony until 1953, from when it became a Danish county until 1979. The communal institutions in Greenland are inspired by—and often copied from—the Danish institutions. Also, environmental issues such as hunting regulations are based on Western concepts. According to the homepage of the Naalakkersuisut—the self-government—of Greenland, their hunting policy has as its "main objective to ensure appropriate and biologically sound use of hunting resources (primarily mammals and birds). The emphasis is on conservation and reproduction of the resources, and the rationally and seasonally best use" (my translation from Danish).

This formulation is in accordance with the Danish (Western) view on management of game populations and on sustainable hunting. It is based on a so-called scientific environmental conservation perspective, also advocated by Western wildlife protection. Scientific conservation is firmly rooted in the doctrine that the world of nature is separate from, and subordinate to, the world of humanity (Ingold 2000:67).

Therefore, as seen from an outsider's point of view, the Greenlandic hunters seem to be performing the difficult task of balancing between two clashing concepts. The Greenlandic hunting culture is rooted in the forager/giving environment concept. According to this concept, human beings do not hold power over nature and animals—human beings are themselves part of nature, and their relationship with animals is social and reciprocal.

The Greenlandic hunting policy and International critics on the other hand are based on the nonforager/scientific conservation and management concept. This perspective sees humans as dominant and animals as a resource, and they talk about sustainable hunting. The hunting policy is concerned with management, while wildlife organizations focus on conservation. They share the same mode of thought but have different interests.

The discussion here is not about differences between Greenlanders and Danes/Westerners. As pointed out by Barnard the foraging mode of thought transcends the boundary between foragers per se and members of other kinds of society. It includes all people who live on a foraging basis, such as foraging in garbage cans and short-term employment (Barnard 2002:6). It is, in other words, not restricted to "traditional" hunting cultures, but can also characterize, for example, the fishermen in Western cultures, who often dispute with biologists and wildlife environmentalists about the rights to fish and hunt, for example, whales. Following Barnard's model, as foragers, they see people as free individuals and the state as a constraining authority. Like the Inuit hunters, they too have to relate to two clashing concepts. For this reason the opposition is not between traditional and Western people, but between foragers and nonforagers (Odgaard 2014).

Negotiation?

It still remains to be explained why there is a bone pattern at most of the old sites reflecting the "nothing is wasted" ethics, whereas at a few sites, there are middens with thick layers of bone in articulated order from the 1600s–1700s. Did the people of the Thule culture share the ethics that "nothing is wasted" and did they change this view, when they needed caribou hides for trading?

This strategy must have presented some kind of concern, since the animals or the animal master would get angry if such an excessive number of animals were killed that their leftovers had to be consumed by foxes and ravens (Kleivan and Sonne 1985:19). And the West Greenlanders believed that a hunter who killed too many caribou calves ran a risk of his own children dying (19–20). However, in a reciprocal relationship there is usually room for some negotiation. At the middens, some of the meat is obviously wasted, but there must have been attention toward the remains of the animals, because they represented the animals' regeneration. And compared to the modern trophy hunters who leave carcasses in the open, there is an obvious difference with the remains in the middens being placed—or sited—there. Practical explanations for collecting the bones, instead of leaving them here and there, could be for aesthetic reasons—that is to keep the rest of the camp clean. But it would not keep flies away, which is the reason for dumping the bones in the fjord at the modern camp in Angujaartorfik.

Logically, the middens must represent negotiation and some kind of "care" for the bones, similar to placing bones under rocks, and they were probably perceived as a kind of "graveyard." However, this aspect still remains to be investigated further. None of the middens mentioned have been fully excavated. In the Aasivissuit midden, a trench has been made, and at L-14, nine test pits were dug. It does not give the full picture of the layout and contents of these middens. With the idea of the animals as guests in mind, items such as hunting tools and glass beads found in the middens might be interpreted as gifts to the animals, in the same way as knives, harpoon heads and other implements—and, after contact time, glass beads—were given as gifts to hunted bears (Kleivan and Sonne 1985:21). To investigate this and other possible patterns of special treatment of the animal bones, single-context excavations of middens might reveal new insights.

CONCLUSION

When Mikiassen reacted against Rosings's interpretation of his ancestors as having hunted with cruelty, the ancestors would probably have agreed with Mikiassen. Their hunting followed an ideology of having a reciprocal relationship with the animals, which were not victims but participants in the hunt. In his artistic vision of a spectacular drama Rosing described the animals as poor, scared, and forced out, which is incompatible with this ideology. Further, the actual hunting probably was less noisy and resulted in less anxiety for both hunters and animals.

It seems, however, that Mikiassen's ancestors did drive animals over the edge of cliffs—at least in the case of the Qinganguaq drive in the Nuuk fjord area. In addition his ancestors during the 1600s and 1700s sometimes killed so many animals that some of the meat would decay, though the reciprocal relationship included the hunters' respectful treating of the animals. Probably the respectful treatment of those animals will be evident in the middens, which in the archaeological record should be treated not as just heaps of "waste" but rather as places for negotiation of the human-animal relationship.

REFERENCES CITED

Bak, Ove. 1982. *Eskimoisk virkelighed.* Copenhagen: Gyldendal.

Barnard, Alan. 2002. "The Foraging Mode of Thought." In *Self and Other-Images of Hunter-Gatherers,* ed. H. Steward, A. Barnard, and K. Omura, 1–24. Senri Ethnological Studies No. 60. Osaka: National Museum of Ethnology.

Bird-David, Nurit. 1990. "The Giving Environment: Another Perspective on the Economic System of Gatherer-Hunters." *Current Anthropology* 31 (2): 189–96. https://doi.org/10.1086/203825.

Birket-Smith, Kaj. 1924. "Ethnography of the Egedesminde District: With Aspects of the General Culture of West Greenland." *Monographs on Greenland* 66:1–486.

Brandstrup, Lasse. 1985. *Dyrenes liv og død: De eskimoiske og sibiriske jægere.* Copenhagen: Borgen.

Dumond, Don. 1984. "Prehistory of the Bering Sea Region." In *Handbook of North American Indians, Arctic,* ed. D. Damas. Vol. 5:94–105. Washington, DC: Smithsonian Institution.

Egede, Hans. 1925. *Relationer fra Grønland 1721–36 (1737) & Det gamle Grønlands ny Perlustration (1741),* ed. L. Bobé 1–304 and 305–404. Monographs on Greenland 54. Copenhagen.

Fienup-Riordan, Ann. 1994. *Boundaries and Passages: Rule and Ritual in Yup'ik Eskimo Oral Tradition.* Norman: University of Oklahoma Press.

Friesen, Max. 2013. "The Impact of Weapon Technology on Caribou Drive System Variability in the Prehistoric Canadian Arctic." *Quaternary International* 297 (May): 13–23. https://doi.org/10.1016/j.quaint.2012.12.034.

Friesen, Max, and Charles Arnold. 2008. "The Timing of the Thule Migration: New Dates from the Western Canadian Arctic." *American Antiquity* 73 (3): 527–38. https://doi.org/10.1017/S0002731600046850.

Gad, Finn. 1969. *Grønlands Historie II:1700–1782.* Copenhagen: Arnold Busck.

Grønnow, Bjarne. 1986. "Archaeological Investigations of West Greenland Caribou Hunting." *Arctic Anthropology* 23 (1–2): 57–80.

Grønnow, Bjarne. 2009. "Caribou Hunting Structures and Hunting Grounds of the Thule Culture in Angujaartorfiup Nunaa, West Greenland." In *On the Track of the Thule Culture from Bering Strait to East Greenland: Proceedings of the SILA Conference 'The Thule Culture—New Perspectives in Inuit Prehistory', Copenhagen, Oct. 26th–28th, 2006. Papers in Honour of Hans Christian Gulløv*, ed. Grønnow, Bjarne. Publications from the National Museum Studies in Archaeology and History, vol. 15:201–10. Copenhagen: National Museum of Denmark.

Grønnow, Bjarne, Morten Meldgaard, and Jørn Berglund Nielsen. 1983. "Aasivissuit: The Great Summer Camp." In *Archaeological, Ethnographical and Zooarchaeological Studies of a Caribou-Hunting Site in West Greenland*. Monographs on Greenland vol. 230; *Man and Society* 5. Copenhagen.

Gulløv, Hans Christian. 1997. *From Middle Ages to Colonial Times: Archaeological and Ethnohistorical Studies of the Thule Culture in South West Greenland 1300–1800* AD. Monographs on Greenland 312; *Man and Society* 23. Copenhagen.

Gulløv, Hans Christian. 2004. *Grønlands Forhistorie*. Copenhagen: Gyldendal.

Hansen, Kjeld. 2002. *A Farewell to Greenland's Wildlife*. Copenhagen: Gad.

Ingold, Tim. 2000. *The Perception of the Environment. Essays in Livelihood, Dwelling and Skill*. London: Routledge. https://doi.org/10.4324/9780203466025.

Jenness, Diamond. 1922. *Report of the Canadian Arctic Expedition 1913–18*. Vol. 12: *The Life of the Copper Eskimos*. Ottawa.

Jensen, Jens Fog. 2006a. "Arkæologien." *Arktisk Station 1906–2006*: 98–111. Copenhagen: University of Copenhagen.

Jensen, Jens Fog. 2006b. *The Stone Age of Qeqertarsuup Tunua (Disko Bugt): A Regional Analysis of the Saqqaq and Dorset Cultures of Central West Greenland*. Monographs on Greenland vol. 336; *Man & Society* 32. Copenhagen.

Kleivan, Inge, and Birgitte Sonne. 1985. *Eskimos: Greenland and Canada: Iconography of Religions, Section VIII, fascicle 2*. Groningen: Institute of Religious Iconography, University of Groningen.

Larsen, H., and J. Meldgaard. 1958. "Palaeo-Eskimo Cultures in Disko Bugt, West Greenland." *Meddelelser om Grønland* 161(2): 1–75.

Mason, Owen. 2009. "Flight from the Bering Strait: Did Siberian Punuk/Thule Military Cadres Conquer Northwest Alaska?" In *The Northern World* AD 1100–1350: *The Dynamics of Climate, Economy and Politics*, ed. H. Maschner, R. McGhee, and O. Mason, 76–128. Salt Lake City: University of Utah Press.

McGhee, Robert. 1996. *Ancient People of the Arctic*. Vancouver: University of British Columbia Press.

Meldgaard, Morten. 1986. *The Greenland Caribou—Zoogeography, Taxonomy, and Population Dynamics*. Monographs on Greenland vol. 25. *Bioscience* 20. Copenhagen: Museum Tusculanum Press.

Mikiassen, Vittus. 1958. Letter to the editor of Atuagagdliutit in *Grønlandsposten* 98. årgang 1958, nr. 22: 12, Greenland.

Møbjerg, Tinna. 1988. "De palæoeskimoiske kulturer i Ammassalik district." In *Palæoeskimoisk forskning i Grønland: Foredrag fra et symposium om de palæoeskimoiske kulturer i Grønland, afholdt på Moesgård i marts 1987*, ed. T. Møbjerg, B. Grønnow, and Schultz-Lorentzen. Aarhus, Denmark: Aarhus University Press.

Nadasdy, Paul. 2007. "The Gift in the Animal: The Ontology of Hunting and Human-Animal Sociality." *American Ethnologist* 34 (1): 25–43. https://doi.org/10.1525/ae.2007.34.1.25.

Nationalmuseet. 1948. "Ethnographic Investigations in Greenland by the National Museum of Denmark (NES)." Questionnaires drawn up by K. Birket-Smith. Written answers collected in the period 1948–1958 (unpublished). Kept at Etnografisk Samling, Nationalmuseet, Copenhagen.

Nellemann, George. 1969/70. "Caribou Hunting in West Greenland." *Folk (Kobenhavn)* 11–12:133–54.

Nellemann, George. 1970. "Rensdyrjagten i Vestgrønland. Jagtmetoder I fortid og nutid." *Tidsskriftet Grønland*, 289–308. Copenhagen.

Nuttall, Mark. 1992. *Arctic Homeland: Kinship, Community and Development in Northwest Greenland*. Toronto: University of Toronto Press.

Odgaard, Ulla. 2007. "Historic and Prehistoric Caribou Hunters in West Greenland." In *Les Civilisations du Renne d'hier et d'aujourd'hui: Approches ethnohistoriques et archéologiques et anthropologiques XXVIIe rencontres internationales d'archéologie et d'histoire d'Antibes*, ed. S. Beyries, and V. Vaté, 1–22, Antibes: APDCA.

Odgaard, Ulla. 2009. "Tent Houses, Territories and Two Generations." In *On the Track of the Thule Culture from Bering Strait to East Greenland: Proceedings of the SILA Conference 'The Thule Culture—New Perspectives in Inuit Prehistory', Copenhagen, Oct. 26th–28th, 2006. Papers in Honour of Hans Christian Gulløv*, ed. Grønnow, Bjarne. Publications from the National Museum Studies in Archaeology and History vol. 15:185–99. Copenhagen: National Museum Studies in Archaeology and History.

Odgaard, Ulla. 2014. "Clash of Concepts: Hunting Rights and Ethics in Greenlandic Caribou Hunting." In *Northern Worlds: Landscapes, Interactions and Dynamics*, ed. Hans Christian Gulløv. Publications from the National Museum. Studies in Archaeology and History 22:157–73.

Odgaard, Ulla, Pauline Knudsen, Hans Christian Petersen, and Agnete Lemcke. 2005. *Bosættelsesmønstre i det centrale Vestgrønland. Rapport om undersøgelserne i Angujaartorfiup Nunaa, Maniitsoq Kommune, sommeren 2003. SILA—Feltrapport 20.*

Pasda, Kerstin, and Ulla Odgaard. 2011. "Nothing is Wasted: The Ideal 'Nothing is Wasted' and Its Divergence in Past and Present among Caribou Hunters in Greenland." *Quaternary International* 238 (1–2): 35–43. https://doi.org/10.1016/j.quaint.2010.12.036.

Powers, William R., and Richard H. Jordan. 1990. "Human Biogeography and Climate Change in Siberia and Arctic North America in the Fourth and Fifth Millennia BP." *Philosophical Transactions of the Royal Society of London: Series A, Mathematical and Physical Sciences* 330 (1615): 665–70. https://doi.org/10.1098/rsta.1990.0047.

Rink, Henry J. 1974. *(org. 1875). Tales and Traditions of the Eskimo.* Montreal: McGill-Queen's University Press.

Rosing, Jens. 1958a. "Drivjagt på vildren." *Atuagagdliutit, Grønlandsposten* 98. årgang 1958, nr. 18:13–20.

Rosing, Jens. 1958b. "Tanker ved et 'Viftested.'" *Tidsskriftet Grønland, Det grønlandske Selskab* 1958:385–92.

Schmidt, Jeremy J., and Martha Dowsley. 2010. "Hunting with Polar Bears: Problems with the Passive Properties of the Commons." Human Ecology 38 (3): 377–87.

Sonne, Birgitte. 2004. Sagn og Myter. Arktisk Institut. Accessed May 12, 2006. https://arktiskinstitut.dk/vidensdatabaserne/groenlandske-sagn-myter/soeg-i-sagn-myter/.

Thalbitzer, William. 1914. "Ethnographical Collections from East Greenland (Angmagsalik and Nualik) Made by Holm, Amdrup and Petersen, Described by Thalbitzer." In *The Ammassalik Eskimo: Contributions to the Ethnology of the East Greenland Natives,* ed. Thalbitzer. Part. Monographs on Greenland no. 39. Copenhagen.

Wright, James V. 1995. "A History of the Native People of Canada." In *10,000–1000 BC Archaeological Survey of Canada,* vol. 1. Mercury Series Paper No. 152. Hull: Canadian Museum of Civilization.

5

Are Models of Ancient Bison Population Structure Valid?

David Maxwell
and Jonathan Driver

The impetus for writing this paper is our continuing curiosity about the low representation of bison calves and yearlings in archaeological assemblages from the northwestern plains of North America. Decades of research support the hypothesis that the indigenous peoples of these regions were heavily dependent on bison for food, shelter, and the raw materials of daily life, and that bison featured prominently in social and ideological behavior (Brink 2008). Understanding the history of people in this region therefore also requires an understanding of bison and their relationships with both the natural environment and their human predators. Archaeologists began the systematic examination of seasonality and population structure in bison death assemblages more than forty years ago, and it soon became apparent that young animals were underrepresented (and sometimes completely absent) in many sites. We believe that exploring this phenomenon can improve our understanding of the human and natural past in regions where bison was the dominant species during the Holocene.

We have summarized the history of this research and explored possible hypotheses for this phenomenon elsewhere (Driver and Maxwell 2013). Interpretations of bison death assemblages have been based on a standard, idealized model of bison population structure, derived from modern observations of bison, accounts from Native Americans' and First Nations' oral histories, written documents by early European

DOI: 10.5876/9781607326823.c005

colonists, and general models borrowed from ecological studies of large mammals. Most archaeologists predict that if mass kills of bison herds were made, the population structure in the kill site should reflect a "natural" population structure that would result from the simultaneous death of an entire social unit, a pattern often referred to as "catastrophic" mortality. The normal assumption is that catastrophic mortality would result in the deaths of significant numbers of calves and yearlings, because natural populations normally include large numbers of individuals in these two age classes. However, most population structures in archaeological bison death assemblages do not conform to this pattern, because young animals are underrepresented. Explanations have fallen into two general categories. The first is that taphonomic processes selectively removed the bones of young animals after death but before excavation. Examples of such process include differential destruction of immature bone by scavengers, or greater susceptibility of immature bones to destruction by mechanical and chemical agents. The second is that some unknown component of ancient human behavior affected the percentage of young animals in the archaeological assemblage. Examples of such behavior include separation of calves from the herd prior to a kill, or removal of complete calf carcasses after a kill had been made. These hypotheses assume that the living herd had a particular population structure, and that we have to explain why that population structure is not preserved at a kill site. We propose an alternative explanation: that our models of bison population structure are inadequate, and the reason that we do not find the predicted patterns is because the basis for the predictions is incorrect.

In a previous paper, we suggested that our models might be incorrect because archaeologists had modeled bison population structure as it would appear immediately after the calving season in the late spring. We suggested that a range of factors would remove calves from the population after the birth season but prior to the times of year when mass kills of bison seem to have been most prevalent (fall through early spring). We also suggested that predation by wolves might be a particularly important factor in removal of young animals from the bison population available for human hunters.

In this chapter we first discuss the extent to which archaeologists have used standard or idealized models of the ecology and behavior of ancient bison, and evaluate the validity of using such models. We ask whether widely accepted accounts of bison behavior and ecology are too general, and if it would be better to model greater variation. We do this by examining a number of behaviors that should be important in understanding human interactions with bison. We will suggest that some behaviors are appropriately modeled with little variation, and that in other cases archaeologists have already incorporated realistic levels of variation into their behavioral models. We then explore the concept that ancient bison population structures ought to conform to a standard model by examining whether or not modern animal populations have predictable structures. We conclude that the known variation in population structures of modern ungulates has not been incorporated adequately into models used by archaeologists. We then examine the implications of this conclusion for understanding the age structure of bison death assemblages.

BISON BEHAVIORS RELEVANT TO ANALYSIS OF MASS KILLS

In this section we examine a series of examples to assess whether archaeologists use realistic models of bison behavior. Many features of bison behavior and ecology would have been significant to the people who relied so heavily on this species, but we will focus on phenomena likely to be most relevant for interpreting mass kill sites. We have selected behaviors that are discussed widely in the literature, that are measurable through archaeological remains, and that seem most relevant to ancient human decision-making about hunting. The behaviors we have selected for analysis are seasonality of reproduction, social structure, and seasonal movement. Each of these aspects of bison behavior can be examined directly from bison specimens preserved in archaeological sites. Other important behaviors that would affect human hunting decisions, such as population density or intensity of predation by nonhuman predators or bison response to the presence of humans, are much more difficult to assess from archaeological data.

SEASONALITY OF REPRODUCTION

Interpretation of the timing of mass kills of bison depends upon the assumption that calves were born in a relatively restricted time frame, and therefore that rutting was also concentrated in a restricted season. Allen Rutberg (1984) argued that the demonstrable synchrony of births on the National Bison Range, Montana, could not be explained as a response to predation, and that it was an adaptation to minimize stress on calves and mothers by timing births to coincide with better weather and more nutritious food. Researchers who rely more on historic period observations and oral traditions of indigenous peoples also support the hypothesis of restricted rutting and birth seasons (e.g., Arthur 1974; Binnema 2001; Brink 2008; Cooper 2008; Frison 2004; Frison and Todd 1987; Geist 1996; Hamilton, Nicholson, and Wiseman 2006; McHugh

1972). Furthermore, the presence of numerous mandibles with identical stages of tooth eruption and wear in ancient mass kills (e.g., Reher 1973) provides good evidence that births were highly synchronous. Less often discussed is the overall success of reproduction in relation to variation in seasonal weather. For example, poor weather at the birth season could have a deleterious effect on the percentage of calves that survive for a particular year. Similarly, disruption to the rut resulting from unusual weather might affect the percentage of pregnant females, and a change in timing of the rut might result in calves being born at less than optimal times. While all accounts of bison reproduction mention the presence of births at other seasons, there is overwhelming evidence from a variety of direct observations and archaeological analysis to support the idea that bison births were highly seasonal during the Holocene. Of course, the birth date varied according to location, and southern dates were typically earlier than those in the north. However, we suggest that modeling a highly seasonal reproductive cycle is justified and that variation from this model is well understood and likely to have minimal impact on archaeological interpretation.

SOCIAL STRUCTURE

Mass kills are usually assumed to be the result of killing either an entire social unit, or a portion of a social unit, and the archaeological remains are often compared to idealized models of bison herds. Herd structure can be described in terms of the age and sex of animals that associate together, and whose cohesion may be expressed through other behaviors, such as group defense or coordinated movement. It would be expected that herd structures could vary seasonally and in relation to the habitat occupied (e.g., woodland versus open grassland).

The most widely discussed aspects of bison herd structure are age and sex composition, together with seasonal variation in those components. Virtually all authors agree that the two primary divisions of bison herds throughout much of the year are larger cow-calf herds (cows, calves of both sexes, and sexually immature males) and smaller groups of bulls (Berger and Cunningham 1994; Binnema 2001:42; Cooper 2008:103, 113–14; Hamilton, Nicholson, and Wiseman 2006:297; McHugh 1972:156–57; Shaw and Meagher 2000). This pattern changes during the primary breeding season, when herds merge and sexually mature bulls seek and guard mates. This pattern appears to be reasonably well documented in archaeological sites. Most mass kills reflect the successful hunting of a female-dominated group. This is usually interpreted as a cow-calf herd, even though calves and yearlings may be underrepresented.

A number of authors note that barren females might join bull groups, and John Speth (1983) attributes the presence of females in a predominantly male assemblage at Garnsey (on the southern plains) to this phenomenon. He also suggests that the rather high proportion of females might indicate a period when fewer females were carrying calves, suggesting poorer environmental conditions. With the exception of the reduced presence of young animals in cow-calf herds (which we discuss later), we again suggest that archaeologists have created a viable model for herd structures, that they understand the seasonal nature of herd structure, and that they are aware of possible exceptions to the model. There is evidence that group size and composition may have been influenced by topography (Berger and Cunningham 1994:84), and this is something that perhaps should be given greater consideration when comparing bison from different regions (e.g., Rocky Mountain foothills versus open plains).

SEASONAL MOVEMENT

Another issue of considerable importance to understanding bison behavior is seasonal movement. Hugh Dingle (1996:23–25) notes that migration is only one of a number of different types of animal movement. Migrations have most or all of the following characteristics: persistent movement beyond the original habitat; "straightened out" movement; migrating animals ignore stimuli such as opportunities to feed; distinctive behaviors are associated with leaving one habitat and entering another; and energy is reallocated to support the moving period. Migrations may be of various kinds, including "to-and-fro," circular, nomadic, or one-way (Dingle 1996:40–63). A.R.E. Sinclair (1983:241) reserved *migration* for round-trip movements and argued that ungulates migrated primarily to improve their reproductive potential, typically by moving to high-value food sources at critical times in the reproductive cycle when pulses of energy or protein would be most valuable. He noted that one of the key characteristics of most ungulate migrations was that animals could remain on their nonbreeding habitat (and breed there) throughout the year if necessary, but normally could not survive year-round on the breeding range. Archaeologists need to be cautious about using the term *migration*, when they may be referring to other kinds of seasonal movement.

Whether or not bison undertook migrations, and the nature of those migrations and other movements, has been a subject of considerable debate. Virtually all archaeological writers recognize that bison were mobile and that the timing, distance, and causes of movement varied geographically and temporally (e.g., Arthur 1974; Binnema 2001:38–39; Brink 2008:62; Cooper

2008:109–17; Hamilton, Nicholson, and Wiseman:290–97). As a result, the general assumption is that most bison participated in seasonal migrations of varying lengths, with the possible exception of populations in the boreal forest, where movement may have been largely within a home range. However, bison populations had declined catastrophically well before modern methods of movement analysis, such as those listed by Keith Hobson and Ryan Norris were available (Hobson and Norris 2008:table 1.1). In addition, there were no systematic, long-term studies of bison in a single region prior to decimation of the population that could establish causes of movement and the predictability of movement.

There is no doubt that some bison undertake seasonal migrations in the sense used by Dingle (1996). For example, Jason Bruggeman et al. (2009) demonstrate that some bison in Yellowstone National Park undertake a seasonal migration in a to-and-fro pattern. Not all bison individuals participate in this activity, and some remain on their home range for the entire year. The longitudinal study at Yellowstone also demonstrates some medium-term and short-term variation in bison migration. For example, in the medium term, as the numbers of bison have increased, the size of the nonmigratory herd also increased until a saturation point was reached on the home range, at which point the number of migrating animals continued to rise, while the home population remained stable. However, migratory patterns are also affected by short-term considerations, such as the depth of the snowpack in the home range. James Shaw and Mary Meagher propose that on open grasslands bison were probably nomadic, rather than migratory (Shaw and Meagher 2000). In other words, rather than displaying a predictable seasonal movement to take advantage of known areas of high forage values, they would react to threats and opportunities whose location would be random. For example, a heavy snowstorm or a fire might induce them to move away from a location, while seasonal rainfall might accelerate vegetation growth and attract animals. Richard Hart (2001) analyzed historical records and concluded that there was little evidence for true migration on the plains, nor evidence that bison grazed briefly in one area and then moved on. He suggested that bison could be found in the same locale for many months, and that movements were essentially unpredictable. Clare Duncan et al. (2012) propose that migratory and nomadic ungulate species are less likely to be to be at risk from drought conditions than sedentary species. Douglas Bolger et al. (2008) state that human disruption of migratory routes often leads to population collapse, noting an 88 percent decrease in wildebeest populations at Tarangire National Park (Tanzania) between 1988 and 2001 due to human impacts on migration routes.

Various archaeological and historical analyses have tried to develop general models for bison movement, particularly in the 1980s. R. Grace Morgan (1980) argued for a regular pattern of movement on and off the northern Plains, with winter (off-plains) herds being larger. Jeffrey Hanson (1984) suggested that movements were less predictable and that local conditions would influence the timing, duration, and direction of bison movement. Henry Epp (1988; Epp and Dyck 2002) used modern wildlife data to support the idea that bison formed both residential and migratory herds, with human hunters depending on the former year-round and taking advantage of seasonal pulses resulting from the arrival of migrants. Douglas Bamforth (1987) used modern ungulate behavior as the basis for modeling bison. He also suggested that it would be important to understand the influence of local or unpredictable conditions on a more general pattern of movement of the kind proposed by Morgan. Brian Chisholm et al. (1986) pioneered the use of stable carbon isotope analysis of bison collagen to assess the extent to which individuals were moving across major vegetation zones. They were able to demonstrate that individual bison found in certain vegetation zones must have consumed plants found in a different vegetation zone at some point during their lives, and drew the conclusion that a cyclical movement from open grasslands to more sheltered locales was a plausible pattern. However, they were unable to specify routes and could not comment on the regularity of such movement. Hopcraft et al. (2014) note that wildebeest move in response to food quality, paying little regard to predation risk; it is possible that bison movements were similar.

In spite of more than a century of debate about the question, there seems little likelihood that the nature of bison seasonal movement can be resolved into a simple model, and archaeologists are aware of this. Researchers seem to have accepted that bison movement had the following characteristics: First, regardless of the general predictability of seasonal movements, these could be disrupted by unpredictable events such as fires or drought. Second, if there was any predictability of movement, it would only apply to bison in a particular area and not universally across the bison range. Third, there is a strong likelihood that both resident and mobile populations were present in many regions. More sophisticated analyses of stable isotopes and trace elements in bison skeletons should allow archaeologists to study the actual movements of ancient bison populations. Research by Graves (this volume) provides an excellent example of the potential of these techniques, and shows that considerable variation in bison movements occurred on the southern Plains during Folsom times.

MODELS FOR BISON POPULATION STRUCTURES TESTED AGAINST LIVING POPULATIONS

The first part of this chapter suggested that some aspects of bison behavior and ecology were reasonably modeled on well-supported information from historical and contemporary accounts of bison, including the pronounced seasonality of the reproductive cycle and the social structure of bison herds. In these cases, it is reasonable to apply a consistent model of expectations to past situations. The previous discussion also established that archaeologists are aware that some behaviors, notably seasonal movement patterns, are likely to be highly variable and contingent on local factors, such as topography, vegetation, fire and weather. When bison movement is discussed, archaeologists are not prone to simplistic "one size fits all" models; instead, they use principles from historical and modern information in order to use hypotheses about past bison movements for further testing and evaluation.

In the case of the population structure of bison herds, as we have shown elsewhere (Driver and Maxwell 2013), archaeologists have adopted a model of bison age structure that is derived from very general models of large mammal age structures. It is difficult to test the validity of that model, because of a lack of detailed information about bison age structures in historical records, and the lack of free-ranging bison herds today that live under comparable conditions to their ancestors on the northern Plains. We therefore propose to examine the "goodness of fit" of a general ungulate age structure model against the reality of living populations of large social grazing ungulates that have been intensively studied by contemporary researchers.

Sinclair and A. E. Byrom describe blue wildebeest (*Connochaetes taurinus*) as a keystone species in the Serengeti, playing a considerable role in determining the abundance and diversity of the large mammal community, along with the physical structure and the species composition of grasses and herbs, and ultimately all related biota, including birds (see also Sinclair and Byrom 2006:66; Sinclair et al. 2007). We suggest using that species as an example of a very well-studied grazing ungulate, in order to understand the expected range of variation in population structures.

Wildebeest are highly migratory, with an annual range of roughly 25,000 sq. km (Norton-Griffiths 1973:136; Pascual, Kareiva, and Hilborn 1997). Larger herds are usually broken into smaller groups, at least some of which tend to be nonmigratory or resident (Ndibalema 2009). Calves make up a relatively small portion of wildebeest herd populations, typically ranging from 13 to 21 percent (Ndibalema 2009:table 1; Rudnai 1974:table 6; Sinclair 1973:102;) and are less abundant in migratory herds than in resident populations. Wildebeest usually give birth to a single calf, typically during March or April (Sinclair, Mduma, and Arcese 2000:2101). Vedasto Ndibalema (2009:579) calculates that the mean annual calf survivorship rate for migratory herds is 84.4 ± 3.4 percent (compared with 44% ± 4.7% for resident herds); yearling survival is 31 ± 3.8 percent for migratory herds (39% ± 2.3 percent for resident herds). Simon Mduma (1996:40–41) demonstrates that there are wide fluctuations in survival rate from year to year and that yearlings (like calves) frequently survive best during wet seasons. Yearlings appear to be the least-common age group in modern wildebeest populations (Mason 1990) and are present in low numbers in all available population data. Migratory herds are composed of nearly equal numbers of male and female adults (Ndibalema 2009:table 1), with adult females slightly more common. Resident herds are composed primarily of adult females (47%), with adult males much less abundant (12%). Subdominant adult males in resident herds tend to congregate together, forming bachelor herds.

A. Mysterud, T. Coulson, and N. C. Stenseth note that adult males play a significant role in ungulate populations, with their numbers playing an important role in overall population resilience (Mysterud, Coulson, and Stenseth 2002). Males can be responsible for a variety of reproductive issues, including the timing of synchronous births, a key adaptive strategy for many migratory ungulates.

Wildebeest have undergone a tremendous resurgence in population over the past fifty years, after suffering through considerable population loss during the 1960s and before (Foster and Kearney 1967; Pascual, Kareiva, and Hilborn 1997; Sinclair 1973:table 8). G. J. Chirima, N. Owen-Smith, and B.F.N. Erasmus show that even when wildebeest populations remain relatively constant over a period of several years, these animals have a very patchy distribution, being abundant in some areas of Kruger National Park, and scarce in others (Chirima, Owen-Smith, and Erasmus 2012). This is the case even when these areas are immediately adjacent to each other.

MORTALITY AND PREDATION

Lions are the predominant predators affecting the wildebeest population. J. B. Foster and D. Kearney note that wildebeest comprised only 6.5 percent of the total game population in Nairobi National Park, yet made up 26 percent of all discovered kills (Foster and Kearney 1967). These authors suggest that at least part of this is due to lions being "habit" killers, who will target wildebeest regardless of whatever other types of game may be available. Judith Rudnai (1974) reports that lions do not exhibit any preference toward age or sex selection bias when hunting wildebeest, despite selecting male and juvenile zebra.

Rudnai (1974:table 6) observes that juvenile wildebeest in the observed population account for 15.2 percent of the population, but make up 18.3 percent of the animals observed in lion kills. Thus, there is a slight bias toward the taking of juveniles by lions, but probably not severe enough to remove this age group from the population. M.G.L. Mills and T. M. Shenk report the same thing (Mills and Shenk 1992:698), pointing out that there was no difference in the frequency of juvenile and adult wildebeest killed by lions, and the observed proportions of these age groups in the population; this was not true for zebra. "No selection for wildebeest calves could be shown and adult males and females were taken in proportion to their presence in the population" (Mills and Shenk 1992:700).

Wildebeest are a particularly important component of the lion diet during the calving period in March and April, though Rudnai (1974) does not think there is preferential predation on calves. Rudnai (1974:223) reports that wildebeest calves frequently survive lion attacks, as the predators choose larger game, but are left to fend for themselves thereafter, and probably do not survive long in the wild.

Cheetahs, on the other hand, show a marked tendency to hunt juvenile wildebeest preferentially over adults. J. S. Hunter, S. M. Durant, and T. M. Caro note that forty-five of forty-seven wildebeest taken by cheetahs were juvenile, compared with only two adults (Hunter, Durant, and Caro 2007:1035). Although this undoubtedly reflects the smaller body size of cheetahs compared to lions, it does demonstrate that juvenile wildebeest have multiple predators and that the presence of multiple predators should influence population age distribution.

Hyenas also hunt wildebeest on a regular basis. K. E. Holekamp et al. (1997) observed hyenas hunting outside of a wildebeest calving area, and note that hyenas typically hunt adult wildebeest in the Masai Mara National Reserve, with success roughly one-third of the time, primarily during the month of August. Juvenile wildebeest were hunted as well, though usually by packs of hyenas (as opposed to single individuals or pairs), with a slightly lower success rate (29 percent). Although neither hyenas nor cheetahs are primary wildebeest predators, both can serve to remove animals from the population, and do so in different fashions.

Wild dogs (*Lycaon pictus*) also hunt wildebeest (Fanshawe and Fitzgibbon 1993), and not surprisingly these predators focus upon younger individuals. Fanshawe and Fitzgibbon (1993:figure 5.1a) report that of 100 hunting attempts by wild dogs on wildebeest over a two-year period, 80 percent were focused on calves or yearlings, with calves accounting for 80 percent of these hunts. Wild dogs were successful between 60 and 70 percent of the time when hunting these younger wildebeest, compared with roughly 40 percent success in hunting adult wildebeest.

M.G.L. Mills and T. M. Shenk argue that lion predation is *not* the only factor influencing calf mortality, though they do not suggest specific alternative predators (Mills and Shenk 1992:694). They (Mills and Shenk 1992:700) also comment that female fecundity is almost as sensitive a parameter in the population dynamics of prey species as is the kill rate, and argue that changes in ecological conditions can result in changes in kill rate. A.R.E. Sinclair and A. E. Byrom comment that predators can have the effect of reducing diversity in prey species, as well as causing it to increase (Sinclair and Byrom 2006:66). Raymond Dasmann and A. S. Mossman note that higher frequencies of young animals are typically found in circumstances where predators are most abundant and argue that this is a response to heavy mortality and high turnover rates (Dasmann and Mossman 1962).

Mills and Shenk (1992:694) suggest that "predators can regulate resident herbivores at low population densities, whereas such regulation is rare for migratory herds." These authors also note that both wildebeest and zebra underwent population declines during a period with unusually *high* rainfall (emphasis ours). Mills and Shenk propose that this relates to tall grass conditions, and a tendency of herds to fragment, perhaps leading to increased vulnerability to predation. These authors further comment that wildebeest may have been preyed upon at a relatively low intensity by both lions and spotted hyenas.

OTHER CAUSES OF MORTALITY

Wildebeest are particularly susceptible to poor environmental conditions and rapid changes in the environment. M. H. Knight (1995:383) reports that wildebeest is the most common game animal to die during periods of drought in the Kalahari. Contrary to the pattern observed in lion hunting (Mills and Shenk 1992; Rudnai 1974), Knight (1995) points out that adult males (40%) and calves (32%) are the animals that die most often due to drought. Adult females appear less susceptible to adverse conditions caused by drought, with die-off frequencies lower than that observed even for calves (24%–28%). Subadults are always poorly represented in die-off populations (Knight 1995:fig. 5.3), which likely reflects their relatively low survivorship and frequency within the overall population (Ndibalema 2009). Knight (1995:383) argues that the first animals to die during a drought are those in the worst physical condition; those animals observed dying during the first phase of a three-stage drought in the 1980s all had the lowest quality of bone marrow.

Mortality frequencies for different age and sex groups are quite different from what might be expected. Knight (1995:table 2) notes that 48 percent of adult female wildebeest were expected to die due to drought, but observed only a 27.2 percent mortality rate in this age/sex group. Conversely, adult males were expected to die at a rate of 22.8 percent, but 42.6 percent were actually observed. This may indicate that adult females are better able to withstand harsh conditions brought on by drought than adult males. Knight argues that the relatively high frequency of calves in the initial die-off phase might relate to the cessation of lactation by adult females. Knight also suggests that adult males included within the die-off population probably contained members of migratory bachelor herds, which would be in poorer condition than resident herds. Knight further points out that nearly half (45%) of adult male wildebeests to die were in the older age groups of eight to ten years.

Explaining mortality is anything but straightforward. Norman Owen-Smith and M.G.L. Mills argue that changes in prey abundance are a result of a complex interplay of a wide variety of factors, including climate, food production, habitat conditions, vulnerability to predation, and spillover effects from other species (Owen-Smith and Mills 2006). Sinclair and Byrom (2006:67) note that "the dynamics of predation affect prey species differently depending on the role that prey play in the system." They note that the primary prey in one ecosystem can become a secondary prey item in a different ecosystem, with the latter actually having more dramatic effects on that species' abundance.

In particular, Sinclair and Byrom (2006) argue for what they refer to as "multiple states," reasoning that "communities can exist in different combinations of species abundance under the *same* environmental conditions" (emphasis original). Multiple states occur when a perturbation radically alters the abundance of species within the community, and these do not immediately return to their original numbers when the perturbation is removed. The process works in a nonlinear fashion, with initially slow changes followed by fast, catastrophic changes, due to the dynamics between trophic levels (Sinclair and Byrom 2006:68–69).

One of the most unusual wildebeest populations is that described by H. H. Berry (1997) for Etosha National Park (ENP) in Namibia. The Etosha population *was* migratory until fencing was introduced in the early 1970s. This resulted in the wildebeest population being unable to migrate and in a dramatic increase in deaths resulting from disease, particularly anthrax. Berry further notes that this process resulted in nutritional issues, with seasonal fluctuations of crude protein and inorganic phosphorous at levels below that required by grazing herbivores.

Age Distributions

Unlike archaeologists, who break herd animals into discrete age groups (Frison and Reher 1970)—or into groups of juveniles, prime-age adults, and old individuals (Stiner 1990)—wildlife biologists studying modern wildebeest herds typically only report three age groups: calves less than a year old, yearlings between 1 and 2 years, and adults that are older than 2 years. Modern herd structures are presented using stacked bar graphs and these three age categories (figures 5.1 and 5.2). Using D. R. Mason's (1990) annual data collected over a six-year period from Kruger National Park (KNP; figure 5.1), we see that there is some fluctuation in the relative frequency of age groups. Over this period, calves fluctuate between 20 and 30 percent of the population, and yearlings from as low as roughly 10 percent to more than 20 percent.

Even more variation is present when we expand our sample to include different periods of time and geographic locations. Craig Tambling and Johan Du Toit's data from Pilanesberg National Park (PNP) in South Africa shows the most extreme variation in wildebeest population we have been able to find (Tambling and Du Toit 2005). At PNP, calves represent roughly 5 percent of the population of some 600 animals. At the opposite extreme, Etosha National Park in Namibia (Berry 1997) shows a two-year population value with calves approaching 40 percent.

Yearlings are present in all modern samples, ranging from as low as 10 percent (KNP January 1978—Mason 1990) to as high as roughly 25 percent (PNP 2002—Tambling and Du Toit 2005) of the total population. This appears to be a significant factor in modern wildebeest populations, a point which we will return to below.

Idealized Populations

As pointed out above, archaeologists have long tended to compare kill site population structures not to *living* herd structures, but to *idealized* population structures. These idealized patterns (see, for example, Klein 1982; Lubinski 2000; Stiner 1990) are typically either presented as bar graphs or as triangle plots. However, to facilitate comparison with living population structures, we suggest using simple stacked bar graphs grouping the animals into classes of calves, yearlings, and adults (figure 5.3). A *catastrophic* mortality profile consists

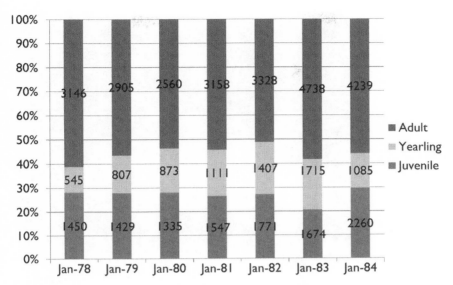

FIGURE 5.1. *Time series of wildebeest population, Kruger National Park: variation in age ratios and population size. (Data from Mason 1990.)*

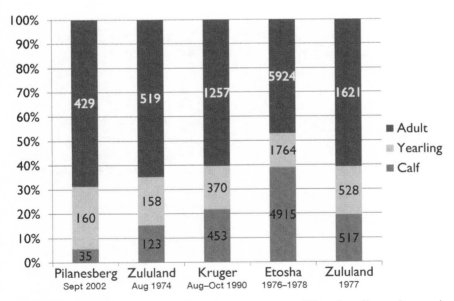

FIGURE 5.2. *Variation in wildebeest population structure at Pilanesberg (September 2002), Zululand (August 1974), Kruger (August to October 1990), Etosha (1976–78) and Zululand (1977). (Data from Tambling and Du Toit 2005 and Berry 1997.)*

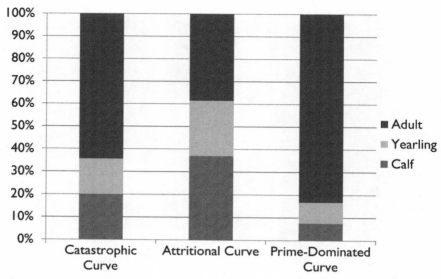

FIGURE 5.3. *Idealized mortality patterns.*

of roughly 20 percent calves and 15 percent yearlings; an *attritional* mortality profile consists of roughly 35 percent calves and 20 percent yearlings; and a prime-dominated (see Stiner 1990) profile consists of more than 80 percent adult animals.

It is worth noting that the idealized catastrophic mortality pattern does resemble *some* living herd structures. Indeed, we see very similar patterns in the wildebeest herd structures at KNP. But the idealized models used by archaeologists exclude any real variation in age structure in herd animals. It is interesting to consider the data from Etosha National Park (Berry 1997), representing a composite of living herds. If these herds suffered a catastrophic death event, the age structure of the death assemblage would be closest to what is typically expected by archaeologists in a death assemblage that has suffered attritional loss.

SUMMARY

While we recognize that wildebeest cannot be used as an exact analogue for bison, we propose that there is sufficient evidence from modern population studies to suggest that archaeologists should expect to find considerable variation in proportions of animals of different ages in circumstances where a mass kill occurred. An idealized model of large mammal age structures is rarely representative of reality due to the many factors that can affect rates of reproduction and survivorship in a particular population at a particular point in time. Thus, assemblages produced by the simultaneous death of all the individuals in a population should not be expected to resemble the classic catastrophic mortality pattern used by most archaeologists, because the classic model does not account for variation. We now return to bison kill sites and reexamine the age structure of the death assemblages in light of this knowledge.

BISON KILL SITES AND LIVING POPULATIONS

Bison death assemblages rarely resemble any *idealized* herd structure. When bison kill site population data are presented in the same fashion as living wildebeest herd structure (figures 5.4 and 5.5), two patterns are immediately apparent: (1) bison kill sites are generally (although not always) lacking in calves, a well-documented phenomenon; and (2), bison kill sites almost always have fewer than the expected number of yearlings.

When bison kill site population data are divided into calves, yearlings, and adults, we see that most sites contain prime-dominated assemblages. However, three sites—Hudson-Meng, Horner, and Carter/Kerr-McGee—more closely resemble the age structure seen in living herds, and thus reflect the catastrophic mortality pattern.

Hudson-Meng (Agenbroad 1978) is the bison kill site that most closely resembles a wildebeest living population structure, using the age groups discussed above. This is perhaps unusual, given that Hudson-Meng has *never* fit the pattern observed at other bison kill sites, nor the pattern of a catastrophic kill as this is traditionally presented. However, comparisons with living wildebeest populations strongly suggest that Hudson-Meng is indeed a catastrophic mortality event.

Horner (Todd and Hofman 1987) has a small sample. However, the relatively high frequency of yearlings within this collection also make Horner resemble a living wildebeest herd, particularly that recorded at PNP in 2002 (Tambling and Du Toit 2005). It seems plausible to argue that Horner also represents a catastrophic kill.

Despite having a small sample ($n = 32$), Carter / Kerr-McGee (Frison 1984) also exhibits an age structure consistent with a catastrophic mortality profile. Carter / Kerr-McGee is very similar in structure to the herd reported from Zululand in 1977 (Berry 1997), again suggesting the possibility of a catastrophic kill.

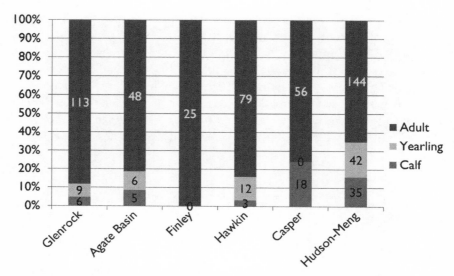

FIGURE 5.4. *Selected bison mass kill site age frequencies. (Data from Driver and Maxwell 2013.)*

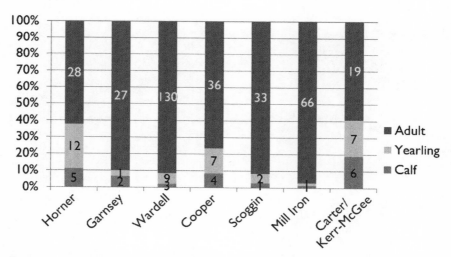

FIGURE 5.5. *Additional bison kill sites. (Data from Driver and Maxwell 2013.)*

PRIME-DOMINATED BISON KILL SITES

The majority of bison kill sites for which we have age structures are best described as prime-dominated, following Stiner (1990). It is both significant and perplexing that these sites all contain age structures that bear little or no resemblance to *any* herd structure reported among living wildebeest. Several bison kill sites—including Glenrock, Finley, Garnsey, Wardell, Scoggin, and Mill Iron—have age structures where calves and yearlings *combine* to account for barely 10 percent or less of the total population. Although our wildebeest herd samples do not include all possible variations, we have no examples of any living herd where these young animals comprise less than 30 percent of the total population. Simply put: most bison kill sites *do not resemble any living herd structure* that we have seen reported in a species that we consider a reasonable analogue for precontact bison.

Most of these sites resemble the idealized prime-dominated pattern that is thought to result from deliberate targeting of animals in prime condition, rather than a mass kill. Elsewhere (Driver and Maxwell 2013) we have argued that the prime-dominated pattern may be the result of catastrophic mortality following a prolonged period of attritional mortality that removed many younger animals from the herd prior to a catastrophic kill. This prekill attrition might be caused by human hunting, or by noncultural agents, including carnivores, disease, and unfavorable weather.

DISCUSSION

In the first part of this chapter we have shown that archaeologists justifiably model some aspects of bison behavior, such as a seasonally constrained reproductive cycle, with a narrow range of variation and a high degree of predictability. On the other hand, other aspects of bison behavior, such as seasonal movement, are understood by archaeologists to be influenced by a wide range of factors, and a high degree of variation should be anticipated. Modeling different degrees of variation in different bison behaviors can be justified by analysis of ancient and modern data. We note that there is little reliable data on the age structure of bison herds living under conditions that would have been prevalent in precontact times, yet analysis of age structure has been a common feature of archaeological studies of death assemblages. Earlier observers of bison did not record information about age structure in sufficient detail, and studies of modern bison are of populations that do not live in conditions that are similar to precontact bison on the Plains. Perhaps because of the lack of good data, archaeologists have assumed that bison age structure was typically very similar to a highly idealized model of large mammal population structures, and have not explored how much variation to expect in living populations.

Using wildebeest as an analogue, we have shown that one should expect considerable variation in the relative proportions of calves, yearling, and adults. Therefore, one should not expect that bison (or, for that matter, any large ungulates) would necessarily display a classic "catastrophic" mortality pattern in circumstances where human hunters killed an entire social group. This means that we must be cautious in applying highly generalized or idealized age structures as a means of comparison with archaeological sites.

If we look at archaeological herd population structures in the same way that biologists look at living herd structures, we see a slightly different picture than what we are typically accustomed to seeing on the Plains. In particular, sites with populations that were previously perplexing, such as Hudson-Meng, are now much more clearly representative of catastrophic mortality patterns. And sites such as Horner and Carter / Kerr-McGee, which were ambiguous, are now best explained as either catastrophic or a close variant of this pattern.

More perplexingly, it is also clear that *most* bison kill populations known from archaeological sites not only deviate from the classic, generalized model of ungulate herd structures but also bear little resemblance to any reported living wildebeest herd structure. That no modern wildebeest population even approaches the low frequency of calves and yearlings reported at most bison kill sites strongly suggests that the majority of these kill sites do not contain typical living herd populations, even when we take into account the fact that modern herds display more variation than archaeologists have typically modeled. However, the evidence of tight seasonality of death, the physical location (arroyo traps, jumps, corrals, etc.), and the nature of bone beds all strongly support the hypothesis that these are mass kills, and not palimpsests of individual hunting episodes. While we have good archaeological evidence for mass killing of bison, using hunting methods that seem consistent with written and oral accounts, the population structure of most of the death assemblages is inconsistent with both the idealized model of ungulate population structure used by many archaeologists and the kinds of variation that modern analogues would lead us to expect.

We propose the following hypotheses for future consideration, and make a few comments about the viability of each hypothesis. Hypothesis 1: mass kills were undertaken primarily when natural phenomena (e.g., predation, bad weather, drought) had already removed a high proportion of calves and yearlings from the herd. This is a more general version of our previous hypothesis—that wolf predation removed calves from herds prior to the seasons of intensive human hunting. In this scenario, mass kills were a human response to a perception that bison numbers were declining, and were thus an "insurance policy" to create stores against the possibility of future bison declines. The primary argument against accepting this hypothesis is that it requires us to account for most bison mass kills as a special response to abnormal conditions, and there are a number of problems with this interpretation. Many mass kill sites were used multiple times, and some had associated landscape modification (e.g., drive lanes or wooden structures); it seems unlikely that this would occur if mass kills were the product of random environmental events, such as drought or cold. Accounts from oral history and ethnography make no mention of this reason for undertaking mass kills. In contrast, those same accounts suggest that considerable skill and knowledge (both practical and ritual) were required to conduct successful hunts, implying that hunters practiced these methods on a regular basis.

Hypothesis 2: indigenous hunters preferred to hunt bison social units with high proportions of adults, especially adult females. Herds with low percentages of calves and yearlings were therefore the preferred targets of regularly conducted mass kills. This hypothesis is consistent with the widely documented human preference for larger and fatter animals. A lack of reliable, abundant sources of carbohydrates over much bison range would increase the incentive for people to secure supplies of fat. The ability to distribute or share fat might also have implications for social status or trade. In a previous paper (Driver and Maxwell 2013), we documented the tendency of wolves to focus on bison herds with calves, and newly reported data support this (Mech, Smith, and MacNulty 2015:108–28); the human decision to hunt herds with fewer calves would potentially reduce competition between people and their major competitors. We distinguish this hypothesis from the previous hypothesis (above) by assuming that under normal conditions there would be opportunities to choose between herds, or perhaps subgroups within herds, that had experienced different levels of success in producing and protecting calves.

Hypothesis 3: hunting techniques that are not well documented in oral histories allowed hunters to segregate calves or calf/cow pairs from the herd prior to the kill occurring, resulting in a death assemblage that did not reflect the original frequency of calves in the herd. This hypothesis would be very difficult to test, and we believe that accounts of bison behavior also make it unlikely.

Hypothesis 4: bison death assemblages originally contained more calves and yearlings, but these were preferentially removed from the kill site, either by natural processes (e.g., weathering, scavenging) or by deliberate human actions (e.g., for special processing of hides or meat). One could test the impact of many natural processes on differential survival of bones of different age classes through comparative taphonomic analysis of bone beds; currently there is insufficient data for a thorough evaluation, but we see no evidence from studies that have been done that percentage representation of calves is correlated with preservation conditions. Furthermore, one of us has shown that the preservation of teeth, on which most population studies depend, does not seem to be as strongly affected by adverse conditions (Driver 1995:29). With regard to human removal of calves and yearlings after a kill, there has been a failure to demonstrate that calves and yearlings are better represented at camp/processing sites associated with mass bison kills.

All of these hypotheses require a more rigorous examination than we have offered here, and all will be difficult to test convincingly. Overall, we believe that the second hypothesis is the most likely, because it is consistent with human dietary needs and with the principle of niche differentiation.

REFERENCES CITED

Agenbroad, L. D. 1978. *The Hudson-Meng Site: An Alberta Bison Kill in the Nebraska High Plains.* Washington, DC: University Press of America.

Arthur, George W. 1974. "An Introduction to the Ecology of Early Historic Communal Bison Hunting among the Northern Plains Indians." MA thesis, University of Calgary.

Bamforth, Douglas B. 1987. "Historical Documents and Bison Ecology on the Great Plains." *Plains Anthropologist* 32 (115): 1–16.

Berger, Joel, and Carol Cunningham. 1994. *Bison: Mating and Conservation in Small Populations.* New York: Columbia University Press.

Berry, H. H. 1997. "Aspects of Wildebeest *Connochaetes taurinus* Ecology in the Etosha National Park—A Synthesis for Future Management." *MADOQUA* 20 (1): 137–48.

Binnema, Theodore. 2001. *Common and Contested Ground: A Human and Environmental History of the Northwestern Plains.* Norman: University of Oklahoma Press.

Bolger, Douglas T., William D. Newmark, Thomas A. Morrison, and Daniel F. Doak. 2008. "The Need for Integrative Approaches to Understand and Conserve Migratory Ungulates." *Ecology Letters* 11 (1): 63–77. doi: 10.1111/j.1461-0248.2007.01109.x.

Brink, Jack W. 2008. *Imagining Head-Smashed-In: Aboriginal Buffalo Hunting on the Northern Plains.* Edmonton: Athabasca University Press.

Bruggeman, Jason E., P. J. White, Robert A. Garrott, and Fred G. Watson. 2009. "Partial Migration in Central Yellowstone Bison." In *The Ecology of Large Mammals in Central Yellowstone,* ed. Robert A. Garrott, P. J. White and Fred G. Watson, 217–35. New York: Elsevier.

Chirima, G. J., N. Owen-Smith, and B.F.N. Erasmus. 2012. "Changing Distributions of Larger Ungulates in the Kruger National Park from Ecological Aerial Survey

Data." *Koedoe* 54 (1): Art. #1009, 11 pages. https://doi.org/10.4102/koe
doe.v54i1.1009.

Chisholm, Brian, Jonathan Driver, Sylvain Dube, and Henry P. Schwarz. 1986.
"Assessment of Prehistoric Bison Foraging and Movement Patterns via Stable-
Carbon Isotopic Analysis." *Plains Anthropologist* 31 (113): 193–205.

Cooper, Judith Rose. 2008. "Bison Hunting and Late Prehistoric Human Subsistence
Economies in the Great Plains." PhD dissertation, Dedman College, Southern
Methodist University.

Dasmann, Raymond F., and A. S. Mossman. 1962. "Abundance and Population
Structure of Wild Ungulates in Some Areas of Southern Rhodesia." *Journal of
Wildlife Management* 26 (3): 262–68. https://doi.org/10.2307/3798701.

Dingle, Hugh. 1996. *Migration.* Oxford: Oxford University Press.

Driver, Jonathan C. 1995. "Social Hunting and Multiple Predation." In *Before Farming:
Hunter-gatherer Society and Subsistence,* ed. Douglas V. Campana, 23–38. Philadelphia:
MASCA, University of Pennsylvania Museum of Archaeology and Anthropology.

Driver, Jonathan C., and David Maxwell. 2013. "Bison Death Assemblages and the
Interpretation of Human Hunting." *Quaternary International* 297 (May): 100–109.
https://doi.org/10.1016/j.quaint.2012.12.038.

Duncan, Clare, Aliénor L. M. Chauvenet, Louise M. McRae, and Nathalie Pettorelli.
2012. "Predicting the Future Impacts of Droughts in Ungulate Populations in Arid
and Semi-Arid Environments." *PLoS One* 7 (12): e51490. https://doi.org/10.1371/jo
urnal.pone.0051490.

Epp, Henry T. 1988. "Way of the Migrant Herds: Dual Dispersion Strategy among
Bison." *Plains Anthropologist* 33 (121): 309–20.

Epp, Henry T., and Ian Dyck. 2002. "Early Human-Bison Population
Interdependence in the Plains Ecosystem." *Great Plains Research* 12 (2):323–37.

Fanshawe, John H., and Clare D. Fitzgibbon. 1993. "Factors Influencing the Hunting
Success of an African Wild Dog Pack." *Animal Behaviour* 45:479–90. https://doi
.org/10.1006/anbe.1993.1059.

Foster, J. B., and D. Kearney. 1967. "Nairobi National Park Game Census, 1966." *East
African Wildlife Journal* 5 (1): 112–20. https://doi.org/10.1111/j.1365-2028.1967.tb00
766.x.

Frison, George C. 1984. "The Carter/Kerr-McGee Paleoindian Site: Cultural
Resource Management and Archaeological Research." *American Antiquity* 49 (2):
288–314. https://doi.org/10.2307/280020.

Frison, George C. 2004. *Survival by Hunting: Prehistoric Human Predators and
Animal Prey.* Berkeley: University of California Press. https://doi.org/10.1525/ca
lifornia/9780520231900.001.0001.

Frison, G. C., and C. A. Reher. 1970. "Age Determination of Buffalo by Teeth Eruption and Wear." In *The Glenrock Buffalo Jump, 48CO304: Late Prehistoric Period Buffalo Procurement and Butchering on the Northwest Plains,* ed. G. C. Frison, 46–50. *Plains Anthropologist Memoir 7.* Topeka, KS: Plains Anthropologist.

Frison, George C., and Lawrence C. Todd. 1987. *The Horner Site: The Type Site of the Cody Cultural Complex.* Orlando: Academic Press.

Geist, Valerius. 1996. *Buffalo Nation: History and Legend of the North American Bison.* Markham, ON: Fifth House Publishers.

Hopcraft, J. Grant C., J. M. Morales, H. L. Beyer, Markus Borner, Ephraim Mwangomo, A.R.E. Sinclair, Han Olff, and Daniel T. Haydon. 2014. "Competition, Predation, and Migration: Individual Choice Patterns of Serengeti migrants Captured by Hierarchical Models." *Ecological Monographs* 84 (3): 355–72. https:// doi.org/10.1890/13-1446.1.

Hamilton, Scott, B. A. Nicholson, and Dion Wiseman. 2006. "Extrapolating to a More Ancient Past: Ethnohistoric Images of Northeastern Plains Vegetation and Bison Ecology." *Plains Anthropologist* 51 (199): 281–302. https://doi.org/10.1179/pan .2006.026.

Hanson, Jeffery R. 1984. "Bison Ecology in the Northern Plains and a Reconstruction of Bison Patterns for the North Dakota Region." *Plains Anthropologist* 29 (104): 93–113.

Hart, Richard H. 2001. "Where the Buffalo Roamed—or Did They?" *Great Plains Research* 11 (1): 83–102.

Hobson, Keith A., and D. Ryan Norris. 2008. "Animal Migration: A Context for Using New Techniques and Approaches." In *Tracking Animal Migration with Stable Isotopes,* ed. Keith A. Hobson and Leonard I. Wassenaar, 1–19. Amsterdam: Elsevier. https://doi.org/10.1016/S1936-7961(07)00001-2.

Holekamp, K. E., L. Smale, R. Berg, and S. M. Cooper. 1997. "Hunting Rates and Hunting Success in the Spotted Hyaena (*Crocuta crocuta*)." *Journal of Zoology* 242 (1): 1–15. https://doi.org/10.1111/j.1469-7998.1997.tb02925.x.

Hunter, J. S., S. M. Durant, and T. M. Caro. 2007. "To Flee or Not to Flee: Predator Avoidance by Cheetahs at Kills." *Behavioral Ecology and Sociobiology* 61 (7): 1033–42. https://doi.org/10.1007/s00265-006-0336-4.

Klein, R. G. 1982. "Age (Mortality) Profiles as a Means of Distinguishing Hunted Species from Scavenged Ones in Stone Age Archaeological Sites." *Paleobiology* 8(2): 151–58. https://doi-org.proxy.lib.sfu.ca/10.1017/S0094837300004498.

Knight, M. H. 1995. "Drought-Related Mortality of Wildlife in the Southern Kalahari and the Role of Man." *African Journal of Ecology* 33 (4): 377–94. https://doi.org/10.1111/j.1365-2028.1995.tb01047.x.

Lubinski, P. M. 2000. "A Comparison of Methods for Evaluating Ungulate Mortality Distributions." *Archaeozoologica* 11:121–34.

Mason, D. R. 1990. "Juvenile Survival and Population Structure of Blue Wildebeest and Warthogs in the Central Region of the Krueger National Park during the Mid-summer Drought of 1988/89." *Koedoe* 33 (1): 29–44. https://doi.org/10.4102/koedoe.v33i1.450.

McHugh, Tom. 1972. *The Time of the Buffalo*. New York: Alfred A. Knopf.

Mduma, Simon A. R. 1996. "Serengeti Wildebeest Population Dynamics: Regulation, Limitation and Implications for Harvesting." PhD dissertation, Department of Zoology, University of British Columbia, Vancouver.

Mech, L. David, Douglas W. Smith, and Daniel R. MacNulty. 2015. *Wolves on the Hunt: The Behavior of Wolves Hunting Wild Prey*. Chicago: Chicago University Press. https://doi.org/10.7208/chicago/9780226255286.001.0001.

Mills, M.G.L., and T. M. Shenk. 1992. "Predator—Prey Relationships: The Impact of Lion Predation on Wildebeest and Zebra Populations." *Journal of Animal Ecology* 61 (3): 693–702. https://doi.org/10.2307/5624.

Morgan, R. Grace. 1980. "Bison Movement Patterns on the Canadian Plains: An Ecological Analysis." *Plains Anthropologist* 25 (88): 143–60.

Mysterud, A., T. Coulson, and N. C. Stenseth. 2002. "The Role of Males in the Dynamics of Ungulate Populations." *Journal of Animal Ecology* 71 (6): 907–15. https://doi.org/10.1046/j.1365-2656.2002.00655.x.

Ndibalema, Vedasto G. 2009. "A Comparison of Sex Ratio, Birth Periods and Calf Survival among Serengeti Wildebeest Sub-populations, Tanzania." *African Journal of Ecology* 47 (4): 574–82. https://doi.org/10.1111/j.1365-2028.2008.00994.x.

Norton-Griffiths, M. 1973. "Counting the Serengeti Migratory Wildebeest Using Two-Stage Sampling." *East African Wildlife Journal* 11 (2): 135–49. https://doi.org/10.1111/j.1365-2028.1973.tb00079.x.

Owen-Smith, Norman, and M.G.L. Mills. 2006. "Manifold Interactive Influences on the Population Dynamics of a Multispecies Ungulate Assemblage." *Ecological Monographs* 76 (1): 73–92. https://doi.org/10.1890/04-1101.

Pascual, Miguel A., Peter Kareiva, and Ray Hilborn. 1997. "The Influence of Model Structure on Conclusions about the Viability and Harvesting of Serengeti Wildebeest." *Conservation Biology* 11 (4): 966–76. https://doi.org/10.1046/j.1523-1739.1997.95437.x.

Reher, C. A. 1973. "The Wardell *Bison bison* Sample: Population Dynamics and Archaeological Interpretations." In *The Wardell Buffalo Trap 48SU301: Communal Procurement in the Upper Green River Basin, Wyoming*, ed. G. C. Frison, 89–105.

University of Michigan Anthropological Papers 48. Ann Arbor: University of Michigan.

Rudnai, Judith. 1974. "The Pattern of Lion Predation in Nairobi Park." *East African Wildlife Journal* 12 (3): 213–25. https://doi.org/10.1111/j.1365-2028.1974.tb00114.x.

Rutberg, Allen T. 1984. "Birth Synchrony in American Bison (*Bison bison*): Response to Predation or Season?" *Journal of Mammalogy* 65 (3): 418–23. https://doi.org/10.2307/1381088.

Shaw, James H., and Mary Meagher. 2000. "Bison." In *Ecology and Management of Large Mammals in North America*, ed. Stephen Demarais and Paul R. Krausman, 447–66. Upper Saddle River, NJ: Prentice Hall.

Sinclair, A.R.E. 1973. "Population Increases of Buffalo and Wildebeest in the Serengeti." *East African Wildlife Journal* 11 (1): 93–107. https://doi.org/10.1111/j.1365-2028.1973.tb00075.x.

Sinclair, A.R.E. 1983. "The Function of Distance Movements in Vertebrates." In *The Ecology of Animal Movement*, ed. Ian R. Swingland and Paul J. Greenwood, 240–58. Oxford: Clarendon.

Sinclair, A. R. E., and A. E. Byrom. 2006. "Understanding Ecosystem Dynamics for Conservation of Biota." *Journal of Animal Ecology* 75 (1): 64–79. https://doi.org/10.1111/j.1365-2656.2006.01036.x.

Sinclair, A. R. E., Simon A. R. Mduma, and P. Arcese. 2000. "What Determines Phenology and Synchrony of Ungulate Breeding in Serengeti?" *Ecology* 81 (8): 2100–2111. https://doi.org/10.1890/0012-9658(2000)081[2100:WDPASO]2.0.CO;2.

Sinclair, A. R. E., Simon A. R. Mduma, J. Grant C. Hopcraft, John M. Fryxell, Ray Hilborn, and Simon Thirgood. 2007. "Long-Term Ecosystem Dynamics in the Serengeti: Lessons for Conservation." *Conservation Biology* 21 (3): 580–90. https://doi.org/10.1111/j.1523-1739.2007.00699.x.

Speth, John D. 1983. *Bison Kills and Bone Counts: Decision Making by Ancient Hunters.* Chicago: University of Chicago Press.

Stiner, M. C. 1990. "The Use of Mortality Patterns in Archaeological Studies of Hominid Predatory Adaptations." *Journal of Anthropological Archaeology* 9:305–51. https://doi.org/10.1016/0278-4165(90)90010-B.

Tambling, Craig J., and Johan T. Du Toit. 2005. "Modelling Wildebeest Population Dynamics: Implications of Predation and Harvesting in a Closed System." *Journal of Applied Ecology* 42 (3): 431–41. https://doi.org/10.1111/j.1365-2664.2005.01039.x.

Todd, L. C., and J. L. Hofman. 1987. "Bison Mandibles from the Horner and Finley Sites." In *The Horner Site*, ed. G. C. Frison and L. C. Todd, 493–539. Orlando: Academic Press.

6

The purpose of this chapter is to discuss the predictability of *Bison antiquus* movement, and the strategies involved in hunting them. Early historic accounts (e.g., Allen 1876; Arthur 1975; Roe 1951; Seton 1910) argued that bison seasonally migrated hundreds or thousands of miles. J. A. Allen (1876:59–61) reported, "I have . . . been assured by former agents of the American Fur Company that before the great overland emigrations to California . . . divided the buffalo into two bands, the buffaloes that were found in summer on the Plains of Saskatchewan and the Red River of the North spent winter in Texas."

Later historians, though discounting these very long migrations, argued that bison seasonally moved hundreds of miles. E. T. Seton (1910:266) stated, "I conclude with Hornaday that the buffalo did migrate 300 to 400 miles northward in the spring, and as far southward again in the autumn." These kinds of statements dominate most ethnohistoric records (see Bamforth 1987; Hornaday 1889; Roe 1951; Soper 1941).

Researchers have questioned these early ethnohistoric accounts. F. G. Roe (1951:78) concluded that the idea of long bison migrations is based on analogies to the cattle drives of the late nineteenth century in which domestic cattle were annually moved vast distances. As Roe (1951:77) stated, "a careful study . . . reveals how flimsy is much of the evidence upon which various forms of the migration argument are based." Several researchers have outlined problems with these early

Microanalytical Evidence of Folsom–Aged Communal Hunting on the US Southern Great Plains

ADAM C. GRAVES

DOI: 10.5876/9781607326823.c006

models of long-distance bison mobility (Bamforth 1987; Hanson 1984; Roe 1951). First, no definitive evidence exists that an individual bison will walk 1,400 miles from Texas to southern Canada in a single year. Second, none of these models explain the impetus for such a long-distance migration.

Based on the definitions outlined by R. R. Baker (1978), bison are neither nomadic (i.e., having no apparent fixed pattern of direction) nor long-distance movers (Lott 1991). There are several reasons why bison move, including the search for food and water, search for other bison, and escape from danger or uncomfortable conditions (e.g., cold temperatures, snowfall, insects, and predators; (Hanson 1984; Krasińska, Kasiński, and Bunevich 2000; Lott 1991; Morgan 1980; Roe 1951; Senft et al. 1987). Random events, such as inclement weather or attacks by predators (including humans), also cause bison to take flight. But these moves usually occur over short distances, usually less than 10 km (Bamforth 1988).

In addition to the distance of movement, modern bison also appear to have predictable movements to the same geographic location. A multiyear tracking study of European bison, for example, saw a high proportion of bison returning to the same summer and winter ranges over multiple consecutive years (Krasińska, Kasiński, and Bunevich 2000). Similarly, a number of accounts suggest that Plains and wood bison repeatedly move back and forth between the same summer and winter forager areas (Lott 1991; Meagher 1973; Soper 1941). Baker (1978) identified this type of movement as "seasonal latitudinal return migrations" (see Lott 1991). T. McHugh (1958:13) observed that the Yellowstone National Park Lamar Herd bison move approximately twenty-five miles from the meadows at 8,000 to 9,000 feet to the lower Lamar Valley at 6,000 feet during the winter. The bison vacate the lower Lamar Valley and return to the higher elevation meadows in May or June. J. D. Soper (1941:380) described the bison herds at Wood Bison National Park, Canada, move from the Plains of the Western Slave River in the spring to the uplands of the Alberta Plateau. The bison return to the Western Slave River Plains in the fall. The bison at Henry Mountain, Utah, also move into their winter range in September and return to their summer range (approximately 15 km away) in May and June (Nelson 1965:24–29). Recent isotopic analyses (e.g., strontium, stable carbon) of archaeological bison remains suggest that prehistoric bison, like their modern counterparts, probably did not range over vast territories, but instead were restricted to relatively small seasonal and annual patches (Widga 2006a, 2006b).

H. Epp and I. Dyck's research regarding behavioral ecology and its implications for bison mobility takes a slightly different approach to bison movement

(Epp and Dyck 2002). Epp and Dyck (2002) identify two distinct, but not mutually exclusive, bison herd populations: resident and migrant herds. Their research shows that behavioral ecological views regarding bison numbers and population dynamics should be reassessed on three bases: (1) there were often two discrete populations of bison species within any area at any given time; (2) the migratory population moved between two distinct home ranges; and (3) migrant herds tended to have larger home ranges vastly outnumbering resident herds, often by 4:1 or more (Epp and Dyck 2002:324,325).

BISON ANTIQUUS PREDICTABILITY

So were Folsom-aged (10,800–10,200 BP) bison populations comprised of both resident and migrant bison? Studies conducted by the author at the University of Oklahoma, the University of Texas, and California State University Long Beach indicate that detecting trace elemental differences of bison teeth by Laser Ablation Inductively Coupled Plasma Mass Spectrometry (LA-ICP/MS) methods is appropriate for examining bison movements and that modern geographical trace element distributions on the southern Plains resemble prehistoric concentrations. In other words, the teeth of modern bison provide a shortcut in determining the differential distribution of trace elements around the southern Plains, which ultimately can be used to explain Folsom-age bison migration patterns. LA-ICP-MS is an analytical technology that enables acute elemental and isotopic analysis to be performed directly on solid samples. LA-ICP-MS begins with a laser beam focused on the sample surface to generate fine particles (Laser Ablation). The ablated particles are transported to the secondary excitation source of the ICP-MS instrument for digestion and ionization of the sample. The excited ions in the plasma torch are subsequently introduced to a mass spectrometer detector for both elemental and isotopic analysis. Trace elements and stable isotopes reflect the compositions of the soil, grasses, and water where the bison grazed during the period of amelogenesis (the forming of tooth enamel) (figure 6.1). Once initiated, enamel placement takes approximately 300 days and begins at the top of the tooth and progresses toward the root, essentially trapping an elemental snapshot of the grasses being grazed. Samples taken down the tooth at five-millimeter intervals analyze enamel content at roughly sixty-day (two-month) intervals (figure 6.2).

Seventeen *Bison antiquus* teeth derived from southern Plains archaeological sites that are Folsom age were sampled. The prehistoric samples included animals from the early Paleoindian Cooper and Jake Bluff sites (stratified bison kills in northwestern Oklahoma); Badger Hole, Oklahoma; the Folsom

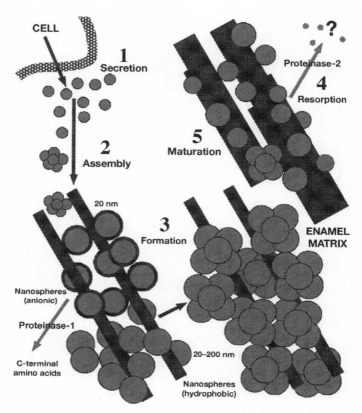

FIGURE 6.1. *Schematic diagram of enamel biomineralization. Note that at the formation stage (stage 3), enamel is only lightly mineralized. Full mineralization (expansion of crystallites) only occurs during the maturation stage (stage 5). (Redrawn from Fincham, Moradian-Oldak, and Simmer 1999.)*

site, New Mexico; Lubbock Lake, Texas; Blackwater Draw, New Mexico; and Lake Theo, Texas (figure 6.3). These sites were chosen because they are all found in the same general area of the plains and because of the dominating presence of Alibates and Edwards chert in the assemblages. Modern bison tooth samples were sought from a variety of regions of the southern Plains because they possessed the potential to give a broad spatial characterization (a map) of the elemental composition of bison from a variety of regional settings. Most samples analyzed were the complete, unworn fourth premolar (P4) from

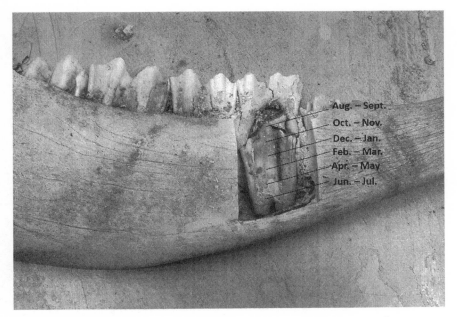

Aug. – Sept.
Oct. – Nov.
Dec. – Jan.
Feb. – Mar.
Apr. – May
Jun. – Jul.

FIGURE 6.2. *Three-year-old bison mandible showing full enamel placement of an unerupted P4 premolar.*

three- to four-year-old animals. The P4 is selected because, at this age, the elements for enamel production are obtained through ingestion of plants, soil on the plants, and water, rather than through the biofilter that produces mother's milk. In addition, occlusal surface wear has not generally begun.

The study employed multivariate analysis to define interrelationships among elemental concentrations down-tooth among both modern and prehistoric samples to assess *Bison antiquus* movement. Dietary elements examined included boron (B), sodium (Na), chlorine (Cl), potassium (K), zinc (Zn), the strontium isotope Sr87/Sr86, and lead (Pb). Selected elements were chosen because of their presence in enamel, their detectability based on previous pilot studies conducted by the author, their nutritional role, and their probability of being geographical indicators.

Laser ablation data from most of the archaeological sites studied show a pattern of movement on and off of the Llano Estacado in accordance with changing seasons (figure 6.4). The down-tooth elemental analysis provides a window into one year of movement, and it appears that teeth representing migratory animals have similar elemental concentrations at the crown and

FIGURE 6.3. *Locations from which modern (circle) and prehistoric (square) bison teeth derived for the elemental analysis.*

cementum enamel junction. In other words, the bison grazed similar areas when amelogenesis began as they did when mineralization of enamel was complete, indicating a circular movement pattern. In addition, bison herds from various Folsom-age archaeological sites seemingly had overlapping ranges, or were potentially a single moving population (Graves 2010).

Patterns in the data emerged that indicate a presence of both resident and migratory herds during the Folsom period. The Jake Bluff bison appear to have either not moved a great distance, not moved away from the Jake Bluff locale for very long, and/or remained in a homogenous geologic environment throughout the year the P4 premolar enamel mineralized. The Lubbock Lake individuals reflect this trend as well. The remaining prehistoric samples showed a high degree of down-tooth variation with spikes in the data during the spring and fall, which is consistent with the behavior of known herds in Yellowstone that have greater flexibility in their movement patterns (Graves 2010).

FOLSOM HUNTING STRATEGY

What can we infer about human strategies as it relates to the presence of both residential and predictable migrant herds? This study is not the only one to suggest that humans exploited migratory and residential bison herds.

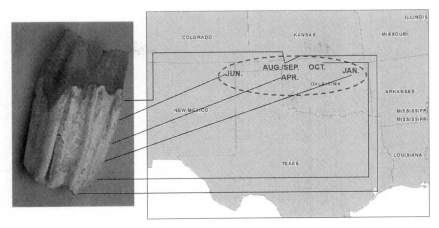

FIGURE 6.4. *Typical Folsom-aged Bison antiquus movement pattern on the southern Plains.*

Epp and Dyck (2002:332–34) offer an optimal foraging model that suggests people continuously exploited resident bison populations and seasonally exploited migrant bison populations in order to have an enormous supply of a high-quality protein resource and to ensure resident and migrant bison herd numbers. This subsistence strategy had several important implications for both humans and bison because the combined use of these herds would have ensured that the people had almost constant access to bison. As well, it ensured that neither the resident nor the migrant population was eliminated. Consequently, hunting both resident and migrant bison populations was an optimal subsistence strategy.

The elemental summation above, illustrates an apparent east-to-west movement of migratory bison herds and the presence of residential herds during the Folsom period. Folsom groups on the southern Plains exhibit a close relationship to those areas where they obtained lithic raw materials. Humans at this time quite obviously obtained raw materials for the tools they needed in Texas and successfully hunted bison on the Llano Estacado adjacent to these toolstone sources. What then was the impetus drawing these same individuals to the periphery of the Llano Estacado hundreds of kilometers away from a reliable lithic acquisition area? The answer is that bison were nearly as reliable a resource as the knappable stone they used to dispatch and process the animals. Hunters operating in an environment where residential bison herds were present in various ecological patches, and where migratory bison regularly wintered on the Rolling Hills, moved west to the Llano Estacado through the summer

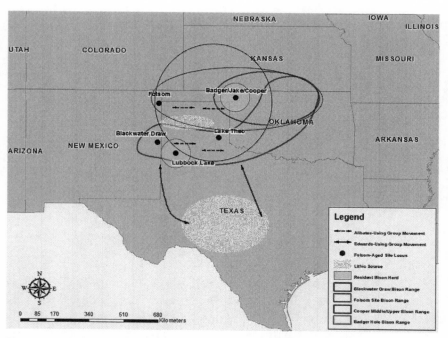

FIGURE 6.5. *Folsom human movements on the southern Plains for the purposes of communal hunting of Bison antiquus.*

and fall, and returned to the Rolling Hills again for the following winter would have had little trouble predicting where and when they could organize their own movement to best take advantage of seasonally available resources.

I submit that Folsom hunters-gatherers whose toolkits were composed primarily of Alibates spent much of the year on the Llano Estacado taking advantage of the numerous available resources, and moved to the landform's peripheries during the fall bison rut. Small bison herds or individual bison on the Llano Estacado that were sought in the spring would be difficult to hunt if they were undertaking their spring migration. A more likely scenario is one where residential herds or individual bison are dispatched, because their whereabouts would be predictable during the spring. Anticipating large, but temporarily preoccupied bison herds during the late summer rut near or on the dissected peripheries of the Llano Estacado would be feasible and the best time and place to successfully hunt, trap, and dispatch large groups of bison. In addition, these locations would be the best places to meet groups of people moving north from the Edwards Plateau source area (figure 6.5).

Why, though, if residential herds were present during the Folsom period on the southern Plains would it be necessary to move so far away from their seemingly preferred lithic acquisition locales? Two reasons come to mind: one is basic conservation of the residential herds, and the other is to meet with other groups for the purposes of conducting social activities. As with other human colonization sequences, the first arrivals take the best locations and hang on to them. As the best locations become occupied and the resources become patchy during Folsom times, strategies for obtaining resources must change. Human groups using Alibates developed seasonal rounds in the middle of a bison-rich ecosystem, and Edwards Plateau groups developed movement to interact with Alibates groups and procure a highly valuable resource in an efficient manner. The Edwards group or groups may have been small bands who needed to gather with other bands seasonally to make large bison kills, trade, and exchange marriage partners. The former reason for communal gatherings is the focus of the discussion below.

Communal hunting is part of a larger pattern of predation in which the strategy is to acquire an adequate amount of animal resources for a group larger than those participating in the hunt in as efficient a manner as possible. In this study, J. C. Driver's (1990) definition of communal hunting is used. He characterized communal hunting by the following traits (Driver 1990:12):

1. Participation by more than two hunters (usually many more than this).
2. Active cooperation between hunters such that they work together, as opposed to passive cooperation in which hunters agree not to interfere with each other's activities.
3. A system of hunting that requires all hunters to participate in a previously conceived plan.

For large game animals, such as bison, habitat, migration route, population density, meat, fat, and hide quality vary seasonally (Driver 1990:13). Consequently, incorporating information about certain environmental features and the adaptive strategies people use to optimize their foraging practices can help reveal variation in social behavior as is made evident by the current study.

The characteristics of the animal often will determine the hunting strategy adopted. Mobile, clumped prey, such as migratory bison, require an aggregated group strategy, whereas stable, evenly distributed prey, such as deer, require that the hunters be dispersed (Winterhalder 1981:31). Driver (1990:23) maintains that "the widespread use of communal hunting in association with concentrated groups of animals suggests that the relative ease of killing may have been an important factor." When considering how bison herd composition can vary according to the patchiness of a particular region, the optimal goal of search and handling time efficiency may lead to behavior that may not make the best use of labor efficiency. In fact, labor productivity may not be important when considering time efficiency if the goal is to take advantage of a seasonally available resource that may require a group of people to expend large amounts of labor for a short period of time (Jochim 1981:52). Due to the mobile nature of some bison, pursuit distances probably fluctuated on a seasonal basis, causing hunting groups to travel farther in order to obtain this highly sought resource. On the other hand, periods of prey aggregation may be highly predictable for migratory herd animals. In those cases, search times would be reduced, particularly if hunters employed communal hunting techniques (Driver 1990:27). The evidence presented in the current study suggests a predictable pattern of bison behavior, and it can be inferred that the species was an excellent candidate for employing communal hunting techniques.

Hunter-gatherers were selective about which animal body parts were transported from the kill site back to the residential camp or village, and the transport distance was an important variable in determining how much of the animal was transported (Metcalfe and Barlow 1992:341). As a result, transport and processing decisions vary according to the animal species being exploited. Increasing the use of an aggregate resource such as bison would increase protein yields for any group of people. But, considering the large size of bison, people would also have to increase their return rate costs due to increased transport costs. Transport costs include prey size and distance from the kill site to the camp and the proportion of elements transported. Undoubtedly, in regards to hunting bison, search and handling time costs would increase given that the farther people go to hunt bison, the greater the amount of field processing required in order to average out the costs of return travel due to the increased load size. In order to decrease transport costs, hunters butchered bison at kill sites and then made decisions regarding which parts of the animal would be transported back to the camp. Folsom hunter-gatherers who were highly mobile during the fall months on the southern High Plains, presumably, were not planning to haul their meat long distances, as it would be impractical to carry such an enormous load.

It is generally accepted that Paleoindian population density was very low and the residential mobility was high, at least seasonally (e.g., Kelly and Todd 1988). Living in a very large, relatively unbound landscape, Folsom-aged people's need for information exchange, economic cooperation, mates, group rituals or ceremonies, and access to trade goods was likely at a premium. Archaeologists have long assumed that Paleoindians satisfied these needs through periodic and temporary aggregations (i.e., fusion) of different groups (e.g., Bamforth 1988, 1991; Greiser 1985; Wilmsen and Roberts 1978), and D. B. Bamforth (1991) suggested Paleoindian social aggregations were tied to communal bison hunts. J. L. Hofman (1994) is critical of any perspective that argues for aggregations as a single type of site or event. He suggests that Paleoindian demography, subsistence, and land-use patterns may not fit any existing model as to why hunter-gatherer groups aggregate. Instead, he proposes that hunter-gatherer aggregations were a mechanism by which different groups could solve problems that were beyond the capacities of any single group, such as finding spouses, conducting necessary spiritual rituals, and gaining information about very large geographic regions (Hofman 1994:342). As a result, he sees aggregations arising for a wide variety of reasons and under diverse conditions. Therefore, multiple archaeological expressions of aggregation localities may exist depending on when, where, and why the fusion of different groups occurred. M. E. Hill (2007) believes it unlikely that social aggregations would have involved large communal hunts, because (1) they would have occurred in landscapes with no major landscape features (Plains), (2) very few additional resources would have been available (high risk), (3) there may be no correlation between the number of bison killed and the number of people it would take to dispatch and process them (see also Hofman 1994), and (4) there is little evidence (lack of lithic and camp debris) for large numbers of people coming together.

One may infer from the findings presented in the current study that aggregations for the purposes of social activity provide an excellent opportunity to hunt large herds of bison in a landscape that provides numerous traps, landmarks, and resources for such an endeavor. The predictable nature of bison, residential herds coupled with migratory herds, with regular and scientifically testable movement of bison, has been known by Plains bison hunters for at least 11,000 years. Further, the evidence for a large number of people coming together may be found at the large kill sites themselves. For example, the middle level of the Cooper site contained at least twenty-nine *Bison antiquus*. The approximate meat weight yield from a modern cow bison using a Cooper-type butchering strategy yields approximately 61.7 kg or about half of the total meat weight of the animal (Johnson and Bement 2009:1445). Even a conservative measure (using modern cow bison size as opposed to *Bison antiquus*) of the total meat yield during the Cooper middle kill would be 1,790 kg (about 4,000 lb.). Presumably, human groups present at or near the Cooper locale, even while operating in a highly mobile manner, would not likely have packed up that much meat and immediately hauled it back to the Llano Estacado. It would have taken several groups of people several trips from kill to a campsite far enough away to avoid the pleasure of twenty-nine rotting bison carcasses and the scavengers that accompany decomposition. Furthermore, a few good hunters would have little reason to process over 4,000 lb. of meat.

CONCLUSION

The results of elemental analysis using laser ablation indicate that Folsom-age bison were moving moderate distances, albeit not all of them. The evidence presented in this study suggests a latitudinal movement of bison on and off the southern High Plains according to seasonal changes during the Folsom period. I posit that the manner in which humans located bison on the southern Plains and organized their movement strategies (aggregation and dispersal) to hunt bison took advantage of the locations of bison across the landscape during different times of the year. Further, Folsom hunters structured their settlement in a way whereby residential mobility was low throughout much of the year, but high during the fall when moving to the periphery of their territory on the southern Plains was advantageous for meeting other groups and procuring large numbers of bison. Herd composition and mobility always affect the amounts and kinds of mobility for humans, which is why the relationship between Plains hunter-gatherers and the bison they hunted remained unchanged for 11,000 years.

REFERENCES CITED

Allen, J. A. 1876. "The American Bison, Living, and Extinct." Memoir of the Geological Survey of Kentucky 1 (pt. 2). Cambridge: University Press. https://doi.org/10.5962/bhl.title.12249.

Arthur, G. W. 1975. "An Introduction to the Ecology of early Historic Communal Bison Hunting among the Northern Plains Indians." *Archaeological Survey of Canada*, Paper 37, Ottawa.

Baker, R. R. 1978. *The Evolutionary Ecology of Animal Migration.* London: Hodder and Stoughton.

Bamforth, D. B. 1987. "Historical Documents and Bison Ecology on the Great Plains." *Plains Anthropologist* 32 (115): 1–16.

Bamforth, D. B. 1988. *Ecology and Human Organization on the Great Plains: Interdisciplinary Contributions to Archaeology.* New York: Plenum Press. https://doi.org/10.1007/978-1-4899-2061-4.

Bamforth, D. B. 1991. "Flintknapping Skill, Communal Hunting, and Paleoindian Projectile Point Typology." *Plains Anthropologist* 36 (137): 309–22.

Driver, J. C. 1990. "Meat in Due Season: The Timing of Communal Hunts." In *Hunters of the Recent Past*, ed. Leslie B. Davis and Brian O. K. Reeves, 11–33. London: Unwin Hyman.

Epp, H., and I. Dyck. 2002. "Early Human-Bison Population Interdependence in the Plains Ecosystem." *Great Plains Research* 12 (615): 323–37.

Fincham, A. G., J. Moradian-Oldak, and J. P. Simmer. 1999. "The Structural Biology of the Developing Dental Enamel Matrix." *Journal of Structural Biology* 126 (3): 270–99. https://doi.org/10.1006/jsbi.1999.4130.

Graves, A. C. 2010. "Investigation Resource Structure and Human Mobility: An Example from Folsom-Aged Bison Kill Sites on the U.S. Southern Great Plains." Dissertation on file at the University of Oklahoma, Norman.

Greiser, S. T. 1985. ""Predictive Models of Hunter-Gatherer Subsistence and Settlement Strategies on the Central High Plains." Plains Anthropologist Memoir 20." *Plains Anthropologist* 30 (110): 1–134.

Hanson, J. R. 1984. "Bison Ecology in the Northern Plains and a Reconstruction of Bison Patterns for the North Dakota Regions." *Plains Anthropologist* 29 (104): 93–113.

Hill, M. E. 2007. "Causes of Regional and Temporal Variation in Paleoindian Diet in Western North America." PhD dissertation, Department of Anthropology, University of Arizona, Tucson.

Hofman, J. L. 1994. "Paleoindian aggregations on the Great Plains." *Journal of Anthropological Archaeology* 13 (4): 341–70. https://doi.org/10.1006/jaar.1994.1018.

Hornaday, W. T. 1889. "The Extermination of the American Bison, with Sketch of Its Discovery and Life History." Report of the U.S. National Museum, Part 2, 367–548. Washington, DC: US Government Printing Office.

Jochim, M. A. 1981. *Strategies for Survival: Cultural Behavior in an Ecological Context*. New York: Academic Press.

Johnson, E., and L. C. Bement. 2009. "Bison Butchery at Cooper, a Folsom Site on the Southern Plains." *Journal of Archaeological Science* 36 (7): 1430–46. https://doi.org/10.1016/j.jas.2009.02.007.

Kelly, R. L., and L. C. Todd. 1988. "Coming into the Country: Early Paleoindian Hunting and Mobility." *American Antiquity* 53 (02): 231–44. https://doi.org/10.2307/281017.

Krasińska, Malgorzata, Zbigniew A. Kasiński, and Aleksei N. Bunevich. 2000. "Factors Affecting the Variability in Home Range Size and Distribution in European Bison in the Polish and Belarussian Parts of Bialowieza Forest." *Acta Theriologica* 45 (3): 321–34. https://doi.org/10.4098/AT.arch.00-32.

Lott, D. F. 1991. "American Bison Socioecology." *Applied Animal Behaviour Science* 29 (1–4): 135–45. https://doi.org/10.1016/0168-1591(91)90242-P.

McHugh, T. 1958. "Social Behavior of the American Buffalo (*Bison bison bison*)." *Zoologica* 43:1–40.

Meagher, M. M. 1973. *The Bison of Yellowstone National Park*. National Park Service Scientific Monograph Series 1:1–161. Washington, DC: National Park Service.

Metcalfe, D., and K. Renee Barlow. 1992. "Model for Exploring the Optimal Trade-Off between Field Processing and Transport." *American Anthropologist* 94 (2): 340–56. https://doi.org/10.1525/aa.1992.94.2.02a00040.

Morgan, R. G. 1980. "Bison Movement Patterns on the Canadian Plains: An Ecological Analysis." *Plains Anthropologist* 25 (88): 142–60.

Nelson, K. L. 1965. *Status and Habit of the American Buffalo (Bison bison) in the Henry Mountain Areas of Utah*. Publication No. 65-2. Salt Lake City: Utah State Department of Fish and Game.

Roe, F. G. 1951. *The North American Buffalo*. Toronto: University of Toronto Press.

Senft, R. L., M. B. Coughenour, D. W. Bailey, L. R. Rittenhouse, O. E. Sala, and D. M. Swift. 1987. "Large Herbivore Foraging and Ecological Hierarchies." *Bioscience* 37 (11): 789–99. https://doi.org/10.2307/1310545.

Seton, E. T. 1910. *Life-Histories of Northern Animals*. Vol. 2. New York: Scribner's.

Soper, J. D. 1941. "History, Range, and Home Life of the Northern Bison." *Ecological Monographs* 11 (4): 347–412. https://doi.org/10.2307/1943298.

Widga, C. C. 2006a. "Niche Variability in Late Holocene Bison: A Perspective from Big Bone Lick, KY." *Journal of Archaeological Science* 33 (9): 1237–55. https://doi.org/10.1016/j.jas.2005.12.011.

Widga, C. C. 2006b. "Bison, Bogs, and Big Bluestem: The Subsistence Ecology of Middle Holocene Hunter-Gatherers in the Eastern Great Plains." PhD dissertation, Department of Anthropology, University of Kansas, Lawrence.

Wilmsen, E. N., and F.H.H. Roberts, Jr. 1978. *Lindenmeier, 1934–1974: Concluding Report on Investigations: Contributions to Anthropology 24*. Washington, DC: Smithsonian Institution.

Winterhalder, B. 1981. "Optimal Foraging Strategies and Hunter-Gatherer Research in Anthropology: Theory and Models." In *Hunter-Gatherer Foraging Strategies: Ethnographic and Archaeological Analyses*, ed. Bruce Winterhalder and Eric A. Smith, 13–35. Chicago: University of Chicago Press.

7

The research reported in this chapter compares southern and northern Plains' early Paleoindian period communal bison hunting using bison bone stable carbon and nitrogen isotopes from samples selected from well-dated context. The isotopic results are then used to reconstruct levels of bison mobility and the environment.

This research focuses on the early Paleoindian time period, 11,100–10,000 radiocarbon years before present (BP), when large-scale bison hunting is prevalent across the northwestern and southern Plains, enabling an interregional comparison. Large-scale kill events may exist prior to this period; however, the archaeological record of such events is sparse (Kornfeld, Frison, and Larsen 2010). For this research we collected data from three southern Plains early Paleoindian sites with comparable sites on the northwestern Plains (figure 7.1). The southern Plains sites include the Beaver River kill complex of northwestern Oklahoma, which contains three arroyo trap kill sites; Cooper (34HP45; Bement 1999), Jake Bluff (34HP60; Bement and Carter 2010), and Badger Hole (34HP194; Bement et al. 2012). The northwestern Plains sites are Mill Iron, Montana (24CT30; Frison 1996); Agate Basin, Wyoming (48NA201; Frison and Stanford 1982; Hill 2008); and Carter/Kerr-McGee (CKM), Wyoming (48CA12; Frison 1984).

The Development of Paleoindian Large-Scale Bison Kills

An Isotopic Comparison

KRISTEN CARLSON
AND LELAND C. BEMENT

DOI: 10.5876/9781607326823.c007

135

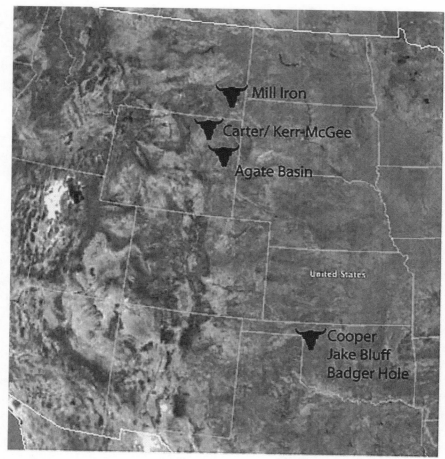

FIGURE 7.1. *Sites included in analysis.*

BACKGROUND

Social organization is a key component to understanding large game hunting behavior. Although it has been suggested that small groups may have carried out arroyo trap kills, the large amount of resources procured provides the ideal setting for a large group aggregation (Kornfeld, Frison, and Larsen 2010). The purposes of band aggregation allows otherwise dispersed groups to perform acts outside their usual capabilities. These acts include communal activities such as hunting, feasting, and social networking, including information exchange, mate selection, trade relations, and social bond reinforcement.

To be successful, the dispersed groups require a predetermined time and place to meet. This meeting place, referred to as a node, is needed in a predictable location on the landscape in order to draw groups of people together at a set time during the year, when a resource surplus is available to support the aggregation of a large number of people. A bison kill site provides this predictable node.

More recent kill/camp/ritual site complexes found at Late Prehistoric northwestern High Plains jump sites provide examples of aggregation around bison kills. These sites consist of one or more repeatedly used bison jumps, a processing site (generally at the base of the jump), a campsite (generally a fair distance from the jump) and evidence of ritual activity, which can be integrated into any of the aspects of the bison kill (Zedeño, chapter 2; Zedeño et al. 2014). The complex and extensive drive lanes associated with jumps reflect the social investment in these sites (Carlson 2011). The rise of social complexity is seen in the emergence of expedient leaders for specific tasks. Emergent hierarchies to handle information transference and population control develop temporarily (Fawcett 1987).

Aggregation at a particular node on the landscape requires a surplus of food to support various groups for the duration of the aggregation, in this case the bison hunt and subsequent butchering of the animals. In considering the use of communal bison hunts as the subsistence intensification required for aggregation, the immovable bison kill site is proposed to serve as the node around which the system functions. Special landscape requirements must be met for a successful communal bison kill, including bison milling area, drive path, and containment or kill structure (pound, jump, arroyo trap; Carlson 2011; Fawcett 1987; Frison 2004). For our research this becomes possible when bison herds reach the numbers in which they can be manipulated by the requisite number of hunters into arroyos at predictable locations. The special requirements of the kill site, especially the proximity to a bison population, anchor the system to areas where the requisite landform types (e.g., cliff or arroyo) are found where bison congregate or are concentrated such as along established migration paths. Bison are considered gregarious herd animals with tight-knit family units (Berger and Cunningham 1994; Post et al. 2001; Rosas, Engle, and Shaw 2005). The basic unit is the cow/calf bond with an extended group composed of immature cows and bulls less than four years of age. Mature bulls often form bachelor herds or, in the case of dominant breeding bulls, singles, or pairs. Mature bulls only mingle with the cow/calf/juveniles animal groupings during the rut. Depending on the time of year, bison may be dispersed widely because of these behavior units.

In order to reconstruct the behavioral aspects of the prey animal, in this case bison, we employ stable carbon and nitrogen isotopes from bison bone from southern and northwestern Plains bison kills. Stable carbon and nitrogen isotopes can be directly linked to grassland composition and environmental conditions of temperature and humidity (Chisholm et al. 1986). There are two kinds of grasses in which bison consume, C_3 and C_4 grasses, and each grass indicates a different kind of environment. C_3 grasses generally grow in wet, cool environments, whereas C_4 grasses are hardier and grow in dryer hotter environments. Bison are obligate grazers, but they are not selective. This means that bison consume grasses in the same proportion as the grasses are distributed in a pasture. Bison grazing within a restricted area will have stable C and N isotopic signatures that directly relate to the areas grasslands (with trophic level adjustment). Bison that are free to move between different grassland areas will have differing isotopic values, depending on how long each individual grazes in each area. The greater the heterogeneity of grassland composition, the greater the range of C and N isotopic signatures between individual free-ranging animals.

In regions where grasses have homogeneous distributions, all bison will ingest the same grass types in the same proportions and have similar isotopic signatures. However, in areas where grass types are distributed heterogeneously, some animals may graze grass species that are distinct from what other animals graze, and thereby acquire a significantly different isotopic signature (Post et al. 2001; Rosas, Engle, and Shaw 2005). Bison cow/calf/juveniles have been found to have similar isotopic diets dominated by C_3 grasses in areas where C_3 and C_4 grasses segregate. Bulls tend to have higher C_4 diets in this same landscape. The difference is attributed to bison behavior in which the bulls move away from cow/calf/juvenile groups, which often prefer lowland areas, areas that tend to be dominated by C_3 grasses, into upland areas where C_4 grasses tend to be dominant. The bulls are marginalized not because of a preference for C_4 grasses, but because of behavioral patterns that inadvertently place them in C_4-rich settings (Berger and Cunningham 1994; Rosas, Engle, and Shaw 2005).

Individual isotopic signature variation is expected on the basis of sexual segregation in heterogeneous grassland settings. This pattern is expected in modern as well as prehistoric bison, if we accept similar behavior patterns in the past. A similar process leading to differential isotopic signatures among individuals may be at work in highly mobile or migratory bison. In migratory settings, some individuals linger in nutrient-rich patches before continuing on to the designated endpoint (Holdo, Holt, and Fryxell 2009). In these instances any subgroup of the herd could obtain an isotopic signature deviant from another group. This situation allows greater range of individual isotopic signature in cow/calf/juvenile subgroupings where sexual segregation is not visible, including bison kill sites targeting cow/calf/juvenile groups. It is expected, then, that a bison kill site targeting cow/calf/juvenile animals during a season when bulls are typically not present could contain significant variability in isotopic signatures if the animals are regularly migrating across heterogeneous (diverse) grasslands, allowing some groups to persist in isotopically distinct areas passed by other groups.

Today the Great Plains of North America display latitudinal and elevational differences in grassland composition (Tieszen 1998). The latitudinal variation has been demonstrated in bison isotopic signatures from various modern bison herds and linked to temperature gradients (Tieszen 1998). The overall trend is for increasing C3 grassland composition with increasing latitude and/or elevation, particularly related to increasing precipitation levels and decreasing temperatures.

Our research strives to compare southern and northern Plains' early Paleoindian period communal bison hunting by characterizing bison stable isotope signatures. Stable carbon and nitrogen isotopic analyses of bison bone from well-dated contexts are analyzed to reconstruct the environment and possible level of mobility.

METHODS: STABLE ISOTOPES

Bison are grazing animals whose trophic level is one step removed from the level of the grasses consumed. These plants leave a stable isotope signature in the bones and teeth, which provides a means to analyze environmental settings of extinct species (Hoppe, Paytan, and Chamberlain 2006; Larson et al. 2001; Tieszen 1991). Archaeologically this is a useful means of analysis because bison bone and teeth are often well preserved and can be studied to reconstruct environments that are difficult to understand by other means such as pollen or phytolith analysis. However, there are many factors that can affect the preservation of bone and tooth remains, and the process in which stable isotopes find their way into bone collagen and tooth enamel must also be understood to ensure that the samples under analysis contain information related directly to the animals and environment and not to the process of degradation that has occurred since the animals' death. This degradation process is known as diagenesis.

The following section provides a brief outline of the photosynthesis process of CO_2 in the atmosphere and how it affects the carbon value of plants. These carbon values are significant because they are the main element analyzed to determine environment. The amount of CO_2 in the atmosphere has not been consistent through time, which leads to variation in stable C isotopes. Carbon isotope ratios of plants have changed through evolutionary time, and this will also be discussed as a result of changes in the atmospheric levels of CO_2.

Variation, Carbon, and CO_2

Carbon (C), Nitrogen (N), and Oxygen (O) contain stable isotopes often studied archaeologically in animal remains (DeNiro and Epstein 1978; Hoppe, Paytan, and Chamberlain 2006; Tieszen 1991). This section discusses C found in plants and the process in which photosynthesis drives the variation between plants (Julien et al. 2012; Tieszen 1991, 1994). C_3 grasses generally grow in wet, cool environments, whereas C_4 grasses are hardier and grow in dryer hotter environments. But what drives the variation between C_3 and C_4 grasses?

CO_2 in the atmosphere is absorbed into plants differently dependent upon the plant (DeNiro and Epstein 1978; Larson et al. 2001). There are three groups of plants that process CO_2 through photosynthesis; these plants are C_3, C_4, and CAM. C_3 plants represent the most common plant type. They use a simple photosynthesis process that leads to a 3 Carbon compound, giving these plants their names. These plants typically are successful in a mesic environment. C_4 plant photosynthesis conserves water, is more energy efficient, and more complex. C_4 plants typically grow in xeric environments. CAM's can fluctuate between C_3 and C_4 but are not typically ingested by bison. They do, however, use photosynthesis similar in complexity to that of C_4.

When CO_2 in the atmosphere increases as it has since the industrial revolution, the amount of CO_2 increases the C parts per million in the plant (Larson et al. 2001; Tieszen 1991). This has led to changes of C in plants through evolutionary time. This is significant when studying Carbon isotopes in archaeological contexts because the amount of increase in CO_2 in the atmosphere must be corrected for, similarly to the way in which archaeologists correct for CO_2 increase when conducting radiocarbon dating.

In order to make sense of C results, archaeologists and biologists analyze the $\delta^{13}C$, which is obtained from the ratio of ^{13}C to ^{12}C. The $\delta^{13}C$ of the sample will break into two groups if C_4 and C_3 plants are present. The $\delta^{13}C$ for C_3 plants will be in the range of −24 parts per million to −34 parts per million, while C_4 plants will usually group in −6 parts per million to −9 parts per million (DeNiro and Epstein 1978). Due to the increase in CO_2 in the atmosphere since the Industrial Revolution prehistoric, samples are expected to be more negative than modern samples (Larson et al. 2001). These numbers fluctuate dependent on materials tested. Everything from hair, to bone collagen, tooth appetite, and feces can be analyzed for stable isotopes. Archaeologically we typically focus on remains buried for extended periods of time, usually bone and tooth remains.

Degradation of Samples

Degradation of sample quality is another issue necessary to consider when studying stable isotopes from prehistoric contexts. This process of degradation and change of sample composition is called diagenesis and is closely related to taphonomy. In the case of bone samples, archaeologists study the collagen in the bone. The apatite in the enamel is under analysis when studying teeth. The dentine in teeth is rarely used because it has a greater risk of being altered by diagenetic processes (Tütken and Vennemann 2011). Collagen in bone has a higher likelihood of being altered through diagenesis than tooth enamel and by extension apatite. Tooth enamel has a larger crystalline structure, making it stronger and more likely to retain its original composition when compared to the crystalline structure of collagen (Tütken and Vennemann 2011).

From the time an animal dies, the remains are subject to alteration from the environment; this process is known as taphonomy. When studying isotopes, researchers hope to isolate the original stable isotopes from the bone or tooth, which indicate the grazing patterns of the animal while alive (Hoppe, Paytan, and Chamberlain 2006; Julien et al. 2012; Tieszen 1994). This can aid in understanding past grazing range and be used to reconstruct past environments (Julien et al. 2012; Tieszen 1991). Diagenesis can alter those results by introducing or degrading the elements under study. The first stage of diagenesis can occur during decomposition and burial. Decomposition is a chemical process, which, under some conditions, changes or destroy collagen or tooth enamel. Understanding the environment of deposition is a key factor in being able to determine the degree to which diagenesis could be a possibility for the samples under study (Tieszen 1991). For example, acidic environments rarely preserve good samples for isotopic analysis. Also factors—such as distance from coal seams, which could increase the overall C composition of the bone or tooth material—must be taken into account.

Testing of prehistoric samples to determine the extent to which they have been altered through diagenesis is necessary. Collagen can be tested by taking the C to N ratio of the prehistoric sample and comparing it to a modern sample (Tieszen 1991; Tütken and Vennemann 2011). Modern C:N ratios range from 2.90 to 3.60. If the ratios are similar, the collagen has been preserved. If the ratios are different, the sample is likely degraded and cannot be used for accurate analysis.

Tooth enamel as mentioned above is far less likely to be impacted by diagenetic process; it is also more difficult to check for diagenesis. Comparing apatite to collagen can determine if the sample has degraded, but the collagen must first be tested with the abovementioned method. If the difference between $\delta^{13}C$ apatite and $\delta^{13}C$ collagen exceeds fourteen parts per million, the apatite has degraded too much to be useful for analysis (DeNiro and Epstein 1978).

Many steps are involved in the process of CO_2 moving from the atmosphere and being processed by plants in the form of photosynthesis. These plants are then ingested by large herbivores, and C is then laid down in the bones and teeth of the grazing animals. If diagenesis has not degraded the collagen and apatite of a sample, then they can be studied to gain an understanding of the C_3 or C_4 plants consumed by grazers. This information can then be used to reconstruct ranging patterns such as migration and paleoenvironmental reconstruction is areas such as the Plains, where pollen and other means of paleoenvironmental reconstruction are unavailable.

THE SITES

Southern Plains Sites

The Beaver River bison hunting complex consists of large (> twenty bison), late summer / early fall, arroyo trap kills manned by groups using lithics from various southern Plains regions, including the western Oklahoma panhandle, Texas panhandle, and central Texas. Occasional inclusion of individuals or groups from the central Plains is suggested by the occasional occurrence of tools or points made from sources in northwestern Kansas and eastern Colorado (Bement 1999). These sites provide the samples from the southern Plains research due to the long hunting duration at the kill complex.

Three arroyo trap bison kill sites located along the Beaver River in Harper County, Oklahoma, constitute the Beaver River complex (figure 7.2). The earliest record of arroyo trap kills within the Beaver River drainage is found at the Clovis-age Jake Bluff Site (34HP60; Bement and Carter 2010). The kill event at Jake Bluff dates to 10,821 ± 17 BP (Bement and Carter 2010; table 7.1), postdating all known Clovis mammoth kills and earning Jake Bluff a position as one of the latest Clovis sites in North America (Holliday and Meltzer 2010; Waters and Stafford 2007). The timing of this site is significant because it marks a period when mammoth were dying off and reflects methods by which Paleoindian hunters began to adapt to the next high-ranking species left on the landscape, bison. Geologic coring along the north margin of the Beaver River floodplain terraces found that the requisite arroyos for bison

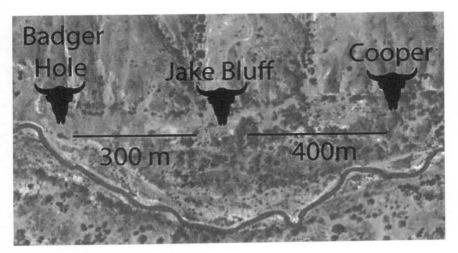

FIGURE 7.2. *Beaver River complex sites.*

traps formed by 11,200 BP (Bement and Brosowske 1999) and began filling with sediment until full, shortly after 10,000 BP. This sequence parallels similar landscape histories identified in nearby regions (Holliday 1995). The development of the arroyo trap technique in this area was possible because of the existence of suitable short, steep-walled arroyos, large numbers of bison—at least seasonally—and the requisite number of hunters with the knowledge of bison trap hunting methods. The minimum number of bison individuals (MNI) killed at Jake Bluff is twenty-two, based on the area excavated (Bement and Carter 2010). The kill took place during late summer/fall.

Cooper (34HP45) consists of three separate kill events spanning roughly sixty radiocarbon years. The state of Oklahoma purchased the property in 1992 and created the Cooper Wildlife Area. Excavations at Cooper began in 1993 after turkey hunters discovered a Folsom point eroding near bison bones (Bement 1999). The seasonality of all three kill sites based on tooth eruption and wear pattern analysis indicated the kills occurred during the late summer early fall. The MNIs from each kill level are described below; the actual number of bison killed during this event are unknown due to excessive erosion occurring well before the discovery of the site. The lowest kill dating to 10,589 ± 16 BP contained an MNI of twenty individual bison. The middle kill dating to 10,563 ± 19 BP contained an MNI of twenty-nine. The upper kill dating to 10,532 ± 19 BP had an MNI of twenty-nine (table 7.1).

TABLE 7.1. Radiocarbon assays for southern and northwestern Plains sites

Site		^{14}C age bp*	1 sig.	Lab number	Reference
Jake Bluff		10750	40	CAMS-79940	*Bement and Carter 2010*
		10840	45	CAMS-90968	
		10810	25	UCIAMS-61657	
		10885	35	PSU-4129/UCIAMS-59874	
	Mean†	10821	17	$X_2 = 6.87$; df = 3, Tcrit = 7.81	
Cooper					
Lower		10600	40	CAMS-94850	*Johnson and Bement 2009*
		10560	30	PSU-6077/UCIAMS-14089	
		10570	30	PSU-6078/UCIAMS-140850	
		10630	30	PSU-6079/UCIAMS-140851	
	Mean	10589	16	$X_2 = 3.28$; df = 3, Tcrit = 7.81	
Middle		10530	45	CAMS-82407	*Johnson and Bement 2009*
		10565	30	PSU-6075/UCIAMS-14847	
		10575	30	PSU-6076/UCIAMS-140848	
	Mean	10563	19	$x_2 = 0.70$; df = 2, Tcrit = 5.99	
Upper		10505	45	CAMS-94849	*Johnson and Bement 2009*
		10550	30	PSU-6073/UCIAMS-140845	
		10525	30	PSU-6074/UCIAMS-140846	
	Mean	10532	19	$X_2 = 0.77$; df = 2, Tcrit = 5.99	
Carter/ Kerr-McGee		10600	25	UCIAMS-122572	
		10520	25	UCIAMS-122573	
	Mean	10560	18	$X_2 = 3.84$; df = 1, Tcrit = 5.12	
Mill Iron		10450	25	UCIAMS-61659	*Waters and Stafford 2014*
		10465	20	UCIAMS-98370	*Waters and Stafford 2014*
		10435	25	UCIAMS-98371	*Waters and Stafford 2014*
		10440	25	UCIAMS-122577	

continued on next page

TABLE 7.1—*continued*

Site		*14C age bp**	*1 sig.*	*Lab number*	*Reference*
		10465	25	UCIAMS-122578	
	Mean	10452	11	X2 = 9.49; df = 4, Tcrit = 1.39	
Agate Basin		10430	25	UCIAMS-122570	
		10135	25	UCIAMS-122571	
	Mean	10283	18	X2 = 3.84; df = 1, Tcrit = 69.62	

* All dates on XAD purified bison bone.

† Weighted mean following Ward and Wilson (1978).

Badger Hole (34HP194), the most recent bison kill site on the Beaver River complex, sites dates to 10,347 ± 16 BP. The site was discovered in 2010 after a brush fire cleared the vegetation exposing the eroding bison bone bed. Excavations carried out in 2011 and 2012 revealed a partially intact arroyo trap, with a section severely eroded and displaced to the west of the intact deposits. An MNI of 10 was determined from excavated remains. Seasonality follows the Beaver River complex pattern of late summer / early fall.

NORTHWESTERN PLAINS SITES

The sites chosen for comparison on the northwestern Plains include Mill Iron, MT (Frison 1996), Agate Basin, WY (Frison and Stanford 1982), and Carter/Kerr-McGee, WY (Frison 1984). Mill Iron and Agate Basin have been extensively analyzed over the years; less data is available on the Folsom level at Carter/Kerr-McGee. Early dating techniques at the three northwestern Plains sites produced dates with wide ranges of error, which have been reevaluated with radiocarbon dates from bone samples.

Mill Iron (24CT30), located in eastern Montana, was discovered in 1979 and excavated extensively from 1984 through 1988 by multiple academic and avocational groups. The principal investigator on the majority of the projects was Dr. George Frison, who later produced a publication concerning the findings at Mill Iron, summarized below (Frison 1996). Dr. Michael Waters and Dr. Tom Stafford recently undertook a project redating bison bone from the Mill Iron site, resulting in an average of 10,450 ± 15 BP (Waters and Stafford 2014). Additional samples from Mill Iron were collected and analyzed and produced dates averaging 10,453 ± 18 BP. When the Waters and Stafford dates were calibrated with the additional samples run with this analysis, the average was 10,452 ± 11 BP (table 7.1). The actual trap used to kill the bison at Mill Iron is missing but was assumed to be an arroyo trap. The bone bed excavated at Mill Iron produced an MNI of twenty-nine individuals, assumed to be mostly cows killed in a single event (Haynes et al. 1992). Seasonality was determined to be late spring/early summer during or just after calving based on tooth eruption (Todd, Rapson, and Hofman 1996).

Agate Basin (48NA201), a multicomponent kill site and camp located in Wyoming, was first excavated in 1942 by Smithsonian archaeologists and then in 1961, 1975–80 by University of Wyoming archaeologists. The Paleoindian use of Agate Basin spanned a period of significant climatic change from the Late Pleistocene to the early Holocene (Frison and Stanford 1982). Three kill levels are evident within the arroyo: a Folsom level with an MNI of 9, an Agate Basin level, and a Hell Gap level. The Folsom level appears to be a winter kill based on tooth eruption patterns. Agate Basin's Folsom component was dated from a small amount of charcoal producing the date of 10,430 ± 570 BP (Frison and Stanford 1982). Bone samples collected for this research produced dates of 10,283 ± 18 BP from the Folsom level (table 7.1).

Carter/Kerr-McGee (48CA12) is also a multicomponent kill site located in Wyoming. Four cultural levels include Clovis, Folsom, Agate Basin-Hell Gap, and Alberta-Cody (Frison 1984). The site was discovered in 1975 and excavated in 1977 as part of a cultural resource management salvage project. Headward erosion destroyed the majority of the kill deposits within the arroyo prior to excavation. Frison (1984) published predominately on the more extensive Cody-Alberta level but makes little remark to the Folsom levels. It is likely that the remains excavated at Carter/Kerr-McGee were not in the location of the kill event but were removed from the nearby kill area to the excavated area for further butchering (Frison 1984). A hearth located at the Folsom level, in addition to Folsom fluted points and channel flakes, led to the dating of the Folsom level. A charcoal sample from the Folsom hearth of Carter/Kerr-McGee produced a date of 10,400 ± 600 BP. Bone samples collected for this analysis produced two groups of dates, indicating the possibility of two use periods. The oldest group dates (averaged two dates) to 10,560 ± 18 BP and is aligned with the Folsom use of the site (table 7.1). The younger group, not reported in table 7.1, aligns with the overlying Cody use of the site. Given the extended use of the site, these two groups are not surprising. The earliest dates provide a reasonable range for the Folsom period. A bison bone assemblage analysis is currently underway for both the Folsom and Cody levels to determine MNI and seasonality.

RESULTS/DISCUSSION

The five kill episodes at the Beaver River complex define one of the highest-density Folsom site concentrations on the southern Plains. This Folsom bison hunting complex is structured on bison concentration, arroyo formation, and seasonally redundant intercept patterns by Folsom hunters. These sites provide the focus of the southern Plains research because of the long duration of hunting at the sites and the Clovis site Jake Bluff, which may mark the transition from Clovis to Folsom and the beginning of large-scale communal hunting of bison herds on the southern Plains. Three comparable sites on the northwestern Plains were included in this study. These three early Paleoindian sites are spread across the landscape and through roughly the same time period of use as the southern Plains sites. Overall this collection of sites provides a means to compare changes in bison herd diet through time on the northern and southern Plains.

To obtain reliable stable isotope data, the atomic Carbon and Nitrogen ratio of the samples were compared to modern C and N ratios to determine if the collagen had undergone diagenesis. $\delta^{13}C$ and $\delta^{15}N$ also provide two slightly different measures to determine environment and vegetation. For paleoenvironmental reconstruction C4 indicates a hot, dry short-grass prairie environment, while C3 indicates a cool, wet taller-grass prairie.

Based on the stable isotope results (figure 7.3), there is a clear separation between the Clovis kill at Jake Bluff, the three Folsom kills at Cooper, and the later Folsom kill at Badger Hole. Due to the poor preservation of the majority of the bone remains from Jake Bluff, only two samples provide sufficient preservation for analysis. The three Cooper kills group as well and lastly the Badger Hole results, which are more dispersed, but do not overlap the results from Cooper and Jake Bluff. These trends suggest an increase in diet variation through time. The overall trend depicted here indicates a shift from hot and dry C4 grasses at Jake Bluff to increasingly wetter and cooler C3 conditions seen in the Badger Hole results, with the three Cooper kills in intermediate positions.

When comparing the carbon isotopes variance in relation to time, a shift is apparent from resident to more wide-ranging migratory herds between the periods of Jake Bluff, Cooper, and Badger Hole. This change in diet demonstrates that these animals go from a restricted possibly resident diet at Jake Bluff with minimal variation to more variation implying increased migration of the animals during the time of Badger Hole.

These findings are significant because we know that animals under pressure will often pack together and minimize their range area to stay close to predictable necessary resources such as water and grasslands (Gadbury et al. 2000).

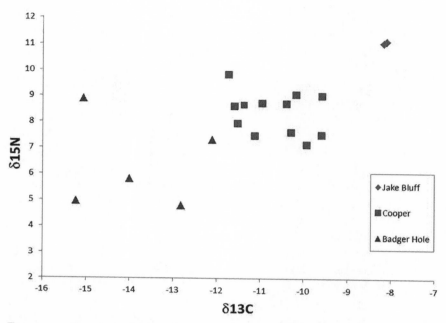

FIGURE 7.3. *Increase in diet variation through time at southern Plains Beaver River complex sites.*

The bison at Jake Bluff are clearly a species under stress. When compared to the skeletal remains of the later Folsom bison kills in the same arroyo trap complex, the bison at Jake Bluff are gracile and thin boned in comparison. It is our opinion that Jake Bluff, currently the earliest large-scale bison kill site on the Plains, marks a period of extreme environmental duress at 10,800 BP as is indicated by the gracile bones of the bison (figure 7.4) and the high value of δ15N and C4 grasses indicated from the isotope analysis. During this time we know that the mammoth are dying out and the bison species itself are under pressure as their numbers bottleneck, as is seen in DNA studies (O'Shea 2012).

During this period of rapid environmental change, the Paleoindian hunters also had to adapt to a rapidly changing environment and a change in the high-rank prey species on the landscape. Bison provide a prey source drastically different from mammoth. Bison pack together and flee as a herd when frightened. This tendency enables the bison to be maneuvered in large numbers to a location predetermined by the hunters. This resident herd at Jake Bluff enabled the development of one of the earliest large-scale bison kill events in the southern Plains.

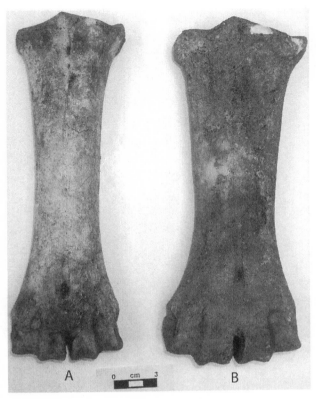

FIGURE 7.4. *Comparison of three-year-old male bison left metacarpals from Jake Bluff (A) and Cooper site (B). Note the gracile form of the Clovis-age example from Jake Bluff (A) compared to the robust form of the Folsom-age example from the Cooper site (B).*

The stable isotopes at the three northwestern Plains sites appear more complex than the clear patterns from the southern Plains (figure 7.5). The oldest remains analyzed come from CKM at 10,560 ± 18 BP. Mill Iron, a Goshen kill site, produced dates of 10,452 ± 18 BP. The most recent Folsom kill event occurred at Agate Basin at 10,283 ± 18 BP. The isotopes indicate a relatively stable environment of cool/moist adapted prairie through all three kill events. There appears to be a trend from a wider range of isotopic diversity among the animals at Carter/Kerr-McGee compared to those at Mill Iron and Agate Basin.

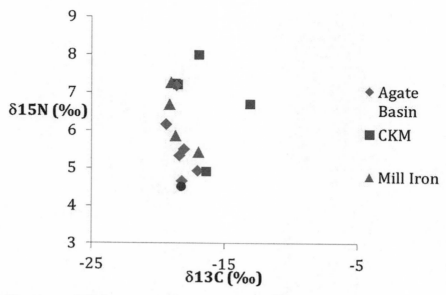

FIGURE 7.5. *Stable isotope results from northwestern Plains sites.*

RELATING δ¹³C VALUES TO HERD MOBILITY

The study of modern bison on restricted ranges provide a baseline from which prehistoric bison mobility can be gauged. Studies conducted at the Tallgrass Prairie Preserve (TPP) in northeastern Oklahoma are particularly applicable, since the TPP is within the migration range of prehistoric bison of northwestern Oklahoma, at least during Folsom times (Graves, chapter 6; Graves 2010). The TPP is contained within the Osage Plains of the Central Lowland Physiographic Province (Fenneman 1938). This region supports lush tall grass prairies and is home to approximately 2,500 free-ranging bison, which have been extensively studied (Rosas, Engle, and Shaw 2005 and citations within; Shaw and Carter 1990). The TPP bison follow the same general patterns observed elsewhere, with bulls and cows forming separate groups throughout most of the year, integrating only during the summertime rut (Berger and Cunningham 1994). This sexual segregation has been found to affect the content and quality of diet between these two groups, with bulls subsisting on lower-quality grasses than cows and, by extension, juveniles. This variation in diet has been quantified using δ¹³C (Rosas, Engle, and Shaw 2005). The results are that bulls have significantly higher C_4 grasses in their diet (Ave = −12.6 ‰, std. dev. 0.32; p = 0.0470) while cows have slightly lower C_4 content

TABLE 7.2. δ¹³C values for bison from the Tallgrass Prairie Preserve, Oklahoma

	N	Mean (‰)	Std. dev.	Variance (Std. dev./mean × 100)
Bulls	7	−12.6	0.32	2.54
Cows	15	−13.4	0.21	1.57
Combined	22	−13.15	0.38	2.90

After Rosas et al. 2005.

(Ave = −13.4 ‰ std. dev. 0.21). The range of variation displayed between cows and bulls expressed by the lower standard deviation for cows and higher standard deviation for bulls can be quantified by the statistic Coefficient of Variation (CV). CV is calculated by dividing the standard deviation by the mean and, for ease of comparison, multiplying the result by −100 (table 7.2). Bulls have a higher CV (CV = 2.54) compared to cows (CV = 1.57). The lesser CV in cows is because cows form large groups that stay together, whereas bulls are more solitary or paired and tend to disperse widely. Together, the bulls (n = 7) and cows (n = 15) have a weighted mean δ¹³C of −13.15 ‰, std. dev. 0.38, and CV of 2.90.

The TPP herd, then, provides an expected range of variance for a resident herd that is either sexually segregated or integrated. The TPP provides baseline quantification for a resident herd within a distinctive grassland type, in this case, tall-grass prairie. We expect to find a similar pattern of variance between cows and bulls and combined groups in other grassland types (mixed and short grasses), since bison everywhere follow similar behavioral patterns of sexual segregation (Berger and Cunningham 1994; Halloran 1968; McHugh 1972). If these values can be projected back in time, we would expect a bison kill of only resident bulls to display a variance of 2.54; whereas a bison kill of resident cows would have a variance of 1.57. A bison kill of a resident herd during the rut, when bulls and cows are integrated, would display a variance of 2.90.

The variation in stable carbon isotopes among individuals from a single kill reflect the variation in the grassland structure available to individuals and, as illustrated by the TPP bison, by the sexual composition of the herd. Where grassland variation is low (homogeneous distribution of species), the δ¹³C coefficient of variation (CV) will also be low. Where grassland variation is high (heterogeneous distribution of species across a greater area traversed by the individuals), the δ¹³C coefficient of variation will be high. It is predicted that the CV of a resident herd in a restricted range of grass species will be low, and CV will increase as individuals cross ever-increasing numbers of

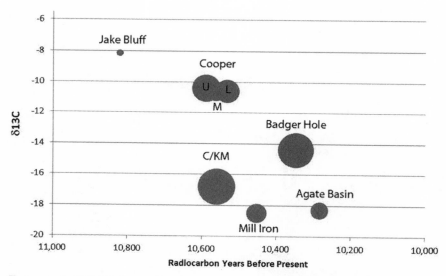

FIGURE 7.6. *δ¹³C CV changes through time for southern and northwestern Plains bison kills.*

areas as migration distance. Lesser variation will be reflected in resident cow/calf herds than in resident bull groups; and will be highest at kill sites conducted during the rut when cows and bulls are together. Greater coefficient of variation will occur in all herd types (cow/calf, bull, combined) as mobility increases through migration.

Computing the CV for the various southern and northwestern Plains kill sites provides new patterns for interpretation (table 7.3) and provides a quantification of the patterns seen in the scatter plots of data (figures 7.3 and 7.5).

On the southern Plains, CV analysis supports the visual dispersion of $\delta^{13}C$ and $\delta^{15}N$ ratios (figure 7.6). In particular, the limited distribution of Jake Bluff data points is accompanied by the lowest CV values of any kill sites in our analysis, southern or northwestern Plains bison kills. This pattern suggests the Jake Bluff bison are indeed very residential with low mobility. Breaking out the Cooper site data into the three kill episodes indicates low to moderate levels of mobility with the lowest kill animals with the highest level of mobility (greatest CV) and the middle kill with the lowest (smallest CV). The Badger Hole animals display far and above the highest level of mobility (greatest CV) of any kill on the southern Plains. The southern Plains CV data is fairly similar for both $\delta^{13}C$ and $\delta^{15}N$, suggesting that both elements have similar distributions across the landscape and both elements can be used to model mobility.

TABLE 7.3. Coefficient of variation for northwestern and southern Plains bison kills

	Age bp	δ15N	δ13C	Mean	Standard deviation	Coefficient of variance
CKM	10,560 ± 18	6.695726	−13.0771			
		7.208015	−18.5366			
		4.916849	−16.3775			
		7.985939	−16.9301			
		7.235724	−18.6761			
			d13C	−16.7195	2.267098	13.55961
			d15N	6.808451	1.153208	16.9379
Mill Iron	10,452 ± 18	7.261388	−19.0247			
		5.86482	−18.682			
		6.679776	−19.1502			
		5.429137	−16.9479			
			d13C	−18.4512	1.021558	5.536545
			d15N	6.30878	0.81975	12.9938
Agate Basin	10,283 ± 18	5.496118	−18.0313			
		4.653536	−18.1894			
		5.334375	−18.3686			
		6.149945	−19.4112			
		4.921575	−17.0379			
		7.183929	−18.5981			

continued on next page

TABLE 7.3—*continued*

	Age bp	δ15N	δ13C	Mean	Standard deviation	Coefficient of variance
			d13C	-18.2728	0.774768	4.240015
			d15N	5.62346	0.921459	16.3866
Jake Bluff	10,821 ± 17	11.1	-8.1			
		11.02	-8.17			
			d13C	-8.135	0.049497	0.608451
			d15N	11.06	0.056569	0.51147
Cooper Lower	10,589 ± 16	9.83	-11.74			
		7.5	-9.6			
		10.10241	-9.17587			
		8.96962	-10.2033			
		7.94	-11.53			
			d13C	-10.4498	1.144255	10.94998
			d15N	8.868407	1.139315	12.8469
Cooper Middle	10,563 ± 19	8.7	-10.4			
		7.6	-10.3			
		9.06	-10.18			
		9.035036	-11.3961			
			d13C	-10.569	0.558646	5.285697
			d15N	8.598759	0.685772	7.975246

continued on next page

TABLE 7.3—*continued*

	Age bp	δ15N	δ13C	Mean	Standard deviation	Coefficient of variance
Cooper Upper	10,532 ± 19	8.6	-11.6			
		7.14	-9.94			
		8.380369	-10.9292			
		8.047061	-9.862			
			d13C	-10.5828	0.834153	7.88216
			d15N	8.041857	0.642777	7.992892
Badger Hole	10,347 ± 16	8.88	-15.06			
		4.95	-15.23			
		4.79	-12.82			
		7.3	-12.1			
		5.8	-14			
		6.092308	-19.3855			
		8.16953	-12.113			
			d13C	-14.3869	2.554574	17.75623
			d15N	6.568834	1.583318	24.10349

The northwestern Plains bison kills CV results suggest the opposite pattern of mobility level through time (figure 7.6). The oldest bison kill is at CKM and has a $\delta^{13}C$ CV value that is the highest level for the three kill sites, suggesting the animals at 10,540 BP were highly mobile. By 10,452 BP, the bison mobility level was reduced to that seen at the temporally roughly contemporaneous middle kill at the Cooper site. The lowest CV and hence lowest mobility level is expressed at the Agate Basin site (10,283 BP), which is when bison on the southern Plains were the most mobile. Unlike the situation on the southern Plains, where $\delta^{15}N$ CV values varied in step with $\delta^{13}C$ values, on the northwestern Plains there is very little variation in $\delta^{15}N$ values between the three time periods. These values, however, are intermediate between those at Cooper and Badger Hole, suggesting the grassland structure on the northwestern Plains maintained a constant level of high nitrogen variability. Such high levels of variability in nitrogen may be the result of sustained drought conditions or possibly the common occurrence of fire. Both drought and fire use are known to produce heterogeneous nitrogen patterns.

With the exception of the Jake Bluff kill (and the Jake Bluff value is probably the result of inadequate sample size), none of the Paleoindian bison kill $\delta^{13}C$ CV values match those of a cow herd on the TPP, even though all these kills are reported as cow/calf herds. This pattern indicates that Paleoindian period grassland structure on both the southern and northwestern Plains was more diverse than that present today on the TPP.

Through isotope analysis of three northwestern and three southern Paleoindian sites, a clear pattern of changing environment and changes in herd migration emerges with consistent exploitation of migrating herds by Paleoindian hunters. At the Beaver River complex over a span of 500 radiocarbon years the environment moves from hot and dry to cool and wet with an increase in bison migration range. The results from the northwestern Plains indicate a change in herd behavior through time with a relatively stable environmental setting. Herds potentially move from a larger migratory range to a smaller migratory range on the northern Plains. This data enables a deeper understanding of adaptation of prey behavior to changing environmental settings. Hunters also would have to adapt to the changing environment, and the communal hunting of large game provides a means for Clovis hunters on the Plains to switch prey species to bison. After the switch is made, the communal hunting of bison in arroyo trap kills continues across North America through the Paleoindian period into the late prehistoric. The time depth of this kill technique speaks to its advantage and success for hunting populations.

REFERENCES CITED

Bement, Leland C. 1999. *Bison Hunting at Cooper Site: Where Lightning Bolts Drew Thundering Herds.* Norman: University of Oklahoma Press.

Bement, Leland C., and Scott D. Brosowske. 1999. "Paleoindian Bison Hunting along the Beaver River, Harper County, Oklahoma." Archaeological Resource Survey Report no. 40. Norman: Oklahoma Archeological Survey, University of Oklahoma.

Bement, Leland C., and Brian J. Carter. 2010. "Jake Bluff: Clovis Bison Hunting on the Southern Plains of North America." *American Antiquity* 75 (4): 907–33. https://doi.org/10.7183/0002-7316.75.4.907.

Bement, Leland C., Brian J. Carter, PollyAnna Jelley, Kristen Carlson, and Scott Fine. 2012. "Badger Hole: Towards Defining a Folsom Bison Hunting Complex along the Beaver River, OK." *Plains Anthropologist* 57 (221): 53–62. https://doi.org /10.1179/pan.2012.006.

Berger, Joel, and Carol Cunningham. 1994. *Bison: Mating and Conservation in Small Populations.* New York: Columbia University Press.

Carlson, Kristen A. 2011. "Prehistoric Bison Procurement: Human Agency and Drive Lane Topography on the Northwestern Plains." MA thesis, Department of Anthropology, Northern Arizona University.

Chisholm, B., J. C. Driver, S. Dube, and H. P. Schwarcs. 1986. "Assessment of Prehistoric Bison Foraging and Movement Patterns via Stable Carbon Isotopic Analysis." *Plains Anthropologist* 31 (113): 193–205.

DeNiro, Michael J., and Samuel Epstein. 1978. "Influence of Diet on the Distribution of Carbon Isotopes in Animals." *Geochimica et Cosmochimica Acta* 42 (5): 495–506. https://doi.org/10.1016/0016-7037(78)90199-0.

Fawcett, William B., Jr. 1987. "Communal Hunts, Human Aggregations, Social Variation, and Climatic Change: Bison Utilization by Prehistoric Inhabitants of the Great Plains." PhD dissertation, Department of Anthropology, University of Massachusetts, Amherst.

Fenneman, N. M. 1938. *Physiography of Eastern United States.* New York: McGraw-Hill.

Frison, George C. 1984. "The Carter/Kerr-McGee Paleoindian Site: Cultural Resource Management and Archaeological Research." *American Antiquity* 49 (2): 288–314. https://doi.org/10.2307/280020.

Frison, George C. 1996. *The Mill Iron Site.* Albuquerque: University of New Mexico Press.

Frison, George C. 2004. *Survival by Hunting: Prehistoric Human Predators and Animal Prey.* Berkeley: University of California Press. https://doi.org/10.1525 /california/9780520231900.001.0001.

Frison, George C., and Dennis J. Stanford. 1982. *The Agate Basin Site: A Record of the Paleoindian Occupation of the Northwestern High Plains.* New York: Academic Press.

Gadbury, C., L. Todd, H. H. Jahren, and R. Amundson. 2000. "Spatial and Temporal Variations in the Isotopic Composition of Bison Tooth Enamel from the Early Holocene Hudson-Meng Bone Bed, Nebraska." *Palaeogeography, Palaeoclimatology, Palaeoecology* 157 (1–2): 79–93. https://doi.org/10.1016/S0031-0182(99)00151-0.

Graves, Adam C. 2010. "Investigation Resource Structure and Human Mobility: An Example from Folsom-Aged Bison Kill Sites on the U.S. Southern Great Plains." PhD dissertation, Department of Anthropology, University of Oklahoma, Norman.

Halloran, Arthur F. 1968. "Bison (Bovidae) Productivity on the Wichita Mountains Wildlife Refuge, Oklahoma." *The Southwestern Naturalist*: 23–26.

Haynes, C. Vance, Jr., R. P. Beukens, A. J. T. Jull, and O. K. Davis. 1992. "New Radiocarbon Dates for Some Old Folsom Sites: Accelerator Technology." In *Ice Age Hunters of the Rockies*, ed. D. J. Stanford and J. S. Day, 83–100. Niwot: Denver Museum of Natural History and University Press of Colorado.

Hill, Matthew G. 2008. *Paleoindian Subsistence Dynamics on the Northwestern Great Plains, Zooarchaeology of the Agate Basin and Clary Ranch sites. BAR International Series 1756.* Oxford: British Archaeological Reports.

Holdo, Ricardo M., Robert D. Holt, and John M. Fryxell. 2009. "Opposing Rainfall and Plant Nutritional Gradients Best Explain the Wildebeest Migration in the Serengeti." *American Naturalist* 173 (4): 431–45. https://doi.org/10.1086/597229.

Holliday, Vance T. 1995. *Stratigraphy and Paleoenvironments of Late Quaternary Valley Fills on the Southern High Plains. Memoir 186.* Boulder: Geological Society of America.

Holliday, Vance T., and David J. Meltzer. 2010. "The 12.9-ka ET Impact Hypothesis and North American Paleoindians." *Current Anthropology* 51 (5): 575–607. https://doi.org/10.1086/656015.

Hoppe, K. A., A. Paytan, and P. Chamberlain. 2006. "Reconstructing Grassland Vegetation and Paleotemperatures Using Carbon Isotope Ratios of Bison Tooth Enamel." *Geology* 34 (8): 649–52. https://doi.org/10.1130/G22745.1.

Johnson, Eileen, and Leland C. Bement. 2009. "Bison Butchery at Cooper, a Folsom Site on the Southern Plains." *Journal of Archaeological Science* 36 (7): 1430–46.

Kornfeld, Marcel, George C. Frison, and Mary Lou Larsen. 2010. *Prehistoric Hunter-Gatherers of the High Plains and Rockies.* 3rd ed. Walnut Creek, CA: Left Coast Press.

Larson, R., L. Todd, E. Kelley, and J. Welker. 2001. "Carbon Stable Isotopic Analysis of Bison Dentition." In *Bison: The Past, Present, and Future of the Great Plains:*

Papers from the Center for Great Plains Studies' 24th Annual Interdisciplinary Symposium. Great Plains Research 11 (1): 25–64.

Julien, Marie-Anne, Hervé Bocherens, Ariane Burke, Dorothée G. Drucker, Marylène Patou-Mathis, Oleksandra Krotova, and Stéphane Péan. 2012. "Were European Steppe Bison Migratory? 18O, 13C and Sr Intra-Tooth Isotopic Variations Applied to a Palaeoethological Reconstruction." Quaternary International 271:106–19. https://doi.org/10.1016/j.quaint.2012.06.011.

McHugh, Tom. 1972. The Time of the Buffalo. Lincoln: University of Nebraska Press.

O'Shea, Lauren. 2012. "Southern Plains Bison mtDNA and What It Says about the Past." MA thesis, Department of Anthropology, University of Oklahoma, Norman.

Post, Diane M., Trent S. Armbrust, Eva A. Horne, and Jacob R. Goheen. 2001. "Sexual Segregation Results in Differences in Content and Quality of Bison (Bos Bison) Diets." Journal of Mammalogy 82 (2): 407–13. https://doi.org/10.1644/1545 -1542(2001)082<0407:SSRIDI>2.0.CO;2.

Rosas, Claudia, David Engle, and James Shaw. 2005. "Potential Ecological Impact of Diet Selectivity and Bison Herd Composition." Great Plains Research 15 (1): 3–13.

Shaw, James H., and Tracy S. Carter. 1990. "Bison Movements in Relation to Fire and Seasonality." Wildlife Society Bulletin 18 (4): 426–30.

Tieszen, L. L. 1991. "Natural Variations in the Carbon Isotope Values of Plants: Implications for Archaeology, Ecology, and Paleoecology." Journal of Archaeological Science 18 (3): 227–48. https://doi.org/10.1016/0305-4403(91)90063-U.

Tieszen, L. L. 1994. "Stable Isotopes on the Plains: Vegetation Analyses and Diet Determinations." In Skeletal Biology in the Great Plains: A Multidisciplinary View, ed. D. W. Owsley and R. L. Jantz, 261e282. Washington, DC: Smithsonian Press.

Tieszen, L. L. 1998. "Stable Isotopic Determination of Seasonal Dietary Patterns in Bison at Four Preserves across the Great Plains." In International Symposium on Bison Ecology and Management in North America, ed. L. Irby and J. Knight. Bozeman: Montana State University Press.

Todd, Lawrence C., David J. Rapson, and Jack L. Hofman. 1996. "Dentition Studies of the Mill Iron and Other Early Paleoindian Bison Bonebed Sites." In The Mill Iron Site, ed. George C. Frison, 145–75. Albuquerque: University of new Mexico Press.

Tütken, Thomas, and Torsten Walter Vennemann. 2011. "Fossil Bones and Teeth: Preservation or Alteration of Biogenic Compositions?" Palaeogeography, Palaeoclimatology, Palaeoecology 310 (1): 1–8. https://doi.org/10.1016/j.palaeo.2011.06.020.

Ward, Greame K., and Steven R. Wilson. 1978. "Procedures for Comparing and Combining Radiocarbon Age Determinations: A Critique." Archaeometry 20 (1): 19–31.

Waters, Michael R., and Thomas W. Stafford, Jr. 2007. "Redefining the Age of Clovis: Implications for the Peopling of the Americas." *Science* 315 (5815): 1122–26. https://doi.org/10.1126/science.1137166.

Waters, Michael R., and Thomas W. Stafford, Jr. 2014. "Redating the Mill Iron Site, Montana: A Reexamination of Goshen Complex Chronology." *American Antiquity* 79 (3): 541–48. https://doi.org/10.7183/0002-7316.79.3.541.

Zedeño, Maria Nieves, Jesse A. M. Ballenger, and John R. Murray. 2014. "Landscape Engineering and Organizational Complexity among Late Prehistoric Bison Hunters of the Northwestern Plains." *Current Anthropology* 55 (1): 23–58. https://doi.org/10.1086/674535.

8

A New Look at Old Assumptions

Paleoindian Communal Bison Hunting, Mobility, and Stone Tool Technology

John D. Speth

I am honored to have been asked to write a concluding chapter for this wonderful collection of papers on communal hunting. My only regret is that I wasn't able to be at the actual session where these papers were presented, or at the informal discussions that surely followed. Communal hunting has always been one of my favorite topics, one that began during my graduate student days when George Frison and I overlapped at the University of Michigan and for a while even shared lab space. Although at the time I was focused on stone tools, Neanderthals, and the Near Eastern Middle Paleolithic, and knew next to nothing about either communal bison kills or Paleoindians, I found George's work on both topics to be captivating, a fascination that played an important role in my eventual "conversion" from stones to bones and my lifelong interest in many of the other topics touched upon in this chapter.

Presentations at symposia by discussants, and their concluding chapters in the volumes that often result, can come in many different forms. Some simply recapitulate what the authors have already said. I know from my own experience that I tend to "zone out" when discussants take that route, thinking instead of the beer that will follow shortly, and I seldom read those sorts of overviews when they finally appear in print. Or the discussant can launch into a diatribe about all that he or she (usually the former) sees as wrong in the session, and I find "contributions" of that

DOI: 10.5876/9781607326823.c008

sort to be counterproductive, if not downright off-putting. So the problem is to find a way to relate one's comments to broader themes of the session and the volume, but in such a way that they don't simply reiterate what has already been said, and that (one hopes) will add something that is both constructive and useful to the whole.

There are obviously quite a few different themes that one could zero in on in an eclectic volume such as this one, so not surprisingly I found I had to be selective. I want to emphasize at the outset, however, that there is no hidden agenda implied by the particular topics I have chosen and those that I have omitted. Quite the contrary, my choices simply reflect the intersection of the book's contents with the path along which my own thinking has been going of late, and hence topics about which I might be able to say something that is not already "old hat." However, a bit like the "Surgeon General's Warning," I should also add that many of my thoughts these days, and hence what I have written here, tend to be rather "unorthodox"; or, as I like to put it, "more than three standard deviations from the mean." In short, I enjoy questioning assumptions, particularly those seemingly unassailable ones that are seldom put under the spotlight.

Inadequate attention to assumptions was always a pet peeve of mine with *Processualism* during the heady days of the "New Archaeology." Too much emphasis was put on "testing" and "confirming" hypotheses. I always had the nagging feeling that if one already knew the answer at the start, the outcome wasn't going to be very interesting or informative, because to me the real issue was not whether you found what you expected to find (there was a good chance that was equifinality, anyway), but whether the initial hypotheses made any sense in the first place. More often than not, the hypotheses that guided the research were lifted uncritically from some hot new "theory" that happened to be the bandwagon at the moment, or from "inherited wisdom" that was largely immune from examination. Thus, we tested hypotheses about whether society "X" was patrilocal or matrilocal, but never really asked what postmarital residence was really all about, or why anyone should be interested in it in the first place. The focus was squarely on the "testing" end of things, usually with no alternative or competing hypotheses offered should the "preferred" one fail, and I'm willing to bet that nine times out of ten if the results of the "test" turned out negative, we never heard about it.

For me, things start to get interesting when your results don't fit what you expect to find, or when you get some results that do, but others that clearly don't. That's when you are forced back to the "drawing boards" and have to start questioning the basic assumptions that you began with. To say the least, that stage can be very frustrating, akin to beating your head against the proverbial wall. But it can also be an exciting and rewarding point in one's thinking, because the new framework that eventually (one hopes) surfaces is often quite unexpected, even counterintuitive, and may well lead to all sorts of new and productive avenues of research. Unfortunately, for junior scholars who are struggling to get tenure, it is also a risky way to launch one's career, because in my experience the one thing that is certain about the whole process is that the light bulb never goes off when you want it to, or when you need it.

In any case, what follows are a few ideas that have been gestating for quite some time in my own thinking and that were sparked anew by chapters in the present volume. They don't all deal directly with communal hunting, nor do they all deal with Paleoindians, but in one way or another they are all concerned with the assumptions we make in reconstructing the lifeways of hunting peoples in the past. As this chapter unfolds, I hope at a minimum that I have succeeded in weaving them together into something that is reasonably coherent and perhaps even interesting. Many of the ideas aren't necessarily new or original to me, but they haven't received the attention they deserve in large part because they run counter to much mainstream thinking in the field today. I offer them, not out of any conviction that they are right, but as "food for thought." If nothing else, I hope they help convince the reader that there is still much we can learn by questioning some of the basic assumptions regarding communal hunting and related issues of technology, mobility, and land use that we all too often simply take for granted.

THE TIME-DEPTH OF COMMUNAL BISON HUNTING

Since many of the chapters in this volume are concerned in one way or another with bison hunting in North America, let me begin with a few comments to place these chapters in a broader geographical and temporal context. For many of us, North American bison kills are the quintessential kill sites, emblematic of communal hunting worldwide. In the classic northern Plains kills, dozens, even hundreds of animals were driven off cliffs, and into an amazing variety of traps including sinkholes, artificially constructed corrals, steep-sided dead-end arroyos, parabolic sand dunes, snowdrifts, and rivers (Kornfeld, Frison, and Larson 2010). Hundreds of these kills have been documented, scores sampled, and many thoroughly excavated and reported in marvelously detailed books and monographs (e.g., Bement 1999; Frison 1974, 1996; Frison and Stanford 1982; Meltzer 2006; Wheat 1972). In a rapidly growing number of cases we know the age and sex of the animals that were killed, and with these sorts of data we can approximate the time of year when the drives took place. Thanks to the pioneering work of Joe Ben Wheat at Olsen-Chubbuck in Colorado and George Frison at a number of kills in Wyoming and Montana, both scholars weaving together insights from the rich ethnohistoric record and the findings of archaeology, as well as information from wildlife biology and ethology, we now have sophisticated models of how the animals were manipulated into these traps and some idea of the reasons why the animals were hunted at particular times of year (see Kornfeld, Frison, and Larson 2010).

These communal bison drives are a remarkable phenomenon, both for their sophistication and for their antiquity, some dating back to North America's early Paleoindian period, 12,000 years ago or more (Bement and Carter 2010, 2015). Yet, despite the romance and mystique of the Paleoindian period, by Old World standards these intrepid hunters of the Great Plains are essentially the distant "backwoods" cousins of Prepottery Neolithic protoagriculturists in the Near East, peoples who were already living year-round in villages, some of them exceptionally large, constructing monumental shrines and other architectural features, and well on their way toward domesticating both plants and animals (e.g., Dietrich et al. 2012). Communal bison hunting actually began much earlier in the Old World. So, if we want to look at its real antiquity, we have to go back at least as far as the Middle Paleolithic and even the latter stages of the Lower Paleolithic. We now know that Neanderthals were communally driving steppe bison (*Bison priscus*) into traps and perhaps even jumping them from cliffs well over 40,000 years ago (Gaudzinski 2006; Jaubert and Delagnes 2007; Jaubert et al. 2005; Rendu and Armand 2009; Rendu et al. 2011; Rendu et al. 2012). They may also have been communally driving both horses and reindeer (Blasco, Peris, and Rosell 2010; Gaudzinski and Roebroeks 2000). And just recently the beginnings of communal bison hunting have been pushed back by a full order of magnitude to some 400,000 years ago! The new kill/processing site was found in the TD10.2 subunit of the Gran Dolina site at Atapuerca in northern Spain (Rodríguez-Hidalgo 2015). Since Neanderthals don't appear in Europe until sometime after about 300,000 years ago, the Middle Pleistocene hominins operating the TD10.2 drive were ancestors of Neanderthals, very likely members of the archaic hominin taxon that paleoanthropologists commonly classify as *Homo heidelbergensis* (Rightmire 1998). In other words, it is quite clear that the cooperation and coordination required to successfully carry out a communal hunt of animals as large and dangerous as bison are certainly not an invention of North American Paleoindians and not even of anatomically modern humans, but one that predates the appearance of *Homo sapiens* in Europe by literally hundreds of thousands of years.

Interestingly, the Middle Pleistocene, even in its latter stages, is also a time period when there are few lithics that would unambiguously qualify as projectile points on the combined basis of morphology, use-wear, tip damage, and clear traces of hafting (Rots 2013, 2016; Rots and Plisson 2014). And, in light of the remarkable finds of nine well-preserved spears and spear fragments and one lance-like weapon—most or all of them apparently very effective throwing weapons, at the 300,000–335,000-year-old site of Schoeningen (Schöningen, Schö 13 II–4), located in an opencast lignite mine near Hannover, Germany—big-game hunting (at least thirty-five very large horses in the Schoeningen case) was routinely being conducted using weapons tipped only with wooden points (Julien et al. 2015; Maki 2013; Richter and Krbetschek 2015; Rieder 2000, 2003; Schoch et al. 2015; Steguweit 1999; Thieme 1997; van Kolfschoten 2014). The revelations at Schoeningen were foreshadowed many years earlier by the discovery (in 1911) of the tip of a wooden spear at Clacton, England. Made of yew wood, this spear, like those at Schoeningen, was never designed to bear a stone projectile point. Although less well known than the Schoeningen spears, the Clacton specimen is currently thought to be at least 400,000 years old (Allington-Jones 2015). The somewhat later Lehringen spear or lance (~120,000 years), found near Bremen, Germany, had a fire-hardened tip and, like the earlier examples, was also never designed to hold a stone point (Gaudzinski 2004; Thieme and Veil 1985; Wenzel 2002).

Cooperative hunting by hominins, though of single animals rather than groups of animals, almost certainly has considerably greater antiquity than the already remarkably early date suggested by the TD10.2 bison kill. Even chimpanzees, our closest living relatives, hunt cooperatively and share meat widely, though the degree, goals, and payoffs of such cooperation remain unclear and controversial (Boesch 2002; Mitani and Watts 2001, 2005; Muller and Mitani 2005). Thus, groups of male chimpanzees coordinate their efforts to surround individual monkeys, drive them into a tree from which they are unable to escape, and then kill them. And they engage in an analogous sort of activity—often dubbed "chimpanzee warfare"—when a group of males silently patrols the borders of their territory in search of isolated or otherwise vulnerable individuals from neighboring groups. Once encountered, such chimpanzees are quickly dispatched. These sorts of behavior suggest that cooperative hunting strategies may already have been part of the behavioral package inherited by both early hominins and chimpanzees from their last common ancestor (Gilby et al. 2013; Mitani, Watts, and Amsler. 2010; Wrangham and Peterson 1996). In other words, it would not be surprising if cooperative hunting may have a time depth measured in millions, not thousands, of years. Although no one yet knows when hominins began directing their cooperative efforts at groups of animals, it may not have been that momentous a cognitive step, and based on the Atapuerca evidence, we know it was already in place nearly half a million years ago and quite likely much earlier.

HIGH-QUALITY LITHICS AND PALEOINDIAN PROJECTILE POINTS

Before proceeding I should clarify a minor but potentially confusing issue of terminology. When talking about spears in what follows, I use the term *projectile point* to refer to the more or less triangular-shaped piece of stone attached to the tip of the weapon, regardless of whether the spear was thrust or thrown. Some authors (e.g., Shea 2006) use the term in a more restrictive sense, referring only to the stone tips of spears that were thrown.

Stone projectile points are conspicuous by their absence throughout most of the long Eurasian Middle Pleistocene, despite a rapidly growing body of evidence for big-game hunting, particularly after about 500,000 years ago, at sites such as Atapuerca (Gran Dolina TD6-2 and TD10.2), Bilzingsleben (possibly), Boxgrove, Schoeningen (Schöningen), and a steadily growing number of others (e.g., Hosfield 2011; Huguet et al. 2012; Mania and Mania 2005; Roberts 1997; Saladié et al. 2011; Serangeli and Böhner 2012; G. Smith 2013). During the subsequent Middle Paleolithic, stone points were clearly present, as demonstrated, for example, by a Levallois point fragment solidly embedded in the vertebra of a wild ass (*Equus africanus*) at the site of Umm el Tlel in Syria (Boëda et al. 1999; see also Rots 2009). But considerable controversy still surrounds the functional interpretation of many of the unretouched and retouched triangular flakes that have been identified as likely candidates, including those identified as spear points on the basis of their overall symmetry, basal thinning, lateral hafting damage or wear, "tip cross-sectional area" (TCSA), and even those with putative "impact" damage on their tips (see Rots 2016:180–83). This has led many to conclude that stone projectile points, while present, were not a core part of the weapon technology used by Neanderthals and their contemporaries, even though these hunters are widely touted as Eurasia's quintessential "top predators" (Beyries and Plisson 1998; Clarkson 2016; Sánchez, Bao, and Vallejo 2011:244; Costa 2012; Groman-Yaroslavski, Zaidner, and Weinstein-Evron 2016; Moncel et al. 2009; Newman and Moore 2013; Rots 2013; Rots and Plisson 2014; Shea 1988; Thiébaut et al. 2014:290; Villa and Lenoir 2006; Villa and Soriano 2010).

Interestingly, not only is there uncertainty about the projectile points themselves, but equally striking is the almost total absence of lesions (wounds) in
bones that can be attributed with reasonable certainty to thrusts or impacts
by stone-tipped spears. While such lesions are commonly produced in
experimental studies involving animal carcasses, their counterparts in the
archaeological record remain exceedingly rare throughout the entire span
of the Lower and Middle Paleolithic (Gaudzinski-Windheuser 2016; Leduc
2014:478; Smith 2002, 2003). One of the few notable exceptions, of course, is
the justly famous Levallois point segment embedded in an equid vertebra at
Umm el Tlel (Boëda et al. 1999). Another might be the puncture wound in
the ninth rib of the Shanidar 3 Neanderthal, quite possibly the product of a
thrown spear of some sort tipped with a stone point (Churchill et al. 2009;
Solecki 1992; Zollikofer et al. 2002). Although extensive butchering and processing of animal carcasses, together with a variety of subsequent taphonomic
alterations, can make such wounds difficult to recognize in highly fragmented
faunal remains, at least in the case of Neanderthals one would nonetheless
expect diagnostic lesions to be reasonably evident if stone points were routinely hafted to the end of their hunting spears. Reacting to the noteworthy
scarcity of such evidence, Sabine Gaudzinski-Windheuser (2016:96) came
to the interesting conclusion that "one way to explain the virtual absence of
hunting lesions caused by tipped lithic projectiles in the Lower, Middle and
major parts of the Upper Palaeolithic is to suggest that it was simply not part
of the regular weaponry system used."

Recently published prey mortality data from the site of FLK-*Zinj* in
Olduvai Gorge (Tanzania) now pushes the entire debate about spears and
projectile points well back into the Early Pleistocene. Work by Henry Bunn
and Alia Gurtov (Bunn and Gurtov 2014; see also Pickering and Bunn 2012)
suggests that hominins (probably *Homo ergaster* or *H. erectus*) may already have
been engaged in ambush hunting of mostly prime-adult medium- to large-
sized prey, presumably using wooden-tipped spears, nearly 2 million years ago.
Unlike classic Mousterian assemblages, the Oldowan assemblage found at
FLK-*Zinj* is essentially devoid of suitably shaped triangular flakes that might
have served as projectile points. Thus, if the prey mortality pattern is telling us
what we think it does, wooden-tipped spears very likely already appeared early
in the Pleistocene (see also Hayden 2015). Hunting of broadly comparable
antiquity (~2.0 MYA), again very likely using wooden-tipped spears, is also
suggested by both faunal and use-wear evidence from Kanjera South in Kenya,
though in this case the prey were mostly young individuals of goat-sized and
somewhat larger antelopes (Lemorini et al. 2014:22).

But even the FLK-*Zinj* data, surprising as it might be, may not mark the beginnings of the use of simple spears. Jill Pruetz and Paco Bertolani observed chimpanzees using wooden sticks with tips that they had deliberately sharpened with their teeth to stab bush babies (small nocturnal prosimians) hidden in cavities and hollows in trees (Pruetz and Bertolani 2007). Thus, like cooperative hunting, the use of simple thrusting spears may have begun millions of years ago.

Given the virtual absence of stone projectile points prior to about 300,000 years ago, and if one accepts the likelihood that hominins were already ambush hunting with wooden-tipped weapons by at least 1.8–2.0 million years ago at FLK-*Zinj* and Kanjera South, and in light of the controversy swirling around the functional role of triangular flakes even during the Middle Paleolithic, the heyday of Eurasia's supposed "top predators," one can't help but be drawn to the rather heretical conclusion that stone points are not (functionally) essential to the successful hunting of big game. It would appear that in the hands of experienced hunters, spears, darts, and arrows tipped only with sharpened wooden points make very effective weapons (Waguespack et al. 2009). The first 30,000+ years of the Australian archaeological record underscores the fact that hunting peoples can be very successful without recourse to stone-tipped projectiles (Allen 1996; Allen and Akerman 2015; Balme and O'Connor 2014; Johnson and Wroe 2003:943; O'Connell and Allen 2004; White 1977:26). Stone spear and dart points don't appear there until the end of the Pleistocene or during the subsequent Holocene, tens of thousands of years after the continent was colonized by fully modern humans (Allen 2011; Allen and Akerman 2015; Moore 2013; White 1977). And it would seem that some of these points (e.g., Kimberley points), once finally present, often were more important as items of ritual, prestige, and exchange, as well as symbols of adult male status, than as weapon tips (Akerman et al. 2002; Taçon 1991). The use of wood-tipped projectiles is also widely documented elsewhere in the ethnohistoric and ethnographic literature, and the frequent discovery of spears, darts, and arrows in dry caves in western North America that were never intended to carry stone tips, further underscores the fact that hunting, whether of animals or fellow humans, can be done quite effectively with points of sharpened wood and a great variety of other perishable materials (Waguespack et al. 2009, and references therein; see also Brugge 1961:13; Hibben 1938; O'Connor et al. 2014:117).

But if one doesn't need a stone projectile point to arm one's spear or dart, then one certainly doesn't need a stone point made of some especially high-quality flint of the sort that is so characteristic of North America's Paleoindian period (Goodyear 1979), a conclusion underscored, for example, by the much less prominent role played by high-quality toolstones in many parts of South America during the same period of time (Borrero 2006:19; Nami 2009:11). Points made from basalt or other fine-grained volcanics—as well as quartzite, silicified limestone, argillite, even granite and various metamorphic rocks—should do just fine, a fact made evident by the panoply of raw materials used to fashion projectile points throughout the post-Paleoindian archaeological record of North America (e.g., Ellis 1989:141; Gardner 1989:14; Gramly and Summers 1986:100; and Vierra 2013; see discussion in Speth et al. 2013:122).

The archaeological record of the Southwestern United States provides a useful case in point. Paleoindians in the region focused heavily on a very limited array of raw materials, with two Southern Plains materials—Alibates and Edwards—figuring prominently in many assemblages. These materials were often transported hundreds of kilometers from their sources in the Texas panhandle and central Texas to the places where they were ultimately lost or discarded. In one fascinating case, Folsom people transported Edwards chert in fair measure from an unknown but apparently nonlocal source to the Adair-Steadman site in central Texas, where they used it to fashion a substantial number of fluted points, but while there made only a handful of points using Edwards chert of more or less equivalent quality from a well-known source that was located almost at their doorstep (Hurst and Johnson 2016).

In striking contrast, the Archaic foragers who followed immediately after the Paleoindians *in the same areas of the Southwest* were quite content to make their points, first mostly from basalt, then increasingly from obsidian, as well as from quartzites and other toolstones, making only minimal use of cherts and often eschewing even locally available high-quality varieties (e.g., Judge 1973:144–45; Thoms 1977:66; Newman 1994:494; Vierra 2013).

The "ancestral pueblo" or Anasazi folk who came next in the same areas, like their Paleoindian forebears, seemed to prefer cryptocrystalline siliceous materials but, unlike Paleoindians, usually focused on sources that were located much closer to home (i.e., within tens of kilometers rather than hundreds). Prominent among these are the translucent multicolored chalcedonies from the Cerro Pedernal in north-central New Mexico, a wide variety of petrified woods, and pink-colored Washington or Narbona Pass chert from the Chuska Mountains along the Arizona–New Mexico border, to name but a few of the many materials that were available and used (e.g., Cameron 2001; Harro 1997; Newman 1994:493–94; Thoms 1977:66).

Then, curiously, some pueblo folk, as in Chaco Canyon (northwestern New Mexico) and Homol'ovi (north-central Arizona), rather suddenly became fond of obsidian, often obtained from quite distant sources and which they had previously ignored or used only sparingly (Cameron 2001; Harry 1989). The pueblo communities scattered across the Pajarito Plateau in north-central New Mexico are particularly interesting in this regard. Although they were situated very close to several of the largest and most important obsidian flows in the Southwest (referred to collectively as the Jemez sources), materials that were traded widely across the entire Southwest and deep into the Southern Plains, the Pajaritans nonetheless made surprisingly limited use of this quint-essential high-quality toolstone until after about AD 1325, when they too quite suddenly developed a fondness for shiny black volcanic glass (Brosowske 2004, 2005; Harro 1997;).

In other words, eminently flakable cherts, fine-grained quartzites, and obsidian have always been available in the Southwest, but at times one or the other was mostly ignored, as in the Paleoindian period and during much of the Archaic. Why then did Paleoindian foragers feel obliged to travel vast dis-tances to obtain materials in the Southern Plains that are no more knappable and, when flaked into projectile points, arguably no better at penetrating the hide of a large ungulate, or the flesh of one's enemy, than many of the cherts, chalcedonies, jaspers, agates, petrified woods, quartzites, and obsidians that are widely available in many parts of the Southwest (see, e.g., the diversity of flakable cherts painstakingly documented by Larry Banks 1990)?

In this context it is perhaps worth briefly digressing to consider the func-tional relevance of "high-quality" toolstone to prehistoric hunters. For a given weapon system such as a thrusting spear, hand-thrown spear, or atlatl dart, if the function of the point is simply to penetrate the hide and muscle of an animal (or a human) to a lethal depth, any sharp-edged, pointed, roughly tri-angular- to ogival-shaped flake of any reasonably durable material will do the job (e.g., Nieuwenhuis 1998). I have seen nothing in the literature to suggest that an unmodified sharp flake of fine-grained basalt, argillite, or even silici-fied limestone would do significantly worse at delivering the needed strike than a sharp flake of Alibates or Edwards chert.

I think it fair to say that most archaeologists would assume, almost with-out question, that the quality of the material *does* become a key factor in the knapping process the moment the hunter decides to shape the point into some desired form, particularly if the knapping involves finely controlled pressure-flaking (not to mention a difficult and failure-prone fluting process as in the case of Folsom points). But even this seemingly obvious assump-tion is not as straightforward as it might at first appear, as indicated both by the Paleoindian record itself and by the somewhat counterintuitive results of recent replicative studies.

Looking first at the artifacts, Paleoindian flintknappers, in both eastern and western North America, fashioned fluted points from an amazing array of materials, many of which one would hardly classify as "high-quality" toolstones (e.g., argillite, basalt, chalcedony, chert, felsite, jasper, metaquartzite, obsidian, ophiolite, orthoquartzite, quartz [crystal and drusy] rhyolite, silicified breccia, silicified gneiss, silicified siltstone, silicified slate, petrified wood, and possibly taconite; Tankersley 1994:504–6; see also Meltzer 1985). Reinforcing Kenneth Tankersley's observations, Briggs Buchanan and Marcus Hamilton analyzed a large sample of Early Paleoindian projectile points from sites across the United States and over this vast area found no statistically significant difference in form that could be attributed to raw material quality (Buchanan and Hamilton 2009:284–85). Michael Bever and David Meltzer came to a similar conclusion in a detailed analysis of Clovis fluted point data from the state of Texas (Bever and Meltzer 2007:88). It would seem that the successful making of a fluted point of a given morphology was not seriously constrained by the physical properties of the raw material beyond such basics as being brittle, isotropic, and reasonably free of major flaws and imperfections. Judging from the archaeological record itself, many materials clearly fit the bill.

Recent experimental replication studies reinforce this conclusion. Thus, Metin Eren and colleagues (2011) showed quite convincingly that the knapper's skill was more important than raw material quality in replicating classic Levallois core reduction. In a similar vein, but using archaeological data, Aleix Eixea, Valentin Villaverde, and João Zilhão show that Neanderthals in Spain and elsewhere in western Europe not uncommonly chose to apply Levallois reduction techniques to quartzite, silicified limestone, and other less-than-ideal raw materials, even in contexts where higher-quality flint was readily available (Eixea, Villaverde, and Zilhão 2016). More recently, Eren and colleagues (2014) replicated the morphology of a handaxe using three different materials—flint, basalt, and obsidian—again finding that skill outweighed toolstone quality in achieving the desired morphology. They conclude that "our results show that assuming the primacy of raw material differences as the predominant explanatory factor in stone tool morphology . . . is unwarranted" (Eren et al. 2014:472).

In short, neither "high-quality" toolstone, nor masterful shaping and fluting, are needed to produce a lethal projectile tip (e.g., Bamforth 2009:146; Bradley 1993:256, 261; MacDonald 2010). Again, nothing makes this more apparent than the archaeological record of Australia and most of the Paleolithic record of East and Southeast Asia, where raw materials were often of mediocre quality and almost nothing was retouched, and yet hunting was clearly an important economic pursuit (Moore 2013; Pawlik 2012; White 1977).

Not only does one not need high-quality raw material or great craftsmanship to fashion an effective weapon tip, the piece of stone stuck on the end of the shaft need not even conform to our conventional ideas of what a projectile point should look like. All that really matters is that its morphology be such that, when the spear is thrust or thrown with sufficient force, its tip is capable of piercing or cutting its way through an animal's (or a fellow human's) hide and well into the tissues that lie beneath. An interesting example is provided by Robert Dinnis, Alfred F. Pawlik, and Claire Gaillard. These authors have made a fairly convincing case that French Aurignacian hunters at times hafted bladelet cores to the business end of their spears using birch tar as a mastic (Dinnis, Pawlik, and Gaillard 2009). An even more striking example of just how flexible one can be in choosing one's weapon tips is provided by the bizarre assortment of "points" found in and among the skeletal remains buried in a Sudanese Final Palaeolithic cemetery. These "projectile points" consisted of nothing more than a hodgepodge of mostly unmodified "debitage" (Wendorf 1968:991–92):

> The most impressive feature is the high frequency of unretouched flakes and chips. In a normal assemblage all of these would be classified as debitage or debris, and none would be considered tools. Yet many of these pieces were recovered in positions where their use as parts of weapons is irrefutable. They were found imbedded in several bones, inside skulls, and in many positions where any other explanation seems unreasonable . . . Most of the remaining artifacts must be regarded as weapons, in spite of the variety of tool "classes" represented. It is obvious that the system of descriptive classification employed here has very little reality in terms of probable use. One function was apparently fulfilled through a broad range of tool classes. Evidently, any pointed thin flake was on occasion employed as a point, and any piece with a thin edge could serve as a barb. Retouch was not required, but when it was used the placement of the retouch, of major significance in the classification system, had little meaning in the ultimate use of the piece.

Thus, if Paleoindians felt compelled to travel hundreds of kilometers to a remote source in order to obtain special high-quality material to fashion their elegant points, such behavior was unlikely to have been driven by some underlying functional necessity, *regardless of how it might have been perceived by the participants*, but by religious, social, and/or political needs or obligations (e.g., Bradley 1993; Bradley, Collins, and Hemmings 2010; Ellis 2013). And such behavior is by no means unique to Paleoindians or to North American hunter-gatherers more generally; one can find similar examples in the archaeological record of foragers across the globe (e.g., Borrazzo 2012; Borrazzo et al. 2015; Flegenheimer et al. 2003, 2015; Kuzmin 2017; Nash et al. 2013:287). As Mary Helms (1988:119) eloquently put it many years ago in *Ulysses' Sail: An Ethnographic Odyssey of Power, Knowledge, and Geographical Distance*: "sheer distance and the magical or symbolic potency associated with distance or with distant places and polities can be important factors in the value assigned to some resource." In short, I see the deliberate long-distance pursuit of special high-quality raw material as a cultural choice, not a functional necessity. Admittedly, such explanations are much less tractable than economically based ones of the type most of us have been weaned on. But in my opinion one cannot judge the veracity of an explanation, parsimony notwithstanding, by the apparent ease with which we can conjure up test implications (Sober 2015:58–59; Yengoyan 2004:59).

If such arguments about the socioreligious and/or sociopolitical significance of exotic high-quality flints during North America's Paleoindian period are at least reasonably on target, and given that the actual amounts, expressed in kilograms, of such flints in most sites from this time period are surprisingly modest (an assertion I will justify more fully below; see also Bamforth 2009:152), then the location of their sources may well have had little or nothing to do with the annual foraging range of most Paleoindian bands (Bamforth 2013). Instead, special high-quality flints from distant sources should probably be viewed more like other valued goods or "exotica," such as turquoise, mica, and marine shells (Speth et al. 2013). Such items and materials most likely would have been acquired, not by procurement embedded in the annual subsistence round, but by special task groups—probably composed of one or more adult men—who periodically (perhaps once a year) made the long trek directly to the source, and/or by intergroup exchanges and gifting in the context of social or ceremonial aggregations and visitations (Bamforth 2002:84, 2013; Ellis 2013; Newlander 2015; G. Smith et al. 2016:559). Mobility for reasons other than the needs of one's stomach is fundamental to the forager way of life for a host of social, informational, and reproductive reasons, a fact that all too frequently seems to slip from sight when Paleoindianists try to envision what life was like in the vast North American wildernesses at the end of the Pleistocene and during the early stages of the Holocene. Without what Robert Whallon has dubbed "non-utilitarian" mobility, those intrepid "pioneers" of the Paleoindian period would have quickly vanished (e.g., MacDonald and Hewlett 1999; Whallon 2006:260; Wiessner 1982; Wobst 1974; Yengoyan 1968:199).

Many archaeologists counter that the abundance of exotic cherts in Paleoindian sites is far too great to have been obtained by such infrequent visits to distant quarries or by occasional ad hoc intergroup exchanges among small, highly mobile bands. After all, exotic flints often comprise more than a third to half of many Paleoindian assemblages, and in quite a few cases nearly all of the material comes from distant sources (Boulanger et al. 2015; Burke 2006:table 1; Meltzer 1989:32). But in most publications these amounts are expressed as percentages, not absolute weights, and percentages can be extremely misleading if the average weight of most flakes is only a few grams or less, as seems to be the case in at least the handful of sites for which complete assemblage-wide weight data are available (Bamforth 2009; Speth et al. 2013). For example, at the Fisher Site, a large Middle Paleoindian (Parkhill phase) encampment in southern Ontario, the weight of the entire lithic assemblage recovered from the studied portion of the site, numbering over 32,000 artifacts and pieces of debitage, adds up to just 29.5 kg (Storck 1997:185). The reason the weight of the material at Fisher, and at other sites such as Parkhill, is so modest, despite the presence of tens of thousands of flakes, is that most pieces of debitage (> 99%) weigh less than 1.0 g (Ellis 1989:147–48; Ellis and Deller 2000; see also Gramly and Summers 1986:120 and Loebel 2009:229 for additional debitage weight data).

Similar arguments can be made about the Paleo Crossing Site in northeastern Ohio where a substantial proportion of the assemblage was fashioned on Wyandotte chert obtained from sources located some 450–510 km away in south-central Indiana (Boulanger et al. 2015). The authors estimate that the total weight of nonlocal chert across the site was—at a minimum—37 kg and, adjusted for broken pieces and assuming uniform distribution across the occupation, could easily have been double or triple that value. Nevertheless, at both Fisher and Paleo Crossing, when total weights are thought of in terms of probable group sizes, lengths of occupations, and numbers of repeat visits to the same locale, the amount of exotic flint on a per capita per year basis is actually quite small, in fact small enough that the entire assemblage at both sites, not just the exotics, could have been brought to these locales by several adults in just one or a few trips to the sources.

In short, the magnitude of the weight of toolstone at Fisher and Paleo Crossing may tell us little about how the flints were actually procured. While "gearing up" via embedded procurement involving an entire social group is certainly one possibility, these data in no way rule out other means by which the material might have been acquired—either by single individuals or small task groups making one or more long-distance treks directly to the quarries, and/or through intergroup exchange and gifting (see, e.g., Bamforth 2013; M. Smith 2013:270–71).

But there is more at stake here than just explaining how Clovis foragers went about getting their flint. A more interesting question is why they went to such lengths to get "exotic" materials when equally suitable (in a functional sense) flint sources were often available much closer at hand? Paleo Crossing provides an interesting case in point. Why would Clovis foragers, faced with (putatively) routine subsistence tasks, ones that should require nothing beyond the standard utilitarian toolkit of the period (i.e., points, endscrapers, sharp flakes, and some additional raw material in reserve), have felt compelled to "gear up" for these activities some 500 km from their destination, and schlepp all that flint across the better part of two large U.S. states, when they were fully aware of (and actually made use of) another equally high-quality flint source (Flint Ridge) that was located only 140 km from the site (Boulanger et al. 2015)? As already noted earlier, something beyond the purely functional and utilitarian must have motivated these herculean long-distance treks. In purely functional or utilitarian terms, there was simply no reason to do it.

Even if these Clovis foragers knew nothing about the landscape that lay before them, a view that becomes increasingly unlikely the more we come to accept a pre-Clovis presence in North America's interior (see, e.g., Politis, Prates, and Perez 2015), what are the odds of walking 500 km and not finding rocks that could be broken by direct percussion or even simple bipolar "smashing" into flakes sharp enough to haft as a point (assuming one needed a stone point at all), or slice open an animal's hide, or butcher the meat from its carcass? If archaic and later folks throughout North and South America could make do with all manner of much more readily available rocks to kill deer, moose, elk, bison, caribou, muskox, peccaries, camelids, and even other humans—unquestionably the most dangerous adversary on the landscape— what was so special about the prey hunted by Paleoindians that in order to survive they had to have very unusual rocks that could only be obtained from a handful of very distant quarries? To assume that such exotic flints were an absolute *functional* necessity to successful hunting by Paleoindians, but not so for the millennia of foragers who came after them, is one of Paleoindian archaeology's most cherished fairy tales.

Let us now look at some real numbers to back up the assertions I made earlier about transport loads, and what they might imply about mode of tool-stone procurement. As a baseline figure, the weight of the average Clovis point commonly falls somewhere between twenty and thirty-five grams (see, for e.g., Jennings 2013:652 and Bamforth 2009:152). Errett Callahan (1979:65) replicated a large number of full-sized Clovis points, which upon completion ranged in weight from thirty to sixty grams, but he notes that his replicas turned out to be thicker and heavier than most of the archaeological specimens with which he was familiar. Richard (Michael) Gramly and Carl Yahnig, reporting on the Adams Site, a Clovis-age workshop in Kentucky, provide weight data for 473 "bifaces," a category that includes "preforms" of various sorts, as well as unfinished points that had been rejected at various stages of manufacture; these average about eighty grams each (Gramly and Yahnig 1991:137). Cores and large core fragments ($N = 140$) from the Adams Site average about 350 g each. Folsom points are generally much smaller and thinner than Clovis points and weigh as little as ten grams or less (Speth et al. 2013).

With these archaeological figures in mind, let us look at the magnitude of the loads routinely carried by physically fit adult males, starting with evidence provided by the military. The normal load of the modern foot soldier on typical marches (20–30 km/day)—loads that were often carried directly into combat as well—averages between 30 kg and 40 kg. Surprisingly, this figure has remained remarkably constant for at least the last 2,500 years, despite steady changes in weapon systems and logistics (Knapik and Reynolds 2012; Orr 2010). In many cases, these load estimates are minimum values, because they do not include the weight of the soldier's personal gear—for example, water-filled canteens, boots, rain-soaked clothing, and so forth. Following the Vietnam War, western militaries began to break with tradition, equipping foot soldiers with loads that commonly exceeded 40–45 kg (Dean 2004; Drain et al. 2010:45; Orr 2010). Assuming a typical (and what turns out to be a comparatively modest) load of 35 kg, an adult male Paleoindian forager could easily have carried anywhere from 1,000 to 3,500 or more fluted points, or more than 430 Clovis-sized "preforms," or up to about 100 cores, or the equivalent weight in raw material, plus his own personal gear, over a distance of 300 km in just two weeks, assuming he traveled at a leisurely pace of about 2.2–2.6 km/hour and covered a normal distance of 20 km/day (e.g., Orr 2010; Walker and Churchill 2014:222). Western militaries, however, typically consider a "normal" march rate to be about 4.0 km/hour (Harper, Knapik, and Pontbriand 1996). At that pace a Paleoindian forager could easily have covered 30 km/day and completed the 300 km trip in ten days or less.

Interestingly, 30 km was the standard training distance for Roman infantry, who were expected to cover the course in five hours (i.e., at a pace of ~6 km/hour) while carrying a 30 kg load (Sabin, van Wees, and Whitby 2007a:288–89, 329; Stout 1921:427). Based on observations spanning the centuries from the ancient Greeks to modern campaigns, on "forced marches" foot soldiers often had to traverse distances well in excess of 30 km/day and on rare occasions covered as much as 60–70 km/day, all the while burdened with 20–30 kg loads plus personal gear (Neumann 1971; Sabin, van Wees, and Whitby 2007b:161). While such highly pressured marches, lasting for ten to twelve hours or longer, some even continuing through the night, are unlikely to be found in the normal hunter-gatherer world, treks of 20–30 km/day at a pace of 4.0 km/hour or more are fairly common among foraging peoples. For example, Hetty Jo Brumbach and Robert Jarvenpa note that Dene hunters covered an average of 34 km/day, mostly on foot, while pursuing game and checking traplines (Brumbach and Jarvenpa 1997:423). Herman Pontzer and colleagues (2015:634), working among the Hadza, documented a series of somewhat shorter daily hunts (average 11.7 km), during which the hunters moved at a median walking speed of about 4.3 km/hour. A similar average pace (4.0–4.5 km/hour) was observed among Venezuelan foragers by Charles Hilton and Russell Greaves (Hilton and Greaves 2008:149). Finally, Louis Liebenberg (2006:1018) documented eight San (Bushman) "persistence hunts" ranging in length from 17.3 km to 35.2 km (average 27.8 km). On these hunts the pursuers maintained a steady clip of 6.2 km/hour.

Returning now to our look at bifaces and the kinds of loads that Paleoindians might reasonably be expected to carry, consider the Acheulian handaxe, the Paleoindian biface's Old World cousin on steroids. On the basis of data for a sample of 531 handaxes drawn from sites in both Africa and western Asia, Ceri Shipton and Michael D. Petraglia arrive at an average weight per biface of 634 g (Shipton and Petraglia 2010:51). Assuming a standard 35 kg load, our Paleoindian forager, in a matter of a few days or weeks, could easily have carried fifty-five or more of these sizeable tools, plus his own personal gear, over distances of dozens or even hundreds of kilometers. According to data recently provided by Kathleen Kuman, Hao Li, and Chaorong Li, European handaxes are even lighter than the African and western Asian specimens (average weight = 341 g; Kuman, Li, and Li 2016), such that our forager, again carrying a 35 kg load, would have been able (ignoring problems of bulk) to transport over one hundred of these bifaces.

Incidentally, these load estimates raise an interesting question about the likely function of Clovis caches, a fair number of which have been discovered over the years in the Great Plains and adjacent regions, as well as in the Great Lakes area. Although a few of the caches were almost certainly ritual offerings or burial accompaniments, most are viewed as "stockpiles" of finished tools, preforms, and raw material intended to provision Paleoindian foragers when they entered areas where high-quality toolstone was either difficult to obtain or was altogether unavailable (Asher 2016:130; Huckell and Kilby 2014; Meltzer 2002:38). Many of the items placed in these caches were fashioned from exotic flints, materials that had been transported literally hundreds of kilometers before being placed in the ground. David Kilby (2014:205; personal communication, February 2017) provides detailed weight data for the lithic assemblages recovered from each of nineteen well-documented Clovis caches. Quite surprisingly, the average weight of the contents of these caches is only about 5.0 kg. One clear outlier is Anzick, at 16.6 kg, but that one is a burial offering and clearly not a case of provisioning (Rasmussen et al. 2014). If we exclude Anzick from the calculation, the mean weight per cache drops to just 4.3 kg. I found weight data for one additional Early Paleoindian cache, this one at the DEDIC/Sugarloaf Site in the Connecticut Valley in Massachusetts. This cache contained "a fluted point preform, an unfinished fluted point (broken in fluting), and 31 additional implements, consisting mostly of flake blanks" (Lothrop and Bradley 2012:35). The total weight of the DEDIC/Sugarloaf cache was less than a kilogram (0.96 kg) and, when added to the others, the average weight per cache drops to just 4.1 kg. Small as this figure is, it still gives an inflated impression of the weight of material in many of the caches. The overall average is pushed up substantially by a single outlier—the Sailor-Helton cache—whose contents weigh nearly 14 kg. Five of the other caches contain less than 1.0 kg of flint and an additional two have less than 2.0 kg.

When these figures are looked at from the perspective of the 2,500-year record of loads routinely carried by foot soldiers on long-distance, often multi-day marches, and not uncommonly during actual combat as well, does it make sense for a forager to carry barely 4.0 kg of flint 200–300 km or more in order to provision himself with high-quality material when he anticipates, at the outset, that he may be heading into territory that lacks adequate supplies of toolstone vital to the success of his mission? I seriously doubt such small-scale provisioning would provide him with much of a backup. And what happens when his limited supply of cached material runs out? Does he retrace his 200–300+ km route back to the quarry just to get another 4.0 kg load of flint? That doesn't make sense. Such small caches make even less sense if they were intended as a reserve, not just for a solitary hunter far from any of his preferred flint sources, but for a larger party of cooperating hunters.

Richard Gould (1978:822) and Barbara Luedtke (1979:260–61) independently attempted to estimate the total amount of flint a forager would need over the course of a year (for further discussion of these estimates, see below). While the values they came up with were obviously little more than educated guesses (Gould, 20 kg/year; Luedtke, 40–50 kg/year), and I suspect Gould's figure errs on the light side, they nonetheless help put the Clovis caches in perspective. If we add the further assumption that our forager uses up his flint at a uniform rate, and (arbitrarily) opt for Luedtke's 40 kg/year figure as the most reasonable of the estimates, the average amount of material found in the caches (4.1 kg) would fulfill the hunter's needs for about five weeks, a rather short period considering the tremendous round-trip distance the hunter would have to travel to replenish his supply.

If these arguments have any merit, one can't help but conclude that most Clovis caches were probably not intended as reserves of material to replenish the hunter's toolkit. Instead, it seems far more likely that they were earmarked for other purposes, probably much less mundane ones. Given their extremely small weights, not to mention the widespread presence of red ocher, the commingling in the same cache of points and bifaces made from more than a single exotic raw material source (Bamforth 2013), the presence of numerous oversized or "hypertrophic" points, and of course the spectacular points fashioned from large quartz crystals, it would seem far more likely that these caches were: (1) votive or ritual offerings (e.g., Gillespie 2007:183; Reher and Frison 1991; Roper 1989; Zedeño 2009; see also Salazar et al. 2011 and Stafford et al. 2003 for evidence of the importance of red ocher mining during Paleoindian times in both North and South America, respectively); or (2) items that were removed from circulation, in some instances even deliberately destroyed, because they were deemed spiritually too powerful or too dangerous to leave exposed or accessible to the uninitiated (see discussion in Adams and Fladd 2017 and McAnany and Hodder 2009; see also Deller and Ellis 2001; Deller, Ellis, and Keron 2009; Ellis 2009); or (3) items that were in transit in some sort of long-distance gifting or exchange network, but were temporarily cached and, for reasons unknown, never retrieved (see, for example, Hiscock 1988:69).

Many Paleoindianists are certain to object to this reasoning by noting that a number of the caches contain seemingly quite mundane artifacts, some used, some broken, and some left unfinished or even unmodified. These are not the kinds of things they would expect a forager to transport vast distances as items of exchange or as ritual offerings. However, the key when dealing with the sacred or the spiritually charged is not the actual or potential utility of the items, the explanatory thread followed by many Paleoindianists, but the values, beliefs, and meanings attached to the items, or to the sources of the material from which the items were fashioned, or to the context in which the items were used, regardless of how mundane they might appear (Brück 1999; Fogelin 2007; Groleau 2009:398). Australian Aborigines transported "ordinary" human hair over hundreds of kilometers as items for exchange. What could be more mundane than that? But it wasn't the hair itself that mattered; it was the spiritual power associated with the hair or the donor of the hair. Bread is just bread until it is blessed by a priest and offered to the devout during observances of the sacrament of the Eucharist or Holy Communion. While it still looks the same, from that point on the bread "becomes" the *Body of Christ*—the extent of the transformation depending on the depth of one's beliefs (Visser 1992:36–37). Once so transformed, the bread must be treated with the utmost reverence, and leftovers disposed of in a dedicated place and manner as prescribed by church doctrine and tradition. The same is true of the wine, the *Blood of Christ*, used in these observances—quite ordinary in appearance and taste but, for the believers, charged with spiritual meaning and potency.

Thus, the fact that Clovis points found in a cache match the size, morphology, and workmanship of those found in direct association with mammoth kills would in no way negate the spiritual potency of the items in the cache (or, for that matter, those with the mammoth), a misguided dichotomy between what is presumed to be "mundane" and what is presumed to be "spiritually charged" that one finds with surprising frequency in the Paleoindian literature (e.g., Buchanan et al. 2012). It is almost a given that Clovis and later Paleoindian hunters would have imbued the very act of pursuing, killing, and subsequently consuming the meat of such an imposing and intelligent animal with a deep sense of respect and spiritual meaning (for classic examples illustrating the spiritual matrix within which traditional subsistence hunting typically is embedded, see Bodenhorn 1990:61; Brightman 1993; Lewis-Williams and Biesele 1978; McNiven and Feldman 2003; and Tanner 1979). The Denésuliné, a First Nation caribou-hunting peoples along the boreal forest-tundra interface in northern Saskatchewan and the Northwest Territories of Canada, provide an excellent example of the depth and closeness of the spiritual connection that exists between hunters and hunted, a relationship that mandates particular behaviors and observances on the part of the hunters if they are to have—or in their view if they are to be granted—continued hunting success in the future:

> In Denésuliné thought, animals are simultaneously spiritual and physical beings who consensually sacrifice their physical forms to human hunters to enable them to survive . . . The power that exists in this relationship rests entirely with the animals. The concept of a contest between human and animal/spirit would simply be without meaning and probably beyond comprehension. It is far closer to the reality of Denésuliné thought to try and understand the hunt as a ritual sacrifice of the god . . . that occurs only because the actions and state of the

hunter elicit the consent of the animal . . . The hunt is a cooperative mutual performance between Denésuliné and animal. (Sharp and Sharp 2015:23)

The relationship between them is one in which the animal/spirits have assumed the responsibility to help the Denésuliné to survive by exposing themselves to contact with the Denésuliné and allowing themselves to be killed by them. This relationship engenders a trust within the Denésuliné: a trust that holds that if they behave as they should, if they show the respect to the animal/spirits that they should, then the animal/spirits will provide them with the opportunity to survive. (Sharp and Sharp 2015:25)

Isabel McBryde (2000) documents a classic example of the great lengths to which Aborigines would go in order to acquire a valued raw material—in this case red ocher—from one particular source—Pukardu Hill. This ocher quarry held special symbolic value for many different tribes that were spread out over a vast region of southern Australia. Members of each group made the long journey *annually* even though materially comparable ocher was readily available to the participants closer to home. Although McBryde's focus is on ocher, not flint, one can easily imagine a similar scenario applying to the exotic toolstones that circulated over distances of hundreds of kilometers among North American Paleoindian groups.

Pukardu Hill itself is a place of great traditional importance for local people and to those of the Cooper, Lake Eyre and the Simpson Desert as well as northwestern New South Wales who made the journey to Pukardu Hill to acquire ochre. These expeditions were part of ceremonial life for these groups associated with song and ritual performances en route and following the return. They are still remembered as significant, though it is eighty years since such journeys were made. Of the ochre itself symbolic values were paramount, derived from the quarry place itself and from the spiritual importance of the journey. Any rarity value of the ochre is associated with these two aspects. Certainly the colour is distinctive, clearly an important quality. These physical and symbolic values ensured that Pukardu ochre was reserved for special use. Ochres are readily obtainable in the local environments of those who travelled to Pukardu Hill . . . as well as from Aroona near Pukardu Hill . . . However they were not seen to hold symbolic values, and were used in more mundane contexts. (McBryde 2000:161, 164)

In sum and by way of example, it seems likely in the Paleoindian context that widely known quarries such as those at Alibates in the Texas panhandle may have been important to bands operating in and around the southern

Plains, not because the toolstone obtained there could be transformed into *singularly* effective killing weapons unmatched in penetrating power by points fashioned out of lesser-quality materials, but because the quarries, or the colorful material extracted from the quarries, or the ceremonies and oral traditions associated with the quarries, held some special meaning that was recognized and shared across a wide network of interacting peoples in the region (see also Bamforth 2013; Bradley 2000:84; Bradley and Collins 2014; Brumm 2010; Helms 1988; Spielmann 2002:199).

Let us return now from this digression into the nature of Clovis caches to our discussion of normal transport loads. As already pointed out, foot soldiers over the centuries have routinely carried loads weighing anywhere from 30 kg to as much as 45 kg or more, not counting the additional weight of whatever personal gear they needed during a campaign. Such loads are by no means unique to the military. Broadly comparable figures are widely documented in the ethnographic and ethnohistoric literature. What follows is a sample of these, drawn from many different parts of the world and observed in a wide range of social and economic contexts. Of particular note is how closely these "civilian" examples match the loads routinely carried by infantry.

- Western Mono hunter-gatherers in California transported basket loads of acorns that weighed about 36 kg (Bettinger, Malhi, and McCarthy 1997:892).

- Nineteenth-century "hod-carriers" routinely carried back-loads of bricks and mortar weighing 35–45 kg up ladders on construction sites in order to keep bricklayers supplied with building materials (Mason 1889:31–32).

- Otis Mason (1896:445–46, 451) described 45 kg loads carried distances of ~35 km in a single day by Chinese porters, and similar 45 kg loads carried over portages and steep mountain passes in Canada and Alaska by professional carriers.

- According to Vilhjalmur Stefansson (1956:226–28), the standard unit (or "piece") of pemmican used in the fur trade throughout the eighteenth and nineteenth century by both the Hudson's Bay Company (HBC) and the North West Company was a flat bison rawhide bag about the size of an ordinary pillow that, when filled, weighed about 90 lb. (~41 kg). In an example of a long portage well known in the fur trade, a man carried the "piece" on his back, plus his own personal gear, over a rough 130 km trail in approximately four and a half days. Stefansson indicates that it was not uncommon for men to carry two such "pieces," and gear, over this portage. Similarly, English goods destined for the fur trade were sent from major HBC supply hubs to inland posts in packages that weighed between 80 and 90 lb. (36–41 kg). As was the case for the standardized bags or "pieces" of pemmican, these "packages are of this limited weight from the necessity of 'portaging' them from river to river, sometimes a long distance, upon the shoulders of boatmen" (Robinson 1879:78–79).

- Felix McBryde (1947) described the activities of traditional merchants in Guatemala, noting that 45 kg loads were commonplace there as well.

- Pre-Hispanic Tarascan porters (*tlameme*) in western Mexico routinely carried loads of copper ingots weighing between 32 and 72 kg over distances averaging about 30 km/day from the smelters to centers where the raw metal was fashioned into elite goods (Pollard 1987:748–50). Kenneth Hirth (2016:239–42) provides additional information about the remarkable loads carried by Mesoamerican porters, for the most part using only tumplines, and compares their loads with the burdens transported by historic and recent porters elsewhere in the world.

- Horst Jäger et al. (1997:475–76) studied degenerative changes in the cervical spine of male porters who over many years carried head-loads that averaged about 50 kg. They also noted in passing that professional carriers in developing countries often transport loads as heavy as 100 kg.

- The Native inhabitants who traveled with Samuel Hearne (1795:89–90) during his explorations of the Canadian subarctic and arctic told him that they particularly valued wives who were "capable of dressing all kinds of skins, converting them into the different parts of their clothing, and able to carry eight or ten stone [112–140 lb., or 50–64 kg] in Summer, or haul a much greater weight in Winter."

- Gair Tourtellot (1978:75), summarizing a variety of information about loads and distances for men, concluded that "daily travel distance for professional porters throughout the world appears to be at least 20 kilometers per day (observed range 10–32) with an average maximum load of about 45 kilograms (observed range 22–64)."

- At the upper end of the ethnographically documented values, the average load carried by Nepalese male porters (age twenty–forty-nine years) is 73 kg (Malville 2001). They make the nearly 190 km round trip in just two weeks traversing extremely steep, dissected mountainous terrain with a cumulative elevation gain of 6,500 m. Many of the porters repeat the same journey up to twenty times each year.

- Even heavier loads were routinely carried by traditional porters, or *hamals*, in Turkey. Although I have had difficulty finding concrete numbers for the weights they typically transported, numerous observers during the nineteenth and early twentieth century explicitly commented on having seen them hauling upright pianos on their back through the streets of Istanbul, a sight I also personally witnessed in 1968 (Cox 1887:182–83; Grosvenor 1915:476). Upright pianos typically weigh at least 150 kg and often more.

- The Australian literature provides a number of hunter-gatherer examples that point to transport loads of the same magnitude (averaging around 30–35 kg) carried by adult males in a matter of weeks over distances measured in hundreds of kilometers. Curr (1886:70–72, cited in Mulvaney 1976:79–80, see also Horne and Aiston 1924:130; Peterson and Lampert 1985:6), for example, describes an annual 500 km–long trek, totally unrelated to subsistence, in order to procure a material of great symbolic importance to Australian Aborigines—red ocher. Alfred Howitt (1904:710–12) provides a similar account of these annual expeditions for the sole purpose of acquiring ocher, and others for gathering a highly prized native tobacco-like narcotic known as pitcheri or pituri (*Duboisia hopwoodii*—McBryde 1987:258–61; see also Thomas 1886:342 and Howitt 1891:77–78). Again there is no hint that such treks involved the entire band, nor were they embedded within the group's annual subsistence rounds. One additional ethnohistoric example from Australia will suffice, in this case a 500 km trek for the express purpose of obtaining suitable rock for making groundstone axes or hatchets (Morgan 1852; see also Smyth 1878:359). Finally, Australia offers up a very interesting Late Pleistocene example of long-distance transport that seems pertinent to this discussion. The skeleton of the 40,000-year-old Lake Mungo burial (III) was completely covered in red ocher, an amount estimated to have weighed about 1 kg. The nearest source that can be identified for the particular type of ocher found in the burial is located some 200 km distant (Bowler 1998:151). Given the historically documented ritual importance of ocher and ocher quarries throughout Aboriginal Australia, and the particular context in which ocher was used at Lake Mungo, it seems quite likely that the quarry had been deliberately visited at some point prior to the burial event by one or more individuals for the express purpose of obtaining the mineral.

Focusing again specifically on flint, Arthur Spiess and Deborah Wilson tried to estimate an individual's total annual needs based on data from a Paleoindian site in eastern North America, and came to the conclusion that perhaps as little as 10 kg would suffice (Spiess and Wilson 1989:90). And as already discussed above, Richard Gould (1978:822), working in Australia, and Barbara Luedtke (1979:260–61), drawing on data from the North American Eastern Woodlands, both attempted similar calculations, and while their estimates are higher than those of Spiess and Wilson, their figures are nonetheless relatively modest, falling between 20 kg at the low end (Gould) and 40–50 kg at the high end (Luedtke 1979). These estimates are surprisingly modest and, in fact, are roughly equivalent to what one Australian forager might carry each year in a single load from a quarry located several hundred kilometers away. Even if these estimates are off by a fairly wide margin, the values certainly do not justify the common assumption that the demand for high-quality flint by Paleoindian foragers was so great that the sources had to be located (i.e., embedded) within their annual foraging range. In short, I think we need to divorce the locations of exotic flint sources from our reconstructions of Paleoindian band territories (see also Bamforth 2013). In many, perhaps most, cases they probably had little or nothing to do with each other.

Pursuing this line of thinking a little further, if the exotic high-quality flints that adult men used to fashion their projectile points were acquired in ways akin to the manner in which other exotica would have been obtained—that is, through exchange or by parties of men traveling directly to the source—then the points made of these special materials that we as archaeologists encounter in communal bison kills are likely to be equally uninformative about the hunters' homeland. If the hunters had to "gear up" prior to the kill, it was most likely to obtain "sacred" or "potent" flint, not "utilitarian" flint, and that could have been done at whatever source was deemed by the hunters to possess the spiritual properties or potency appropriate to the activity. In other words, we are going to have to devise ways other than locations of exotic flint sources to track the seasonal movements of the hunters themselves. Were we to find an *Olivella* shell bead necklace in a bison kill that had been made of shells obtained from Baja California, we would certainly not conclude that the hunters likewise came from Baja. Yet I worry this is precisely what we are doing when we use points made of exotic raw materials to decide where our Paleoindian bison hunters came from.

If I were to venture still farther out on the proverbial limb, I would follow the gendered path pointed out many years ago by Joan Gero (1991), and more recently by Khori Newlander (2012), and suggest that if any flint procurement might have been embedded in the annual subsistence round, it was the tool-stone used and probably also acquired by women. For example, identifying the sources of the flint from which endscrapers were made—tools presumably most commonly employed by women in preparing hides (e.g., Albright 1982:115–20; Sharp and Sharp 2015:195–97)—might tell us more about overall band movements than the sources of the lithics procured and used by men to fashion points (e.g., Amick 1999; Iceland 2013; Jodry 1999:303; Morrow 1997; Robinson and Ort 2011:220; and Ruth 2013:5; Deller and Ellis 1984:51 and Langford 2015 may provide other examples). However, even with the raw materials used to make women's tools such as endscrapers, we have to be cautious—the grinding slabs used by Australian Aboriginal women to process wild seeds were often procured, not by women at local outcrops, but by men on long treks to distant quarries. We will have to look for tendencies in the data, not rigidly bounded dichotomies.

BIG-GAME HUNTING, MOBILITY, AND PALEOINDIAN BIFACES

The conventional view of Paleoindian lifeways is one of highly mobile big-game hunting specialists, relentlessly pursing their prey, be they mammoth, bison, or caribou, over vast swathes of territory. As I have already noted, success in these endeavors is commonly assumed to have required exquisitely made projectile points, most often fashioned from flints of the highest quality, as well as a variety of sharp cutting tools for butchering the prey and for making and repairing other essential equipment. But locating and pursuing game over such vast terrains might well take our nomadic foragers deep into areas where suitable flint to replace broken points or exhausted cutting tools was scarce or unavailable. Anticipating such "flint deserts," the hunters had to carry with them whatever replacement toolstone they might need and, in the conventional wisdom, that's where weight enters the picture.

Stones *are* heavy, a decided problem for mobile foragers, and especially problematic for Paleoindian foragers who are assumed to have moved more or less continually over vast tracts of land in their relentless pursuit of game. The solution to this conundrum, an idea developed nearly thirty years ago by Robert Kelly (1988), is to rely on the "biface"—the Paleoindian's flint equivalent of the "Swiss army knife." In Kelly's view, a biface was not a finished point but a prior stage in the flaking process that, if continued, would ultimately lead to the point, a stage often referred to as a *preform*. The preform is far less fragile than a finished point and thus can be transported with little danger of accidental breakage. And, though not finished, much of the initial weight reduction, such as removing cortex and unwanted exterior material, was accomplished prior to the hunt so that the preform became a lightweight "ready-to-go" core, able to provide a supply of sharp cutting flakes, but also equally usable in its own right as a robust, easily resharpened knife, and finally, should the need arise, a tool that could be further reduced in order to transform it into a finished projectile point.

This was, and continues to be, a very influential idea. And rightfully so. The biface argument provided a clear link between stone tools—often the predominant and sometimes the only class of artifact recovered on Paleoindian sites—and mobility, one of the key dimensions of the presumed big-game hunting way of life. Over the many years since the article first appeared, "Three Sides of a Biface" has stimulated a great deal of constructive thinking and research, and it remains one of the most widely cited papers in the Paleoindian literature today. That to me is the sign of scholarship at its best.

But that doesn't mean the arguments are right. While over the years there have been a handful of reevaluations of Kelly's original arguments (e.g., Borrero 2006:19; Eren and Andrews 2013; Gingerich and Stanford 2016; Kuhn 1994; Jennings, Pevny, and Dickens 2010; Prasciunas 2007), some of which I will discuss shortly, they have been too few and far between. The majority of Paleoindianists today—at least in North America—seem to treat the biface argument as though it were an "established fact," an idea so secure and solid in its foundations that it no longer needs to be reexamined (see discussion in Eren and Andrews 2013:166–67). However, any argument that was put together nearly three decades ago is surely in need of a closer look. Such a reevaluation in no way denigrates the scholarship embodied in the original paper. In 1988 it was a brilliant contribution, one that played an invaluable role in moving lithic specialists away from their obsession with description and typology toward thinking in more anthropological terms about how hunter-gatherer technologies were organized and how they fit into the broader adaptive and cultural fabric. So what follows is directed, not at Kelly's original contribution, which stands as a classic in the field, but at the "business as usual" posture so common among North American Paleoindianists today. The biface-mobility package is not as neatly and tightly wrapped up as many would seem to think (a point even raised in a recent paper by the originator of the biface argument—see Kelly 2014:1122). In fact, there is ample reason to believe that the presence or absence of bifaces may have little or nothing to do with mobility. It is time to have another look.

As already alluded to above, several aspects of the Paleoindian biface argument have been questioned in previous studies, and I will touch on these only briefly here. For example, Steven Kuhn (1994:437) developed a model suggesting that utility relative to weight was actually better served if foragers carried toolkits comprised, not of bifaces or larger cores, but of "numerous relatively small implements, between 1.5 and 3.0 times their minimum usable sizes." Toby Morrow (1996) provided an interesting counterargument to Kuhn's, but one that also brought into question the primacy of the carefully shaped and thinned biface as the ideal core form for mobile peoples. Morrow concluded that potential utility would actually be maximized by transporting larger cores, not flakes. More recently, Douglas Bamforth (2002:88) concurred, concluding that "Paleoindian technology is best described as largely, although certainly not exclusively, a core/flake-based rather than a fundamentally biface-based industry." Mary Prasciunas (2007) evaluated the idea that in serving as a core, a biface would produce more cutting edge per unit weight than an amorphous core. She showed that bifaces in fact only yielded more cutting edge if one included very small "waste" flakes that would have been of limited functional value in most real-world activities (see also Bamforth 2003:210). Thomas Jennings, Charlotte D. Pevny, and William A. Dickens expanded these core reduction studies, showing that bifaces were no more efficient than blade cores in the number of potentially usable flakes they produced (Jennings, Pevny, and Dickens 2010). Metin Eren and Brian Andrews approached the biface-as-core issue from a different angle. They reasoned that, if bifaces were being used as a source of flakes for unifacial tools, the average maximum flake thickness (and standard deviation) of these tools should decline with increasing distance from the raw material source (Eren and Andrews 2013). In a sample of Great Lakes region Clovis sites, they found the reverse to be the case and concluded that bifaces probably were not being used as cores. Juliet Morrow (1997) looked at the morphology of endscrapers and, like Eren and Andrews, found that these flake tools too did not pattern as expected with increasing distance from source if they had been made on flakes derived from bifaces. Finally, Briggs Buchanan et al. (2015) showed that Clovis points in the Ohio-Indiana-Kentucky area did not display the expected degree of resharpening with increasing distance from the sources on which the points had been fashioned.

All of the studies just noted came to the same general conclusion—that bifaces do not necessarily represent the most efficient or effective way for Paleoindian foragers to cope with uncertain tool needs and raw material availability in a context of high mobility. One might be tempted to argue that the finished bifaces and preforms found in many caches, particularly those attributed to the Clovis period, provide evidence to the contrary—that bifaces were in fact being transported around the landscape for precisely the reasons proposed by Kelly (1988). However, as suggested earlier I seriously doubt the form, quantity, or source of the artifacts in the caches tell us much, if anything, about the transport constraints that confronted the people who put those items in the ground. Thus, core forms other than bifaces, as well as unmodified large flakes, may have done the job just fine, if not better.

Here I want to bring in two additional dimensions to the biface discussion that have not been considered as closely. The first of these concerns weight, a topic that we have already looked at in more general terms, but not specifically as it concerns bifacial technology—the hallmark of the Paleoindian period. Paleoindianists all agree that stones are heavy and must therefore have been a constraining factor in the design and content of a mobile forager's (lithic) toolkit. But few ask what to me seems like the most obvious question with which to begin: "How heavy is heavy?" The second dimension to bring to the table here concerns the ubiquity (or lack thereof) of bifacial technology among prehistoric foragers on a global scale, and over a much longer temporal span than the few millennia represented by the North American Paleoindian period.

Turning first to the issue of weight—given the normal loads transported by foot soldiers, porters, explorers, foragers such as Australian Aborigines, and many others—loads that typically fall around 35 kg and often considerably more (and often not including personal gear), one can't help but wonder whether the almost negligible weight of a typical Paleoindian (Clovis) biface (20–35 g), or its partially worked preform or "blank" (mean weights seldom exceeding 250–300 g; Bamforth and Becker 2000; Jennings 2013; McAvoy 1992; Verrey 1986), would have been sufficient to have had any significant impact on the transport decisions of a mobile band of Clovis or Folsom hunters (Bamforth 2009:152). Aided by simple carrying technology—such as a shoulder bag, backpack, or tumpline, or balancing the load on one's head—the paltry weights (up to a few hundred grams) that archaeologists have been worried about in formulating the "biface argument" fall short of normal human transport loads by two full orders of magnitude.

There is another problem with the way Paleoindianists conceive of the biface argument. In the literature there is a widespread tendency to talk about Paleoindian "lithic technology" as though it were more or less isomorphic with "the technology" of the prehistoric societies in question, a misapprehension of what a "technology" actually embraces when looked at in its many strategic, organizational, social, and symbolic dimensions (Lemonnier 1992). In point of fact, most Paleoindianists are concerned only with the *material component* of the technology, and in reality almost solely with that limited part of the material technology that relates to subsistence (Gell 1988:6).

But the problem goes deeper still. What the Paleoindian record actually offers up for study is not even the material component of the "subsistence technology" but an assemblage of flakes, retouched pieces, and discarded waste, some portion of which were used for a limited range of operations related to the acquisition and preparation of food, while others—likely the majority—were used in one way or another in the *manufacture or repair* of the actual tools and equipment that comprised the material component of the subsistence technology. Among ethnographically and ethnohistorically documented hunter-gatherers, and I see no reason why this would not also have been the case with Paleoindians (Miller 2014), most tools and equipment, even those devoted to subsistence activities, were fashioned, not from flint, but from *perishable* materials such as wood, hide, sinew, gut, bone, horn, antler, fur, human hair, bark, and various plant fibers (Adovasio et al. 2014; Adovasio and Hyland 2000:36; Hurcombe 2014; Oswalt 1976:34; Shott 1986:36). For the most part, the lithics are the "razor blades," the cutting and piercing tools, not "the technology," not even "the subsistence technology."

Now, following this line of reasoning back to our original concern about bifaces and mobility, if weight really was a serious constraint, it would have been the weight of their *overall material technology* that mattered, not just their "razor blades." Thus, while Paleoindianists devote the lion's share of their efforts to the lithics, and especially to bifaces and their reduction products, these items—*in terms of weight*—constituted a minor, likely even a trivial, part of the material technology. It is the latter we need to be concerned about, not the former.

Incidentally, the same critique can be extended to the frequent discussions in the lithics literature about the maintainability, reliability, versatility, flexibility, and other design characteristics of mobile toolkits (e.g., Bamforth and Bleed 1997; Bleed 1986; Bousman 1993; Carr and Bradbury 2011:310–11; Nelson 1991). Granted, these are interesting topics, but too much of the focus has been at the wrong level. Like weight, these are features that matter much more at the level of the overall material technology, not at the level of the "razor blades." Again, one need only look at the Mode-1 lithics that typify most stone tool assemblages from East and Southeast Asia and Australia over the entire span of hominin presence in these vast regions of the globe to see that what presumably mattered was not their dismal assortment of minimalist cutting and chopping tools, but the (mostly) perishable technology fashioned with the aid of those "crude, colourless, and unenterprising" rocks (White 1977; see also Bar-Yosef 2015:89 for an interesting comment about the likely futility of attempting to infer the level of human technological sophistication or cognitive capacity from the lithics).

There is another issue that Paleoindianists may need to pay more attention to when considering the transport decisions of mobile foragers, and the manner in which toolstone constraints might fit into the picture. Virtually all of the discussions that I have seen about transport constraints treat the lithic-using (usually male) forager as though he moved about the landscape alone (or in small all-male hunting parties), far removed from any other members of his family or band. In other words, whatever gear he would need while away from home he had to carry himself. This would seem to be the most widely shared image of logistical mobility that archaeologists have garnered from Lewis Binford's (1980) classic work among the Alaskan Nunamiut, an image that has now (mistakenly, in my opinion) been (over)generalized to a near universal in contemporary archaeological thinking.

One reason for worrying about the universality of this particular image of logistical mobility is that the very idea grew out of work among Inuit peoples, northern foragers whose very way of life depended upon complex dog-sled technology (Sheppard 2004). Binford saw the Nunamiut's hunting strategies and mobility patterns—for example, their long-distance caribou-focused hunting treks from fixed winter settlements; their practice of freeze-caching meat close to kills with the expectation of retrieving it later—as part and parcel of "the arctic way of life," a sort of timeless view of the way northern peoples anywhere, anytime, would have organized themselves in response to the temporal and spatial constraints and incongruities posed by their resources. Unfortunately, in his model building Binford didn't adequately consider the extent to which such practices would have been common, or even feasible, in the absence of dog traction (Morey and Aaris-Sørensen 2002; Savelle and Dyke 2014; Sheppard 2004). This is obviously an important issue that in some ways is reminiscent of trying to imagine what life was like on the North American Great Plains prior to the introduction of the horse (Secoy

1953; Oliver 1962). Thus, quite possibly the particular form of logistical mobility that Binford saw as a universal necessity of arctic life was instead a pattern that only became possible with the introduction of dog sleds (Sheppard 2004).

If so, this immediately brings to the fore the question of the antiquity of this technology. Has it always been part of life in the north, or did it become available at some more recent point in time? The evidence—archaeological (Sheppard 2004), faunal (Morey and Aaris-Sørensen 2002), and ethnohistoric (Savishinsky 1975; Sharp 1976:26)—clearly favors the latter, though the precise dating remains contentious. Nonetheless, most believe that dog sleds (and breeds of dogs suitable for pulling heavy loads) were introduced fairly recently—in the high arctic perhaps hand-in-hand with the expansion of Thule culture a thousand years ago or so; and even later in the subarctic, perhaps not until the early stages of the fur trade (McCormack 2014; Morey and Aaris-Sørensen 2002; Savelle and Dyke 2014; Savishinsky 1975; Sharp 1976:26; Sheppard 2004).

Thus, whatever its exact age, the logistical mobility that Binford universalized on the basis of his work among the Nunamiut would seem to be a fairly recent phenomenon. Without dog sleds (and the dogs capable of pulling them), mobility in the arctic may have looked much more like the pattern we see in the early postcontact period among neighboring subarctic Athabaskan and Algonkian groups—small numbers of dogs, some used for hunting, others carrying packs strapped to their backs, and women dragging or pushing heavily laden sleds or sledges (e.g., de Laguna 2000:326; Loovers 2015; McCormack 2014; Osgood 1936:65, 112; Perry 1979:365; Savishinsky 1975; Sharp 1976:26). And if women were responsible for hauling most of the gear and supplies needed to make long-distance hunting feasible, and for transporting meat, hides, and gear back to the home base, what does that do for our conception of the personnel who would have been present on many, if not most, of these "logistical" hunts? The typical "as the crow flies" distance of these hunting forays from home? The viability of a strategy of routinely caching frozen meat at distant kills? The very size, composition, and duration of the winter settlements? And of particular interest to us here, the weight constraints posed by the items men normally carried while out on the hunt?

> The Archithinue [Blackfoot] Natives . . . are all well mounted on light, Sprightly Animals . . . They likewise use pack-Horses, which give their Women a great advantage over the other Women who are either carrying or hauling on Sledges every day in the year [December 4, 1772]. (Cocking 1909:111)

The Nascopies [Naskapi] practise polygamy more from motives of convenience than any other—the more wives, the more slaves. The poor creatures, in fact, are in a state of relentless slavery; every species of drudgery devolves upon them. When they remove from camp to camp in winter, the women set out first, dragging sledges loaded with their effects, and such of the children as are incapable of walking . . . (McLean 1849:121; see also Turner 1894:271)

[Dene] When moving camp, clothing and bedding were put into large skin bags which, in winter, were dragged, toboggan-like, over the snow or pulled by hand on small double-ended sleds . . . Women did this heavy work, leaving the men free to hunt and to protect them from enemies or dangerous animals. Other loads, women carried on their backs with a tumpline over the shoulders and/or over the forehead. (de Laguna 2000:326)

It seems quite likely that the logistical mobility Binford saw as a universal key to survival in arctic environments may actually be a comparatively recent development, one that only became feasible with the introduction of dog-sled technology. If so, how might hunting, particularly in winter, have been organized without the benefit of dog traction? Obviously, to find game the hunter would likely have to cover a lot of terrain, 10 to 20 or more kilometers per day not being uncommon (e.g., Grove 2010; Kelly 1983; Sharp and Sharp 2015:123). However, the farther his "straight-line" distance from home, the more difficult it will be, without additional help (and especially without the aid of dog sleds), to field process the carcass and get the meat and hide back to camp in usable condition. Thus, in thinking about logistically based hunting, it is critical to keep in mind the distinction between, on the one hand, the total distance that a hunter might travel while searching for game and, on the other hand, the shortest route separating him (and his kill) from the place where his foraging efforts will be transformed from raw material into food, clothing, and other life-supporting necessities. Unfortunately, archaeologists all too often fail to recognize this distinction, one that clearly has a bearing on the nature and quantity of equipment and supplies (including lithics) the hunter will be compelled to carry, and how far he can afford to hunt without the aid of additional helpers (discussed further below). The subarctic Denésuliné provide an interesting perspective on this issue: "Their routine travel can well exceed 15 miles [24 km] in a single day, but the range of their movements will almost always fall within that 7.5-mile [12 km] radius. We suspect that 7.5 miles is about the maximum range at which an individual could make a caribou kill and still pack back enough meat to make a difference to a hungry family" (Sharp and Sharp 2015:123).

The Hadza, though generally not thought of as operating "logistically" on their hunting forays, nonetheless illustrate this same point quite nicely. While Hadza hunters typically cover some 15 km per day in their search for game (Bartram 1997:335), the vast majority of their kills actually occur within a 3 km radius of home, and almost none are made beyond 5–6 km (Bunn, Bartram, and Kroll 1988:439, fig. 15; Lupo 2006:43; O'Connell, Hawkes, and Jones 1992:329, fig. 4).

Thus, if the hunter is working alone, and at substantial distances from home, he very likely will either have to abandon parts of the carcass or temporarily cache some of the meat at or near the site of the kill (Sharp and Sharp 2015). If he decides on the caching option, he may also have to sacrifice the hide in order to wrap or cover the meat, which will probably preclude its subsequent use for clothing, shelter, or equipment. In addition to the labor involved in preparing the cache, by leaving the meat unguarded while he seeks help he runs the risk of losing valuable food to predators and bacterial spoilage, particularly if the meat is inadequately dried, the cache hastily constructed, the gut pile not made sufficiently attractive to predators, and strategically placed, to keep them well away from the cache itself during his absence, or if the hunter is unable to return with helpers in a timely fashion (and assuming, of course, that freezing the meat was not invariably an option at all times and places). Moreover, the farther away from home the hunter operates, the greater the need for him to make more than a single kill while on the hunt so that his investment of time and effort is worthwhile. Needless to say, multiple kills exacerbate the logistical problems of preserving the meat and hides until others arrive to help transport everything home.

Spoilage of meat that is temporarily cached at a kill isn't the only problem facing the hunter. The farther the kill is from camp, the greater the risk the meat will spoil on the trip home, because of heat during the days the meat is in transit, and because of insect infestations, humidity, or rain (Sharp and Sharp 2015). Spoilage can be prevented by thoroughly drying (jerking) the meat prior to transport. Doing this properly, however, is not only labor-intensive, it is also very time consuming (even with the use of fire), and may well preclude further hunting for two to three days or more until the processing is completed (see below).

Before the meat can be dried, it must be carefully sliced into uniformly thin strips to increase surface area relative to volume. This assures that the meat not only dries quickly, but also evenly. Proper drying is essential to inhibit bacterial and fungal growth, retard undesirable oxidation of fats within or still adhering to the meat, and prevent insects from laying their eggs in it (e.g., Warriss 2000:182–91). If the strips are too thick or cut unevenly, the rapidly drying outer surface may block evaporation of moisture from the interior, thereby fostering internal bacterial spoilage of the meat and oxidation (rancidity) of the lipids (FAO 1990). According to Gene Weltfish (1977:217), just slicing the meat to the proper thickness is a very tedious process, even for a skilled butcher. Drawing on ethnographic information from the Pawnee, she estimates that preparing the strips from a single bison, one that has already been butchered at the kill and brought back to camp, would still require some five to six hours to complete (Weltfish 1977:217). The drying strips also need constant vigilance to assure that the meat is protected from predator/scavengers such as rodents, foxes, cats, bears, wolves, wolverines, and aerial pests such as ravens and jays. In addition, the strips need to be flipped over periodically to assure sufficient drying on both sides. And, obviously, the meat must be protected from rain and dew throughout the process, not necessarily an easy task in the bush.

Henry and Karyn Sharp, people with extensive firsthand knowledge of Denésuliné techniques of meat drying, provide a vivid description of the labor and skill involved in properly drying meat; their observations are worth quoting in full here:

> The people cutting the dry meat and attending to it while it is drying have to spend hours around the dry meat rack. It is therefore desirable to build the rack where it is protected from wind and blowing sand . . . Cut meat in the process of drying has to be watched and attended. It is turned periodically to promote more uniform drying. It has to be protected from moisture and is brought inside if it starts to rain. It is brought inside each evening as the day begins to cool and darken and is kept inside overnight. It is not placed back on the racks until any morning dampness or fog has dissipated. . . Dry meat that is improperly dried is vulnerable to rapid spoilage. If the meat has been cut too thickly, the outside may appear to be properly dried while the inside still retains too much moisture for it to keep for lengthy periods. Spots on the improperly dried meat that have too high a moisture content are vulnerable to bacterial growth and can become fly blown . . . The skill of the person cutting the meat is a crucial factor in successfully preparing the meat to be dried. There is a premium on getting a rough uniformity of thickness in the raw meat if it is to attain a uniform state of dryness. Skill and effort play a similar role in the actual drying of the meat. If it is not turned regularly or if it is improperly turned, or if there are places where the meat has become folded, it will not dry to a uniform state. Successfully drying meat demands a great deal of skill, work, and experience. (Sharp and Sharp 2015:43–45)

So how much time is actually needed to dry the strips of meat once they have been hung on a specially constructed rack or tree branch? Judging from both ethnohistory and ethnography, the process typically requires at least two to three days, even when the drying strips are heated from beneath with a fire. Again, the observations of the Sharps are helpful here:

There is variation in practice in determining how long the meat has to hang before it is ready to pack away. Assuming reasonable conditions—no rain or dampness, moderate temperatures, etc.—the meat needs to hang for three days to reduce its weight by roughly 50 percent. It can be consumed by the second day before it is completely dried, but at that point it cannot be stored except by freezing it. There is variation in Denésuliné practice—as well as the opinions of the authors—about hanging the meat for a fourth day. Unless conditions have been ideal, meat packed away on the third day is more vulnerable to damage while stored and will not last as long as meat hung for a fourth day. The fourth day of hanging further reduces its moisture content, making it better suited for long-term storage. It also makes the meat harder and more brittle—whether this is desirable is a matter of individual preference—and better preserves any fat within the meat. Obviously the length of time the meat needs to be hung depends upon the specific situation. Variations in temperature or humidity can lengthen or shorten the amount of time the meat needs to be hung before it reaches a state suitable for long-term storage. Variations in the skill of the person cutting the meat and the uniformity with which it has been prepared have similar effects upon the drying process. (Sharp and Sharp 2015:44–45)

The Sharps' observations echo those made in the subarctic by James Isham more than two centuries earlier (1740s): "They then take some poles, on which they hang the meet [sic], making a good fire under, which is Kept turning, tell itt's thoroughly Dryd. which will be a bout 4 Day's they then tie itt in Bundles, and will Keep for years" (Rich 1949:155).

According to Kerstin Pasda and Ulla Odgaard (2011:36), it took Greenland Inuit at least two days to dry thin, carefully prepared strips of caribou meat: "Agnethe explained the whole process and told how she learned this traditional practise in her youth. She emploied [sic] a special technique of cutting the lumps of meat into thin, but very big pieces . . . In this way the meat could be dried in only a couple of days, in the sun and the wind, and could be preserved for a long period."

Farther south in the North American Great Plains, Arthur Ray (1984:265), in a study of the early fur trade, noted that properly drying bison meat to prepare it for transport or storage required two to three days, but that an additional day was needed to get the meat brittle enough to be pounded up and used in pemmican. According to Clark Wissler (1920:27–28), meat will dry in the sun, if kept free of moisture, "in the course of a few days." Gilbert Wilson (1914:16) says of the Hidatsa: "stages were built in the camp, and for two days, every body was busy drying meat or boiling bones for marrow fat." Also commenting on meat drying in the Plains, George Catlin (1841:124) noted that

> having prepared it all in this way, in strips about half an inch in thickness, it is hung up by hundreds and thousands of pounds on poles resting on crotches, out of the reach of dogs or wolves, and exposed to the rays of the sun for several days, when it becomes so effectually dried, that it can be carried to any part of the world without damage. This seems almost an unaccountable thing, and the more so, as it is done in the hottest months of the year, and also in all the different latitudes of an Indian country.

Finally, moving well away from the northern latitudes, a Food and Agriculture Organization manual outlines simple methods for sun-drying meat in warm, modest-humidity portions of rural Africa. The compilers of the manual recommend a total drying time of at least four to five days to achieve a stable, storable product (FAO 1990: unpaginated document). Even in the arid Kalahari Desert in southern Africa, more than a day and a half are required to dry the strips sufficiently to prevent the onset of bacterial spoilage: "In the space of thirty-six hours the meat was sufficiently case-hardened to stand travelling, only requiring to be hung out at each camping-place during the two subsequent days, to give it the necessary dryness to preserve it for a long period" (Schulz and Hammar 1897:23).

Thus, logistical hunting is not just a matter of one or more men traveling long distances to find game and killing it. As the Sharps so aptly put it, killing an animal is actually the easy part. To the extent that the hunter's family or larger social unit is dependent for its well-being or very survival on the outcome of the hunt, it is the time and effort that go into assuring that both meat and hides reach camp without undue spoilage, loss, or damage that ultimately determine the success or failure of the entire enterprise (Sharp and Sharp 2015:198). Thus, even on what archaeologists would classify as "logistical hunts," it is in the hunter's best interest to either make his kills as close to home as possible (in which case lithics are unlikely to pose much of a constraint); or to bring helpers with him (or have them follow shortly behind him)—most often his wife or wives and perhaps siblings and other female relatives—to take care of the processing of both meat and hides while he continues to hunt (in which case—as outlined more fully below—the women carry most of the hunter's belongings and supplies, except his weapons, and again lithics may pose much less of a constraint than archaeologists routinely assume).

In other words, mobility, even logistical mobility, often involved an entire family unit, or at least the wife or wives and perhaps other female relatives, not just the hunter; and the entire retinue would relocate to an area where prior information indicated hunting prospects were favorable. While away from home, the women managed the temporary camps and processed the meat and hides procured by the hunter. These camps might be moved several times over the course of weeks until the hunting group returned home.

Of particular interest, therefore, to the present discussion are the numerous tantalizing examples in the ethnohistoric and ethnographic literature suggesting that at times women, while en route on the hunt, not only carried their own personal possessions, but also most of the needed supplies and equipment—*including the husband's lithics, or their modern counterparts.* I illustrate this point with examples drawn from vastly different contexts and habitats—Australia, the Kalahari, the Canadian arctic and subarctic, late eighteenth-century eastern North America, and the South American rainforest. Obviously, a handful of examples of this sort remains anecdotal since neither I, nor to my knowledge anyone else, has systematically combed the ethnohistoric literature to see just how common this sort of gender-biased transport behavior might have been among foragers. Nevertheless, these examples are a valuable reminder that we may not be able to understand the impact of mobility on a man's toolkit, including his lithics, if we think only of the hunter, or an all-male hunting party, traveling over vast distances in isolation.

Australian Aborigines

At a respectful distance behind him follow the women; a long stick . . . is in each of their hands, a child or two fixed in their bags or upon their shoulders, and in the deep recesses of these mysterious bags they carry . . . [a] flat stone to pound roots with; earth to mix with the pounded roots; *quartz for the purpose of making spears and knives; stones for hatchets;* prepared cakes of gum to make and mend weapons and implements; kangaroo sinews to make spears and to sew with; needles made of the shin-bones of kangaroos, with which they sew their cloaks, bags, &c.; opossum hair to be spun into waist-belts; shavings of kangaroo skins to polish spears, &c.; the shell of a species of mussel to cut hair, &c., with; native knives; a native hatchet; pipe-clay; red-ochre, or burnt clay yellow-ochre; a piece of paper-bark to carry water in; waist-bands and spare ornaments; pieces of quartz which the native doctors have extracted from their patients, and thus cured them of diseases. . . . Banksia cones . . . , or pieces of a dry white species of fungus, to kindle fire with rapidly, and to convey it from place to place; grease . . . ; the spare weapons of their husbands, or the pieces of wood from which these are to be manufactured; the roots, &c., which they have collected during the day. Skins not yet prepared for cloaks are generally carried between the bag and the back, so as to form a sort of cushion for the bag to rest on. In general, each woman carries a lighted fire-stick or brand under her cloak and in her hand. (Smyth 1878:131–33, italics added)

Kalahari Ju / 'Hoansi (San)

We heard that "many women," including those of the previous generation, had "for a long time" accompanied their husbands on hunting trips. Some took nursing infants along, as they do when gathering. (Biesele and Barclay 2001:78)

Women accompany their husbands on about half of their hunting days. Women gather on these trips but also take an active role in hunting. They spot game, take part in the chase, retrieve arrows, bring water to flood armadillo holes, encourage dogs, strike animals with sticks or machetes, participate in orienting the party, and carry meat home. (Biesele and Barclay 2001:79)

Denésuliné (Canadian Subarctic)

Traditional Denésuliné did not use dog teams. Dogs were pack animals. The Denésuliné used toboggans, but as mentioned earlier they were pulled by women rather than by dogs. When camps moved, the men ranged out searching for game while the women moved the camp. It was women's year-round responsibility to pack, load, and then pull or pack the entire camp and everyone in it to the location of the next camp. (Sharp and Sharp 2015:197)

Chipewyan (Canadian Subarctic)

While males often performed the actual killing, husband-wife partnerships facilitated the timely and uninterrupted flow of travel, tracking, killing, butchering, processing, and meat distribution . . . Most reported examples of male-female hunting teams involve husband-wife pairs, although cases of father-daughter, grandfather-granddaughter, and other team combinations are known . . . [S]uch teams tend to concentrate on the pursuit of large mammals such as caribou and moose, but other resources can be involved. (Brumbach and Jarvenpa 1997:426)

[In] . . . mixed male-female teams . . . husband-wife pairs and their children, especially during the summer and fall months, conduct moose-hunting forays of two days' to two weeks' duration in a radius of 10–45 km of staging communities or villages. (Brumbach and Jarvenpa 1997:428)

Iglulik Inuit (Canadian Arctic)

A successful hunter required a wife travelling along with him . . . and when a wife was unable to travel a daughter or another woman from the camp might fill in. Women would be charged with such tasks as keeping the snow-house warm, helping to tend the dog team, processing the skins of freshly butchered animals, drying the hunters' wet clothing upon their return, repairing seams and holes in garments, chewing stiffened boot soles and softening other hardened clothing to have them ready for the next day. (Wachowich 2014:138)

Inupiat Inuit (Alaskan Arctic)

Inland, men typically left heavy, bulky meat behind while hunting in the mountains, packing home valuable skins and what little meat they could carry. But when accompanied by a woman, she dried the meat, put it on her back and hauled the heavy loads home. (Starks 2011:304)

Eighteenth-Century Lenni-Lenape and Neighboring Tribes (Pennsylvania and Ohio)

A man who wishes his wife to be with him while he is out hunting in the woods, needs only tell her, that on such a day they will go to such a place, where he will hunt for a length of time, and she will be sure to have provisions and every thing else that is necessary in complete readiness, and well packed up to carry to the spot; for the man, as soon as he enters the woods, has to be looking out and about for game, and therefore cannot be encumbered with any burden; after wounding a deer, he may have to pursue it for several miles, often running it fairly down. The woman, therefore, takes charge of the baggage, brings it to the place of encampment, and there, immediately enters on the duties of housekeeping, as if they were at home; she moreover takes pains to dry as much meat as she can, that none may be lost; she carefully puts the tallow up, assists in drying the skins, gathers as much wild hemp as possible for the purpose of making strings, carrying-bands, bags and other necessary articles, collects roots for dyeing; in short, does every thing in her power to leave no care to her husband but the important one of providing meat for the family. (Heckewelder [1818] 1876:157)

Ache (Paraguayan Tropical Rainforest)

Men left the settlement carrying only bows and arrows and machetes . . . The direction of departure was usually guided by expectations about peccary hunting. Women (usually wives) and children followed, the women carrying infants and children up to age four, as well as axes, carrying baskets, and sometimes a pet (usually a monkey or coati). Each basket held all the household gear brought by a single family, including one or more knives and pots, a plate or cup, matches, a sewing kit, extra clothing, and a mat or blanket. Most women began these trips with several kilos of manioc or corn, and someone always brought sugar and salt . . . An hour or so before dark, a camp was established by the women. (Hawkes et al. 1982:384)

Now let us turn to the second dimension in the biface argument that has not been adequately considered in most accounts of why North American Paleoindians were so fond of bifaces. As someone who works in the Old World, perhaps the first thing that strikes me is how many vast regions (continental-sized ones), and how many millennia (measured in tens to hundreds of thousands of years), reveal little or no evidence of bifaces, whether diminutive ones like those of the Paleoindian period or jumbo-sized bifaces like those of the Acheulian (Araujo 2015; Araujo and Pugliese 2009:173; Bar-Yosef and Belfer-Cohen 2001:21; 2013:38; Chabai 2003:73; Hovers and Belfer-Cohen 2013:S337; Jennings, Pevny, and Dickens 2010; Kuhn 1994; Moore 2015; Moore and Brumm 2007; Pawlik 2012; Prasciunas 2007; Rabett 2011; White 2000:37; Wu and Cui 2010). Simple core-flake industries—Mode 1 in Robert Foley and Marta Lahr's terminology (Foley and Lahr 1997)—can be found among prehistoric foragers almost everywhere, and across the entire span of the Paleolithic from the first tool-using hominins right into the Holocene. When looked at on a global scale, there is very little correlation between the presence or absence of bifaces and such factors as paleoclimate, availability of workable raw materials, or mobility strategies insofar as they can be inferred from the archaeological record.

Moreover, mobile foragers worldwide over the millennia seem to have managed quite well with a bewildering array of different core types and reduction strategies, ranging from totally amorphous forms to block-on-block and bipolar reduction, discoidal systems, a variety of Levallois reduction schemes, macro- and microblade cores, and others (Boëda et al. 1990; Meignen, Delagnes, and Bourguignon 2009).

In terms of achieving functional flexibility, it is quite clear that many foraging systems in the past were able to address their multiple needs while on the fly without recourse to bifaces. Nowhere is this better seen than in the vast temporal span and spatial extent of the Eurasian Middle Paleolithic (ca. 300,000–40,000 years ago). Bifaces of the type that Kelly had in mind, when they occur at all, tend to be late and very patchy in their distribution. Instead, most stone tools most of the time were flakes, with very little correlation between overall morphology and tool function as assessed by use-wear (Anderson-Gerfaud 1990;

Beyries 1988b; Turq et al. 2013). And in Australia over much of the record even marginal retouch is rare, suggesting that a broad range of functions was performed without altering the shape of the tool at all (e.g., Balme and O'Connor 2014; Holdaway and Douglass 2012; Holdaway, Douglass, and Phillipps 2015; Moore 2013; White 1977). Thus, while humans have been mobile for a very long time, bifaces of the sort envisioned by Kelly are an anomaly, in fact a rather specialized one that develops quite late in the overall scheme of things.

There are of course many ways one can try to explain away the absence of bifaces, whether large or small, in many of these areas and over such vast spans of times. Use of bamboo, a favored explanation for their absence in East and Southeast Asia, remains entirely hypothetical as yet. Moreover, bamboo knives may not be capable of performing heavy-duty butchery and hide-processing tasks, particularly when dealing with large to very large prey. And finally, the bamboo argument is simply not applicable to the vast desert stretches of Australia or to the more northerly reaches of East Asia (Bar-Yosef et al. 2012:19; Pawlik 2012; Xhauflair et al. 2016), let alone those parts (and periods) of Central and Southwest Asia where bifaces are also noteworthy for their overall scarcity, patchy distribution, or complete absence. One might grant such sweeping dismissals for the Lower Paleolithic on the grounds of fundamental cognitive differences, but when we come to the Middle Paleolithic we are dealing with "top predators" who were regularly killing quite an array of very large ungulates. Surely, Neanderthal hunters could not have taken all of these animals within a day's round-trip walk from home unless there were game parks conveniently placed in their front yards. In other words, logistical hunting strategies had to be part of their repertoire of mobility strategies. And given the expectations of the traditional biface-mobility argument, many of these Neanderthals should have been routinely transporting bifaces around the landscape. But, as already noted, substantial segments of the Eurasian Middle Paleolithic record—both temporally and spatially—are largely or entirely devoid of such tools.

Interestingly, although Neanderthals were clearly very capable hunters of even the largest and most dangerous prey on the landscape, taking down mammoth, rhino, bison, aurochs, horses, red deer, ibex, and reindeer, most of their lithics were derived from local sources, usually within 5–10 km of the sites where the artifacts were recovered and seldom from distances greater than 20–30 km (Brenet et al. 2017; Féblot-Augustins 2009:28; Frahm et al. 2016; Geneste 1988, 1989; Macdonald et al. 2009:213; Mester and Moncel 2006:224; Moncel et al. 2015; Turq et al. 2013:644, 651). Transport of lithics from more remote sources is of course known, but the percentages of such nonlocal materials are generally quite small, especially when juxtaposed to the proportions of exotic raw materials moving around the landscape in North American Paleoindian contexts (e.g., Bourguignon, Delagnes, and Meignen 2006).

So here we have an interesting conundrum. In Paleoindian North America, the abundance of lithics from sources hundreds of kilometers away is argued to be a logical outcome of embedded procurement within the context of high mobility, which in turn is assumed to be necessitated by an economy focused on hunting large animals. The theoretical underpinning of this perspective can be traced back to "Damuth's rule," the idea that the larger the ungulate, the lower its local abundance (Damuth 1981; see also Peters 1986). The expectation that arises from this, of course, is that hunters who focus their foraging efforts on large prey will have to exploit bigger areas than hunters who are content to rely on smaller game (Morin, Speth, and Lee-Thorp 2016). Neanderthals were hunting an even more impressive array of big game than Paleoindians were, so they too should have been moving over comparably large tracts of land. And such mobility should have provided them with ample access to distant sources of high-quality lithics much like our North American Paleoindians. Yet what shows up in Neanderthal sites for the most part is locally derived (i.e., from distances under 20–30 km and usually considerably less). So which do we believe—the ungulates and the implications of Damuth's rule, or the lithics?

Uncomfortable as the following conclusion might seem, I suspect the problem lies more with the way we interpret the lithics than the animals. In both archaeological contexts—Neanderthal and Paleoindian—it would seem that the source locations of the predominant toolstones are probably not providing us with a reliable map of the annual subsistence rounds of the site's prehistoric inhabitants, either in terms of the size of their home range (far too large in many if not most Paleoindian cases, far too small in many if not most Neanderthal cases), or with regard to its location in geographic space (Amick 1996:418–20, 423; Jones et al. 2003:31, fig. 13; Seeman 1994:276, fig. 2; Walker and Churchill 2014). And if there is any validity to that conclusion, it raises an even thornier question—how often was flint procurement *not* embedded in the foragers' seasonal rounds? Binford (1979:259), drawing on his work in the arctic among the Nunamiut, people with absolutely no recent tradition of flaked stone tool use, together with observations he made during a fleeting two-week sojourn among the Alyawara in Australia in June 1974, nonetheless felt justified in asserting that "raw materials used in the manufacture of implements are normally obtained incidentally to the execution of basic subsistence tasks. Put another way, procurement of raw materials is embedded in basic subsistence schedules. Very rarely, *and then only when things have gone wrong*, does one go out into the environment for the express and exclusive purpose of obtaining raw material for tools" (emphasis added).

Judging from this quote, Binford clearly viewed embedded toolstone procurement as a universal principle applicable to hunter-gatherers everywhere and at all times. And, in the decades since his article first appeared, most Paleoindianists have accepted the universality of his proclamation with scarcely the bat of an eye. Yes, embedded procurement may well be common, even the norm, in many day-to-day situations, but the moment a finished tool, or the raw material from which the tool was made, or the quarry from which the stone was obtained, or the context in which the tool or stone was used, takes on culturally significant meaning, acquisition through gifting, exchange, and dedicated treks directly to the source (Binford's "direct procurement") may become much more common, at times even the predominant mode of toolstone acquisition.

> One cannot assume embeddedness of the lithic technology solely in relation
> to the subsistence economy, as Binford would have us do, even though . . . this
> is a logically parsimonious argument . . . The only real differences from the
> reported behavior of the Nunamiut have to do with the clear and openly
> stated primary goals of these resource-procurement trips and the fact that
> they occurred frequently and not simply during emergencies or at times when
> the raw materials were scarce. This latter point is especially important because
> every single observed case . . . involved a situation in which usable—and as now
> known, as a result of experiments—often technically superior lithic materials
> were already abundantly present in camp at the time when this procurement
> took place . . . Unlike the Nunamiut, the Western Desert Aborigines made
> trips whenever possible to localities of sacred significance, even when these
> trips represented detours from the primary routes of movement to water and
> food sources . . . In 1966–1967 the senior author observed special, all-male
> groups making such trips, often over hundreds of kilometers from their home
> areas, to introduce novices to sacred landmarks and the myths associated with
> them. These special, long-distance trips were called *panalipi* (literally: "all over
> the earth") and the tracks followed on such trips were a favorite theme for
> depiction in rock and cave art. Visitors on these occasions camped together in
> distinct, all-male enclaves within the main concentration of campsites occupied
> by the locally resident population. Such trips established the introductions nec-
> essary for later use of the resources of these distinct areas by the visitors with
> their families, and lithic materials were often obtained and transported over
> long distances during the course of such trips. (Gould and Saggers 1985:118–22)

Scraper manufacture among the Chukchi, on the other hand, is character-ized by embedded raw material procurement as mobile groups move across the tundra with reindeer herds during the summer grazing season. Since the manu-facture and maintenance of leather items is an ongoing process, scraper use is frequently required during residential moves, and it is difficult to anticipate in terms of its location. Lithic raw material is acquired during residential moves and logistical trips made for the collection of other resources. *This is perhaps the only true case of embedded lithic raw material collection by a mobile group for which there is ethnoarchaeological data.* (McCall 2012:178; emphasis added)

No doubt, Binford had a brilliant idea when he came up with the con-cept of embedded procurement, but what he thought was the rule among lithic-using foragers may actually have been much less the universal than he imagined. While there is no way we can resolve this issue here, one thing does seem clear. For more than three decades, most archaeologists have sim-ply accepted Binford's proclamation as though it were an irrefutable fact. Yet we have a substantial ethnographic and ethnohistoric literature showing that members of small-scale societies across the globe—be they foragers or hor-ticulturalists—went to extraordinary lengths to acquire all sorts of culturally meaningful items and materials such as turquoise, amber, mica, quartz crystals, ocher, copper, sandstone grinding slabs, marine shells, sharks' teeth, stingray spines, pigs' tusks, feathers, furs, pituri, minerals and plants with medicinal or psychoactive properties, special woods and reeds, songs and entire ceremo-nies, and even obsidian and flint (as amply documented throughout Australia, California, and elsewhere; see, e.g., Akerman, Fullagar, and van Gijn 2002:29; Basgall 1979:180; Brumm 2010; Dillian 2002:265–66, 286–92; Jackson 1986:121–22, 1988; Paton 1994; Ross, Anderson, and Campbell 2003:77; Taçon 1991). Acquiring these things commonly involved long-distance treks, often annually, many covering hundreds of kilometers over difficult terrain and sometimes through enemy territories. Some of these trips were to participate in social and ceremonial gatherings, others to visit sacred shrines and landmarks, oth-ers to acquire materials directly at the source or from groups that controlled access to the source. And, though hard data are not abundant, the actual loads transported back on these treks commonly exceeded 30–35 kg (not including personal gear). Played out year after year over generations, remarkable quan-tities of raw materials, finished goods, and intangibles such as songs, rituals, ceremonies, and, yes, even procedures for "properly" making fluted points, are likely to have moved widely through complex social networks that crisscrossed the North American continent.

Why then do most Paleoindianists assume, for the most part implicitly, that flint was essentially devoid of any such culturally significant meaning, and hence was seldom if ever the target of dedicated trips, even though much of the exotic flint in Paleoindian sites was specifically earmarked for the manufacture of weapon tips? In a foraging society where men were both hunters and warriors, what item could possibly be more emblematic of adult male status than large, beautifully crafted projectile points made from unusual, often colorful materials that could only be obtained with considerable effort from distant sources? It would seem that the majority of Paleoindianists steadfastly, almost doggedly, adhere to the idea that embedded procurement was the universal norm, despite both evidence and logic to the contrary, largely because one hugely influential scholar declared it was so more than a third of a century ago!

One final line of thought might be of interest here. Bearing in mind the expectations arising from Damuth's rule, it seems highly unlikely that Neanderthals could have successfully acquired the quantity and especially the diversity of large and very large prey commonly found side-by-side in the same sites and stratigraphic horizons given the comparatively small to modest territories often implied (under the logic of embedded procurement) by their mostly locally acquired lithics.

I see two intriguing—and not necessarily mutually exclusive—ways one might account for this curious conundrum. One is that many of the lithics were actually acquired locally by women, not by men, and were fashioned and used by women as they carried out domestic activities in and around the home base (see Gero 1991 for the classic exposition of this perspective; see also Albright 1982:115–20; Beyries 2008:25; Bird 1993:27; Butler 1975; Weedman 2005:188–90; and Weedman Arthur 2010 for several interesting ethnographic examples and one likely archaeological case of women procuring their own toolstone, both locally and nonlocally, and fashioning it into hide working and other tools).

Venturing way out on the proverbial limb, one might suggest that we may be seeing hints of just such a gender-based distinction in the oft-noted dichotomy between, on the one hand, discoidal approaches to core reduction, not uncommonly, though not invariably, occurring together with more locally acquired materials; versus Levallois forms of core reduction, often in conjunction with higher-quality, nonlocal materials, on the other hand (e.g., Bourguignon, Delagnes, and Meignen 2006; Brenet et al. 2017; de la Torre, Martínez-Moreno, and Mora 2013:S330; Duran and Soler 2006; Faivre 2011; Faivre et al. 2014:236; Gravina and Discamps 2015; Leroyer et al. 2014:29; Meignen, Delagnes, and Bourguignon 2009:16; Moncel 2001:611; Moncel et al. 2015; Peresani 2003; Pettitt 2003; Picin and Carbonell 2016; Picin and Vaquero 2016; Thiébaut et al. 2014:286–87, 292; Turq et al. 2013:645–46; 2017). Likewise, Middle Paleolithic sites that display contemporary yet spatially discrete assemblages comprised of functionally distinct subsets of tools might be seen in the same light (see e.g., Bosquet, Giner, and Jadin 2004:273 and other cases cited therein). Thus, from a gendered perspective one might not only expect Neanderthal men and women to have performed different tasks, but one might also anticipate that at times they might have done the same tasks differently, each gender using somewhat different types of tools, or perhaps the same types of tools but produced on different raw materials that had been reduced according to different *chaînes opératoires* and, where deemed culturally appropriate, put to tasks carried out in discrete "gendered" spaces.

> Indigenous [Australian Aboriginal] emphases on separation recognize it as a defining and differentiating dimension of types of activity. For example, many . . . productive tasks are gender-typed: on this basis we commonly find metonymic references to women as "digging sticks" and men as "woomeras" (spear-throwers)—so highly stylized are these productive identifications . . . Similarly, ritual activity is strenuously gender-differentiated into men's and women's "business," sites and parts of camps are defined in terms of association with one sex or the other, and so forth. (Merlan 1992:171)
>
> It is interesting to note that, where there is sufficiently detailed data available [from Aboriginal Australian ethnography and ethnohistory], there seem to be differences between men and women in choice of raw materials, manufacturing techniques and toolkit. One reason women have been perceived as less visible than men is that . . . women seem to make and use fewer heavily retouched tools than men and indeed in some instances women use unmodified or minimally modified stones as tools. (Bird 1993:27)

Gender-based distinctions, though remarkably varied, are universal in modern hunting-and-gathering societies, and perhaps the rudiments of such distinctions emerged already during the Middle Paleolithic. Unfortunately, recognizing a gender-based division of labor in the distant past, particularly when having to rely largely on lithic data, is severely handicapped by an almost complete lack of workable middle-range theory. As a result, only a handful of courageous souls have thus far ventured off into what is surely a scholarly minefield (e.g., Balme and Bowdler 2006; Binford and Binford 1969:81–82; Hayden 2012; Keeley 2010; Kuhn and Stiner 2006; Soffer 2009; Zilhão 2010:11–12; 2015:36). Nonetheless, a recent look at tooth wear in a sample of late Neanderthals found tantalizing evidence that males and females habitually performed different sorts of tasks with their teeth (Estalrrich and Rosas 2015). This result is sufficient to suggest that a division of labor of some sort might already have been in place (see also Ruff 1987:411; 2005:207), increasing the likelihood that at least some gendered tasks might have been linked in various ways to different work spaces, raw materials, chaînes opératoires, and sets of tools. Speculative, yes, but certainly within the realm of possibility.

I hasten to add that I am not suggesting that we should try to explain the diverse array of Middle Paleolithic stone tool production strategies solely in terms of gender. Quite the contrary. We are clearly dealing with variability that stems from many different sources, some social, some economic, some climatic, some chronological, some imposed by raw material properties and availability, and so forth (e.g., Thiébaut et al. 2014). Nor am I suggesting that products of discoidal reduction will reflect only the activities of women, and those produced by Levallois techniques solely the activities of men. Judging by the complex ways in which gender plays out in modern hunting-and-gathering societies, if gender is in fact involved in some manner in these lithic distinctions, I anticipate tendency, not rigidly bounded dichotomy. Small dispersed bands of foragers eking out a livelihood in harsh, unpredictable environments are dependent on the combined efforts of a relatively small number of productive adults—both male and female. Should one or more of these individuals become temporarily incapacitated through illness or injury, an ever-present threat in difficult environments (e.g., Steegmann 1983), the viability of the entire group might be placed in jeopardy if tools and tasks were that rigidly structured and inflexibly ascribed to just one or the other sex. Thus, a man away from home on a winter hunt must be capable, not just of hunting, but of preparing hides and sewing to repair or replace his own damaged clothing in order to stave off hypothermia; a woman must be capable, not just of preparing hides, sewing, and cooking food, but of supplying her family with meat if the family's principal hunter is injured or sick (Sharp and Sharp 2015:193–95; see also Brumbach and Jarvenpa 2006). And I would expect the use of tools to reflect that sort of overlapping contingent flexibility, regardless of how formally structured the gendered ideals might be under more "normal" circumstances.

However, it would seem that when Middle Paleolithic archaeologists acknowledge the likely existence of a "social" component to the variability in their lithic assemblages, gender seldom gets so much as a nod, let alone any sort of serious consideration, despite its fundamental importance among all historically and ethnographically known foraging societies (e.g., Frink 2009:21–22). In fact, when it comes to conceptualizing the social domain, what many lithic practitioners seem to have in mind is so vague and weakly grounded in any sort of anthropological reality that it boils down to little more than a "black box." What social realities are actually in the box remain unknown, but, either by dint of habit or convenience, the box is simply given a generic label—"contents: cultural tradition"—as though the act of putting this ill-defined label on the outside of the box is sufficient to serve as explanation of all that is contained within it. The current passion for painstakingly reconstructing chaînes opératoires, a largely descriptive endeavor that provides the empirical foundation for many of these cultural traditions (sometimes referred to as technical or technological traditions), has hardly brought us any closer to knowing what is in the box than conventional typological approaches (e.g., Soressi and Geneste 2011:340). Thus, one is left wondering how it is that two or more of these putative cultural (or technological) traditions could end up co-occurring, not just within the same site, but side-by-side within the very same archaeological horizon? What would produce patterning of this sort in any "real world" hunter-gatherer context?

> Indistinctive Quina and discoid flaking are documented in quartzite and flint, while Levallois is consistently made in the highest quality raw materials available . . . Beyond recurrence of this pattern, and despite the wealth of Mousterian assemblages in the Cantabrian region, no clear correlations are yet available between knapping methods and other contextual elements. (de la Torre, Martínez-Moreno, and Mora 2013:S330)
>
> A challenge in current studies of intrasite variability is to decipher why changing technological behaviors are documented in contexts where raw material sources were fixed and biotic resources would have been similar through time; that will surely help explain the apparently random changes detected in some archaeological sequences. (de la Torre, Martínez-Moreno, and Mora 2013:S332)

If the usual *external* suspects (raw material, paleoclimate, chronology)—the *dei ex machina* of the lithics world—don't provide convincing explanation for the coexistence of these "traditions," what then? Is it not conceivable that such patterning might have arisen from *internal* sources, from somewhere within the very fabric of Neanderthal social life? This is the kind of thorny but critical question that most archaeologists seem content to avoid by recourse to the "cultural tradition" label, though by doing so we are left with familiar echoes of François Bordes's famous "tribes" of more than half a century ago (Bordes 1961; Bordes and de Sonneville-Bordes 1970). As an explanation, the idea of multiple "tribes" vying with one another over centuries, even millennia, for occupancy of the same caves made little anthropological sense. Today, armed with an almost overwhelming amount of technological, functional, spatial, and chronological data, is the idea of multiple coresiding cultural (or technological) traditions any more compelling? What I am suggesting here is that at least some part of this complex web of variability is likely to be gender based. But we'll never find out if the idea is not even put on the table for consideration.

A second possible way that one might account for the predominance of local toolstone in most Middle Paleolithic assemblages is that Neanderthals simply attributed little or no symbolic significance to particular toolstones or to their sources. As a consequence, they saw little reason to seek out colorful or otherwise unusual flints or cherts from "special" places whose very remoteness added to their perceived value. In this respect, Neanderthals appear to have been "lithic pragmatists" and thus very unlike their Upper Paleolithic, Paleoindian, and later successors who often went to great lengths to obtain toolstone for reasons that make little sense if looked at in purely economic or functional terms.

I hasten to add, however, that Neanderthals were anything but lithic pragmatists when it came to the production of their stone tools. Nothing illustrates this better than their frequent use of sophisticated Levallois reduction strategies. This suite of techniques—complex enough to keep many an archaeologist gainfully employed attempting to decipher the chaînes opératoires that were employed—is blatant "overkill" when viewed in purely functional terms. One need only look to the first 40,000 years of stone tool-making in Australia—notable for a suite of minimalist lithic industries that J. Peter White (1977) humorously dubbed "crude, colourless and unenterprising"—as a way of highlighting the remarkable craftsmanship (and deliberate showmanship?) that Neanderthals (males?) displayed in producing tools whose real purpose was to fulfill the most mundane of functions—slicing, scraping, and piercing—the same functions that Australian Aborigines and many other foragers worldwide accomplished with the most rudimentary stone tool technologies imaginable. To me, this—perhaps more than anything else—underscores the likelihood that gender played a role, perhaps a prominent one, in Middle Paleolithic societies.

Steven Churchill (2014) offers a rather different and very interesting way of estimating the size of Neanderthal home ranges, an approach that ultimately leads him to conclusions that differ quite markedly from the one I have just reached here. His approach draws on the ecology of carnivores, particularly gray wolves, as the basis for modeling the likely amount of space needed to support a modest-sized band of robust, heavily meat-dependent Neanderthals living under subarctic to arctic conditions in Late Pleistocene Europe. The model builds on a series of well-reasoned estimates for male and female body size, basal metabolic needs, and the additional energy expenditures that arise from mobility and other essential life-supporting activities. At the heart of Churchill's model is an interesting ecological relationship, one first recognized by Chris Carbone and John Gittleman (Carbone and Gittleman 2002), which shows that it takes a standing crop of about 10,000 kg of prey to support 90 kg of carnivore, regardless of the actual body mass of the carnivore in question (Churchill 2014:252, 302). Weaving various ecological and energetic threads together, Churchill estimates that the likely foraging range of European Neanderthals would have been quite modest, in fact of a size that matches quite closely the small to moderate ranges commonly envisioned by archaeologists on the basis of the mostly local lithics found in Neanderthal sites. Not surprisingly, Churchill (2014:301, 306–8) also sees the outcome of his modeling efforts as a strong endorsement of Binford's classic vision of embedded toolstone procurement.

Churchill's arguments make for rewarding reading, providing a comprehensive and compelling look at the energetic constraints that framed the lifeways of Late Pleistocene European Neanderthals. However, I believe there are two important factors that are missing from his calculations that must be included if we are to arrive at a realistic understanding of the scale of Neanderthal foraging.

The first of these concerns the carnivores that form the basis of Carbone and Gittleman's original study. These animals are *hypercarnivores*—that is, they are obligate meat-eaters who are fully capable of subsisting on a diet with as much as 70 percent of total energy coming from protein. While human foragers such as traditional Inuit can also subsist on an all-meat diet, they are unable to handle protein intakes in excess of about 35 percent of total energy (Speth 2010). In other words, at most they can consume barely half of the protein that a hypercarnivore can thrive on. At higher intakes humans would quickly perish, a condition widely known in the ethnohistoric literature as "rabbit starvation." I assume, as does Churchill (2014:85), that Neanderthals, metabolically speaking, were Inuit-like meat eaters, not hypercarnivores. Thus, where a hypercarnivore might do well consuming old, largely fat-depleted reindeer, bison, or aurochs, a meat-dependent human might starve to death on the same fare. In short, human foragers have to be far more selective than a hypercarnivore in the age and sex of the prey they target, since some 65 percent or more of their energy has to come from fat, not protein. Our much lower tolerance for protein may be key to why human hunters in the past habitually targeted prime adults, the individuals likely to carry the most fat, while large predators are often more prone to take very young and very old individuals, the animals with the least fat. The individuals at either end of the age spectrum are not only less risky for the hypercarnivore to hunt, the fat-poor (young) or fat-depleted (old) state of these prey is not likely to be of much concern to them. For the human hunter, however, the condition of the prey may be absolutely critical to survival. And, not surprisingly, the more selective the human hunter has to be with regard to the fat status of his prey, the larger the range he is likely to have to cover to find suitable targets.

There is a second factor at work that is also likely to have favored larger foraging ranges for Neanderthal hunters. Carnivores don't wear clothes or wrap their infants in soft hides, nor do they wear soft-soled moccasins on their feet, or sleep in hide tents, or cover themselves with skin blankets, or drag kills home on hide tarpaulins, or depend on leather carrying bags, tumplines, or other such items of equipment. All the carnivore is after is meat (and not getting killed or injured while acquiring it). But hides are a different story. Not all hides are created equal (see Hatt and Taylor 1969; Klokkernes 2007; Manning and Manning 1944; Michel 2014; Oakes 1992; Stenton 1991b). There are times of year when hides are in good condition and times when they are unusable. Some hides provide excellent insulation, others do not. Some provide better waterproofing than others. Some stand up to heavy use better than others. Some hides, like those of caribou and reindeer, provide superb insulation, but also don't last very long because they lack natural oils to prevent the guard hairs from becoming brittle and breaking or falling off (Wachowich 2014:131). Such hides may also stiffen excessively and even begin to rot fairly quickly if they become damp—even from perspiration—and are not properly dried in a timely fashion (Wachowich 2014:133). Some hides are inherently very stiff regardless of treatment, others softer and more pliable. Some are better for making footwear, others better for baby clothing. Hides vary in thickness, suppleness, and other properties, not just according to the species of animal, but also according to the animal's age and sex. Male hides tend to be thicker and stiffer, female hides thinner and more supple. Hides from older animals tend to be stiffer, hides from calves softer and more pliable. The characteristics of the hide also vary across the anatomy of an animal, such that the skin over the neck is often thick, stiff, and sometimes so heavily wrinkled that it is difficult to flatten out, while that from the abdomen is thinner, smoother, and softer. The configuration, density, length, and other properties of the hair also vary according to position on the body. Finally, a single complete outfit of clothing may require hides, or parts of hides, from half a dozen or more animals, and are likely to need replacing at least once a year (Gramly 1977:602; Lothrop 1929:4, 11–12; Manning and Manning 1944:160; Oakes 1992:52; Rasmussen 1931:174–75; Stenton 1991a:19–20; Wachowich 2014:141).

Since the utility of hides varies significantly by species, season, sex, age, anatomical location, and the animal's overall health, one hunts for hides to fulfill specific needs, and hence one must deliberately choose one's prey with those purposes in mind (Burch 1972:362; 2006:139; Dean 2008:147; Wachowich 2014:134). Hide hunting therefore may be anything but random or haphazard (Hatt and Taylor 1969:8). In short, a useful hide for a given purpose is not a guaranteed byproduct of each and every kill. And it is easy to see that one's choices in terms of hide needs may at times be at odds with one's food needs (e.g., Sharp and Sharp 2015:184–85). For example, the hides of male reindeer may be in excellent condition in the fall and well suited for making certain kinds of clothing or equipment, but if the bulls have entered the rut their fat stores may be depleted, making them poor or unsuitable as food. Likewise, calves may be ideal targets for soft skins in the spring, but their lactating mothers, generally in poor condition at that time of year, would not be an ideal source of food for a hungry subarctic or arctic hunter. That may be precisely the time of year when males are in better overall condition than females, but they may be unavailable where the calves are. As a consequence, the hunter is often faced with complex choices and trade-offs, necessitating selectivity that again can only serve to increase his overall foraging range well beyond that of the typical hypercarnivore.

Some readers will undoubtedly object to the implication in this discussion that Neanderthals might have worn fairly complex forms of hide clothing. While I suspect no one doubts that during glacial episodes Neanderthals wore at least some kind of clothing, many envision their attire as amounting to little more than a minimally processed robe or hide cape draped or wrapped around the body (e.g., Gilligan 2007). The basis for this view stems in substantial measure from the noteworthy absence of eyed needles in the Middle Paleolithic, which is widely seen as an indication that Neanderthals were unable to sew more sophisticated form-fitting—and hence better-insulating—types of clothing (e.g., Churchill 2014:144; Hoffecker 2002; Song et al. 2016; Zhang et al. 2016).

The whole "eyed-needle issue," however, may prove to be a "red herring" in Paleolithic archaeology. Many historically documented northern peoples made quite elaborate multilayered tailored clothing without the aid of eyed needles, using just simple bone awls and sinew instead. The end of a sinew thread, when dried and cut or tapered to form a point, serves quite effectively in place of a needle (Amato 2010:202; see also Lothrop 1929:11–12). In many parts of the arctic and subarctic, eyed needles didn't appear at all until Europeans introduced metal needles. These gained popularity especially for fancy embroidery and fine beadwork (Amato 2010:202; Albright 1982:100; see also Hoffman 2002:152), as well as for purposes unrelated to clothing (e.g., the manufacture of netting and basketry). Thus, the absence of eyed needles may tell us little or nothing about the complexity or insulating properties of a people's clothing.

> For most Northern groups (e.g. Native Americans and Siberians), the main sewing tool used was an awl ... Eyed needles were scarcely found in North America ... Those found were mostly on the West coast. In North America, other perforated bone tools of many different shapes, sizes and thicknesses were also sometimes used but generally for other domestic craftwork such as basketry, mat making ... or fishing ... The combination of an awl plus sinew is totally adapted to the craft and a needle is not necessary. The awl effectively perforates skin or fur. Then the sinew joins together the two parts of the soft material. In effect, once dry, the tip of the sinew has the property of being used just like a needle ... Needles became mostly popular in North America among Natives once contact with Europeans was established. Natives swapped the traditional porcupine quillwork made with awls for glass bead embroidery done by needles. (Amato 2010:202)

In short, the presumed one-to-one correlation between the introduction of eyed needles and the development of form-fitting or tailored clothing is at best weak and may in fact be spurious (see Zilhão 2010:11–12). Instead, the presence of eyed needles in the Eurasian Upper Paleolithic, as among many recent northern-latitude foragers, may reflect, not the thermal properties of the clothing, but the importance of fine decorative stitching as a visible means of denoting an individual's, or a family's, social standing, economic well-being, or membership in particular corporate groups or other socially meaningful entities (as exemplified, perhaps, by the elaborately beaded clothing of the Sungir burials—Gilligan 2014:192–93; Kuzmin et al. 2004:731–32; see also Hayden 1990:98–99; and 1993:130–31). Paleoindian eyed needles may likewise be telling us more about display and social differentiation than about clothing needs dictated by deteriorating climatic conditions such as occurred during the Younger Dryas (e.g., Erlandson et al. 2014; Lyman 2015; Osborn 2014).

> Appearance mattered among the Denésuliné. Success and prosperity were judged in part by how the tipis looked as well as by the look of the clothing people wore. All of these were the result of women's labor. Sewing, like preparing hides or drying meat, was seen to reflect variation in the skill, character, and creativity of individual women. Other Denésuliné noticed the quality of the hides women prepared. They would see the hides on the tipi; they would sit on

hides when they visited. Guests would share food and would notice if the dry meat was well prepared. They would notice the clothing worn by the individuals within a camp. Denésuliné women, in particular, paid attention to the quality of the sewing done by other women. Sewing was a task all women performed; a task that interested them. They would examine sewn items, noticing the quality of the stitching and decoration as well as the execution and choice of designs upon the clothing. (Sharp and Sharp 2015:196–97)

Though made to be functional for the hunt, clothing was sewn with design and decorative features that were meant to relay cultural, familial and biographical details, thereby affording social status to the wearer. When worn correctly, garments could authorize and engender social relationships. (Wachowich 2014:130)

While it is true that Neanderthals made no use of bone awls until the very end of the Middle Paleolithic (e.g., during the Châtelperronian; d'Errico et al. 2003), they could easily have performed the same functions with awls fashioned from hard wood, a durable and easily worked material that microwear studies tell us they frequently put to use (Beyries 1988a, 1988b; Beyries and Hayden 1993; Carbonell and Castro-Curel 1992; Lazuén and Delagnes 2014:350; Rots 2009; Schelinski 1993). So, the honest answer is that we have no idea whether Neanderthals did, or did not, possess complex, perhaps multilayered, perhaps even form-fitting tailored clothing. To assume they didn't—hands down the dominant view in Paleolithic archaeology today and in many reconstructions of Neanderthal energetics and land use—is no more justified than to assume they did. We clearly need to develop new ways to find out, but they must be ways that are not based solely upon the presence or absence of eyed needles.

Recently, Mark Collard and colleagues (2016) have introduced an interesting new way of evaluating the thermal effectiveness of Neanderthal clothing under the extreme arctic conditions that gripped northern Europe during the last glaciation. First, they show that many ethnographically documented arctic peoples sewed strips of fur from small mammals, particularly leporids, canids, and mustelids, around the openings of hoods and sleeves, and sometimes around the bottom of garments as well, as a way of reducing the chilling effect of the wind on exposed skin of the face, wrists, forearms, and elsewhere on the body, and as an effective way to prevent the build-up of ice crystals on and around the wearer's face. The authors then turn to archaeological data and show that the bones of these same fur-bearers are relatively common in Aurignacian and Gravettian sites but rare in Middle Paleolithic sites, a difference that they take to mean that Neanderthal apparel lacked the sophisticated thermal properties of the clothing worn by their modern human successors. While there is virtually no evidence that Upper Paleolithic foragers actually used small-mammal furs in the manner seen in historically documented arctic clothing, the idea is certainly plausible and worth exploring further.

But from this interesting possibility, the authors take a flying leap to a conclusion that hardly seems justifiable by their data: "the higher frequency of leporids, mustelids, and canids in early modern human strata than in Neanderthal strata is consistent with the hypothesis that the Neanderthals employed only cape-like clothing while early modern humans used specialized cold weather clothing" (Collard et al. 2016:241). Their conclusion may ultimately prove to be correct, but not because of the fur-bearer data. The correlation between the use of complex, form-fitting, multilayered clothing and the presence or absence of fur ruffs is not as straightforward or clear cut as the authors believe it to be. True, many arctic groups with complex tailored clothing did also make use of fur trim, but others did not, and the correlation becomes weaker among non-Inuit peoples in northern Eurasia (Hatt and Taylor 1969; Murdoch 1892:120). Moreover, in some groups males used fur ruffs but females did not, and in others only certain individuals possessed such trim, presumably a reflection of social standing or wealth. And finally, from at least the eighteenth century onward, the overall importance of small-mammal furs increased dramatically among circumpolar populations as they became enmeshed in the global fur trade, creating considerable uncertainty about the extent to which clothing was routinely trimmed with such fur in earlier periods. So, while Collard et al.'s (2016) approach is both novel and interesting, their sweeping conclusion that Neanderthals did not wear form-fitting or multilayered clothing—*because* they may not have added ruffs made of small-mammal fur around the edges of their sleeves and hoods—is stretching the data far beyond reasonable bounds. As already noted in discussing eyed needles, as far as I'm concerned the whole issue about the nature and thermal effectiveness of Neanderthal clothing remains unresolved.

Returning after a rather lengthy detour to our look at the occurrence of bifaces in both time and space, the Upper Paleolithic provides another interesting case. As in the Middle Paleolithic, there are vast areas and long stretches of time where bifaces are rare or absent. Blades and microblades, not bifaces, were often the tools of choice, and in Southeast Asia the same "Mode-1" tool assemblages that characterized the earlier stages of the Paleolithic continue to the end of the Pleistocene and in some areas well into the Holocene (Rabett 2011).

If bifaces were so important for mobile foragers venturing far from home into areas that lacked (or might lack) adequate supplies of workable flint or chert, why did so few Middle and Upper Paleolithic populations across the Old World hit on the idea (Kuhn 1994:428)? And when they did, as in the

South African Still Bay, why did they abandon the idea well before the end of the Middle Stone Age?

Looking at the issue globally, and over the span of the Paleolithic, bifaces—whether small ones, such as those of the Paleoindian period, or more substantial ones, such as those of the Acheulian—are far less prominent in the archaeological record than they ought to be if they represented the ideal solution to mobility in the face of uncertain tool needs and raw material availability. In fact, given the substantial loads that modern humans are easily capable of transporting (typically on the order of 30–40 kg, not including the weight of personal gear), it seems quite likely that the paltry weight of the lithic component of a forager's toolkit (very likely less than 1.0–1.5 kg) would seldom have posed a major transport issue in the first place. But even if it did, there seem to have been many different ways to deal with the problem, three of which stand out as particularly likely—and not necessarily mutually exclusive—solutions: (1) travel with one or more large cores; (2) carry a supply of suitably shaped large flakes; or (3) travel in the company of one's wife or wives and/or other female helpers. Thus, from this broader perspective, one can't help but come to the conclusion that the presence or absence of carefully shaped bifaces had little or nothing to do with mobility. Nowhere is this clearer than in Australia, where modern human foragers—without the aid of such bifaces—coped for tens of thousands of years with high mobility in the face of marked unpredictability (Moore 2015). Bifaces did appear in Australia, but late, only within the last few thousand years of the Holocene, and in a context that many archaeologists view as one of social and political intensification (Lourandos 1985). Thus, the making of bifaces would appear to be a cultural choice, not a functional necessity arising from the demands of mobility. Their manufacture represents a deliberate investment of time and labor, and a clear display of skill and craftsmanship, that in some manner symbolizes the social, religious, or political identities, values, and/or statuses of individuals or larger culturally meaningful entities (e.g., Bar-Yosef and Belfer-Cohen 2013:32; Kuhn 2014).

While the specific reasons that members of a given culture might choose to make and use bifaces undoubtedly varied widely, there are certain commonalities that pop up repeatedly when looking at the issue cross-culturally. Making a biface clearly required more effort and skill than producing simple unmodified flakes, especially if the final product was shaped and thinned by pressure-flaking. In addition, foragers often fashioned bifaces from materials of higher quality than the toolstones they normally used to produce unmodified or minimally retouched flakes; and they may only have been able to acquire these special materials from distant, often extra-territorial sources, most likely via visitation and gifting, or through more formalized intergroup exchanges during ceremonial gatherings, or by means of deliberate treks to the quarries themselves. While the biface could derive its symbolic potency from any number of different sources, either singly or in combination, some of the more common reasons include (1) the cosmological significance of the quarry itself, or of the stone that comes from the quarry, or of the particular ceremonies that are connected with use of the quarry or the stone; (2) the symbolic association of flint with particular phenomena in the natural or spiritual world such as fire, lightning and rain-making, death, or medicine and healing; and (3) to the extent that the bifaces were ultimately intended as tips for hunting or fighting spears (whether or not they were actually put to use), they may have been the property of men, possibly just initiated men, and may well have served in some capacity as symbols of adult male status (Akerman 2008; Moore 2015; J. Morrow 2011; Taçon 1991).

Needless to say, ideas of this nature are speculative and quite difficult to tease out of the archaeological record, and many other scenarios are of course possible (e.g., Bradley and Collins 2014). But if shifting the primary focus from economic to sociocultural factors is ultimately moving us in a more productive direction, there are broader implications that I believe are worth thinking about. It is interesting, for example, that thinly flaked bifaces of the type envisioned by Kelly don't appear in the Old World until the latter or transitional stages of the Middle Paleolithic (e.g., Blattspitzen, Szeletian, Lincombian-Ranisian-Jerzmanowician) and Middle Stone Age (e.g., Aterian, Still Bay), only sporadically at first, but then gradually increasing in frequency and geographical range during the ensuing Upper Paleolithic (e.g., Streletskian, Solutrean) (Allsworth-Jones 1990; Conard 2011:226; Flas 2013; Hublin and McPherron 2012; Kot 2014; Kozlowski 2003; Moncel and Voisin 2006; Mourre, Villa, and Henshilwood 2010; Richter 2008–9). In broad outline, this pattern follows the same trajectory as the use of pigments, personal ornaments, feathers, long-distance exchange of exotic flints, and other signs of "symbolic" behavior, social differentiation, and widening inter-group connections (Kuhn 2014). Whatever is driving such a remarkable fluorescence of symbolic expression, I would add Paleoindian bifaces as a further, albeit late, manifestation of this same package (Kuhn 2014:46). Although approaching this issue from a very different direction, John Hoffecker and colleagues have come to a remarkably similar conclusion:

A 2007 model, the Beringian Standstill Hypothesis, which is based on analysis of mitochondrial DNA ... in living people, derives Native Americans from a population that occupied Beringia during the LGM. The model suggests a parallel between ancestral Native Americans and modern human populations that retreated to refugia in other parts of the world during the arid LGM. It is supported by evidence of comparatively mild climates and rich biota in south-central Beringia at this time (30,000–15,000 years ago). *These and other developments suggest that the settlement of the Americas may be integrated with the global dispersal of modern humans.* (Hoffecker et al. 2016:64, italics added)

In short, the idea that bifaces served solely, or even primarily, as an economic response to the transport constraints that hunters faced as they pursued big game over the vast wildernesses of North America has long since served its purpose, and continuing to interpret the Paleoindian record in such narrowly economic terms is unlikely to be very fruitful.

WHY HUNT BISON (AND OTHER LARGE GAME) COMMUNALLY?

Why does one hunt bison and other ungulates communally? The standard answer, of course, is for food, with hides and prestige thrown in as added benefits. By hunting larger game whenever the opportunity presents itself, one gets "more bang for the buck" (i.e., higher return rates in the terminology of optimal foraging theory; see, e.g., Winterhalder 2001). And by taking big animals in communal events, the per capita yield is (assumed to be) even greater than if one were to pursue animals individually by stalking or ambushing them. Of course, the per capita yields of a communal hunt actually depend in large measure on the number of animals taken in relation to the number of people who participated in the event and subsequently received shares of meat. It is entirely conceivable that an individual might have done better in terms of per capita yield had he hunted on his own or with just one or two other partners, as is often the case among modern hunter-gatherers (Hayden 1981:371; Smith 1985; Stanford 2001:130–31).

In any case, most archaeologists take for granted that bison hunting, whether singly or communally, was done first and foremost for food, and that the primary goal of the hunter was to provision his family, any surplus then being shared with other members of the group once the basic needs of his family had been met (e.g., Frison 1978). There seems little doubt that food (and hides) are at the heart of what traditional hunting is all about in subarctic and arctic habitats (e.g., Sharp and Sharp 2015). But as one moves into temperate and more moderate climes, what seems almost trivially obvious, a "no-brainer," may in fact be more complex than it might at first seem, and touches on a major and very contentious theoretical debate going on among behavioral ecologists. In brief, the debate can be divided broadly into two "camps" with very different views of what big-game hunting is all about (at least outside of the arctic/subarctic). In one camp are those who see male hunting primarily as a means of family provisioning along the lines of the traditional division of labor (e.g., Wood and Marlowe 2013, 2014); while in the other camp are those who see hunting, especially big-game hunting, more as a political tool, a means by which men acquire a highly valued "public good" (meat) that they then share widely and publicly, not with their own family, but with other unrelated males (and their families) as part of the political dynamics of the local group (Bliege Bird, Codding, and Bird 2009; Hawkes, O'Connell, and Jones 2001, 2014).

As is often the case, there are data that support both positions, so we remain quite far from any clear consensus (Wiessner 2002). However, to lay my cards on the table, I find myself leaning increasingly toward the "public good" side of the argument, though I remain open-minded in light of the complexity of the issue. Nonetheless, several observations are pushing me in that direction. First, counter to what most of us would have expected only a few years ago, most hunter-gatherer groups are composed, not of primary kin and other close relatives, but of unrelated individuals (Hill et al. 2011). Second, when men make a successful kill, much of the meat they bring back to camp is shared, not with their immediate family, but with other unrelated males (Hawkes, O'Connell, and Jones 2001, 2014). And finally, more and more studies are finding that men would actually do better, in terms of the day-to-day reliability of their foraging effort, and in their average return rates, if they did more or less what the women did (Bliege Bird and Bird 2008:657; Cronk 1991; Hawkes 2000:64–65; Hill 1988:165; Kaplan and Hill 1992:189; Marlowe 2007; O'Connell et al. 2002:836).

In case after case, behavioral ecologists are finding that men typically engage in foraging activities that have big payoffs when successful but are very prone to failure. As classic examples, San hunters fail to make a kill more than 75 percent of the time (Hitchcock et al. 1996:182; Lee 1979:267), and Hadza hunters fail to make a kill on a staggering 97 percent of all hunting days (Hawkes, O'Connell, and Jones 1997:573), despite using poisoned arrows and bows with up to 100 lb. draw-weights (Bartram 1997; Henrich 2008:187–88; Neuwinger 1996:90; O'Brien 1994:89; Woodburn 1970). Thus, while men produce occasional bonanzas of highly valued but difficult-to-acquire meat from large game, most of the time they come home with little or nothing to show for the many hours they spent hunting. Women's foraging, on the other hand, seldom produces anything that would rival the bounty resulting from a hunter's successful kill, but women almost never come home empty-handed. In short, while meat from larger animals certainly does provide food (and other important items such as hides), its foremost importance seems to be as a highly valued public good that is distributed widely and mostly among unrelated members of the group. It therefore seems to serve as a critical political mechanism through which a group's most active and successful hunters demonstrate generous, "pro-social" behavior toward others (commonly referred to as "costly signaling" in the literature), thereby helping to assure continued cooperation among a group of otherwise distantly related or unrelated males and their families. Interestingly, a similar argument has been made about hunting and meat-eating in chimpanzees (Mitani and Watts 2001:922). If the analogy with our primate cousin has any validity, we are looking at a political mechanism with considerable time depth.

So how does all this relate to communal hunting of bison or other large ungulates? In a brief survey of the ethnographic literature on communal hunting that I made many years ago with colleague Susan Scott, we found that, outside of the northern latitudes, people most commonly engaged in such practices as part of calendrical and noncalendrical rituals and ceremonies associated with events such as planting, harvesting, initiations and other puberty rites, New Year and world-renewal observances, formation or cementing of intergroup alliances, "big-man" and related mortuary feasts, and so forth (Speth and Scott 1989). Obviously what was killed was eaten, but food was not the raison d'être for such events; instead, the motivations were largely socioreligious and/or political. Generally, communal hunting was only "elevated" to the status of a core economic activity when local game resources were severely depleted, or when the political climate in the region made hunting beyond the immediate surroundings of the camp or village too dangerous to undertake, or when communities became enmeshed in regional exchange systems and broader market economies. These were not hard-and-fast divisions, but clear and quite strong "tendencies" in the data (see also Hayden 1981:371).

If these generalizations have any merit, they actually fit observations about Paleoindian communal bison hunting fairly well. Over and over again in the literature, one finds comments about "gourmet butchering" in descriptions of both Northern and Southern Plains Paleoindian kills—that is, stripping of meat from carcasses, but often incompletely dismembering many of the animals, sometimes even ignoring carcasses altogether, as well as limited evidence of on-site marrow processing or transporting high-utility marrow bones away from the kill for processing elsewhere, and little or no evidence of grease rendering (e.g., boiling pits, fire-cracked rock). These are not just isolated incidences. Instead, "gourmet butchering" would appear to be a recurrent and widespread pattern, sufficiently common in fact that it might almost serve as an identifying signature of Paleoindian communal hunting (Bamforth 2011; Buehler 1997; Frison 1968; Haynes and Hutson 2014; Hill 2002:335; 2007:252; 2008:48; 2010; 2013; Hill and Hofman 1997:75–76, 78; Hofman et al. 1991:184; Johnson and Bement 2009; Kornfeld 2007; Kornfeld and Larson 2008; Kreutzer 1996:136; Sellards, Evans, and Meade 1947:928; Speth 2015:56; Todd 1987; Todd, Hofman, and Schultz 1990:821; Wheat 1972). Similar gourmet butchering is often noted in discussions of earlier Archaic period kills as well (Bamforth 2011; Buehler 1997). Limited processing makes little sense if one is conducting these kills primarily to acquire food, for example, stocking up in the fall to survive the harsh winters of the Northern Plains, a compelling view offered many years ago by George Frison (1978). In fact, truly intensive processing of kills—as evidenced by thoroughly dismembered carcasses, large quantities of comminuted bone, boiling pits, and masses of fire-cracked rock—does not really become clearly evident until the end of the Archaic, and especially during the ensuing Late Prehistoric period after about AD 500 (Bamforth 2011; Bethke et al. 2016; Brink and Dawe 2003; Cooper 2008; Kornfeld 2007; Peck 2011:177–78; Zedeño, Ballenger, and Murray 2014). This is a period when farming communities, and hence potential trading partners, began popping up in many of the river valleys bordering and transecting the Plains, and when hides earmarked for both robes and shields became a key resource in regional and interregional exchange systems both among Plains groups, and between those living on the Plains and those in adjacent culture areas to the east and west (e.g., Brosowske 2005; Creel 1991; Creel, Ferguson, and Kenmotsu 2013; Hanson 1986; Speth and Newlander 2012; Speth and Staro 2012; Spielmann 1983; Wood 1974). In other words, the sociopolitical matrix within which communal hunting was embedded probably differed quite markedly between the Paleoindian period (and earlier portions of the Archaic) on the one hand, and the Late Prehistoric period on the other (see, e.g., Bamforth 2011; see also Bethke et al. 2016).

This does not mean that all communal kills in the earlier period were motivated solely by socioreligious and political factors, with food (and hides) largely irrelevant. Nor does it mean the reverse—that all Late Prehistoric kills were motivated only by economics and that social and political goals were irrelevant. But it does suggest that many early communal kills were conducted more as a means of underwriting socioreligious aggregations than as core components of the subsistence system (e.g., Cooper 2008; Fawcett 1987). If that conclusion holds any water, the location of such aggregation sites could have been literally hundreds of kilometers from home, anywhere in fact that was known and reasonably accessible to all, politically safe, and one with resources that could support a large number of people on a temporary yet longer-than-usual basis (see Balme, chapter 3 in this volume). Hence, like the sources of high-quality exotic flint, the locations of these Paleoindian and perhaps Archaic communal bison kills likely tell us more about periodic intergroup rendezvous points, perhaps of bands speaking closely related languages or sharing particular ceremonies, than about annual home ranges of individual groups engaged in their normal subsistence-related movements and activities. I suspect that clear links between kill loci and annual foraging ranges would remain comparatively rare and ill-defined until the Late Prehistoric period, when intensified communal bison hunting took on a much more economic cast, at times (at least in the Northern Plains) on an almost "industrial" scale (e.g., Kehoe 1973:195; see also Zedeño, chapter 2 in this volume).

NUTRITION AND COMMUNAL BISON HUNTING

Despite our ability to eat a considerable amount of meat (traditional Inuit diet may often have exceeded 90% meat), humans are not hypercarnivores. That is, compared for example to wild felids (e.g., Eisert 2011), we are quite limited in the total amount of protein we can ingest on a daily basis. The reason is that the amino acids from ingested proteins are catabolized (deaminized) in the liver, and the nitrogenous wastes that result from this process must be converted to urea and largely excreted in the urine. However, the ability of the liver to upregulate the enzymes involved in the synthesis of urea is rate limited, such that, at protein intakes above the safe limit, the liver can no longer effectively deaminize the amino acids, leading to a build-up of ammonia (*hyperammonemia*) and excess amino acids (*hyperaminoacidemia*) in the blood. These are the conditions, exacerbated by low carbohydrate intake, ketosis, and concomitant impairment of kidney function, that Vilhjalmur Stefansson (1944) and other explorers recognized as "protein poisoning" or "rabbit starvation" (Speth 2010:76).

For an average modern hunter-gatherer, who would probably weigh around 50 kg (obviously much less than present-day 70–80 kg Euroamericans), the upper safe limit is about 183 g of protein per day (see calculations in Speth 2010:76–77; see also Cordain et al. 2000:688). Thus, at roughly 4 kcal per gram of protein (Food Standards Agency 2002:9), our hypothetical forager can consume about 730 kcal of protein. If the daily energetic needs of such a forager fell between about 2,000–2,500 kcal, protein could constitute up to about 30–35 percent of his or her total caloric intake without negative consequences. Interestingly, this figure is very close to the traditional composition of pemmican, a widely used foodstuff among hunting and trapping peoples across the width and breadth of the Plains, subarctic, and arctic (Allen 1877:567–68; Dunn 1844:75; Ellis 1889:18; Godman 1836:134; Hind 1860:312; Keating 1824:428–29; Lewis 1809:147–48; Richardson 1829:245; Robinson 1879:162–64; Stefansson 1956:138–39; Thompson 1916:434–35).

> The inside fat, and that of the rump, which is much thicker in these wild than our domestic animals, is melted down and mixed, in a boiling state, with the pounded meat, *in equal proportions*; it is then put in baskets or bags for the convenience of carrying it. Thus it becomes a nutritious food, and is eaten, without any further preparation, or the addition of spice, salt, or any vegetable or farinaceous substance. (Mackenzie 1801:cxxi–cxxii, italics added)

> [Pemmican] is composed of buffalo meat, dried and pounded fine, and mixed *with an amount of tallow or buffalo fat equal to itself in bulk*. The tallow having been boiled, is poured hot from the caldron into an oblong bag, manufactured from the buffalo hide, into which the pounded meat has previously been placed. The contents are then stirred together until they have been thoroughly well mixed. When full, the bag is sewed up and laid in store. Each bag when full weighs one hundred pounds. (Hargrave 1871:168, italics added)

> It was a standard calculation of the fur trade that one pound of jerky had the food value of six pounds of lean meat, and they knew from experience that in order to remain healthy and strong indefinitely they needed a pound of suet to go with each six pounds of fresh lean, meaning they would have to have *a pound of suet for each pound of jerky*. (Stefansson 1956:212, italics added)

> The supply of fat was always too small to enable us to convert all the lean pounded or powdered meat into pemmican, *for which equal weights were required*. (Cowie 1913:415, italics added)

One can easily estimate the percentage of protein in a "standard" pemmican mix of the sort described by Mackenzie and others. If we assume that the jerked (dried) lean is mostly protein, an arbitrary amount—say 10 kg—would yield about 40,000 kcal (Food Standards Agency 2002:9). An equal amount of fat (i.e., 10 kg) would yield another 90,000 kcal, for a total energy value in the mix of about 130,000 kcal, with protein therefore contributing slightly over 30 percent of the calories. It is clear from the vast ethnohistoric literature on pemmican that at sustained protein intakes above the 30–35 percent threshold, our hypothetical Paleoindian forager would likely have begun to experience the lethargy, weakness, diarrhea, and other symptoms of classic "rabbit starvation" so vividly described by Randolph Marcy (1863:16), Stefansson (1944:234), and countless others.

Bison, like many other wild ungulates, are notoriously lean animals even at the best of times, with total body fat levels fluctuating from about 10 percent when in peak condition to as low as 3 percent or lower during harsh times of year or during particularly stressful points within their annual reproductive cycle (e.g., pregnancy and lactation, rut) (Crawford 1968; Emerson 1990:512–14; Galbraith et al. 2006; Hoffman and Cawthorn 2012; Hoffman and Wiklund 2006:201; Ledger 1968; Marchello et al. 1989; McDaniel et al. 2013; Morris et al. 1981; Ramanzin et al. 2010; Rule et al. 2002; Speth and Spielmann 1983). They typically have far less subcutaneous fat than domestic animals, and they lack the intramuscular marbling that is so characteristic of the cuts one buys at the supermarket (O'Dea 1991:235–36). Thus, the meat from wild or range-fed bison is highly attractive as a "health food" in the modern world where we are plagued with a surfeit of fat and calories, but for the prehistoric hunter lean bison would have posed a problem, particularly at times of year when adequate sources of nonprotein calories (i.e., carbohydrates and plant oils) were unavailable (Speth and Spielmann 1983).

Using some simple calculations, we can highlight the magnitude of the nutritional problem confronting the Paleoindian bison hunter. If the hunters were limited to only about 183 g of protein per day, a value as noted above based on a 50 kg forager (see Speth 2010:77), that would translate into somewhat less than 0.9 kg (871 g) of meat per day (meat typically has a protein content of ~21%). Looking first at bison at the leaner end of the condition spectrum (about 3% total body fat), such meat would yield only 26 g of fat, or roughly 234 kcal (~9% of one's daily energy intake, estimated at 9 kcal/g of fat). The combined calories from both the protein (730 kcal) and the fat (234 kcal) contained in the meat add up to less than 1,000 kcal (964 kcal), or only about 40 percent of the hunter's average daily energy needs (assumed here to be 2,500 kcal). The remaining ~60 percent of the calories would have to come from other sources. If we now look at bison in peak condition (10% total body fat), meat from these animals would yield approximately 87 g of fat, or roughly 783 kcal. In these animals, the combined calories from both the protein (730 kcal) and the fat (783 kcal) add up to 1,513 kcal, or about 60 percent of the hunter's total energy requirement, still leaving a large gap that must be filled by other means.

While the hunter can obviously focus a lot of his attention on fat-rich organs, the tongue being a prime example, this does not obviate the protein problem. And of course tongues are limited in size and number and alone could hardly provide the missing nonprotein calories needed by an overwintering band. The brain is also a fat-rich organ but, like the tongue, is limited in number and size and thus equally insufficient. There is another problem with brains worth noting, one that I have thus far been unable to find addressed head-on in the food science literature. Brains are definitely edible and quite palatable—a point to which I can personally attest—and they are rich in lipids, particularly the long-chain polyunsaturated fatty acids (LCPUFA's), docosahexaenoic acid and arachidonic acid. Thus, given their fat content one might at least expect brains to be an important *supplementary* source of nonprotein calories in a forager diet that is heavily meat-based, an idea that many archaeologists, biological anthropologists, nutritionists, and others have repeatedly raised (e.g., Cordain et al. 2002; Kuipers et al. 2010). And yet one gets the impression from the ethnographic and ethnohistoric literature that foragers were often more prone to use brains to tan hides than as a supplemental source of food. I certainly don't see much historic or ethnographic evidence from the Plains that bison brains played a prominent role as an overwintering food. I emphasize that my comments here are little more than impressions, ones that may well prove to be wrong. But it may be the case that brains were not widely relied upon because the LCPUFA's are very unstable and readily oxidized, much like the fatty acids in marine resources and, if not handled properly (i.e., deliberately rotted or fermented, as is common practice, for example, in preparing arctic "stink-head"; see Starks 2011:306–7), they may produce hydroperoxides and other byproducts that are potentially toxic. In other words, it is possible that without proper fermentation technology the brains could not be stored for later use and instead had to be eaten relatively soon after a kill. Clearly, the suitability of brains as an overwintering food is an intriguing but unresolved issue, one with behavioral, nutritional, and taphonomic implications that would be well worth looking into further.

Given the limited overall amount of fat in the carcass of a wild bison, one can begin to appreciate the tremendous importance of the lipids in the marrow cavities of the limb bones and the "grease" that could be boiled, or stewed, from the cancellous tissue of limb epiphyses, vertebrae, and flat-bones such as ribs and sternebrae. The highly standardized composition of pemmican, in which fat typically comprised about 65 to 75 percent of the total calories of the lean-fat mixture, underscores just how vital these lipids were to Native Americans and First Nation peoples, not to mention the countless explorers, fur-trappers, and military personnel of the eighteenth and nineteenth centuries who supplied themselves using the same basic formula. And when the mixture wasn't right, or when fat was scarce or missing altogether, the outcome of subsisting on just lean meat could be devastating:

I had no opportunity of seeing him personally, but supposing that his pemmican, like the ordinary preparation, would consist of dried meat and fat in equal quantities, or would contain at least a third part of the latter, I ordered the necessary amount of him. As I was passing through Copenhagen just before we started I learned that his pemmican was carefully purified of all fat. This was an unpleasant surprise; but, as we had a certain quantity of butter, as well as some liver "pâte" of a very fatty nature, I thought we should get on well enough. However, it proved a very short supply, and in the end we suffered from a craving for fat which can scarcely be realised by anyone who has not experienced it. (Nansen 1892:38–39)

We tried the meat of horse, colt, and mules, all of which were in a starved condition, and of course not very tender, juicy, or nutritious. We consumed the enormous amount of from five to six pounds of this meat per man daily, but continued to grow weak and thin, until, at the expiration of twelve days, we were able to perform but little labor, and were continually craving for fat meat. (Marcy 1863:16)

This morning we got our female friends to slice and dry the meat over fires. All of it was very lean, and we could not get any fat or grease to trade from the Indians, which was a bad look out, as it is nearly as hard to live on the dried meat of a lean animal alone without grease, as it is to starve altogether. (Palliser 1863:108)

If you are transferred suddenly from a diet normal in fat to one consisting wholly of rabbit you eat bigger and bigger meals for the first few days until at the end of about a week you are eating in pounds three or four times as much as you were at the beginning of the week. By that time you are showing both signs of starvation and of protein poisoning. You eat numerous meals; you feel hungry at the end of each; you are in discomfort through distention of the stomach with much food and you begin to feel a vague restlessness. Diarrhoea will start in from a week to 10 days and will not be relieved unless you secure fat. Death will result after several weeks. (Stefansson 1944:234)

Thus, without systematically extracting these life-giving nutrients—both marrow and grease—from the bones acquired during a successful kill, or gathering and storing adequate surpluses of carbohydrates and plant-derived oils, it is hard to imagine how highly mobile bands of Paleoindian foragers could have overwintered successfully on the Plains. Subsisting solely or primarily on large quantities of lean meat is simply not a viable option.

The importance of this issue is by no means unique to Paleoindians. No matter how successful Eurasian Middle and Upper Paleolithic foragers might have been as hunters, they would still have faced similar nutritional constraints (assuming of course that their ability to metabolize protein was broadly comparable to our own). They would have needed to obtain more than half of their per capita daily caloric intake from sources other than animal protein—in other words, either from animal-derived lipids such as adipose tissue, internal organ fats, marrow, and bone grease (Costamagno 2013; Marean 2005; Morin and Ready 2013; Speth 2015); or from plant-derived starches and oils such as underground storage organs, seeds, nuts, fruits, and the partly digested stomach contents of their prey (Buck et al. 2016; Buck and Stringer 2014; Hardy 2010; Henry, Brooks, and Piperno 2011, 2014; Jones 2009; Kubiak-Martens 1996; Lippi et al. 2015; Mason, Hather, and Hillman 1994; Power et al. 2015; Pryor et al. 2013; Revedin et al. 2010; Revedin et al. 2015). Even the widely popular perception that Neanderthals were highly carnivorous "top predators," a view based largely on nitrogen isotope studies, is coming under scrutiny as paleoecologists and others begin to raise concerns about the interpretation of the $\delta^{15}N$ values (see discussion in Morin, Speth, and Lee-Thorp 2016). According to Hervé Bocherens, "A small percent of meat already increases very significantly the $\delta^{15}N$ value, and contributions of plant food as high as 50% do not yield $\delta^{15}N$ values lower than 1 standard-deviation of the average hyena collagen $\delta^{15}N$ value . . . This example clearly illustrates that the collagen isotopic values of Neanderthal collagen provide data on the relative contribution of different protein resources, but it does not preclude a significant amount of plant food with low nitrogen content, as high as half the dry weight dietary intake" (Bocherens 2009:244).

Even the graphics used to display the isotope data are misleading. Neanderthal $\delta^{15}N$ values place these hominins cheek-by-jowl with hypercarnivores such as cave lions and hyenas, giving the reader the (false) impression that our ancestors and these nonhuman predators must have been consuming comparable all-meat diets and probably even relying on many of the same taxa. As noted earlier, however, if Neanderthal's capacity to metabolize protein was more or less the same as that of modern foragers such as the Inuit, they would have died in a matter of weeks or months had they been forced to consume the normal fare ingested by the hypercarnivores. The difference? Neanderthals would have had to obtain 65 percent or more of their calories from fat, hypercarnivores less than half that amount. In short, the fact that Neanderthals fall together with cave lions and hyenas on the $\delta^{15}N$ axis of the graph obscures fundamental differences in their nutritional requirements.

Although largely ignored until recently, potential problems with these isotope-based dietary reconstructions have been apparent for many years.

For example, Margaret Schoeninger (1995), in an overview published more than two decades ago in *Evolutionary Anthropology*, showed that European Neanderthals and late prehistoric maize farmers (Pueblo Indians) in the American Southwest had overlapping $\delta^{15}N$ values despite vastly different diets and food ways (compare the Neanderthal $\delta^{15}N$ values in Schoeninger's figure 2C with the Pueblo Indian values in her figure 2D). In a more recent study, Schoeninger (2014:420–21) notes that $\delta^{15}N$ values overlapping those of Neanderthals are observed quite commonly in human populations across a broad range of environments and among peoples known to have consumed only modest amounts of meat.

The bottom line: without an adequate supply of nonprotein calories, big-game hunters—whether Paleolithic or Paleoindian—would have had to face the height of winter subsisting on a high-protein Atkins-like diet, but minus the benefits of the fat marbling that is part and parcel of meat—even "lean" cuts—from most domestic animals (Cordain et al. 2002:186–87). An extreme weight-loss diet of this sort might be cautiously recommended for overweight Euroamericans, but would hardly be an ideal survival strategy for a forager. At worst, our Paleoindian (and Paleolithic) hunter-gatherers would have begun experiencing the far more severe consequences of classic "rabbit starvation."

With this in mind, I can't help but come to the conclusion that if Paleoindians were only superficially processing their kills (i.e., "gourmet butchering"), ignoring much of the marrow and all of the bone grease, then bison simply couldn't have been as central *nutritionally* to their diet as many scholars steadfastly assume, and plant foods—the meager evidence presently available notwithstanding—must have played a far greater role than most of us currently envision. David Meltzer (1993) questioned the primacy of large game such as mammoth and bison in Paleoindian diet a quarter of a century ago, as have many others since, but I don't think I am too far off the mark in saying that the "Paleoindian as big-game-hunting specialist" remains—hands-down—the predominant view. Interestingly, Marcel Kornfeld (2007:42–43) came to a somewhat similar conclusion independently by using data on the number of known kill sites, the number of animals in these sites, their estimated meat yields, and the human populations those animals might be able to feed over the roughly 3,500-year duration of the Paleoindian period. It therefore seems far more likely that the real importance of these kills—and the special raw materials that the hunters used to fashion their exquisitely flaked and often excessively delicate projectile points—lay in the socioreligious and political spheres. Following this thread to its (one hopes) logical conclusion, bison probably could not become a core *nutritional* component of Plains diet until the Late Prehistoric period, when evidence for intensive on-site processing of both marrow and bone grease became the norm, not the exception.

FINAL THOUGHTS

So, where have we come in this rather lengthy undertaking? Throughout I have had one principal goal—to take a fresh look at some of the key assumptions that we routinely make about Paleoindian lifeways in order to point out ways in which they may be flawed and, in at least a few cases, just plain wrong. In the 1970s and 1980s, ideas such as communal bison hunting as overwintering strategy, embedded toolstone procurement, logistical organization of hunting strategies, bifacial technology as response to transport constraints, stone tool caching as insurance, and many others provided exciting new ways to think about the Paleoindian archaeological record, small but bold steps away from the field's traditional obsession with description, typology, and chronology toward a broader and more anthropologically grounded endeavor. But somehow over the intervening years some of these once innovative ideas have become fossilized, transformed from interesting possibilities that called out for further exploration, to unquestioned (and unquestionable) "givens" that now get repeated over and over, almost like religious dogma. The result has been limiting and at times downright stultifying. Many interesting and potentially rewarding avenues of research, ripe for further inquiry, have simply been removed from the table, replaced by boilerplate rehashes of things that have been "old hat" for decades. What has genuinely continued to advance over this period is our understanding of chronology, route of entry, paleoclimate, and various technical matters such as the chemical sourcing of raw materials. But our understanding of Paleoindians as hunters and gatherers, as real peoples with real cultures—the anthropological part of the endeavor—has changed remarkably little in years. Reduced to its bare bones, and taking more than a few liberties in the process, the standard mantra goes something like this: "Paleoindians devoted most of their waking hours to acquiring pretty flint from distant sources and fashioning pretty points without which their big-game hunting economy would not have been viable." How many more Paleoindian sites do we have to dig before the profession finally says "enough"? Along the way the amount of trivia that has been garnered about the morphology and pattern of flake scars on Paleoindian points is almost overwhelming. Would anyone seriously want to know that kind of detail about the arrowheads and spear points of any historically known group of hunter-gatherers? Beyond their possible value in matters of chronology, what interesting anthropological questions are really at stake that require all those mind-numbing minutiae?

In fact, judging from the literature one could easily come to the conclusion that Paleoindian technology amounted to little more than projectile points, with a smattering of sharp flakes thrown in for butchering animals (they of course never cut anything else), and some endscrapers to do something with the hides. Paleoindians, it would seem, had no social or symbolic life, certainly no gender, and essentially no interactions, peaceful or otherwise, with any other human beings (Gero 2000:311; 2002). They were obviously far too busy wandering around the empty North American landscape searching for big game and procuring their precious life-sustaining flint. One wonders how they managed to reproduce, let alone maintain viable cultures and societies. In short, their entire existence revolved around males, meat, and flint. Looked at from the vantage point of anthropology, these big-game hunting "flintivores" were indeed peculiar members of the modern humans club!

Many Paleoindianists will no doubt object by noting the restrictive nature of the archaeological record. With rare exceptions, little is preserved beyond flint and animal bones. True. One can hardly argue with that. But I would add that Paleoindian studies are also seriously handicapped by treating as established fact what should be seen as little more than interesting ideas and plausible hypotheses, thereby closing off whole domains of potentially rewarding inquiry. I would also add that Paleoindian studies are hamstrung by the profession's overwhelming obsession with pretty points. Playing devil's advocate here, it is tempting to suggest that the projectile points are the single greatest obstacle to progress in the field.

In this chapter I have touched upon a number of key assumptions that form the substrate upon which many present-day Paleoindian studies have been built. Most of these assumptions began as limited observations in one or another very specific context, often an ethnographic one, but that were then (over)generalized to the point that they are now seen as universal principles governing the behavior of foragers at all times and in all places. The original observations and their interpretation may have been completely valid. The problems arise when such case- and context-specific observations are elevated to the status of universal "truths" and removed from further scientific scrutiny. A few examples drawn from discussions in the chapter should suffice to illustrate the point.

Why, for example, do Paleoindianists almost invariably treat lithics (raw materials, sources, and products) as purely economic entities that for all practical purposes are devoid of symbolic valuation? While it is certainly a convenient assumption, numerous ethnographic and ethnohistoric cases from both the Old and New World show us that it is often patently false. However, by blanketly treating toolstone as having no symbolic import, Paleoindianists can model its procurement more or less like any other mundane resource—that is, solely in terms of its economic costs and benefits. And since flint sources are highly predictable in both space and time, and toolstone neither flees when pursued nor spoils if not "harvested" at the right time, it is not surprising that foragers would attend to their less predictable food needs first, acquiring their flints as needed along the way. In short, it is taken as self-evident that flint procurement would be "embedded" within a group's annual subsistence rounds, precisely the perspective that Binford promulgated decades ago.

But what if Binford's conception of embedded procurement is an overgeneralization extended far beyond the bounds that were justified by the specific and very limited context in which his original observations were made? What if flint at times did in fact have important symbolic significance to its users? This certainly seems likely in the Paleoindian case given that most of the exotic material was specifically earmarked for the manufacture of hunting and fighting weapons, prime social markers of adult male status. If so, then our ideas about the universality of embedded procurement in Paleoindian times might well collapse. In fact, beyond Binford's evangelical pronouncements more than a third of a century ago, which incidentally were based on just two weeks of "hit and run" fieldwork in Australia in June 1974 (O'Connell 2011:87), what other ethnographic observations actually justify this assumption? Almost none that I am aware of. And if Binford's view of embedded procurement is vastly overgeneralized, what happens to our reconstructions of Paleoindian mobility patterns and band territories? They too might well collapse. In other words, there could be little or no direct relationship between the sources of exotic flint and the locations on the ground where Paleoindians did most of their foraging.

Nearly thirty years ago in a carefully reasoned archaeological look at the same issue, Meltzer (1989) emphasized the ever-present problem of equifinality when trying to figure out how Paleoindians obtained their exotic flints. In the end, after considering the issue from many different angles, he cautiously leaned in the direction of embedded procurement rather than acquisition via gifting or exchange, or dedicated procurement trips by individuals or small task groups. I have no argument with Meltzer's paper. It stands as a major contribution to the field precisely because it was a thoughtful attempt to come to terms with an important but difficult problem. Instead, my concern is with the "business as usual" stance of most Paleoindian studies ever since. Our ideas about the scale of Paleoindian mobility and land use are founded almost entirely on the assumption that embedded procurement was the universal means by which these ancient foragers obtained their exotic flints. Yet, despite the fundamental importance of this assumption, it would seem that most Paleoindianists today are content to no longer think about it, preferring instead to take an intellectual shortcut by simply citing Binford's and Meltzer's classic, but long-outdated papers. This is an unsatisfying way to do science, and a rather flimsy foundation upon which to base what has become the standard view of Paleoindian mobility and use of space. The whole procurement issue is long overdue for a fresh look.

Archaeologists talk a lot about the transport constraints imposed by the (heavy) weight of the toolstone that Paleoindian foragers had to carry about the landscape. Countless papers pay homage to the weight constraint, and yet few ever bother to weigh anything. Instead, they rely on percentages, deceptively simple statistics that can lead to very erroneous conclusions about band movements when most of the exotic flint items turn out to be scrappy little pieces of debitage weighing less than a gram. And while Paleoindianists worry a lot about weight, few ever ask, how much weight is too much? As I've tried to show in this chapter, the normal loads carried by foot soldiers for at least the past 2,500 years of record are quite remarkable, dwarfing by two full orders of magnitude the paltry weights of the points and preforms upon which most Paleoindianists have focused their attention. Moreover, why are Paleoindianists so concerned about a handful of "razor blades," when the real issue for foragers would have been the weight, and bulk, of the actual tools, camping gear, and ritual paraphernalia that they had to carry with them, items that for the most part were made, not of flint, but of perishable materials such as wood, bark, leather, fur, human hair, plant fiber, and bone? Paleoindianists are aiming their heavy artillery at the wrong target.

Discussions of transport constraints are commonly framed in the context of logistical mobility, which for many archaeologists conjures up an image of a single man or small parties of men traveling long distances away from home to hunt. With that scenario in mind, it is not surprising that weight might be a serious constraining factor, since each hunter would have had to carry everything himself. But when one digs deeper into the ethnographic and ethnohistoric literature, one finds that logistically organized hunting expeditions took on a variety of different forms, not just the one that Binford universalized (erroneously, in fact, since what he thought was the norm in the subarctic and arctic very likely only became possible with dog sleds). And one form that is repeatedly mentioned involved not just lone hunters, but also their wives, siblings, even entire families, and guess who did most of the schlepping? Women! Not surprisingly, in those contexts men were far less constrained by the weight of their tools and equipment (including flint), because in a sense there was always a human "supply train" close at hand. In short, Paleoindianists have uncritically bought into one very context-specific view of logistical mobility with little or no serious attempt to assess its universality.

The idea that bifacial technology was the optimum way to provide mobile foragers with needed toolstone when traveling into areas of uncertain raw material availability was compelling, though again mostly from a strictly economic point of view. But hunter-gatherers throughout Eurasia were mobile for hundreds of thousands of years, and yet few hit upon the idea that bifacial technology was the way to go. Instead, bifacial technology, particularly of the sort seen in Paleoindian times, was late, very spotty in its distribution, often quite ephemeral, and in the grand scheme of things is more likely to have been a social marker of some sort than an optimal economic solution to a transport problem.

Finally, Paleoindian bison kills have most commonly been seen as events motivated first and foremost by the food needs of the participants, with their social and political needs taken as "also-rans." But this ignores fascinating developments over the past several decades in human behavioral ecology which see the sharing of meat from big game, not strictly as food provisioning, but as a form of prosocial behavior, a political means by which genetically unrelated or distantly related band members were able to foster cooperation and long-term group cohesion. I'm not arguing here that this view of communal bison hunting is necessarily the only one, or even the right one, but I have seldom seen the issue mentioned, let alone seriously discussed, in the mainstream Paleoindian literature. It would certainly be worthwhile looking at this issue more closely, since there are intriguing lines of evidence from the archaeological record itself that do not jibe well with the traditional food-provisioning view.

So-called gourmet butchering is one of these. If building up food stocks was what these kills were all about, *gourmet butchering* implies that more than trivial amounts of meat were wasted. Why would Paleoindians do that? Moreover, why did they often ignore valuable marrow bones, and apparently eschew grease-rendering altogether? From a nutritional perspective, and particularly when it comes to surviving long harsh winters, these within-bone lipids are not just important sources of calories, but are absolutely vital ones for foragers relying heavily on the naturally lean and seasonally fat-depleted meat of ungulates such as bison. If Paleoindian peoples actually did process bone grease, where is the evidence? Where is the fire-cracked rock? Where are the boiling pits? If on the other hand they didn't routinely utilize these key sources of fat, what does that imply about the nutritional role of bison in

Paleoindian diet? How did they avoid the deleterious health consequences of what early explorers, military officers, and fur-trappers knew all too well as "protein poisoning" or "rabbit starvation"? One can ask these same sorts of questions about communal caribou hunting by Paleoindians in the Northeast and Great Lakes region. How were they getting at the lipids without some form of grease rendering? It is true that conditions have seldom been favorable for the preservation of the caribou bones themselves, but there should be no shortage of fire-cracked rock. Where is it? These are important questions that have hardly ever been broached.

One could go on enumerating issues and problems such as these. I hope the few I've mentioned here, and discussed in more depth in the chapter, are sufficient to show that there are many avenues of inquiry that we still can, and should, pursue. Despite the vagaries of preservation, the data from the Paleoindian period are not as poor or limiting as many would have us believe. In many cases what is actually holding us back is not the quality of the data, but the questionable assumptions to which we doggedly adhere, the limited scope of the questions we ask, and our obsessive "love affair" with pretty points.

ACKNOWLEDGMENTS

I want to thank Kristen Carlson and Lee Bement for their invitation to include a chapter at the end of this volume. While my contribution is neither summary nor critique of the volume's contents, it was directly inspired by what I perceived as some of the key threads that unite a number of the chapters—mobility, communal hunting, and hunting-related technologies. I know my take on these issues is quite unorthodox, and I wouldn't be the least bit surprised if most of my ideas turn out to be wrong. Looking back over half a century from my current vantage point of retirement, I see that most of the explanations I diligently committed to memory as an undergraduate—regardless of discipline (genetics, geology, human evolution)—have either been so thoroughly revised that they are hardly recognizable today, or they have been flat-out rejected in favor of quite different ways of looking at the world. So I have little reason to expect that any of the ideas I offer here will still be standing in another half century. There's no real surprise there. After all, that's the nature of the scientific enterprise. We don't really prove something is right; rather we fail to falsify it, until of course someone comes along with a fresh new perspective and does just that. The exercise is not as futile as it may sound, however. We get rid of lots of ideas that are patently wrong. And with each such step we gain a clearer appreciation of the complexity of the phenomena we are studying, and the many factors previously ignored that we now know we have to consider. My hope in the present endeavor is that the thoughts and ideas developed herein will have some value precisely because they fall outside of the standard "box," and as a result may encourage others to question inherited wisdoms long in need of being looked at afresh. If nothing else, what I hope I've been able to show is that some of our most cherished ideas about foraging lifeways in the past, perspectives and interpretations that have come to be seen by many archaeologists as almost trivially obvious and hence quite beyond the need for questioning, are in fact not so obvious or secure after all. This chapter has been fun to write—my only real excuse for the length of the final product—as it allowed me a chance to give some order to inchoate thoughts and ideas that, in bits and pieces, have been stewing and brewing in my mind for quite some time. I thank the editors for giving me the opportunity to put these ruminations on paper, stimulating CARTA sessions in San Diego where my thoughts about logistical mobility began to cohere, and the University of Arizona's School of Anthropology for two wonderful months in the summer of 2016 as a Residential Scholar, where I was able to add the finishing touches to the manuscript. My thanks also to my two anonymous reviewers who provided valuable suggestions for clarifying some of the arguments, modifying others, and streamlining yet others. While in the end I didn't follow all of their suggestions, their input did lead to many changes and a product that is definitely better overall. I owe a particular debt of gratitude to David Kilby for catching an error in the way I initially calculated average flint weights in Clovis caches. His timing was most fortunate because in about another week the press would have begun formatting the manuscript, and the incorrect values would have become a permanent (and incorrect) part of the published record. Thank you, David! And finally, I am grateful to those dedicated readers who had the patience and stamina to make it all the way to the finish line.

REFERENCES CITED

Adams, E. Charles, and Samantha G. Fladd. 2017. "Composition and Interpretation of Stratified Deposits in Ancestral Hopi Villages at Homol'ovi." *Archaeological and Anthropological Sciences* 9 (6): 1101–14.

Adovasio, James M., and David C. Hyland. 2000. "The Need to Weave: The First Americans Used More Fiber Than Flint." *Discovering Archaeology* 2 (1): 36–37.

Adovasio, James M., Olga Soffer, Jeffrey S. Illingworth, and David C. Hyland. 2014. "Perishable Fiber Artifacts and Paleoindians: New Implications." *North American Archaeologist* 35 (4): 331–52. https://doi.org/10.2190/NA.35.4.d.

Akerman, Kim. 2008. "'Missing the Point' or 'What to Believe—the Theory or the Data': Rationales for the Production of Kimberley Points." *Australian Aboriginal Studies* 2008 (2): 70–79.

Akerman, Kim, Richard Fullagar, and Annelou van Gijn. 2002. "Weapons and *Wunan*: Production, Function and Exchange of Kimberley Points." *Australian Aboriginal Studies* 2002 (1): 13–42.

Albright, Sylvia L. 1982. "An Ethnoarchaeological Study of Tahltan Subsistence and Settlement Patterns." MA thesis, Department of Archaeology, Simon Fraser University, Burnaby, BC.

Allen, Harry. 1996. "Ethnography and Prehistoric Archaeology in Australia." *Journal of Anthropological Archaeology* 15 (2): 137–59. https://doi.org/10.1006/jaar.1996.0005.

Allen, Harry. 2011. "Thomson's Spears: Innovation and Change in Eastern Arnhem Land Projectile Technology." In *Ethnography and the Production of Anthropological Knowledge: Essays in Honour of Nicolas Peterson*, ed. Yasmine Musharbash and Marcus Barber, 69–88. Canberra, Australia: Australian National University E. Press.

Allen, Harry, and Kim Akerman. 2015. "Innovation and Change in Northern Australian Aboriginal Spear Technologies: The Case for Reed Spears." *Archaeology in Oceania* 50 (Supplement): 83–93. https://doi.org/10.1002/arco.5051.

Allen, Joel A. 1877. *History of the American Bison, Bison americanus.* Washington, DC: US Government Printing Office.

Allington-Jones, Lu. 2015. "The Clacton Spear: The Last One Hundred Years." *Archaeological Journal* 172 (2): 273–96. https://doi.org/10.1080/00665983.2015.1008839.

Allsworth-Jones, Philip. 1990. "The Szeletian and the Stratigraphic Succession in Central Europe and Adjacent Areas: Main Trends, Recent Results, and Problems for Resolution." In *The Emergence of Modern Humans: An Archaeological Perspective*, ed. Paul A. Mellars, 160–242. Edinburgh: Edinburgh University Press.

Amato, Penelope. 2010. "Sewing with or without a Needle in the Upper Palaeolithic?" In *Ancient and Modern Bone Artefacts from America to Russia: Cultural, Technological and Functional Signature*, ed. Alexandra Legrand-Pineau, Isabelle Sidéra, Natacha Buc, Eva David, and Vivian Scheinsohn, 201–10. BAR International Series S2136. Oxford: Archaeopress.

Amick, Daniel S. 1996. "Regional Patterns of Folsom Mobility and Land Use in the American Southwest." *World Archaeology* 27 (3): 411–26. https://doi.org/10.1080/004 38243.1996.9980317.

Amick, Daniel S. 1999. "Raw Material Variation in Folsom Tool Assemblages and the Division of Labor in Hunter-Gatherer Societies." In *Folsom Lithic Technology: Explorations in Structure and Variation*, ed. Daniel S. Amick, 169–87. Archaeological Series 12. Ann Arbor: International Monographs in Prehistory.

Anderson-Gerfaud, Patricia C. 1990. "Aspects of Behaviour in the Middle Palaeolithic: Functional Analysis of Stone Tools from Southwest France." In *The Emergence of Modern Humans: An Archaeological Perspective*, ed. Paul A. Mellars, 389–418. Edinburgh: Edinburgh University Press.

Araujo, Astolfo Gomes de Mello. 2015. "On Vastness and Variability: Cultural Transmission, Historicity, and the Paleoindian Record in Eastern South America." *Anais da Academia Brasileira de Ciências* 87 (2): 1239–58. https://doi.org/10.1590/0001 -3765201520140219.

Araujo, Astolfo Gomes de Mello, and Francisco Pugliese. 2009. "The Use of Non-Flint Raw Materials by Paleoindians in Eastern South America: A Brazilian Perspective." In *Non-Flint Raw Material Use in Prehistory: Old Prejudices and New Directions*, ed. Farina Sternke, Lotte Eigeland, and Laurent-Jacques Costa, 169–75. BAR International Series S1939. Oxford: Oxbow Books.

Asher, Brendon P. 2016. "Across the Central Plains: Clovis and Folsom Land Use and Lithic Procurement." *PaleoAmerica* 2 (2): 124–34. https://doi.org/10.1080/20555563.2 016.1172442.

Balme, Jane, and Sandra Bowdler. 2006. "Spear and Digging Stick: The Origin of Gender and Its Implications for the Colonization of New Continents." *Journal of Social Archaeology* 6 (3): 379–401. https://doi.org/10.1177/1469605306067845.

Balme, Jane, and Sue O'Connor. 2014. "Early Modern Humans in Island Southeast Asia and Sahul: Adaptive and Creative Societies with Simple Lithic Industries." In *Southern Asia, Australia and the Search for Human Origins*, ed. Robin Dennell and Martin Porr, 164–74. Cambridge: Cambridge University Press. https://doi.org /10.1017/CBO9781139084741.013.

Bamforth, Douglas B. 2002. "High-Tech Foragers? Folsom and Later Paleoindian Technology on the Great Plains." *Journal of World Prehistory* 16 (1): 55–98. https://doi.org/10.1023/A:1014567313865.

Bamforth, Douglas B. 2003. "Rethinking the Role of Bifacial Technology in Paleoindian Adaptations on the Great Plains." In *Multiple Approaches to the Study of Bifacial Technologies*, ed. Marie Soressi and Harold L. Dibble, 209–28. Philadelphia: University of Pennsylvania, Museum of Archaeology and Anthropology.

Bamforth, Douglas B. 2009. "Projectile Points, People, and Plains Paleoindian Perambulations." *Journal of Anthropological Archaeology* 28 (2): 142–57. https://doi .org/10.1016/j.jaa.2009.01.002.

Bamforth, Douglas B. 2011. "Origin Stories, Archaeological Evidence, and Post-Clovis Paleoindian Bison Hunting on the Great Plains." *American Antiquity* 76 (1): 24–40. https://doi.org/10.7183/0002-7316.76.1.24.

Bamforth, Douglas B. 2013. "Paleoindian Perambulations and the Harman Cache." *Plains Anthropologist* 58 (225): 65–82. https://doi.org/10.1179/pan.2013.005.

Bamforth, Douglas B., and Mark S. Becker. 2000. "Core/Biface Ratios, Mobility, Refitting, and Artifact Use-Lives: A Paleoindian Example." *Plains Anthropologist* 45 (173): 273–90.

Bamforth, Douglas B., and Peter Bleed. 1997. "Technology, Flake Stone Technology, and Risk." *Anthropological Papers of the American Anthropological Association* 7 (1): 109–39. https://doi.org/10.1525/ap3a.1997.7.1.109.

Banks, Larry D. 1990. *From Mountain Peaks to Alligator Stomachs: A Review of Lithic Sources in the Trans-Mississippi South, the Southern Plains, and Adjacent Southwest. Memoir 4.* Norman: Oklahoma Anthropological Society.

Bartram, Laurence E. 1997. "A Comparison of Kua (Botswana) and Hadza (Tanzania) Bow and Arrow Hunting." In *Projectile Technology*, ed. Heidi Knecht, 321–43. New York: Plenum. https://doi.org/10.1007/978-1-4899-1851-2_13.

Bar-Yosef, Ofer. 2015. "Chinese Palaeolithic Challenges for Interpretations of Palaeolithic Archaeology." *L'Anthropologie* 53 (1–2): 77–92.

Bar-Yosef, Ofer, and Anna Belfer-Cohen. 2001. "From Africa to Eurasia: Early Dispersals." *Quaternary International* 75 (1): 19–28. https://doi.org/10.1016/S1040-6182(00)00074-4.

Bar-Yosef, Ofer, and Anna Belfer-Cohen. 2013. "Following Pleistocene Road Signs of Human Dispersals Across Eurasia." *Quaternary International* 285:30–43. https://doi.org/10.1016/j.quaint.2011.07.043.

Bar-Yosef, Ofer, Metin I. Eren, Jiarong Yuan, David J. Cohen, and Yiyuan Li. 2012. "Were Bamboo Tools Made in Prehistoric Southeast Asia? An Experimental View from South China." *Quaternary International* 269:9–21. https://doi.org/10.1016/j.quaint.2011.03.026.

Basgall, Mark E. 1979. "To Trade, or Not to Trade: A Pomo Example." *Journal of California and Great Basin Anthropology* 1 (1): 178–82.

Bement, Leland C. 1999. *Bison Hunting at Cooper Site: Where Lightning Bolts Drew Thundering Herds.* Norman: University of Oklahoma Press.

Bement, Leland C., and Brian J. Carter. 2010. "Jake Bluff: Clovis Bison Hunting on the Southern Plains of North America." *American Antiquity* 75 (4): 907–33. https://doi.org/10.7183/0002-7316.75.4.907.

Bement, Leland C., and Brian J. Carter. 2015. "From Mammoth to Bison: Changing Clovis Prey Availability at the End of the Pleistocene." In *Clovis: On the Edge of a New Understanding*, ed. Ashley M. Smallwood and Thomas A. Jennings, 263–75. College Station: Texas A&M University Press.

Bethke, Brandi, María Nieves Zedeño, Geoffrey Jones, and Matthew Pailes. 2016 (Forthcoming). "Complementary Approaches to the Identification of Bison Processing for Storage at the Kutoyis Complex, Montana." *Journal of Archaeological Science: Reports.* https://doi.org/10.1016/j.jasrep.2016.05.028.

Bettinger, Robert L., Ripan Malhi, and Helen McCarthy. 1997. "Central Place Models of Acorn and Mussel Processing." *Journal of Archaeological Science* 24 (10): 887–99. https://doi.org/10.1006/jasc.1996.0168.

Bever, Michael R., and David J. Meltzer. 2007. "Exploring Variation in Paleoindian Life Ways: The Third Revised Edition of the Texas Clovis Fluted Point Survey." *Bulletin of the Texas Archeological Society* 78:65–99.

Beyries, Sylvie. 1988a. Étude tracéologique des racloirs du niveau IIA. In *Le gisement paléolithique moyen de Biache-Saint-Vaast (Pas-de-Calais)*, Vol. 1. *Stratigraphie, environnement, études archéologiques (1ère Partie)*, ed. Alain Tuffreau and Jean Sommé, 215–30. Mémoires 21. Paris: Société Préhistorique Française.

Beyries, Sylvie. 1988b. "Functional Variability of Lithic Sets in the Middle Paleolithic." In *Upper Pleistocene Prehistory of Western Eurasia*, ed. Harold L. Dibble and Anta Montet-White, 213–24. Philadelphia: University of Pennsylvania, Museum of Archaeology and Anthropology.

Beyries, Sylvie. 2008. "Modélisation du travail du cuir en ethnologie: Proposition d'un système ouvert à l'archéologie." *Anthropozoologica* 43 (1): 9–42.

Beyries, Sylvie, and Brian Hayden. 1993. "L'importance du travail du bois en préhistoire." In *Traces et fonction: Les gestes retrouvés*, Vol. 2, ed. Patricia C. Anderson, Sylvie Beyries, Marcel Otte, and Hugues Plisson, 283–85. Études et Recherches Archéologiques de l'Université de Liège (ERAUL) 50. Liège, Belgium: Université de Liège.

Beyries, Sylvie, and Hugues Plisson. 1998. "Pointes ou outils triangulaires? Données fonctionnelles dans le Moustérien levantin." *Paléorient* 24 (1): 5–24. https://doi.org/10.3406/paleo.1998.4666.

Biesele, Megan, and Steve Barclay. 2001. "Ju/'hoan Women's Tracking Knowledge and Its Contribution to Their Husbands' Hunting Success." *Kyoto University African Study Monographs* 26 (Supplement): 67–84.

Binford, Lewis R. 1979. "Organization and Formation Processes: Looking at Curated Technologies." *Journal of Anthropological Research* 35 (3): 255–73. https://doi.org/10.1086/jar.35.3.3629902.

Binford, Lewis R. 1980. "Willow Smoke and Dogs' Tails: Hunter-Gatherer Settlement Systems and Archaeological Site Formation." *American Antiquity* 45 (1): 4–20. https://doi.org/10.2307/279653.

Binford, Sally R., and Lewis R. Binford. 1969. "Stone Tools and Human Behavior."

Scientific American 220 (4): 70–84. https://doi.org/10.1038/scientificamerican 0469-70.

Bird, Caroline F. M. 1993. "Woman the Toolmaker: Evidence for Women's Use and Manufacture of Flaked Stone Tools in Australia and New Guinea." In *Women in Archaeology: A Feminist Critique*, ed. Hilary du Cros and Laurajane Smith, 22–30. Occasional Papers in Prehistory 23. Canberra, Australia: Australian National University, Research School of Pacific Studies, Department of Prehistory.

Blasco, Ruth, Josep Fernández Peris, and Jordi Rosell. 2010. "Several Different Strategies for Obtaining Animal Resources in the Late Middle Pleistocene: The Case of Level XII at Bolomor Cave (Valencia, Spain)." *Comptes Rendus. Palévol* 9 (4): 171–84. https://doi.org/10.1016/j.crpv.2010.05.004.

Bleed, Peter. 1986. "The Optimal Design of Hunting Weapons: Maintainability or Reliability." *American Antiquity* 51 (4): 737–47. https://doi.org/10.2307/280862.

Bliege Bird, Rebecca L., and Douglas W. Bird. 2008. "Why Women Hunt: Risk and Contemporary Foraging in a Western Desert Aboriginal Community." *Current Anthropology* 49 (4): 655–93.

Bliege Bird, Rebecca L., Brian F. Codding, and Douglas W. Bird. 2009. "What Explains Differences in Men's and Women's Production? Determinants of Gendered Foraging Inequalities among Martu." *Human Nature (Hawthorne, N.Y.)* 20 (2): 105–29. https://doi.org/10.1007/s12110-009-9061-9.

Bocherens, Hervé. 2009. "Neanderthal Dietary Habits: Review of the Isotopic Evidence." In *The Evolution of Hominin Diets: Integrating Approaches to the Study of Palaeolithic Subsistence*, ed. Jean-Jacques Hublin and Michael P. Richards, 241–50. Dordrecht, Netherlands: Springer. https://doi.org/10.1007/978-1-4020-9699-0_19.

Bodenhorn, Barbara. 1990. "'I'm Not the Great Hunter, My Wife Is': Iñupiat and Anthropological Models of Gender." *Études/Inuit/Studies* 14 (1–2):55–74.

Boëda, Eric, Jean-Michel Geneste, Christophe Griggo, Norbert Mercier, Sultan Muhesen, Jean-Louis Reyss, Ahmed Taha, and Hélène Valladas. 1999. "A Levallois Point Embedded in the Vertebra of a Wild Ass (*Equus africanus*): Hafting, Projectiles and Mousterian Hunting Weapons." *Antiquity* 73 (280): 394–402. https://doi.org/10.1017/S0003598X00088335.

Boëda, Eric, Jean-Michel Geneste, and Liliane Meignen. 1990. "Identification de chaînes opératoires lithiques du paléolithique ancien et moyen." *Paléo* 2:43–80.

Boesch, Christophe. 2002. "Cooperative Hunting Roles Among Taï Chimpanzees." *Human Nature (Hawthorne, N.Y.)* 13 (1): 27–46. https://doi.org/10.1007/s12110-002 -1013-6.

Bordes, François. 1961. "Mousterian Cultures in France." *Science* 134 (3482): 803–10. https://doi.org/10.1126/science.134.3482.803.

Bordes, François, and Denise de Sonneville-Bordes. 1970. "The Significance of Variability in Paleolithic Assemblages." *World Archaeology* 2 (1): 61–73. https://doi.org/10.1080/00438243.1970.9979464.

Borrazzo, Karen B. 2012. "Raw Material Availability, Flaking Quality, and Hunter-Gatherer Technological Decision Making in Northern Tierra del Fuego Island (Southern South America)." *Journal of Archaeological Science* 39 (8): 2643–54. https://doi.org/10.1016/j.jas.2012.03.018.

Borrazzo, Karen B., Flavia Morello, Luis Alberto Borrero, Massimo D'Orazio, María Clara Etchichury, Mauricio Massone, and Hernán De Angelis. 2015. "Caracterización de las materias primas líticas de Chorrillo Miraflores y su distribución arqueológica en el extremo meridional de Fuego-Patagonia." In *Intersecciones en antropología*, Volumen Especial 2: *Materias primas líticas en Patagonia. Localización, circulación y métodos de estudio de las Fuentes de Rocas de la Patagonia Argentino-Chilena*, ed. Jimena Alberti and María Victoria Fernández, 155–68. Buenos Aires: Facultad de Ciencias Sociales de la Universidad Nacional del Centro de la Provincia de Buenos Aires, Olavarría.

Borrero, Luis A. 2006. "Paleoindians without Mammoths and Archaeologists without Projectile Points? The Archaeology of the First Inhabitants of the Americas." In *Paleoindian Archaeology: A Hemispheric Perspective*, ed. Juliet E. Morrow and Cristóbal Gnecco, 9–20. Gainesville: University Press of Florida.

Bosquet, Dominique, Paula Jardon Giner, and Ivan Jadin. 2004. "L'Industrie lithique du site paléolithique moyen de Remicourt 'En Bia Flo' (Province de Liège, Belgique): Technologie, tracéologie et analyse spatiale." In *Le Paléolithique Moyen. Actes du XIVème Congrès UISPP, Université de Liège, Belgique, 2–8 Septembre 2001. Section 5, Sessions Générales et Posters*, ed. Philip Van Peer, Patrick Semal, and Dominique Bonjean, 257–74. BAR International Series S1239. Oxford: Archaeopress, British Archaeological Reports.

Boulanger, Matthew T., Briggs Buchanan, Michael J. O'Brien, Brian G. Redmond, Michael D. Glascock, and Metin I. Eren. 2015. "Neutron Activation Analysis of 12,900-Year-Old Stone Artifacts Confirms 450–510+ Km Clovis Tool-Stone Acquisition at Paleo Crossing (33ME274), Northeast Ohio, U.S.A." *Journal of Archaeological Science* 53:550–58. https://doi.org/10.1016/j.jas.2014.11.005.

Bourguignon, Laurence, Anne Delagnes, and Liliane Meignen. 2006. "Systèmes de production lithique, gestion des outillages et territoires au paléolithique moyen: Où se trouve la complexité?" In *Normes techniques et pratiques sociales: De la simplicité des outillages pré- et protohistoriques. Actes des XXVIe rencontres internationales d'archéologie et d'histoire d'Antibes, 20–22 octobre 2005*, ed. Laurence Astruc, François Bon, Vanessa Léa, Pierre-Yves Milcent, and Sylvie Philibert, 75–86. Antibes,

France: Éditions APDCA (Association pour la Promotion et la Diffusion des Connaissances Archéologiques).

Bousman, C. Britt. 1993. "Hunter-Gatherer Adaptations, Economic Risk and Tool Design." *Lithic Technology* 18 (1–2): 59–86. https://doi.org/10.1080/01977261.1993.11720897.

Bowler, James M. 1998. "Willandra Lakes Revisited: Environmental Framework for Human Occupation." *Archaeology in Oceania* 33 (3): 120–55. https://doi.org/10.1002/j.1834-4453.1998.tb00414.x.

Bradley, Bruce A. 1993. "Paleo-Indian Flaked Stone Technology in the North American High Plains." In *From Kostenki to Clovis: Upper Paleolithic—Paleo-Indian Adaptations*, ed. Olga Soffer and Nikolai D. Praslov, 251–62. New York: Plenum Press. https://doi.org/10.1007/978-1-4899-1112-4_18.

Bradley, Bruce A., and Michael B. Collins. 2014. "Imagining Clovis as a Cultural Revitalization Movement." In *Paleoamerican Odyssey*, ed. Kelly E. Graf, Caroline V. Ketron, and Michael R. Waters, 247–55. College Station: Texas A&M University, Center for the Study of the First Americans.

Bradley, Bruce A., Michael B. Collins, and Andrew Hemmings. 2010. *Clovis Technology: Archaeology Series 17*. Ann Arbor, MI: International Monographs in Prehistory.

Bradley, Richard. 2000. *An Archaeology of Natural Places*. New York: Routledge.

Brenet, Michel, Jean Pierre Chadelle, Émilie Claud, David Colonge, Anne Delagnes, Marianne Deschamps, Mila Folgado, Brad Gravina, and Ewen Ihuel. 2017. "The Function and Role of Bifaces in the Late Middle Paleolithic of Southwestern France: Examples from the Charente and Dordogne to the Basque Country." *Quaternary International* 428 (Part A): 151–69.

Brightman, Robert A. 1993. *Grateful Prey: Rock Cree Human-Animal Relationships*. Berkeley: University of California Press.

Brink, John W., and Bob Dawe. 2003. "Hot Rocks as Scarce Resources: The Use, Re-Use and Abandonment of Heating Stones at Head-Smashed-In Buffalo Jump." *Plains Anthropologist* 48 (186): 85–104.

Brosowske, Scott D. 2004. "Obsidian Procurement and Distribution during the Middle Ceramic Period of the Southern High Plains: Evidence for the Emergence of Regional Trade Centers." *Council of Texas Archeologists* 28 (2): 16–28.

Brosowske, Scott D. 2005. "The Evolution of Exchange in Small-Scale Societies of the Southern High Plains." PhD dissertation, Department of Anthropology, University of Oklahoma, Norman, OK.

Brück, Joanna. 1999. "Ritual and Rationality: Some Problems of Interpretation in European Archaeology." *European Journal of Archaeology* 2 (3): 313–44.

Brugge, David M. 1961. "History, Huki, and Warfare—Some Random Data on the Lower Pima." *Kiva* 26 (4): 6–16. https://doi.org/10.1080/00231940.1961.11757614.

Brumbach, Hetty Jo, and Robert Jarvenpa. 1997. "Ethnoarchaeology of Subsistence Space and Gender: A Subarctic Dene Case." *American Antiquity* 62 (3): 414–36. https://doi.org/10.2307/282163.

Brumbach, Hetty Jo, and Robert Jarvenpa. 2006. "Gender Dynamics in Hunter-Gatherer Society: Archaeological Methods and Perspectives." In *Handbook of Gender in Archaeology*, ed. Sarah M. Nelson, 503–36. Lanham, MD: Altamira.

Brumm, Adam. 2010. "'The Falling Sky': Symbolic and Cosmological Associations of the Mt William Greenstone Axe Quarry, Central Victoria, Australia." *Cambridge Archaeological Journal* 20 (2): 179–96. https://doi.org/10.1017/S0959774310000223.

Buchanan, Briggs, Metin I. Eren, Matthew T. Boulanger, and Michael J. O'Brien. 2015. "Size, Shape, Scars, and Spatial Patterning: A Quantitative Assessment of Late Pleistocene (Clovis) Point Resharpening." *Journal of Archaeological Science: Reports* 3:11–21. https://doi.org/10.1016/j.jasrep.2015.05.011.

Buchanan, Briggs W., and Marcus J. Hamilton. 2009. "A Formal Test of the Origin of Variation in North American Early Paleoindian Projectile Points." *American Antiquity* 74 (2): 279–98. https://doi.org/10.1017/S0002731600048605.

Buchanan, Briggs W., David Kilby, Bruce B. Huckell, Michael J. O'Brien, and Mark Collard. 2012. "A Morphometric Assessment of the Intended Function of Cached Clovis Points." *PloS One* 7 (2): e30530. https://doi.org/10.1371/journal.pone.0030530.

Buck, Laura T., J. Colette Berbesque, Brian M. Wood, and Chris B. Stringer. 2016. "Tropical Forager Gastrophagy and Its Implications for Extinct Hominin Diets." *Journal of Archaeological Science: Reports* 5:672–79. https://doi.org/10.1016/j.jasrep.2015.09.025.

Buck, Laura T., and Chris B. Stringer. 2014. "Having the Stomach for It: A Contribution to Neanderthal Diets?" *Quaternary Science Reviews* 96:161–67. https://doi.org/10.1016/j.quascirev.2013.09.003.

Buehler, Kent J. 1997. "Where's the Cliff? Late Archaic Bison Kills in the Southern Plains." *Plains Anthropologist* 42 (159): 135–43.

Bunn, Henry T., Laurence E. Bartram, and Ellen M. Kroll. 1988. "Variability in Bone Assemblage Formation from Hadza Hunting, Scavenging, and Carcass Processing." *Journal of Anthropological Archaeology* 7 (4): 412–57. https://doi.org/10.1016/0278-4165(88)90004-9.

Bunn, Henry T., and Alia N. Gurtov. 2014. "Prey Mortality Profiles Indicate that Early Pleistocene *Homo* at Olduvai Was an Ambush Predator." *Quaternary International* 322–23:44–53. https://doi.org/10.1016/j.quaint.2013.11.002.

Burch, Ernest S. 1972. "The Caribou/Wild Reindeer as a Human Resource." *American Antiquity* 37 (3): 339–68. https://doi.org/10.2307/278435.

Burch, Ernest S. 2006. *Social Life in Northwest Alaska: The Structure of Inupiaq Eskimo Nations.* Fairbanks: University of Alaska Press.

Burke, Adrian L. 2006. "Paleoindian Ranges in Northeastern North America Based on Lithic Raw Materials Sourcing." In *Notions de territoire et de mobilité: Exemples de l'Europe et des Premières Nations en Amérique du Nord avant le Contact Européen. Actes de Sessions Présentées au Xe Congrès Annuel de l'Association Européenne des Archéologues (Lyon, 8–11 septembre 2004),* ed. Céline Bressy, Ariane Burke, Pierre Chalard, and Hélène Martin, 77–89. Études et Recherches Archéologiques de l'Université de Liège (ERAUL) 116. Liège, Belgium: Université de Liège.

Butler, William B. 1975. "Two Initial Middle Missouri Tradition Tool Kits." *Plains Anthropologist* 20 (67): 53–59.

Callahan, Errett. 1979. "The Basics of Biface Knapping in the Eastern Fluted Point Tradition: A Manual for Flintknappers and Lithic Analysts." *Archaeology of Eastern North America* 7 (1): 1–179.

Cameron, Catherine M. 2001. "Pink Chert, Projectile Points, and the Chacoan Regional System." *American Antiquity* 66 (1): 79–101. https://doi.org/10.2307/2694319.

Carbone, Chris, and John L. Gittleman. 2002. "A Common Rule for the Scaling of Carnivore Density." *Science* 295 (5563): 2273–76. https://doi.org/10.1126/science .1067994.

Carbonell, Eudald, and Zaida Castro-Curel. 1992. "Palaeolithic Wooden Artefacts from the Abric Romani (Capellades, Barcelona, Spain)." *Journal of Archaeological Science* 19 (6): 707–19. https://doi.org/10.1016/0305-4403(92)90040-A.

Carr, Philip J., and Andrew P. Bradbury. 2011. "Learning from Lithics: A Perspective on the Foundation and Future of the Organization of Technology." *PaleoAnthropology* 2011:305–19.

Catlin, George. 1841. *Letters and Notes on the Manners, Customs, and Condition of the North American Indians, Written During Eight Years' Travel amongst the Wildest Tribes of Indians in North America in 1832, 33, 34, 35, 36, 37, 38, and 39.* Vol. 1. London: Egyptian Hall, Piccadilly.

Chabai, Victor P. 2003. "The Chronological and Industrial Variability of the Middle to Upper Paleolithic Transition in Eastern Europe." In *The Chronology of the Aurignacian and of the Transitional Technocomplexes: Dating, Stratigraphies, Cultural Implications. Proceedings of Symposium 6.1, XIVth Congress of the UISPP, University of Liege, Belgium, September 2–8, 2001,* ed. João Zilhão and Francesco d'Errico, 71–86. Trabalhos de Arqueologia 33. Lisboa, Portugal: Instituto Português de Arqueologia.

Churchill, Steven E. 2014. *Thin on the Ground: Neandertal Biology, Archeology, and Ecology. Advances in Human Biology.* Chichester: Wiley-Blackwell. https://doi.org/10.1002/9781118590836.

Churchill, Steven E., Robert G. Franciscus, Hilary A. McKean-Peraza, Julie A. Daniel, and Brittany R. Warren. 2009. "Shanidar 3 Neandertal Rib Puncture Wound and Paleolithic Weaponry." *Journal of Human Evolution* 57 (2): 163–78. https://doi.org/10.1016/j.jhevol.2009.05.010.

Clarkson, Chris. 2016. "Testing Archaeological Approaches to Determining Past Projectile Delivery Systems Using Ethnographic and Experimental Data." In *Multidisciplinary Approaches to the Study of Stone Age Weaponry*, ed. Radu Iovita and Katsuhiro Sano, 189–201. Dordrecht, Netherlands: Springer. https://doi.org/10.1007/978-94-017-7602-8_13.

Cocking, Matthew. 1909. "An Adventurer from Hudson Bay: Journal of Matthew Cocking, from York Factory to the Blackfeet Country, 1772–73." In *Transactions of the Royal Society of Canada, Series 3*, vol. 2, ed. Lawrence J. Burpee, 91–121. Ottawa, ON: Royal Society of Canada.

Collard, Mark, Lia Tarle, Dennis Sandgathe, and Alexander Allan. 2016. "Faunal Evidence for a Difference in Clothing Use between Neanderthals and Early Modern Humans in Europe." *Journal of Anthropological Archaeology* 44 (Part B): 235–46. https://doi.org/10.1016/j.jaa.2016.07.010.

Conard, Nicholas J. 2011. "The Demise of the Neanderthal Cultural Niche and the Beginning of the Upper Paleolithic in Southwestern Germany." In *Neanderthal Lifeways, Subsistence and Technology: One Hundred Fifty Years of Neanderthal Study*, ed. Nicholas J. Conard and Jürgen Richter, 223–40. New York: Springer. https://doi.org/10.1007/978-94-007-0415-2_19.

Cooper, Judith R. 2008. "Bison Hunting and Late Prehistoric Human Subsistence Economies in the Great Plains." PhD dissertation, Department of Anthropology, Southern Methodist University, Dallas, TX.

Cordain, Loren, Janette Brand Miller, S. Boyd Eaton, Neil Mann, Susanne H. A. Holt, and John D. Speth. 2000. "Plant-Animal Subsistence Ratios and Macronutrient Energy Estimations in Worldwide Hunter-Gatherer Diets." *American Journal of Clinical Nutrition* 71 (3): 682–92.

Cordain, Loren, Bruce A. Watkins, Gregory L. Florant, Marguerite Kelher, Laura L. Rogers, and Yong Li. 2002. "Fatty Acid Analysis of Wild Ruminant Tissues: Evolutionary Implications for Reducing Diet-Related Chronic Disease." *European Journal of Clinical Nutrition* 56 (3): 181–91. https://doi.org/10.1038/sj.ejcn.1601307.

Costa, August G. 2012. "Were There Stone-Tipped Armatures in the South Asia Middle Paleolithic?" *Quaternary International* 269:22–30. https://doi.org/10.1016/j.quaint.2011.01.044.

Costamagno, Sandrine. 2013. "Bone Grease Rendering in Mousterian Contexts: The Case of Noisetier Cave (Fréchet-Aure, Hautes-Pyrénées, France)." In *Zooarchaeology and Modern Human Origins: Human Hunting Behavior during the Later Pleistocene*, ed. Jamie L. Clark and John D. Speth, 209–25. New York: Springer. https://doi.org/10.1007/978-94-007-6766-9_13.

Cowie, Isaac. 1913. *The Company of Adventurers: A Narrative of Seven Years in the Service of the Hudson's Bay Company During 1867–1874 on the Great Buffalo Plains with Historical and Biographical Notes and Comments.* Toronto: William Briggs.

Cox, Samuel S. 1887. *Diversions of a Diplomat in Turkey.* New York: Charles L. Webster.

Crawford, Michael A. 1968. "Fatty-Acid Ratios in Free-Living and Domestic Animals." *Lancet* 291 (7556): 1329–33. https://doi.org/10.1016/S0140-6736(68)92034-5.

Creel, Darrell G. 1991. "Bison Hides in Late Prehistoric Exchange in the Southern Plains." *American Antiquity* 56 (1): 40–49. https://doi.org/10.2307/280971.

Creel, Darrell G., Jeffrey R. Ferguson, and Nancy A. Kenmotsu. 2013. "A Compositional Analysis of Central Texas Hunter-Gatherer Ceramics and Its Implications for Mobility, Ethnic Group Territory, and Interaction." *Bulletin of the Texas Archeological Society* 84:29–83.

Cronk, Lee. 1991. "Human Behavioral Ecology." *Annual Review of Anthropology* 20 (1): 25–53. https://doi.org/10.1146/annurev.an.20.100191.000325.

Curr, Edward Micklethwaite. 1886. *The Australian Race: Its Origin, Languages, Customs, Place of Landing in Australia, and the Routes by Which It Spread Itself over That Continent.* Vol. 2. Melbourne, Australia: John Ferres.

Damuth, John. 1981. "Population Density and Body Size in Mammals." *Nature* 290 (5808): 699–700. https://doi.org/10.1038/290699a0.

Dean, Charles E. 2004. *The Modern Warrior's Combat Load: Dismounted Operations in Afghanistan, April–May 2003.* Fort Leavenworth, KS: US Army Center for Army Lessons Learned, Task Force Devil Combined Arms Assessment Team.

Dean, Joanna. 2008. "Review Essay—Big Game and the State: The History of the Hunt in Canada." *Left History: An Interdisciplinary Journal of Historical Inquiry and Debate* 13 (1): 143–55.

de Laguna, Frederica. 2000. *Travels among the Dena: Exploring Alaska's Yukon Valley.* Seattle: University of Washington Press.

de la Torre, Ignacio, Jorge Martínez-Moreno, and Rafael Mora. 2013. "Change and Stasis in the Iberian Middle Paleolithic: Considerations on the Significance of

Mousterian Technological Variability." *Current Anthropology* 54 (S8 Supplement 8): S320–36. https://doi.org/10.1086/673861.

Deller, D. Brian, and Christopher J. Ellis. 1984. "Crowfield: A Preliminary Report on a Probable Paleo-Indian Cremation in Southwestern Ontario." *Archaeology of Eastern North America* 12:41–71.

Deller, D. Brian, and Christopher J. Ellis. 2001. "Evidence for Late Paleoindian Ritual from the Caradoc Site (AfHj-104), Southwestern Ontario, Canada." *American Antiquity* 66 (2): 267–84. https://doi.org/10.2307/2694608.

Deller, D. Brian, Christopher J. Ellis, and James R. Keron. 2009. "Understanding Cache Variability: A Deliberately Burned Early Paleoindian Tool Assemblage from the Crowfield Site, Southwestern Ontario, Canada." *American Antiquity* 74 (2): 371–97. https://doi.org/10.1017/S0002731600048642.

d'Errico, Francesco, Michèle Julien, Despina Liolios, Marian Vanhaeren, and Dominique Baffier. 2003. "Many Awls in Our Argument: Bone Tool Manufacture and Use in the Châtelperronian and Aurignacian Levels of the Grotte du Renne at Arcy-sur-Cure." In *The Chronology of the Aurignacian and of the Transitional Technocomplexes: Dating, Stratigraphies, Cultural Implications. Proceedings of Symposium 6.1 of the XIVth Congress of the UISPP, Liege, Belgium, 2001*, ed. João Zilhão and Francesco d'Errico, 247–70. Trabalhos de Arqueologia 33. Lisbon, Portugal: Instituto Português de Arqueologia.

Dietrich, Oliver, Manfred Heun, Jens Notroff, Klaus Schmidt, and Martin Zarnkow. 2012. "The Role of Cult and Feasting in the Emergence of Neolithic Communities: New Evidence from Göbekli Tepe, South-Eastern Turkey." *Antiquity* 86 (333): 674–95. https://doi.org/10.1017/S0003598X00047840.

Dillian, Carolyn D. 2002. "More Than Toolstone: Differential Utilization of Glass Mountain Obsidian." PhD dissertation, Department of Anthropology, University of California-Berkeley, Berkeley, CA.

Dinnis, Robert, Alfred F. Pawlik, and Claire Gaillard. 2009. "Bladelet Cores as Weapon Tips? Hafting Residue Identification and Micro-wear Analysis of Three Carinated Burins from the Late Aurignacian of Les Vachons, France." *Journal of Archaeological Science* 36 (9): 1922–34. https://doi.org/10.1016/j.jas.2009.04.020.

Drain, Jace, Rob M. Orr, Daniel C. Billing, and Stephan Rudzki. 2010. "Human Dimensions of Heavy Load Carriage." In *Full Spectrum Threats: Adaptive Responses. Land Warfare Conference Proceedings, Brisbane 15–19, Australia, November 2010*, ed. Vinod Puri and Despina Filippidis, 43–63, Canberra, Australia.

Dunn, John. 1844. *History of the Oregon Territory and British North-American Fur Trade; with an Account of the Habits and Customs of the Principal Native Tribes on the Northern Continent*. London: Edwards and Hughes.

Duran, Jean-Pierre, and Narcís Soler. 2006. "Variabilité des modalités de débitage et des productions lithiques dans les Industries Moustériennes de la Grotte de l'Arbreda, Secteur Alpha (Serinyà, Espagne)." *Bulletin de la Société Préhistorique Française* 103 (2): 241–62. https://doi.org/10.3406/bspf.2006.13431.

Eisert, Regina. 2011. "Hypercarnivory and the Brain: Protein Requirements of Cats Reconsidered." *Journal of Comparative Physiology. B, Biochemical, Systemic, and Environmental Physiology* 181 (1): 1–17. https://doi.org/10.1007/s00360-010-0528-0.

Eixea, Aleix, Valentin Villaverde, and João Zilhão. 2016. "Not Only Flint: Levallois on Quartzite and Limestone at Abrigo de la Quebrada (Valencia, Spain): Implications for Neandertal Behavior." *Journal of Anthropological Research* 72 (1): 24–57. https://doi.org/10.1086/685265.

Ellis, Christopher J. 1989. "The Explanation of Northeastern Paleoindian Lithic Procurement Patterns." In *Eastern Paleoindian Lithic Resource Use*, ed. Christopher J. Ellis and Jonathan C. Lothrop, 139–64. Boulder, CO: Westview Press.

Ellis, Christopher J. 2009. "The Crowfield and Caradoc Sites, Ontario: Glimpses of Palaeo-Indian Sacred Ritual and World View." In *Painting the Past with a Broad Brush: Papers in Honour of James Valliere Wright*, ed. David L. Keenlyside and Jean-Luc Pilon, 319–52. Mercury Series Archaeology Paper 170. Gatineau, Quebec: Canadian Museum of Civilization.

Ellis, Christopher J. 2013. "Clovis Lithic Technology: The Devil Is in the Details." *Revista de Antropologia* 42:127–60.

Ellis, Christopher J., and D. Brian Deller, eds. 2000. *An Early Paleo-Indian Site near Parkhill, Ontario. Archaeological Survey of Canada, Mercury Series 159*. Gatineau, Quebec: Canadian Museum of Civilization.

Ellis, George E. 1889. "The Hudson Bay Company." In *Narrative and Critical History of America*, vol. 8. ed. Justin Winsor, 1–64. Boston: Houghton, Mifflin and Company.

Emerson, Alice M. 1990. "The Archaeological Implications of Variability in the Economic Anatomy of Bison bison." PhD Dissertation, Department of Anthropology, Washington State University, Pullman, WA.

Eren, Metin I., and Brian N. Andrews. 2013. "Were Bifaces Used as Mobile Cores by Clovis Foragers in the North American Lower Great Lakes Region? An Archaeological Test of Experimentally Derived Quantitative Predictions." *American Antiquity* 78 (1): 166–80. https://doi.org/10.7183/0002-7316.78.1.166.

Eren, Metin I., Stephen J. Lycett, Christopher I. Roos, and C. Garth Sampson. 2011. "Toolstone Constraints on Knapping Skill: Levallois Reduction with Two Different Raw Materials." *Journal of Archaeological Science* 38 (10): 2731–39. https://doi.org/10.1016/j.jas.2011.06.011.

Eren, Metin I., Christopher I. Roos, Brett A. Story, Noreen von Cramon-Taubadel, and Stephen J. Lycett. 2014. "The Role of Raw Material Differences in Stone Tool Shape Variation: An Experimental Assessment." *Journal of Archaeological Science* 49:472–87. https://doi.org/10.1016/j.jas.2014.05.034.

Erlandson, Jon M., Douglas J. Kennett, Brendan J. Culleton, Ted Goebel, Greg C. Nelson, and Craig Skinner. 2014. "Eyed Bone Needles from a Younger Dryas Paleoindian Component at Tule Lake Rock Shelter, Northern California." *American Antiquity* 79 (4): 776–81. https://doi.org/10.7183/0002-7316.79.4.776.

Estalrrich, Almudena, and Antonio Rosas. 2015. "Division of Labor by Sex and Age in Neandertals: An Approach through the Study of Activity-Related Dental Wear." *Journal of Human Evolution* 80:51–63. https://doi.org/10.1016/j.jhevol .2014.07.007.

Faivre, Jean-Philippe, ed. 2011. *Organisation techno-économique des industries du paléolithique moyen récent dans le nord-est Aquitain. BAR International Series S2280.* Oxford: British Archaeological Reports, Archaeopress.

Faivre, Jean-Philippe, Emmanuel Discamps, Brad Gravina, Alain Turq, Jean-Luc Guadelli, and Michel Lenoir. 2014. "The Contribution of Lithic Production Systems to the Interpretation of Mousterian Industrial Variability in South-Western France: The Example of Combe-Grenal (Dordogne, France)." *Quaternary International* 350:227–40. https://doi.org/10.1016/j.quaint.2014.05.048.

FAO (Food and Agriculture Organization). 1990. *Manual on Simple Methods of Meat Preservation. FAO Animal Production and Health Paper 79.* Rome: Food and Agriculture Organization of the United Nations.

Fawcett, William B. 1987. "Communal Hunts, Human Aggregations, Social Variation, and Climatic Change: Bison Utilization by Prehistoric Inhabitants of the Great Plains." PhD dissertation, Department of Anthropology, University of Massachusetts, Amherst, MA.

Féblot-Augustins, Jehanne. 2009. "Revisiting European Upper Paleolithic Raw Material Transfers: The Demise of the Cultural Ecological Paradigm?" In *Lithic Materials and Paleolithic Societies*, ed. Brian Adams and Brooke S. Blades, 25–46. Hoboken, NJ: Wiley-Blackwell. https://doi.org/10.1002/9781444311976.ch3.

Flas, Damien. 2013. "Les industries à pointes foliacées du paléolithique supérieur ancien dans le nord-ouest de l'Europe: Le Lincombien-Ranisien-Jerzmanowicien." In *Le paléolithique supérieur ancien de l'Europe du nord-ouest: Réflexions et synthèses à partir d'un projet collectif de recherche sur le centre et le sud du bassin parisien. Actes du Colloque de Sens (15–18 avril 2009), Paris*, ed. Pierre Bodu, Lucie Chehmana, Laurent Klaric, Ludovic Mevel, Sylvain Soriano, and Nicolas Teyssandier, 445–60. Mémoire 56. Paris: Société Préhistorique Française.

Flegenheimer, Nora, Cristina Bayón, Miguel Valente, Jorge Baeza, and Jorge Femenías. 2003. "Long Distance Tool Stone Transport in the Argentine Pampas." *Quaternary International* 109–10:49–64. https://doi.org/10.1016/S1040-6182 (02)00202-1.

Flegenheimer, Nora, Natalia Mazzia, and Celeste Weitzel. 2015. "Landscape and Rocks in the East-Central Portion of the Tandilia Range (Buenos Aires Province, Argentina)." *PaleoAmerica* 1 (2): 163–80. https://doi.org/10.1179/20555563 15Z.0000000017.

Fogelin, Lars. 2007. "The Archaeology of Religious Ritual." *Annual Review of Anthropology* 36 (1): 55–71. https://doi.org/10.1146/annurev.anthro.36.081406.094425.

Foley, Robert A., and Marta M. Lahr. 1997. "Mode 3 Technologies and the Evolution of Modern Humans." *Cambridge Archaeological Journal* 7 (1): 3–36. https://doi.org /10.1017/S0959774300001451.

Food Standards Agency. 2002. *McCance and Widdowson's* The Composition of Foods, *Sixth Summary Edition*. Cambridge: Royal Society of Chemistry.

Frahm, Ellery, Joshua M. Feinberg, Beverly A. Schmidt-Magee, Keith N. Wilkinson, Boris Gasparyan, Benik Yeritsyan, and Daniel S. Adler. 2016. "Middle Palaeolithic Toolstone Procurement Behaviors at Lusakert Cave 1, Hrazdan Valley, Armenia." *Journal of Human Evolution* 91:73–92. https://doi.org/10.1016/j.jhevol.2015.10.008.

Frink, Lisa. 2009. "The Identity Division of Labor in Native Alaska." *American Anthropologist* 111 (1): 21–29. https://doi.org/10.1111/j.1548-1433.2009.01074.x.

Frison, George C. 1968. "Site 48SH312: An Early Middle Period Bison Kill in the Powder River Basin of Wyoming." *Plains Anthropologist* 13 (39): 31–39.

Frison, George C., ed. 1974. *The Casper Site: A Hell Gap Bison Kill on the High Plains*. New York: Academic Press.

Frison, George C. 1978. *Prehistoric Hunters of the High Plains*. New York: Academic Press.

Frison, George C., ed. 1996. *The Mill Iron Site*. Albuquerque: University of New Mexico Press.

Frison, George C., and Dennis J. Stanford, eds. 1982. *The Agate Basin Site: A Record of the Paleoindian Occupation of the Northwestern High Plains*. New York: Academic Press.

Galbraith, Jayson K., Gerald Hauer, Larissa Helbig, Zhiquan Wang, Martin J. Marchello, and Laksiri A. Goonewardene. 2006. "Nutrient Profiles in Retail Cuts of Bison Meat." *Meat Science* 74 (4): 648–54. https://doi.org/10.1016/j.meatsci .2006.05.015.

Gardner, William M. 1989. "An Examination of Cultural Change in the Late Pleistocene and Early Holocene (circa 9200 to 6800 BC)." In *Paleoindian Research in Virginia: A Synthesis*, ed. J. Mark Wittkofski and Theodore R. Reinhart, 5–51. Special Publication 19. Richmond, VA: Archaeological Society of Virginia.

Gaudzinski, Sabine. 2004. "A Matter of High Resolution? The Eemian Interglacial (OIS 5e) in North-Central Europe and Middle Palaeolithic Subsistence." *International Journal of Osteoarchaeology* 14 (3–4): 201–11. https://doi.org/10.1002/oa.756.

Gaudzinski, Sabine. 2006. "Monospecific or Species-Dominated Faunal Assemblages during the Middle Paleolithic in Europe." In *Transitions before the Transition: Evolution and Stability in the Middle Paleolithic and Middle Stone Age*, ed. Erella Hovers and Steven L. Kuhn, 137–47. New York: Springer. https://doi.org /10.1007/0-387-24661-4_8.

Gaudzinski, Sabine, and Wil Roebroeks. 2000. "Adults Only: Reindeer Hunting at the Middle Palaeolithic Site Salzgitter Lebenstedt, Northern Germany." *Journal of Human Evolution* 38 (4): 497–521. https://doi.org/10.1006/jhev.1999.0359.

Gaudzinski-Windheuser, Sabine. 2016. "Hunting Lesions in Pleistocene and Early Holocene European Bone Assemblages and Their Implications for Our Knowledge on the Use of Lithic Projectile Technology." In *Multidisciplinary Approaches to the Study of Stone Age Weaponry*, ed. Radu Iovita and Katsuhiro Sano, 77–100. Dordrecht, The Netherlands: Springer. https://doi.org/10.1007/978-94-017-7602-8_6.

Gell, Alfred. 1988. "Technology and Magic." *Anthropology Today* 4 (2): 6–9. https://doi.org/10.2307/3033230.

Geneste, Jean-Michel. 1988. "Systèmes d'approvisionnement en matières premières au paléolithique moyen et au paléolithique supérieur en Aquitaine." In *L'Homme de Neandertal, Vol. 8. La Mutation*, ed. Marcel Otte, 61–70. Études et Recherches Archéologiques de l'Université de Liège (ERAUL) 35. Liège, Belgium: Université de Liège.

Geneste, Jean-Michel. 1989. "Economie des Ressources Lithiques dans le Moustérien du Sud-Ouest de la France." In *L'Homme de Neandertal, Vol. 6. La Subsistance*, ed. Marcel Otte, 75–97. Études et Recherches Archéologiques de l'Université de Liège (ERAUL) 33. Liège, Belgium: Université de Liège.

Gero, Joan M. 1991. "Genderlithics: Women's Roles in Stone Tool Production." In *Engendering Archaeology: Women and Prehistory*, ed. Joan M. Gero and Margaret W. Conkey, 163–93. Oxford: Basil Blackwell.

Gero, Joan M. 2000. "The Social World of Prehistoric Facts: Gender and Power in Paleoindian Research." In *Interpretive Archaeology: A Reader*, ed. Julian Thomas, 304–16. London: Leicester University Press.

Gero, Joan M. 2002. "Phenomenal Points of Folsom." In *Folsom Technology and Lifeways*, ed. John E. Clark and Michael B. Collins, 333–41. Walnut Creek, CA: Left Coast Press.

Gilby, Ian C., Lauren J. N. Brent, Emily E. Wroblewski, Rebecca S. Rudicell, Beatrice H. Hahn, Jane Goodall, and Anne E. Pusey. 2013. "Fitness Benefits of Coalitionary Aggression in Male Chimpanzees." *Behavioral Ecology and Sociobiology* 67 (3): 373–81. https://doi.org/10.1007/s00265-012-1457-6.

Gillespie, Jason D. 2007. "Enculturing an Unknown World: Caches and Clovis Landscape Ideology." *Canadian Journal of Archaeology* 31 (2): 171–89.

Gilligan, Ian. 2007. "Neanderthal Extinction and Modern Human Behaviour: The Role of Climate Change and Clothing." *World Archaeology* 39 (4): 499–514. https://doi.org/10.1080/00438240701680492.

Gilligan, Ian. 2014. "Clothing and Modern Human Behaviour: The Challenge from Tasmania." In *Southern Asia, Australia and the Search for Human Origins*, ed. Robin Dennell and Martin Porr, 189–99. New York: Cambridge University Press. https://doi.org/10.1017/CBO9781139084741.015.

Gingerich, Joseph A. M., and Dennis J. Stanford. 2016 (Forthcoming). "Lessons from Ginsberg: An Analysis of Elephant Butchery Tools." *Quaternary International*. https://doi.org/10.1016/j.quaint.2016.03.025.

Godman, John D. 1836. *American Natural History, to Which Is Added His Last Work, the Rambles of a Naturalist, with a Biographical Sketch of the Author*. 3rd ed. Vol. 2. Philadelphia: Hogan and Thompson.

Goodyear, Albert C. 1979. *A Hypothesis for the Use of Cryptocrystalline Raw Materials among Paleo-Indian Groups of North America. Research Manuscript Series Book 156*. Columbia, SC: University of South Carolina, South Carolina Institute of Archeology and Anthropology.

Gould, Richard A. 1978. "The Anthropology of Human Residues." *American Anthropologist* 80 (4): 815–35. https://doi.org/10.1525/aa.1978.80.4.02a00030.

Gould, Richard A., and Sherry Saggers. 1985. "Lithic Procurement in Central Australia: A Closer Look at Binford's Idea of Embeddedness in Archaeology." *American Antiquity* 50 (1): 117–36. https://doi.org/10.2307/280637.

Gramly, Richard M. 1977. "Deerskins and Hunting Territories: Competition for a Scarce Resource of the Northeastern Woodlands." *American Antiquity* 42 (4): 601–5. https://doi.org/10.2307/278933.

Gramly, Richard M., and Garry L. Summers. 1986. "Nobles Pond: A Fluted Point Site in Northeastern Ohio." *Midcontinental Journal of Archaeology, MCJA* 11 (1): 97–123.

Gramly, Richard M., and Carl Yahnig. 1991. "The Adams Site (15Ch90) and the Little River, Christian County, Kentucky, Clovis Workshop Complex." *Southeastern Archaeology* 10 (2): 134–45.

Gravina, Brad, and Emmanuel Discamps. 2015. "MTA-B or Not To Be? Recycled Bifaces and Shifting Hunting Strategies at Le Moustier and Their Implication for the Late Middle Palaeolithic in Southwestern France." *Journal of Human Evolution* 84:83–98. https://doi.org/10.1016/j.jhevol.2015.04.005.

Groleau, Amy B. 2009. "Special Finds: Locating Animism in the Archaeological Record." *Cambridge Archaeological Journal* 19 (3): 398–406. https://doi.org/10.1017/S0959774309000584.

Groman-Yaroslavski, Iris, Yossi Zaidner, and Mina Weinstein-Evron. 2016. "Mousterian Abu Sif Points: Foraging Tools of the Early Middle Paleolithic Site of Misliya Cave, Mount Carmel, Israel." *Journal of Archaeological Science: Reports* 7:312–23. https://doi.org/10.1016/j.jasrep.2016.05.002.

Grosvenor, Edwin A. 1915. "Constantinople and Sancta Sophia." *National Geographic* 27 (January–June): 459–506.

Grove, Matt. 2010. "Logistical Mobility Reduces Subsistence Risk in Hunting Economies." *Journal of Archaeological Science* 37 (8): 1913–21. https://doi.org/10.1016/j.jas.2010.02.017.

Hanson, Jeffrey R. 1986. "Adjustment and Adaptation on the Northern Plains: The Case of Equestrianism among the Hidatsa." *Plains Anthropologist* 31 (112): 93–108.

Hardy, Bruce L. 2010. "Climatic Variability and Plant Food Distribution in Pleistocene Europe: Implications for Neanderthal Diet and Subsistence." *Quaternary Science Reviews* 29 (5–6): 662–79. https://doi.org/10.1016/j.quascirev.2009.11.016.

Hargrave, Joseph J. 1871. *Red River*. Montreal, Quebec: John Lovell.

Harper, William H., Joseph J. Knapik, and Rene de Pontbriand. 1996. *Investigation of Female Load Carrying Performance. MIPR Number 95MM5589*. Frederick, MD: US Army Medical Research and Materiel Command, Fort Detrick.

Harro, Douglas R. 1997. "Patterns of Lithic Raw Material Procurement on the Pajarito Plateau, New Mexico." MA thesis, Department of Anthropology, Washington State University, Pullman, WA.

Harry, Karen G. 1989. "The Obsidian Assemblage from Homol'ovi III: Social and Economic Implications." *Kiva* 54 (3): 285–96. https://doi.org/10.1080/00231940.1989.11758122.

Hatt, Gudmund, and Kirsten Taylor. 1969. "Arctic Skin Clothing in Eurasia and America: An Ethnographic Study." *Arctic Anthropology* 5 (2): 3–132.

Hawkes, Kristen. 2000. "Hunting and the Evolution of Egalitarian Societies: Lessons from the Hadza." In *Hierarchies in Action: Cui Bono?* ed. Michael W. Diehl, 59–83. Occasional Paper 27. Carbondale, IL: Southern Illinois University, Center for Archaeological Investigations.

Hawkes, Kristen, Kim Hill, and James F. O'Connell. 1982. "Why Hunters Gather: Optimal Foraging and the Ache of Eastern Paraguay." *American Ethnologist* 9 (2): 379–98. https://doi.org/10.1525/ae.1982.9.2.02a00100.

Hawkes, Kristen, James F. O'Connell, and Nicholas G. Blurton Jones. 1997. "Hadza Women's Time Allocation, Offspring Provisioning, and the Evolution of Long Postmenopausal Life Spans." *Current Anthropology* 38 (4): 551–77. https://doi.org/10.1086/204646.

Hawkes, Kristen, James F. O'Connell, and Nicholas G. Blurton Jones. 2001. "Hunting and Nuclear Families: Some Lessons from the Hadza about Men's Work." *Current Anthropology* 42 (5): 681–709.

Hawkes, Kristen, James F. O'Connell, and Nicholas G. Blurton Jones. 2014. "More Lessons from the Hadza About Men's Work." *Human Nature (Hawthorne, N.Y.)* 25 (4): 596–619. https://doi.org/10.1007/s12110-014-9212-5.

Hayden, Brian. 1981. "Subsistence and Ecological Adaptations of Modern Hunter-Gatherers." In *Omnivorous Primates: Gathering and Hunting in Human Evolution*, ed. Robert S. O. Harding and Geza Teleki, 344–421. New York: Columbia University Press.

Hayden, Brian. 1990. "The Right Rub: Hide Working in High Ranking Households." In *The Interpretative Possibilities of Microwear Studies. Proceedings of the International Conference on Lithic Use-Wear Analysis, 15–17 February, 1989, Uppsala, Sweden*, ed. Bo Gräslund, Helena Knutsson, Kjel Knutsson, and Jackie Taffinder, 89–102. Aun Archaeological Studies 14. Uppsala, Sweden: Societas Archaeologica Upsaliensis.

Hayden, Brian. 1993. "The Cultural Capacities of Neandertals: A Review and Re-Evaluation." *Journal of Human Evolution* 24 (2): 113–46. https://doi.org/10.1006/jhev.1993.1010.

Hayden, Brian. 2012. "Neandertal Social Structure?" *Oxford Journal of Archaeology* 31 (1): 1–26. https://doi.org/10.1111/j.1468-0092.2011.00376.x.

Hayden, Brian. 2015. "Insights into Early Lithic Technologies from Ethnography." *Philosophical Transactions of the Royal Society (London), Series B. Biological Sciences* 370B (1682): 20140356.

Haynes, Gary, and Jarod M. Hutson. 2014. "Clovis-Era Subsistence: Regional Variability, Continental Patterning." In *Paleoamerican Odyssey*, ed. Kelly E. Graf, Caroline V. Ketron, and Michael R. Waters, 293–309. College Station: Texas A&M University, Center for the Study of the First Americans.

Hearne, Samuel. 1795. *A Journey from Prince of Wales's Fort in Hudson's Bay to the Northern Ocean, Undertaken by Order of the Hudson's Bay Company for the Discovery* of *Copper Mines, A North-West Passage, &c., in the Years 1769, 1771, and 1772.* London: A. Strahan and T. Cadell.

Heckewelder, John G. E. [1818] 1876. *History, Manners, and Customs of the Indian Nations: Who Once Inhabited Pennsylvania and the Neighboring States.* New and Revised ed. Memoir 12. Philadelphia: Historical Society of Pennsylvania.

Helms, Mary W. 1988. *Ulysses' Sail: An Ethnographic Odyssey of Power, Knowledge, and Geographical Distance.* Princeton, NJ: Princeton University Press. https://doi.org /10.1515/9781400859542.

Henrich, Joseph. 2008. "A Cultural Species." In *Explaining Culture Scientifically,* ed. Melissa J. Brown, 184–210. Seattle: University of Washington Press.

Henry, Amanda G., Alison S. Brooks, and Dolores R. Piperno. 2011. "Microfossils in Calculus Demonstrate Consumption of Plants and Cooked Foods in Neanderthal Diets (Shanidar III, Iraq; Spy I and II, Belgium)." *Proceedings of the National Academy of Sciences of the United States of America* 108 (2): 486–91. https://doi.org/10 .1073/pnas.1016868108.

Henry, Amanda G., Alison S. Brooks, and Dolores R. Piperno. 2014. "Plant Foods and the Dietary Ecology of Neanderthals and Early Modern Humans." *Journal of Human Evolution* 69:44–54. https://doi.org/10.1016/j.jhevol.2013.12.014.

Hibben, Frank C. 1938. "A Cache of Wooden Bows from the Mogollon Mountains." *American Antiquity* 4 (1): 36–38. https://doi.org/10.2307/275360.

Hill, Kim. 1988. "Macronutrient Modifications of Optimal Foraging Theory: An Approach Using Indifference Curves Applied to Some Modern Foragers." *Human Ecology* 16 (2): 157–97. https://doi.org/10.1007/BF00888091.

Hill, Kim, Robert S. Walker, Miran Božičević, James Eder, Thomas Headland, Barry Hewlett, A. Magdalena Hurtado, Frank Marlowe, Polly Wiessner, and Brian Wood. 2011. "Co-Residence Patterns in Hunter-Gatherer Societies Show Unique Human Social Structure." *Science* 331 (6022): 1286–89. https://doi.org/10.1126/science.1199071.

Hill, Matthew E. 2002. "The Milnesand Site: Site Formation Study of a Paleoindian Bison Bonebed in Eastern New Mexico." *Plains Anthropologist* 47 (183): 323–37.

Hill, Matthew E. 2007. "Causes of Regional and Temporal Variation in Paleoindian Diet in Western North America." PhD dissertation, Department of Anthropology, University of Arizona, Tucson, AZ.

Hill, Matthew E., Jr. 2008. "Variation in Paleoindian Fauna Use on the Great Plains and Rocky Mountains of North America." *Quaternary International* 191 (1): 34–52. https://doi.org/10.1016/j.quaint.2007.10.004.

Hill, Matthew E. 2010. "Analysis of Site Formation Processes at the Rex Rodgers Bison Bonebed." *Plains Anthropologist* 55 (213): 3–24. https://doi.org/10.1179/pan .2010.009.

Hill, Matthew E. 2013. "Sticking It to the Bison: Exploring Variation in Cody Bison Bonebeds." In *Paleoindian Lifeways of the Cody Complex*, ed. Edward J. Knell and Mark P. Muñiz, 93–117. Salt Lake City: University of Utah Press.

Hill, Matthew E., and Jack L. Hofman. 1997. "The Waugh Site: A Folsom-Age Bison Bonebed in Northwestern Oklahoma." *Plains Anthropologist* 42 (159): 63–83.

Hilton, Charles E., and Russell D. Greaves. 2008. "Seasonality and Sex Differences in Travel Distance and Resource Transport in Venezuelan Foragers." *Current Anthropology* 49 (1): 144–53. https://doi.org/10.1086/524760.

Hind, Henry Y. 1860. *Narrative of the Canadian Red River Exploring Expedition of 1857 and of the Assiniboine and Saskatchewan Exploring Expedition of 1858.* Vol. 1. London: Longman, Green, Longman, and Roberts. https://doi.org/10.5962/bhl .title.82399.

Hirth, Kenneth G. 2016. *The Aztec Economic World: Merchants and Markets in Ancient Mesoamerica.* New York: Cambridge University Press. https://doi.org/10.1017/CBO 9781316537350.

Hiscock, Peter. 1988. "A Cache of Tulas from the Boulia District, Western Queensland." *Archaeology in Oceania* 23 (2): 60–70. https://doi.org/10.1002/j .1834-4453.1988.tb00188.x.

Hitchcock, Robert K., John E. Yellen, Diane J. Gelburd, Alan J. Osborn, and Aron L. Crowell. 1996. "Subsistence Hunting and Resource Management among the Ju/'hoansi of Northwestern Botswana." *African Study Monographs* 17 (4): 153–220.

Hoffecker, John F. 2002. *Desolate Landscapes: Ice-Age Settlement in Eastern Europe.* New Brunswick, NJ: Rutgers University Press.

Hoffecker, John F., Scott A. Elias, Dennis H. O'Rourke, G. Richard Scott, and Nancy H. Bigelow. 2016. "Beringia and the Global Dispersal of Modern Humans." *Evolutionary Anthropology* 25 (2): 64–78. https://doi.org/10.1002/evan.21478.

Hoffman, Brian W. 2002. "Broken Eyes and Simple Grooves: Understanding Eastern Aleut Needle Technology through Experimental Manufacture and Use of Bone Needles." In *Many Faces of Gender: Roles and Relationships through Time in Indigenous Northern Communities*, ed. Lisa Frink, Rita S. Shepard, and Gregory A. Reinhardt, 151–64. Boulder: University Press of Colorado.

Hoffman, Louwrens C., and Donna-Mareè Cawthorn. 2012. "What Is the Role and Contribution of Meat from Wildlife in Providing High Quality Protein for Consumption?" *Animal frontiers* 2 (4): 40–53. https://doi.org/10.2527/af.2012-0061.

Hoffman, Louwrens C., and Eva Wiklund. 2006. "Game and Venison—Meat for the Modern Consumer." *Meat Science* 74 (1): 197–208. https://doi.org/10.1016/j.meat sci.2006.04.005.

Hofman, Jack L., Lawrence C. Todd, C. Bertrand Schultz, and William Hendy. 1991. "The Lipscomb Bison Quarry: Continuing Investigation of a Folsom Site on the Southern Plains." *Bulletin of the Texas Archeological Society* 60:149–89.

Holdaway, Simon J., and Matthew Douglass. 2012. "A Twenty-First Century Archaeology of Stone Artifacts." *Journal of Archaeological Method and Theory* 19 (1): 101–31. https://doi.org/10.1007/s10816-011-9103-6.

Holdaway, Simon J., Matthew Douglass, and Rebecca Phillipps. 2015. "Flake Selection, Assemblage Variability, and Technological Organization." In *Works in Stone: Contemporary Perspectives on Lithic Analysis*, ed. Michael J. Shott, 46–62. Salt Lake City: University of Utah Press.

Horne, George, and George Aiston. 1924. *Savage Life in Central Australia*. London: Macmillan.

Hosfield, Robert. 2011. "The British Lower Palaeolithic of the Early Middle Pleistocene." *Quaternary Science Reviews* 30 (11–12): 1486–1510. https://doi.org/10.1016/j.quascirev.2010.02.026.

Hovers, Erella, and Anna Belfer-Cohen. 2013. "On Variability and Complexity: Lessons from the Levantine Middle Paleolithic Record." *Current Anthropology* 54 (S8): S337–57. https://doi.org/10.1086/673880.

Howitt, Alfred W. 1891. "The Dieri and Other Kindred Tribes of Central Australia." *Journal of the Anthropological Institute of Great Britain and Ireland* 20:30–104. https://doi.org/10.2307/2842347.

Howitt, Alfred W. 1904. *The Native Tribes of South-East Australia*. London: Macmillan.

Hublin, Jean-Jacques, and Shannon P. McPherron, eds. 2012. *Modern Origins: A North African Perspective*. New York: Springer. https://doi.org/10.1007/978-94-007-2929-2.

Huckell, Bruce B., and J. David Kilby. 2014. "Clovis Caches: Discoveries, Identification, Lithic Technology, and Land Use." In *Clovis Caches: Recent Discoveries and New Research*, ed. Bruce B. Huckell and J. David Kilby, 1–9. Albuquerque: University of New Mexico Press.

Huguet, Rosa, Palmira Saladié, Isabel Cáceres, Carlos Díez, Jordi Rosell, María Bennàsar, Ruth Blasco, Montserrat Esteban-Nadal, María Joana Gabuccio, Antonio Rodríguez-Hidalgo, et al. 2012. "Successful Subsistence Strategies of the First Humans in South-Western Europe." *Quaternary International* 247:69–84.

Hurcombe, Linda M. 2014. *Perishable Material Culture in Prehistory: Investigating the Missing Majority*. London: Routledge.

Hurst, Stance, and Eileen Johnson. 2016. "Gearing Up at the Adair-Steadman (41FS2) Folsom Site." *PaleoAmerica* 2 (3): 252–60. https://doi.org/10.1080/20555563.2016.1198215.

Iceland, Harry. 2013. "Refining Paleo-Indian Lithic Technology at Shawnee-Minisink via an Artifact Refitting Study." *North American Archaeologist* 34 (3): 237–67. https://doi.org/10.2190/NA.34.3.b.

Jackson, Thomas L. 1986. "Late Prehistoric Obsidian Exchange in Central California." PhD dissertation, Department of Anthropology, Stanford University, Stanford, CA.

Jackson, Thomas L. 1988. "Amending Models of Trans-Sierran Obsidian Tool Production and Exchange." *Journal of California and Great Basin Anthropology* 10 (1): 62–72.

Jäger, Horst J., Len Gordon-Harris, Ulrich-Martin Mehring, G. Friedrich Goetz, and Klaus D. Mathias. 1997. "Degenerative Change in the Cervical Spine and Load-Carrying on the Head." *Skeletal Radiology* 26 (8): 475–81. https://doi.org/10.1007/s002560050269.

Jaubert, Jacques, and Anne Delagnes. 2007. "De l'espace parcouru à l'espace habité au paléolithique moyen." In *Les néandertaliens: Biologie et cultures*, ed. Bernard Vandermeersch and Bruno Maureille, 263–81. Documents Préhistoriques 23. Paris: Éditions du Comité des Travaux Historiques et Scientifiques (CTHS).

Jaubert, Jacques, Bertrand Kervazo, Jean-Jacques Bahain, Jean-Philip Brugal, Pierre Chalard, Christophe Falguères, Marc Jarry, Marcel Jeannet, Cristina Lemorini, Antoine Louchart, et al. 2005. "Coudoulous I (Tour-de-Faure, Lot), site du Pléistocène Moyen en Quercy: Bilan pluridisciplinaire." In *Données récentes sur les modalités de peuplement et sur le cadre chronostratigraphique, géologique et paléogéographique des industries du Paléolithique Inférieur et Moyen en Europe. Actes du Colloque International de Rennes, 22–25 Septembre 2003*, ed. Nathalie Molines, Marie-Hélène Moncel, and Jean-Laurent Monnier, 227–51. BAR International Series S1364. Oxford: John and Erica Hedges, British Archaeological Reports.

Jennings, Thomas A. 2013. "The Hogeye Clovis Cache, Texas: Quantifying Lithic Reduction Signatures." *Journal of Archaeological Science* 40 (1): 649–58. https://doi.org/10.1016/j.jas.2012.07.016.

Jennings, Thomas A., Charlotte D. Pevny, and William A. Dickens. 2010. "A Biface and Blade Core Efficiency Experiment: Implications for Early Paleoindian Technological Organization." *Journal of Archaeological Science* 37 (9): 2155–64. https://doi.org/10.1016/j.jas.2010.02.020.

Jodry, Margaret A. 1999. "Folsom Technological Organization and Socioeconomic Strategies: Views from Stewart's Cattle Guard and the Upper Rio Grande Basin, Colorado." PhD dissertation, Department of Anthropology, American University, Washington, DC.

Johnson, Christopher N., and Stephen Wroe. 2003. "Causes of Extinction of Vertebrates during the Holocene of Mainland Australia: Arrival of the Dingo, or Human Impact?" *Holocene* 13 (6): 941–48. https://doi.org/10.1191/0959683603hl682fa.

Johnson, Eileen, and Leland C. Bement. 2009. "Bison Butchery at Cooper, a Folsom Site on the Southern Plains." *Journal of Archaeological Science* 36 (7): 1430–46. https://doi.org/10.1016/j.jas.2009.02.007.

Jones, George T., Charlotte Beck, Eric E. Jones, and Richard E. Hughes. 2003. "Lithic Source Use and Paleoarchaic Foraging Territories in the Great Basin." *American Antiquity* 68 (1): 5–38. https://doi.org/10.2307/3557031.

Jones, Martin. 2009. "Moving North: Archaeobotanical Evidence for Plant Diet in Middle and Upper Paleolithic Europe." In *The Evolution of Hominin Diets: Integrating Approaches to the Study of Palaeolithic Subsistence*, ed. Jean-Jacques Hublin and Michael P. Richards, 171–80. Dordrecht, Netherlands: Springer. https://doi.org/10.1007/978-1-4020-9699-0_12.

Judge, W. James. 1973. *PaleoIndian Occupation of the Central Rio Grande Valley in New Mexico*. Albuquerque: University of New Mexico Press.

Julien, Marie-Anne, Florent Rivals, Jordi Serangeli, Hervé Bocherens, and Nicholas J. Conard. 2015. "A New Approach for Deciphering between Single and Multiple Accumulation Events Using Intra-Tooth Isotopic Variations: Application to the Middle Pleistocene Bone Bed of Schöningen 13 II–4." *Journal of Human Evolution* 89:114–28. https://doi.org/10.1016/j.jhevol.2015.02.012.

Kaplan, Hillard, and Kim Hill. 1992. "The Evolutionary Ecology of Food Acquisition." In *Evolutionary Ecology and Human Behavior*, ed. Eric A. Smith and Bruce Winterhalder, 167–201. Hawthorne, NY: Aldine de Gruyter.

Keating, William H. 1824. *Narrative of an Expedition to the Source of St. Peter's River, Lake Winnepeek, Lake of the Woods, &c. &c. Performed in the Year 1823, by Order of the Hon. J. C. Calhoun, Secretary of War, under the Command of Stephen H. Long, Major U. S. T. E. Compiled from the Notes of Major Long, Messrs. Say, Keating, and Colhoun.* Vol. 1. Philadelphia: H. C. Carey and I. Lea.

Keeley, Lawrence H. 2010. "The Probable Sexual Division of Labor in Magdalenian Hide Working: Ethnological Evidence." In *The Magdalenian Household: Unraveling Domesticity*, ed. Ezra Zubrow, Françoise Audouze, and James G. Enloe, 227–34. Albany: State University of New York Press.

Kehoe, Thomas F. 1973. *The Gull Lake Site: A Prehistoric Bison Drive Site in Southwestern Saskatchewan. Publications in Anthropology and History 1*. Milwaukee: Milwaukee Public Museum.

Kelly, Robert L. 1983. "Hunter-Gatherer Mobility Strategies." *Journal of Anthropological Research* 39 (3): 277–306. https://doi.org/10.1086/jar.39.3.3629672.

Kelly, Robert L. 1988. "The Three Sides of a Biface." *American Antiquity* 53 (04): 717–34. https://doi.org/10.2307/281115.

Kelly, Robert L. 2014. "Technology." In *Oxford Handbook of the Archaeology and Anthropology of Hunter-Gatherers*, ed. Vicki Cummings, Peter Jordan, and Marek Zvelebil, 1110–26. Oxford: Oxford University Press.

Kilby, J. David. 2014. "Direction and Distance in Clovis Caching: The Movement of People and Lithic Raw Materials on the Clovis-Age Landscape." In *Clovis Caches: Recent Discoveries and New Research*, ed. Bruce B. Huckell and J. David Kilby, 201–16. Albuquerque: University of New Mexico Press.

Klokkernes, Torunn. 2007. *Skin Processing Technology in Eurasian Reindeer Cultures: A Comparative Study in Material Science of Sàmi and Evenk Methods—Perspectives on Deterioration and Preservation of Museum Artefacts*. PhD dissertation, Museum of Cultural History, University of Oslo, Oslo, Norway. Rudkøbing, Denmark: Langelands Museum, LMR Press.

Knapik, Joseph J., and Katy Reynolds. 2012. "Load Carriage in Military Operations: A Review of Historical, Physiological, Biomechanical, and Medical Aspects." In *Military Quantitative Physiology: Problems and Concepts in Military Operational Medicine*, ed. Karl E. Friedl and William R. Santee, 303–37. Falls Church, VA: United States Army, Office of the Surgeon General; Fort Detrick, MD: Borden Institute.

Kornfeld, Marcel. 2007. "Are Paleoindians of the Great Plains and Rockies Subsistence Specialists?" In *Foragers of the Terminal Pleistocene in North America*, ed. Renee Beauchamp Walker and Boyce N. Driskell, 32–58. Lincoln: University of Nebraska Press.

Kornfeld, Marcel, George C. Frison, and Mary Lou Larson, eds. 2010. *Prehistoric Hunter-Gatherers of the High Plains and Rockies*. 3rd ed. Walnut Creek, CA: Left Coast Press.

Kornfeld, Marcel, and Mary L. Larson. 2008. "Bonebeds and Other Myths: Paleoindian to Archaic Transition on North American Great Plains and Rocky Mountains." *Quaternary International* 191 (1): 18–33. https://doi.org/10.1016/j.quaint.2007.08.004.

Kot, Małgorzata Anna. 2014. "The Earliest Palaeolithic Bifacial Leafpoints in Central and Southern Europe: Techno-Functional Approach." *Quaternary International* 326–27:381–97. https://doi.org/10.1016/j.quaint.2013.10.030.

Kozlowski, Janusz K. 2003. "From Bifaces to Leaf Points." In *Multiple Approaches to the Study of Bifacial Technologies*, ed. Marie Soressi and Harold L. Dibble, 229–49. University Museum Monograph 115. Philadelphia: University of Pennsylvania Museum of Archaeology and Anthropology.

Kreutzer, Lee A. 1996. "Taphonomy of the Mill Iron Site Bison Bonebed." In *The Mill Iron Site*, ed. George C. Frison, 101–43. Albuquerque: University of New Mexico Press.

Kubiak-Martens, Lucyna. 1996. "Evidence for Possible Use of Plant Foods in Palaeolithic and Mesolithic Diet from the Site of Całowanie in the Central Part of the Polish Plain." *Vegetation History and Archaeobotany* 5 (1–2): 33–38. https://doi .org/10.1007/BF00189433.

Kuhn, Steven L. 1994. "A Formal Approach to the Design and Assembly of Mobile Toolkits." *American Antiquity* 59 (03): 426–42. https://doi.org/10.2307/282456.

Kuhn, Steven L. 2014. "Signaling Theory and Technologies of Communication in the Paleolithic." *Biological Theory* 9 (1): 42–50. https://doi.org/10.1007/s13752-013-0156-5.

Kuhn, Steven L., and Mary C. Stiner. 2006. "What's a Mother to Do? The Division of Labor among Neandertals and Modern Humans in Eurasia." *Current Anthropology* 47 (6): 953–81. https://doi.org/10.1086/507197.

Kuipers, Remko S., Martine F. Luxwolda, D. A. Janneke Dijck-Brouwer, S. Boyd Eaton, Michael A. Crawford, Loren Cordain, and Frits A. J. Muskiet. 2010. "Estimated Macronutrient and Fatty Acid Intakes from an East African Paleolithic Diet." *British Journal of Nutrition* 104 (11): 1666–87. https://doi.org/10.1017/S000711 4510002679.

Kuman, Kathleen, Hao Li, and Chaorong Li. 2016. "Large Cutting Tools from the Danjiangkou Reservoir Region, Central China: Comparisons and Contrasts with Western and South Asian Acheulean." *Quaternary International* 400:58–64. https://doi.org/10.1016/j.quaint.2015.07.052.

Kuzmin, Yaroslav V. 2017. "Obsidian as a Commodity to Investigate Human Migrations in the Upper Paleolithic, Neolithic, and Paleometal of Northeast Asia." *Quaternary International* 442 (Part B): 5–11.

Kuzmin, Yaroslav V., George S. Burr, A. J. Timothy Jull, and Leopold D. Sulerzhitsky. 2004. "AMS ¹⁴C Age of the Upper Palaeolithic Skeletons from Sungir Site, Central Russian Plain." *Nuclear Instruments and Methods in Physics Research. Section B, Beam Interactions with Materials and Atoms* 223–24:731–34. https://doi.org/10 .1016/j.nimb.2004.04.135.

Langford, Dale G. 2015. "Interpreting the Spatial Distribution of Lithic Artifacts from the RLF Paleoindian Site (DdJf–13), Thunder Bay Region, Northwestern Ontario." MA thesis, Environmental Studies (Northern Environments and Cultures), Lakehead University, Thunder Bay, Ontario.

Lazuén, Talía, and Anne Delagnes. 2014. "Lithic Tool Management in the Early Middle Paleolithic: An Integrated Techno-Functional Approach Applied to

Le Pucheuil-Type Production (Le Pucheuil, Northwestern France)." *Journal of Archaeological Science* 52:337–53. https://doi.org/10.1016/j.jas.2014.08.029.

Ledger, Horace P. 1968. "Body Composition as a Basis for a Comparative Study of Some East African Mammals." In *Comparative Nutrition of Wild Animals. Proceedings of a Symposium Held at the Zoological Society of London on 10 and 11 November 1966*, ed. Michael A. Crawford, 289–310. Symposia of the Zoological Society of London 21. London: Academic Press.

Leduc, Charlotte. 2014. "New Mesolithic Hunting Evidence from Bone Injuries at Danish Maglemosian Sites: Lundby Mose and Mullerup (Sjælland)." *International Journal of Osteoarchaeology* 24 (4): 476–91. https://doi.org/10.1002/oa.2234.

Lee, Richard B. 1979. *The! Kung San: Men, Women, and Work in a Foraging Society.* Cambridge: Cambridge University Press.

Lemonnier, Pierre. 1992. *Elements for an Anthropology of Technology. Anthropological Paper 88.* Ann Arbor: University of Michigan, Museum of Anthropology.

Lemorini, Cristina, Thomas W. Plummer, David R. Braun, Alyssa N. Crittenden, Peter W. Ditchfield, Laura C. Bishop, Fritz Hertel, James S. Oliver, Frank W. Marlowe, Margaret J. Schoeninger, et al. 2014. "Old Stones' Song: Use-Wear Experiments and Analysis of the Oldowan Quartz and Quartzite Assemblage from Kanjera South (Kenya)." *Journal of Human Evolution* 72:10–25. https://doi .org/10.1016/j.jhevol.2014.03.002.

Leroyer, Mathieu, Pierre Bodu, Hélène Salomon, and Vincent Lhomme. 2014. "The Discoid Techno-Complex (MIS 3) at Ormesson and across the Paris Sedimentary Basin: Consistency and Flexibility of a Singular Technical Choice with Relation to the Lithological Context [Abstract]." In *Middle Palaeolithic in North-West Europe: Multidisciplinary Approaches. Conference, Moulins de Beez, Namur, Belgium, March 20–21, 2014*, ed. Kévin Di Modica, Stéphane Pirson, Michel Toussaint, Grégory Abrams, and Dominique Bonjean, 29. Namur, Belgium: Centre Archéologique de la Grotte Scladina and Service Public de Wallonie.

Lewis, Meriwether. 1809. *The Travels of Capts. Lewis and Clarke, from St. Louis, by Way of the Missouri and Columbia Rivers, to the Pacific Ocean; Performed in the Years 1804, 1805, and 1806, by Order of the Government of the United States. . . .* London: Longman, Hurst, Rees, and Orme.

Lewis-Williams, J. David, and Megan Biesele. 1978. "Eland Hunting Rituals among Northern and Southern San Groups: Striking Similarities." *Africa: Journal of the International Africa Institute* 48 (2): 117–34. https://doi.org/10.2307/1158603.

Liebenberg, Louis. 2006. "Persistence Hunting by Modern Hunter-Gatherers." *Current Anthropology* 47 (6): 1017–26. https://doi.org/10.1086/508695.

Lippi, Marta Mariotti, Bruno Foggi, Biancamaria Aranguren, Annamaria Ronchitelli, and Anna Revedin. 2015. "Multistep Food Plant Processing at Grotta Paglicci (Southern Italy) Around 32,600 cal BP." *Proceedings of the National Academy of Sciences of the United States of America* 112 (39): 12075–80. https://doi.org/10.1073/pnas.1505213112.

Loebel, Thomas J. 2009. "Withington (47Gt158): A Clovis/Gainey Campsite in Grant County, Wisconsin." *Midcontinental Journal of Archaeology, MCJA* 34 (2): 223–48. https://doi.org/10.1179/mca.2009.014.

Loovers, Jan Peter Laurens. 2015. "Dog-Craft: A History of Gwich'in and Dogs in the Canadian North." *Hunter-Gatherer Research* 1 (4): 387–419. https://doi.org/10.3828/hgr.2015.21.

Lothrop, Jonathan C., and James W. Bradley. 2012. "Paleoindian Occupations in the Hudson Valley, New York." In *Late Pleistocene Archaeology and Ecology in the Far Northeast*, ed. Claude Chapdelaine, 9–47. College Station: Texas A&M University Press.

Lothrop, Samuel K. 1929. *Polychrome Guanaco Cloaks of Patagonia*. Contribution 7(6). New York: Museum of the American Indian, Heye Foundation. https://doi.org/10.5479/sil.451440.39088016090524.

Lourandos, Harry. 1985. "Intensification and Australian Prehistory." In *Prehistoric Hunter-Gatherers: The Emergence of Cultural Complexity*, ed. T. Douglas Price and James A. Brown, 385–426. Orlando: Academic Press.

Luedtke, Barbara E. 1979. "Quarrying and Quantification: Estimates of Lithic Material Demand." *Midcontinental Journal of Archaeology, MCJA* 4 (2): 255–66.

Lupo, Karen D. 2006. "What Explains the Carcass Field Processing and Transport Decisions of Contemporary Hunter-Gatherers? Measures of Economic Anatomy and Zooarchaeological Skeletal Part Representation." *Journal of Archaeological Method and Theory* 13 (1): 19–66. https://doi.org/10.1007/s10816-006-9000-6.

Lyman, R. Lee. 2015. "North American Paleoindian Eyed Bone Needles: Morphometrics, Sewing, and Site Structure." *American Antiquity* 80 (1): 146–60. https://doi.org/10.7183/0002-7316.79.4.146.

MacDonald, Douglas H. 2010. "The Evolution of Folsom Fluting." *Plains Anthropologist* 55 (213): 39–54. https://doi.org/10.1179/pan.2010.011.

MacDonald, Douglas H., and Barry S. Hewlett. 1999. "Reproductive Interests and Forager Mobility." *Current Anthropology* 40 (4): 501–23.

Macdonald, Katharine, Wil Roebroeks, and Alexander Verpoorte. 2009. "An Energetics Perspective on the Neandertal Record." In *The Evolution of Hominid Diets: Integrating Approaches to the Study of Palaeolithic Subsistence*, ed. Jean-Jacques Hublin and Michael P. Richards, 211–20. Dordrecht Netherlands: Springer. https://doi.org/10.1007/978-1-4020-9699-0_16.

Mackenzie, Alexander. 1801. *Voyages from Montreal, on the River St. Laurence, through the Continent of North America, to the Frozen and Pacific Oceans; in the Years 1789 and 1793. With a Preliminary Account of the Rise, Progress, and Present State of the Fur Trade of that Country.* Vol. 1. London: T. Cadell, Jun. and W. Davies.

Maki, Julia M. 2013. "The Biomechanics of Spear Throwing: An Analysis of the Effects of Anatomical Variation on Throwing Performance, with Implications for the Fossil Record." PhD dissertation, Department of Anthropology, Washington University in St. Louis, St. Louis, MO.

Malville, Nancy J. 2001. "Long-Distance Transport of Bulk Goods in the Pre-Hispanic American Southwest." *Journal of Anthropological Archaeology* 20 (2): 230–43. https://doi.org/10.1006/jaar.2000.0373.

Mania, Dietrich, and Ursula Mania. 2005. "The Natural and Socio-Cultural Environment of *Homo erectus* at Bilzingsleben, Germany." In *The Hominid Individual in Context: Archaeological Investigations of Lower and Middle Palaeolithic Landscapes, Locales and Artefacts*, ed. Clive Gamble and Martin Porr, 98–114. London: Routledge.

Manning, Thomas H., and Ella W. Manning. 1944. "The Preparation of Skins and Clothing in the Eastern Canadian Arctic." *Polar Record* 4 (28): 156–69. https://doi.org/10.1017/S0032247400041711.

Marchello, Martin J., William D. Slanger, D. B. Milne, A. G. Fischer, and Paul T. Berg. 1989. "Nutrient Composition of Raw and Cooked Bison." *Journal of Food Composition and Analysis* 2 (2): 177–85. https://doi.org/10.1016/0889-1575(89)90079-3.

Marcy, Randolph B. 1863. *The Prairie Traveler: A Handbook for Overland Expeditions.* London: Trubner.

Marean, Curtis W. 2005. "From the Tropics to the Colder Climates: Contrasting Faunal Exploitation Adaptations of Modern Humans and Neanderthals." In *From Tools to Symbols: From Early Hominids to Modern Humans*, ed. Francesco d'Errico and Lucinda Backwell, 333–71. Johannesburg, South Africa: Witwatersrand University Press.

Marlowe, Frank W. 2007. "Hunting and Gathering: The Human Sexual Division of Foraging Labor." *Cross-Cultural Research* 41 (2): 170–95. https://doi.org/10.1177/1069397106297529.

Mason, Otis T. 1889. "The Beginnings of the Carrying Industry." *American Anthropologist* A2 (1): 21–46. https://doi.org/10.1525/aa.1889.2.1.02a00030.

Mason, Otis T. 1896. "Primitive Travel and Transportation." Smithsonian Institution, United States National Museum. Washington, DC: US Government Printing Office. *Annual Report of the Board of Regents of the Smithsonian Institution* 1894:237–593.

Mason, Sarah L. R., Jon G. Hather, and Gordon C. Hillman. 1994. "Preliminary Investigation of the Plant Macro-Remains from Dolni Vestonice II, and Its Implications for the Role of Plant Foods in Palaeolithic and Mesolithic Europe." *Antiquity* 68 (258): 48–57. https://doi.org/10.1017/S0003598X00046184.

McAnany, Patricia A., and Ian Hodder. 2009. "Thinking about Stratigraphic Sequence in Social Terms." *Archaeological Dialogues* 16 (1): 1–22. https://doi.org/10.1017/S1380203809002748.

McAvoy, Joseph M. 1992. *Nottoway River Survey, Part I. Clovis Settlement Patterns: The 30 Year Study of a Late Ice Age Hunting Culture on the Southern Interior Coastal Plain of Virginia. Archeological Society of Virginia Special Publication 28, Nottaway River Publications Research Report 1. Courtland.* Archeological Society of Virginia.

McBryde, Felix W. 1947. *Cultural and Historical Geography of Southwest Guatemala. Institute of Social Anthropology Publication 4.* Washington, DC: Smithsonian Institution.

McBryde, Isabel. 1987. "Goods from Another Country: Exchange Networks and the People of the Lake Eyre Basin." In *Australians to 1788*, ed. Derek J. Mulvaney and J. Peter White, 253–73. Australians: A Historical Library. Broadway, NSW, Australia: Fairfax, Syme and Weldon Associates.

McBryde, Isabel. 2000. "Travellers in Storied Landscapes: A Case Study in Exchanges and Heritage." *Aboriginal History* 24:152–74.

McCall, Grant S. 2012. "Ethnoarchaeology and the Organization of Lithic Technology." *Journal of Archaeological Research* 20 (2): 157–203. https://doi.org/10.1007/s10814-011-9056-z.

McCormack, Patricia A. 2014. "Evolving Accommodations: The Sled Dog in the Canadian Fur Trade." In *Une bête parmi les hommes: Le Chien—De la domestication à l'anthropomorphisme. Actes des Troisièmes Rencontres Internationales "Des Bêtes et des Hommes," Valenciennes, 5 et 6 novembre 2009*, ed. Fabrice Guizard and Corinne Beck, 130–47. Amiens, France: Encrage Édition.

McDaniel, John, Wayne Askew, Danielle Bennett, Jason Mihalopoulos, Sujata Anantharaman, Anette S. Fjeldstad, Dan C. Rule, Nazeem M. Nanjee, Ryan A. Harris, and Russell S. Richardson. 2013. "Bison Meat Has a Lower Atherogenic Risk than Beef in Healthy Men." *Nutrition Research (New York, N.Y.)* 33 (4): 293–302. https://doi.org/10.1016/j.nutres.2013.01.007.

McLean, John. 1849. *Notes of a Twenty-Five Years' Service in the Hudson's Bay Territory.* Vol. 2. London: Richard Bentley.

McNiven, Ian J., and Ricky Feldman. 2003. "Ritually Orchestrated Seascapes: Hunting Magic and Dugong Bone Mounds in Torres Strait, NE Australia."

Cambridge Archaeological Journal 13 (2): 169–94. https://doi.org/10.1017/S09597
7430300018.

Meignen, Liliane, Anne Delagnes, and Laurence Bourguignon. 2009. "Patterns of Lithic Material Procurement and Transformation During the Middle Paleolithic in Western Europe." In *Lithic Materials and Paleolithic Societies*, ed. Brian Adams and Brooke S. Blades, 15–24. Hoboken, NJ: Wiley-Blackwell. https://doi.org /10.1002/9781444311976.ch2.

Meltzer, David J. 1985. "On Stone Procurement and Settlement Mobility in Eastern Fluted Point Groups." *North American Archaeologist* 6 (1): 1–24. https://doi.org/10 .2190/T0JL-P9E8-X45J-QBDX.

Meltzer, David J. 1989. "Was Stone Exchanged among Eastern North American Paleoindians?" In *Eastern Paleoindian Lithic Resource Use*, ed. Christopher J. Ellis and Jonathan C. Lothrop, 11–39. Boulder, CO: Westview Press.

Meltzer, David J. 1993. "Is There a Clovis Adaptation?" In *From Kostenki to Clovis: Upper Paleolithic—Paleo-Indian Adaptations*, ed. Olga Soffer and Nikolai D. Praslov, 293–310. New York: Plenum Press. https://doi.org/10.1007/978-1-4899 -1112-4_21.

Meltzer, David J. 2002. "What Do You Do When No One's Been There Before? Thoughts on the Exploration and Colonization of New Lands." In *The First Americans: The Pleistocene Colonization of the New World*, ed. Nina G. Jablonski, 27–58. Memoirs of the California Academy of Sciences 27. San Francisco, CA: California Academy of Sciences.

Meltzer, David J. 2006. *Folsom: New Archaeological Investigations of a Classic Paleoindian Bison Kill*. Berkeley, CA: University of California Press.

Merlan, Francesca. 1992. "Male-Female Separation and Forms of Society in Aboriginal Australia." *Cultural Anthropology* 7 (2): 169–93. https://doi.org/10.1525 /can.1992.7.2.02a00020.

Mester, Zsolt, and Marie-Hélène Moncel. 2006. "Le site paléolithique moyen d'Erd (Hongrie): Nouvelles données sur les chaînes opératoires et résultats morpho-fonctionnels de la production." *L'Anthropologie* 44 (3): 221–40.

Michel, Amanda. 2014. "Skin Deep: An Outline of the Structure of Different Skins and How It Influences Behaviour in Use: A Practitioners' Guide." In *Why Leather? The Material and Cultural Dimensions of Leather*, ed. Susanna Harris and André J. Veldmeijer, 23–40. Leiden, Netherlands: Sidestone Press.

Miller, G. Logan. 2014. "Lithic Microwear Analysis as a Means to Infer Production of Perishable Technology: A Case from the Great Lakes." *Journal of Archaeological Science* 49:292–301. https://doi.org/10.1016/j.jas.2014.05.019.

Mitani, John C., and David P. Watts. 2001. "Why Do Chimpanzees Hunt and Share Meat?" *Animal Behaviour* 61 (5): 915–24. https://doi.org/10.1006/anbe.2000.1681.

Mitani, John C., and David P. Watts. 2005. "Seasonality in Hunting by Nonhuman Primates." In *Primate Seasonality: Implications for Human Evolution*, ed. Diane K. Brockman and Carel P. van Schaik, 215–42. Cambridge: Cambridge University Press. https://doi.org/10.1017/CBO9780511542343.009.

Mitani, John C., David P. Watts, and Sylvia J. Amsler. 2010. "Lethal Intergroup Aggression Leads to Territorial Expansion in Wild Chimpanzees." *Current Biology* 20 (12): R507–8. https://doi.org/10.1016/j.cub.2010.04.021.

Moncel, Marie-Hélène. 2001. "Le moustérien de type quina de la Grotte du Figuier (Ardèche): Fouilles P. et A. Huchard et R. Gilles: Des occupations en grotte de courtes durées pour une exploitation locale de l'environnement?" *Bulletin de la Société Préhistorique Française* 98 (4): 593–614. https://doi.org/10.3406/bspf.2001.12564.

Moncel, Marie-Hélène, María Gema Chacón, Aude Coudenneau, and Paul Fernandes. 2009. "Points and Convergent Tools in the European Early Middle Palaeolithic Site of Payre (SE, France)." *Journal of Archaeological Science* 36 (9): 1892–1909. https://doi.org/10.1016/j.jas.2009.04.018.

Moncel, Marie-Hélène, David Pleurdeau, Ron Pinhasi, Reuven Yeshurun, Tamar Agapishvili, Tony Chevalier, François-Xavier Lebourdonnec, Gerard Poupeau, Sébastien Nomade, Richard Jennings, et al. 2015. "The Middle Palaeolithic Record of Georgia: A Synthesis of the Technological, Economic and Paleoanthropological Aspects." *L'Anthropologie* 53 (1–2): 93–125.

Moncel, Marie-Hélène, and Jean-Luc Voisin. 2006. "Les 'Industries de Transition' et le mode de spéciation des groupes néandertaliens en Europe entre 40 et 30 ka." *Comptes Rendus. Palévol* 5 (1–2): 183–92. https://doi.org/10.1016/j.crpv.2005.09.010.

Moore, Mark W. 2013. "Simple Stone Flaking in Australasia: Patterns and Implications." *Quaternary International* 285:140–49. https://doi.org/10.1016/j.quaint.2011.09.030.

Moore, Mark W. 2015. "Bifacial Flintknapping in the Northwest Kimberley, Western Australia." *Journal of Archaeological Method and Theory* 22 (3): 913–51. https://doi.org/10.1007/s10816-014-9212-0.

Moore, Mark W., and Adam Brumm. 2007. "Stone Artifacts and Hominins in Island Southeast Asia: New Insights from Flores, Eastern Indonesia." *Journal of Human Evolution* 52 (1): 85–102. https://doi.org/10.1016/j.jhevol.2006.08.002.

Morey, Darcy F., and Kim Aaris-Sørensen. 2002. "Paleoeskimo Dogs of the Eastern Arctic." *Arctic* 55 (1): 44–56. https://doi.org/10.14430/arctic689.

Morgan, John. 1852. *The Life and Adventures of William Buckley, Thirty-Two Years a Wanderer amongst the Aborigines of Then Unexplored Country Round Port Phillip, Now the Province of Victoria.* Hobart, Tasmania: Archibald Macdougall.

Morin, Eugène, and Elspeth Ready. 2013. "Foraging Goals and Transport Decisions in Western Europe during the Paleolithic and Early Holocene." In *Zooarchaeology and Modern Human Origins: Human Hunting Behavior during the Later Pleistocene*, ed. Jamie L. Clark and John D. Speth, 227–69. New York: Springer. https://doi.org /10.1007/978-94-007-6766-9_14.

Morin, Eugène, John D. Speth, and Julia Lee-Thorp. 2016. "Middle Palaeolithic Diets: A Critical Examination of the Evidence." In *The Oxford Handbook of the Archaeology of Diet*, ed. Julia Lee-Thorp and M. Anne Katzenberg. Handbooks in Archaeology. Oxford: Oxford University Press. DOI: 10.1093/oxfordhb/9780199694013.013.24.

Morris, Elizabeth A., W. Max Witkind, Ralph L. Dix, and Judith Jacobson. 1981. "Nutritional Content of Selected Aboriginal Foods in Northeast Colorado: Buffalo (*Bison bison*) and Wild Onions (*Allium* spp.)." *Journal of Ethnobiology* 1 (2): 213–20.

Morrow, Juliet E. 1997. "End Scraper Morphology and Use-life: An Approach for Studying Paleoindian Lithic Technology and Mobility." *Lithic Technology* 22 (1): 70–85. https://doi.org/10.1080/01977261.1997.11754534.

Morrow, Juliet E. 2011. "The Sloan Dalton Site (3GE94) Assemblage Revisited: Chipped-Stone Raw Material Procurement and Use in the Cache Basin." *Missouri Archaeologist* 71:5–40.

Morrow, Toby A. 1996. "Bigger Is Better: Comments on Kuhn's Formal Approach to Mobile Tool Kits." *American Antiquity* 61 (03): 581–90. https://doi.org/10.2307/281842.

Mourre, Vincent, Paola Villa, and Christopher S. Henshilwood. 2010. "Early Use of Pressure Flaking on Lithic Artifacts at Blombos Cave, South Africa." *Science* 330 (6004): 659–62. https://doi.org/10.1126/science.1195550.

Muller, Martin N., and John C. Mitani. 2005. "Conflict and Cooperation in Wild Chimpanzees." *Advances in the Study of Behavior* 35:275–331. https://doi.org/10.1016 /S0065-3454(05)35007-8.

Mulvaney, Derek J. 1976. "'The Chain of Connection': The Material Evidence." In *Tribes and Boundaries in Australia*, ed. Nicolas Peterson, 72–94. Social Anthropology Series 10. Canberra, Australia: Australian Institute of Aboriginal Studies.

Murdoch, John. 1892. *Ethnological Results of the Point Barrow Expedition. Ninth Annual Report for 1887–1888*. Washington, DC: Smithsonian Institution, Bureau of American Ethnology.

Nami, Hugo G. 2009. "Crystal Quartz and Fishtail Projectile Points: Considerations on Raw-Material Selection by Paleo South Americans." *Current Research in the Pleistocene* 26:9–12.

Nansen, Fridtjof. 1892. *The First Crossing of Greenland, Translated from the Norwegian by Hubert Majendie Ge*. London: Longmans, Green, and Company.

Nash, David J., Sheila Coulson, Sigrid Staurset, J. Stewart Ullyott, Mosarwa Babutsi, Laurence Hopkinson, and Martin P. Smith. 2013. "Provenancing of Silcrete Raw Materials Indicates Long-Distance Transport to Tsodilo Hills, Botswana, during the Middle Stone Age." *Journal of Human Evolution* 64 (4): 280–88. https://doi.org/10.1016/j.jhevol.2013.01.010.

Nelson, Margaret C. 1991. "The Study of Technological Organization." In *Archaeological Method and Theory*, vol. 3, ed. Michael B. Schiffer, 57–100. Tucson: University of Arizona Press.

Neumann, C. 1971. "A Note on Alexander's March-Rates." *Historia. Einzelschriften* 20 (2–3): 196–98.

Neuwinger, Hans Dieter. 1996. *African Ethnobotany: Poisons and Drugs—Chemistry, Pharmacology, Toxicology. Translated by Aileen Porter.* Weinheim, Germany: Chapman and Hall GmbH.

Newlander, Khori S. 2012. "Exchange, Embedded Procurement, and Hunter-Gatherer Mobility: A Case Study from the North American Great Basin." PhD dissertation, Department of Anthropology, University of Michigan, Ann Arbor, MI.

Newlander, Khori S. 2015. "Beyond Obsidian: Documenting the Conveyance of Fine-Grained Volcanics and Cherts in the North American Great Basin." *PaleoAmerica* 1 (1): 123–26. https://doi.org/10.1179/2055556314Z.0000000007.

Newman, Jay R. 1994. "The Effects of Distance on Lithic Material Reduction Technology." *Journal of Field Archaeology* 21 (4): 491–501.

Newman, Kim, and Mark W. Moore. 2013. "Ballistically Anomalous Stone Projectile Points in Australia." *Journal of Archaeological Science* 40 (6): 2614–20. https://doi.org/10.1016/j.jas.2013.01.023.

Nieuwenhuis, Channah Jose. 1998. "Unattractive but Effective: Unretouched Pointed Flakes as Projectile Points? A Closer Look at the Abriense and Tequendamiense Artifacts." In *Explorations in American Archaeology: Essays in Honor of Wesley R. Hurt*, ed. Mark G. Plew, 133–63. Lanham, MD: University Press of America.

Oakes, Jill. 1992. "Comparison of Factors Influencing Caribou and Copper Inuit Skin Clothing." *Dress* 19 (1): 47–56. https://doi.org/10.1179/036121192805298391.

O'Brien, Christopher J. 1994. "Determining Seasonality and Age in East African Archaeological Faunas: An Ethnoarchaeological Application of Cementum Increment Analysis." PhD dissertation, Department of Anthropology, University of Wisconsin, Madison, WI.

O'Connell, James F. 2011. "Remembering Lew Binford." *Mitteilungen der Gesellschaft für Urgeschichte* 20:79–89.

O'Connell, James F., and Jim Allen. 2004. "Dating the Colonization of Sahul (Pleistocene Australia–New Guinea): A Review of Recent Research." *Journal of Archaeological Science* 31 (6): 835–53. https://doi.org/10.1016/j.jas.2003.11.005.

O'Connell, James F., Kristen Hawkes, and Nicholas G. Blurton Jones. 1992. "Patterns in the Distribution, Site Structure and Assemblage Composition of Hadza Kill-Butchering Sites." *Journal of Archaeological Science* 19 (3): 319–45. https://doi.org/10.1016/0305-4403(92)90020-4.

O'Connell, James F., Kristen Hawkes, Karen D. Lupo, and Nicholas G. Blurton Jones. 2002. "Male Strategies and Plio-Pleistocene Archaeology." *Journal of Human Evolution* 43 (6): 831–72. https://doi.org/10.1006/jhev.2002.0604.

O'Connor, Sue, Gail Robertson, and Ken P. Aplin. 2014. "Are Osseous Artefacts a Window to Perishable Material Culture? Implications of an Unusually Complex Bone Tool from the Late Pleistocene of East Timor." *Journal of Human Evolution* 67:108–19. https://doi.org/10.1016/j.jhevol.2013.12.002.

O'Dea, Kerin. 1991. ""Traditional Diet and Food Preferences of Australian Aboriginal Hunter-Gatherers." *Philosophical Transactions of the Royal Society of London. Series B, Biological Sciences* 334 (1270): 233–41. https://doi.org/10.1098/rstb.1991.0112.

Oliver, Symmes C. 1962. *Ecology and Cultural Continuity as Contributing Factors in the Social Organization of the Plains Indians.* University of California Publications in American Archaeology and Ethnology 48:1–90. Berkeley: University of California.

Orr, Rob M. 2010. "The History of the Soldier's Load." *Australian Army Journal* 7 (2): 67–88.

Osborn, Alan J. 2014. "Eye of the Needle: Cold Stress, Clothing, and Sewing Technology during the Younger Dryas Cold Event in North America." *American Antiquity* 79 (1): 45–68. https://doi.org/10.7183/0002-7316.79.1.45.

Osgood, Cornelius B. 1936. *Contributions to the Ethnography of the Kutchin. Yale University Publications in Anthropology 14.* New Haven, CT: Yale University.

Oswalt, Wendell H. 1976. *An Anthropological Analysis of Food-Getting Technology.* New York: John Wiley.

Palliser, John. 1863. *The Journals, Detailed Reports, and Observations Relative to the Exploration, by Captain Palliser, of that Portion of British North America, which in Latitude, Lies between the British Boundary Line and the Height of Land or Watershed of the Northern or Frozen Ocean Respectively, and in Longitude, between the Western Shore of Lake Superior and the Pacific Ocean, during the Years 1857, 1858, 1859, and 1860. Presented to Both Houses of Parliament by Command of Her Majesty, 19th May, 1863.* London: Printed by George Edward Eyre and William Spottiswoode for Her Majesty's Stationery Office.

Pasda, Kerstin, and Ulla Odgaard. 2011. "Nothing Is Wasted: The Ideal 'Nothing Is Wasted' and Divergence in Past and Present among Caribou Hunters in Greenland." *Quaternary International* 238 (1–2): 35–43. https://doi.org/10.1016/j.quaint.2010.12.036.

Paton, Robert. 1994. "Speaking through Stones: A Study from Northern Australia." *World Archaeology* 26 (2): 172–84. https://doi.org/10.1080/00438243.1994.9980271.

Pawlik, Alfred F. 2012. "Behavioural Complexity and Modern Traits in the Philippine Upper Palaeolithic." *Asian Perspective* 51 (1): 22–46. https://doi.org/10.1353/asi.2012.0004.

Peck, Trevor R. 2011. *Light from Ancient Campfires: Archaeological Evidence for Native Lifeways on the Northern Plains.* Edmonton, AB: Athabasca University Press.

Peresani, Marco. 2003. "An Initial Overview on the Middle Palaeolithic Discoid Industries in Central-Northern Italy." In *Discoid Lithic Technology: Advances and Implications,* ed. Marco Peresani, 209–23. BAR International Series S1120. Oxford: Archaeopress.

Perry, Richard J. 1979. "The Fur Trade and the Status of Women in the Western Subarctic." *Ethnohistory (Columbus, Ohio)* 26 (4): 363–75. https://doi.org/10.2307/481366.

Peters, Robert H. 1986. *The Ecological Implications of Body Size.* Cambridge: Cambridge University Press.

Peterson, Nicolas, and Ronald Lampert. 1985. "A Central Australian Ochre Mine." *Records of the Australian Museum* 37 (1): 1–9. https://doi.org/10.3853/j.0067-1975.37.1985.333.

Pettitt, Paul B. 2003. "The Mousterian in Action: Chronology, Mobility, and Middle Palaeolithic Variability." In *Lithic Analysis at the Millennium,* ed. Norah Moloney and Michael J. Shott, 29–44. London: University College London, Institute of Archaeology.

Picin, Andrea, and Eudald Carbonell. 2016. "Neanderthal Mobility and Technological Change in the Northeastern of the Iberian Peninsula: The Patterns of Chert Exploitation at the Abric Romaní Rock-Shelter." *Comptes Rendus. Palévol* 15 (5): 581–94. https://doi.org/10.1016/j.crpv.2015.09.012.

Picin, Andrea, and Manuel Vaquero. 2016. "Flake Productivity in the Levallois Recurrent Centripetal and Discoid Technologies: New Insights from Experimental and Archaeological Lithic Series." *Journal of Archaeological Science: Reports* 8:70–81. https://doi.org/10.1016/j.jasrep.2016.05.062.

Pickering, Travis R., and Henry T. Bunn. 2012. "Meat Foraging by Pleistocene African Hominins: Tracking Behavioral Evolution beyond Baseline Inferences of Early Access to Carcasses." In *Stone Tools and Fossil Bones: Debates in the Archaeology of Human Origins,* ed. Manuel Domínguez-Rodrigo, 152–73.

Cambridge: Cambridge University Press. https://doi.org/10.1017/CBO9781139
149327.007.

Politis, Gustavo G., Luciano Prates, and S. Ivan Perez. 2015. "Early Asiatic Migration
to the Americas: A View from South America." In *Mobility and Ancient Society
in Asia and the Americas*, ed. Michael D. Frachetti and Robert N. Spengler, 89–102.
Cham, Switzerland: Springer. https://doi.org/10.1007/978-3-319-15138-0_7.

Pollard, Helen P. 1987. "The Political Economy of Prehispanic Tarascan Metallurgy."
American Antiquity 52 (4): 741–52. https://doi.org/10.2307/281382.

Pontzer, Herman, David A. Raichlen, Brian M. Wood, Melissa Emery Thompson,
Susan B. Racette, Audax Z. P. Mabulla, and Frank W. Marlowe. 2015. "Energy
Expenditure and Activity among Hadza Hunter-Gatherers." *American Journal of
Human Biology* 27 (5): 628–37. https://doi.org/10.1002/ajhb.22711.

Power, Robert C., Domingo C. Salazar-García, Lawrence G. Straus, Manuel R.
González Morales, and Amanda G. Henry. 2015. "Microremains from El Mirón
Cave Human Dental Calculus Suggest a Mixed Plant-Animal Subsistence
Economy during the Magdalenian in Northern Iberia." *Journal of Archaeological
Science* 60:39–46. https://doi.org/10.1016/j.jas.2015.04.003.

Prasciunas, Mary M. 2007. "Bifacial Cores and Flake Production Efficiency: An
Experimental Test of Technological Assumptions." *American Antiquity* 72 (02):
334–48. https://doi.org/10.2307/40035817.

Pruetz, Jill D., and Paco Bertolani. 2007. "Savanna Chimpanzees, *Pan troglodytes
verus*, Hunt with Tools." *Current Biology* 17 (5): 412–17. https://doi.org/10.1016/j
.cub.2006.12.042.

Pryor, Alexander J. E., Madeline Steele, Martin K. Jones, Jiří Svoboda, and David G.
Beresford-Jones. 2013. "Plant Foods in the Upper Palaeolithic at Dolní Věstonice?
Parenchyma Redux." *Antiquity* 87 (338): 971–84. https://doi.org/10.1017/S0003598
X00049802.

Rabett, Ryan J. 2011. "Techno-Modes, Techno-Facies and Palaeo-Cultures: Change
and Continuity in the Pleistocene of Southeast, Central and North Asia." In
Investigating Archaeological Cultures: Material Culture, Variability, and Transmission,
ed. Benjamin W. Roberts and Marc Vander Linden, 97–135. New York: Springer.
https://doi.org/10.1007/978-1-4419-6970-5_6.

Ramanzin, Maurizio, Andrea Amici, Carmen Casoli, Luigi Esposito, Paola Lupi,
Giuseppe Marsico, Silvana Mattiello, Oliviero Olivieri, Maria Paola Ponzetta,
Claudia Russo, et al. 2010. "Meat from Wild Ungulates: Ensuring Quality and
Hygiene of an Increasing Resource." *Italian Journal of Animal Science* 9 (3): 318–31.

Rasmussen, Knud. 1931. *The Netsilik Eskimos: Social Life and Spiritual Culture*. Report
of the Fifth Thule Expedition, 1921–24. The Danish Expedition to Arctic North

America in Charge of Knud Rasmussen 8(1–2). Copenhagen: Gyldendalske Boghandel, Nordisk Forlag.

Rasmussen, Morten, Sarah L. Anzick, Michael R. Waters, Pontus Skoglund, Michael DeGiorgio, Thomas W. Stafford, Simon Rasmussen, Ida Moltke, Anders Albrechtsen, Shane M. Doyle, et al. 2014. "The Genome of a Late Pleistocene Human from a Clovis Burial Site in Western Montana." *Nature* 506 (7487): 225–29. https://doi.org/10.1038/nature13025.

Ray, Arthur J. 1984. "The Northern Great Plains: Pantry of the Northwestern Fur Trade, 1774–1885." *Prairie Forum* 9 (2): 263–80.

Reher, Charles A., and George C. Frison. 1991. "Rarity, Clarity, Symmetry: Quartz Crystal Utilization in Hunter-Gatherer Stone Tool Assemblages." In *Raw Material Economies among Prehistoric Hunter-Gatherers*, ed. Anta Montet-White and Steven R. Holen, 375–97. Publications in Anthropology 19. Lawrence: University of Kansas.

Rendu, William, and Dominique Armand. 2009. "Saisonnalité de prédation du bison du gisement Moustérien de la Quina (Gardes-le-Pontaroux, Charente), Niveau 6c: Apport à la compréhension des comportements de subsistance." *Bulletin de la Société Préhistorique Française* 106 (4): 679–90. https://doi.org/10.3406/bspf .2009.13890.

Rendu, William, Laurence Bourguignon, Sandrine Costamagno, Liliane Meignen, Marie-Cécile Soulier, Dominique Armand, Cédric Beauval, Francine David, Christophe Griggo, Jacques Jaubert, Bruno Maureille, and Seong-Jin Park. 2011. "Mousterian Hunting Camps: Interdisciplinary Approach and Methodological Considerations." In *Hunting Camps in Prehistory: Current Archaeological Approaches*, ed. François Bon, Sandrine Costamagno, and Nicolas Valdeyron, 61–76. P@lethnologie 3. Laboratoire Travaux et Recherches Archéologiques sur les Cultures, les Espaces et les Sociétés (TRACES). Proceedings of the International Symposium, May 13–15, 2009. Toulouse, France: University Toulouse II-Le Mirail.

Rendu, William, Sandrine Costamagno, Liliane Meignen, and Marie-Cécile Soulier. 2012. "Monospecific Faunal Spectra in Mousterian Contexts: Implications for Social Behavior." *Quaternary International* 247:50–58. https://doi.org/10.1016/j .quaint.2011.01.022.

Revedin, Anna, Biancamaria Aranguren, Roberto Becattini, Laura Longo, Emanuele Marconi, Marta Mariotti Lippi, Natalia Skakun, Andrey Sinitsyn, Elena Spiridonova, and Jiří Svoboda. 2010. "30,000 Year Old Flour: New Evidence of Plant Food Processing in the Upper Paleolithic." *Proceedings of the National Academy of Sciences of the United States of America* 107 (44): 18815–19. https://doi .org/10.1073/pnas.1006993107.

Revedin, Anna, Laura Longo, Marta Mariotti Lippi, Emanuele Marconi, Annamaria Ronchitelli, Jiří Svoboda, Eva Anichini, Matilde Gennai, and Biancamaria Aranguren. 2015. "New Technologies for Plant Food Processing in the Gravettian." *Quaternary International* 359–60:77–88. https://doi.org/10.1016/j.quaint.2014.09.066.

Rich, Edwin E., ed. 1949. *James Isham's Observations on Hudsons Bay, 1743 and Notes and Observations on a Book Entitled A Voyage to Hudsons Bay in the Dobbs Galley, 1749. Publications of the Champlain Society, Hudson's Bay Company Series 12.* Toronto: The Champlain Society.

Richardson, John. 1829. *Fauna Boreali Americana or the Zoology of the Northern Parts of British America.* London: John Murray.

Richter, Daniel, and Matthias Krbetschek. 2015. "The Age of the Lower Palaeolithic Occupation at Schöningen." *Journal of Human Evolution* 89:46–56. https://doi.org/10.1016/j.jhevol.2015.06.003.

Richter, Jürgen. 2008–9. "The Role of Leaf Points in the Late Middle Palaeolithic of Germany." *Praehistoria* 9–10:99–113.

Rieder, Hermann. 2000. "Die Altpaläolithischen Wurfspeere von Schöningen, ihre Erprobung und ihre Bedeutung für die Lebensumwelt des *Homo erectus.*" *Praehistoria Thuringica* 5:68–75.

Rieder, Hermann. 2003. "Der Große Wurf der Frühen Jäger: Nachbau Altsteinzeitlicher Speere." *Biologie in Unserer Zeit* 33 (3): 156–60. https://doi.org/10.1002/biuz.200390058.

Rightmire, G. Philip. 1998. "Human Evolution in the Middle Pleistocene: The Role of *Homo heidelbergensis.*" *Evolutionary Anthropology* 6 (6): 218–27. https://doi.org/10.1002/(SICI)1520-6505(1998)6:6<218::AID-EVAN4>3.0.CO;2-6.

Roberts, Mark B. 1997. "Boxgrove: Palaeolithic Hunters by the Seashore." *Archaeology International* 1:8–13. https://doi.org/10.5334/ai.0104.

Robinson, Brian S., and Jennifer C. Ort. 2011. "Paleoindian and Archaic Period Traditions: Particular Explanations from New England." In *Hunter-Gatherer Archaeology as Historical Process*, ed. Kenneth E. Sassaman and Donald H. Holly, Jr., 209–26. Tucson: University of Arizona Press.

Robinson, Henry M. 1879. *The Great Fur Land, or, Sketches of Life in the Hudson's Bay Territory.* London: Sampson Low, Marston, Searle, and Rivington.

Rodríguez-Hidalgo, Antonio. 2015. *Dinámicas subsistenciales durante el pleistoceno medio en la Sierra de Atapuerca: Los conjuntos arqueológicos de TD10.1 y TD10.2.* Tarragona, Spain: Tesis Doctoral, Departamento de Historia e Historia del Arte, Universitat Rovira i Virgili.

Roper, Donna C. 1989. "Red Ochre Use on the Plains during the Paleoindian Period." *Mammoth Trumpet* 5 (3):1, 6.

Ross, Anne, Bob Anderson, and Cliff Campbell. 2003. "Gunumbah: Archaeological and Aboriginal Meanings at a Quarry Site on Moreton Island, Southeast Queensland." *Australian Archaeology* 57 (1): 75–81. https://doi.org/10.1080/03122417.2003.11681764.

Rots, Veerle. 2009. "The Functional Analysis of the Mousterian and Micoquian Assemblages of Sesselfelsgrotte, Germany: Aspects of Tool Use and Hafting in the European Late Middle Palaeolithic." *Quartär* 56:37–66.

Rots, Veerle. 2013. "Insights into Early Middle Palaeolithic Tool Use and Hafting in Western Europe: The Functional Analysis of Level IIa of the Early Middle Palaeolithic Site of Biache-Saint-Vaast (France)." *Journal of Archaeological Science* 40 (1): 497–506. https://doi.org/10.1016/j.jas.2012.06.042.

Rots, Veerle. 2016. "Projectiles and Hafting Technology." In *Multidisciplinary Approaches to the Study of Stone Age Weaponry*, ed. Radu Iovita and Katsuhiro Sano, 167–85. Dordrecht, Netherlands: Springer.

Rots, Veerle, and Hugues Plisson. 2014. "Projectiles and the Abuse of the Use-Wear Method in a Search for Impact." *Journal of Archaeological Science* 48:154–65. https://doi.org/10.1016/j.jas.2013.10.027.

Ruff, Christopher B. 1987. "Sexual Dimorphism in Human Lower Limb Bone Structure: Relationship to Subsistence Strategy and Sexual Division of Labor." *Journal of Human Evolution* 16 (5): 391–416. https://doi.org/10.1016/0047-2484(87)90069-8.

Ruff, Christopher B. 2005. "Mechanical Determinants of Bone Form: Insights from Skeletal Remains." *Journal of Musculoskeletal and Neuronal Interactions* 5 (3): 202–12.

Rule, Daniel C., K. Shane Broughton, Sarah M. Shellito, and Giuseppe Maiorano. 2002. "Comparison of Muscle Fatty Acid Profiles and Cholesterol Concentrations of Bison, Beef Cattle, Elk, and Chicken." *Journal of Animal Science* 80 (5): 1202–11. https://doi.org/10.2527/2002.8051202x.

Ruth, Susan. 2013. "Women's Toolkits: Engendering Paleoindian Technological Organization." PhD dissertation, Department of Anthropology, University of New Mexico, Albuquerque, NM.

Sabin, Philip, Hans van Wees, and Michael Whitby, eds. 2007a. *Rome from the Late Republic to the Late Empire*. Vol. 2. The Cambridge History of Greek and Roman Warfare. Cambridge: Cambridge University Press.

Sabin, Philip, Hans van Wees, and Michael Whitby, eds. 2007b. *Greece, the Hellenistic World and the Rise of Rome*. Vol. A. The Cambridge History of Greek and Roman Warfare. Cambridge: Cambridge University Press.

Saladié, Palmira, Rosa Huguet, Carlos Díez, Antonio Rodríguez-Hidalgo, Isabel Cáceres, Josep Vallverdú, Jordi Rosell, José María Bermúdez de Castro, and Eudald Carbonell. 2011. "Carcass Transport Decisions in *Homo antecessor*

Subsistence Strategies." *Journal of Human Evolution* 61 (4): 425–46. https://doi.org
/10.1016/j.jhevol.2011.05.012.

Salazar, Diego, Donald Jackson, Jean Louis Guendon, Hernán Salinas, Diego
Morata, Valentina Figueroa, Germán Manríquez, and Victoria Castro. 2011. "Early
Evidence (ca. 12,000 BP) for Iron Oxide Mining on the Pacific Coast of South
America." *Current Anthropology* 52 (3): 463–75. https://doi.org/10.1086/659426.

Sánchez, Miguel Cortés, Juan F. Gibaja Bao, and María D. Simón Vallejo. 2011.
"Level 14 of Bajondillo Cave and the End of the Middle Paleolithic in the South
of the Iberian Peninsula." In *Neanderthal Lifeways, Subsistence and Technology:
One Hundred Fifty Years of Neanderthal Study*, ed. Nicholas J. Conard and Jürgen
Richter, 241–47. New York: Springer. https://doi.org/10.1007/978-94-007-0415-2_20.

Savelle, James M., and Arthur S. Dyke. 2014. "Prehistoric Neoeskimo Komatiks,
Victoria Island, Arctic Canada." *Arctic* 67 (2): 135–42. https://doi.org/10.14430
/arctic4383.

Savishinsky, Joel S. 1975. "The Dog and the Hare: Canine Culture in an Athapaskan
Band." In *Proceedings: Northern Athapaskan Conference, 1971*, vol. 2, ed. A. McFadyen
Clark, 462–515. National Museum of Man, Mercury Series, Canadian Ethnology
Service Paper No. 27. Ottawa, ON: National Museums of Canada.

Schelinski, Vyacheslav E. 1993. "Outils pour travailler le bois et l'os au paléolithique
inférieur et moyen de la Plaine Russe et du Caucase." In *Traces et fonction: Le
geste retrouvé*, ed. Patricia C. Anderson, Sylvie Beyries, Marcel Otte, and Hugues
Plisson, 309–16. Études et Recherches Archéologiques de l'Université de Liège
(ERAUL) 50. Liège, Belgium: Université de Liège.

Schoch, Werner H., Gerlinde Bigga, Utz Böhner, Pascale Richter, and Thomas
Terberger. 2015. "New Insights on the Wooden Weapons from the Paleolithic Site
of Schöningen." *Journal of Human Evolution* 89:214–25. https://doi.org/10.1016/j
.jhevol.2015.08.004.

Schoeninger, Margaret J. 1995. "Stable Isotope Studies in Human Evolution."
Evolutionary Anthropology 4 (3): 83–98. https://doi.org/10.1002/evan.1360040305.

Schoeninger, Margaret J. 2014. "Stable Isotope Analyses and the Evolution of
Human Diets." *Annual Review of Anthropology* 43 (1): 413–30. https://doi.org/10
.1146/annurev-anthro-102313-025935.

Schulz, Aurel, and August Hammar. 1897. *The New Africa: A Journey Up the Chobe and
Down the Okovango Rivers—A Record of Exploration and Sport*. London: William
Heinemann.

Secoy, Frank R. 1953. *Changing Military Patterns on the Great Plains: 17th Century
Through Early 19th Century. Monographs of the American Ethnological Society 21*.
Seattle: University of Washington Press.

Seeman, Mark F. 1994. "Intercluster Lithic Patterning at Nobles Pond: A Case for 'Disembedded' Procurement among Early Paleoindian Societies." *American Antiquity* 59 (2): 273–88. https://doi.org/10.2307/281932.

Sellards, Elias H., Glen L. Evans, and Grayson E. Meade. 1947. "Fossil Bison and Associated Artifacts from Plainview, Texas." *Bulletin of the Geological Society of America* 58 (10): 927–64. https://doi.org/10.1130/0016-7606(1947)58[927:FBAAAF]2.0.CO;2.

Serangeli, Jordi, and Utz Böhner. 2012. "Die Artefakte von Schöningen und ihre Zeitliche Einordnung." In *Die Chronologische Einordnung Der Paläolithischen Fundstellen Von Schöningen*, ed. Karl-Ernst Behre, 23–37. Mainz, Germany: Römisch-Germanischen Zentralmuseums.

Sharp, Henry S. 1976. "Man: Wolf: Woman: Dog." *Arctic Anthropology* 13 (1): 25–34.

Sharp, Henry S., and Karyn Sharp. 2015. *Hunting Caribou: Subsistence Hunting along the Northern Edge of the Boreal Forest*. Lincoln: University of Nebraska Press.

Shea, John J. 1988. "Spear Points from the Middle Paleolithic of the Levant." *Journal of Field Archaeology* 15 (4): 441–50.

Shea, John J. 2006. "The Origins of Lithic Projectile Point Technology: Evidence from Africa, the Levant, and Europe." *Journal of Archaeological Science* 33 (6): 823–46. https://doi.org/10.1016/j.jas.2005.10.015.

Sheppard, William L. 2004. "The Significance of Dog Traction for the Analysis of Prehistoric Arctic Societies." *Alaska Journal of Anthropology* 2 (1–2): 70–82.

Shipton, Ceri, and Michael D. Petraglia. 2010. "Inter-Continental Variation in Acheulean Bifaces." In *Asian Paleoanthropology: From Africa to China and Beyond*, ed. Christopher J. Norton and David R. Braun, 49–55. Dordrecht, Netherlands: Springer.

Shott, Michael J. 1986. "Technological Organization and Settlement Mobility: An Ethnographic Examination." *Journal of Anthropological Research* 42 (1): 15–51. https://doi.org/10.1086/jar.42.1.3630378.

Smith, Eric A. 1985. "Inuit Foraging Groups: Some Simple Models Incorporating Conflicts of Interest, Relatedness, and Central-Place Sharing." *Ethology and Sociobiology* 6 (1): 27–47. https://doi.org/10.1016/0162-3095(85)90039-1.

Smith, Geoff M. 2002. "Investigating Wooden Spear Damage on Faunal Remains." BSc dissertation, Archaeology (General), University College London, Institute of Archaeology, London.

Smith, Geoff M. 2003. "Damage Inflicted on Animal Bone by Wooden Projectiles: Experimental Results and Archaeological Implications." *Journal of Taphonomy* 1 (2): 105–14.

Smith, Geoff M. 2013. "Taphonomic Resolution and Hominin Subsistence Behaviour in the Lower Palaeolithic: Differing Data Scales and Interpretive

Frameworks at Boxgrove and Swanscombe (UK)." *Journal of Archaeological Science* 40 (10): 3754–67. https://doi.org/10.1016/j.jas.2013.05.002.

Smith, Geoffrey M., Alexander Cherkinsky, Carla Hadden, and Aaron P. Ollivier. 2016. "The Age and Origin of Olivella Beads from Oregon's LSP-1 Rockshelter: The Oldest Marine Shell Beads in the Northern Great Basin." *American Antiquity* 81 (3): 550–61.

Smith, Mike A. 2013. *The Archaeology of Australia's Deserts.* Cambridge: Cambridge University Press. https://doi.org/10.1017/CBO9781139023016.

Smyth, Robert Brough. 1878. *The Aborigines of Victoria: With Notes Relating to the Habits of the Natives of Other Parts of Australia and Tasmania.* Vol. 1. London: John Ferres.

Sober, Elliott. 2015. *Ockham's Razors: A User's Manual.* Cambridge: Cambridge University Press. https://doi.org/10.1017/CBO9781107705937.

Soffer, Olga. 2009. "Defining Modernity, Establishing Rubicons, Imagining the Other—and the Neanderthal Enigma." In *Sourcebook of Paleolithic Transitions: Methods, Theories, and Interpretations,* ed. Marta Camps and Parth R. Chauhan, 43–64. New York: Springer. https://doi.org/10.1007/978-0-387-76487-0_3.

Solecki, Rose L. 1992. "More on Hafted Projectile Points in the Mousterian." *Journal of Field Archaeology* 19 (2): 207–12.

Song, Yanhua, Xiaorong Li, Xiaohong Wu, Eliso Kvavadze, Paul Goldberg, and Ofer Bar-Yosef. 2016. "Bone Needle Fragment in LGM from the Shizitan Site (China): Archaeological Evidence and Experimental Study." *Quaternary International* 400:140–48. https://doi.org/10.1016/j.quaint.2015.06.051.

Soressi, Marie, and Jean-Michel Geneste. 2011. "The History and Efficacy of the Chaîne Opératoire Approach to Lithic Analysis: Studying Techniques to Reveal Past Societies in an Evolutionary Perspective." *PaleoAnthropology* 2011:334–50.

Speth, John D. 2010. *The Paleoanthropology and Archaeology of Big-Game Hunting: Protein, Fat or Politics?* New York: Springer. https://doi.org/10.1007/978-1-4419-6733-6.

Speth, John D. 2015. "When Did Humans Learn to Boil?" *PaleoAnthropology* 2015:54–67.

Speth, John D., and Khori Newlander. 2012. "Plains-Pueblo Interaction: A View from the 'Middle." In *The Toyah Phase of Central Texas: Late Prehistoric Economic and Social Processes,* ed. Nancy A. Kenmotsu and Douglas K. Boyd, 152–80. College Station: Texas A&M University Press.

Speth, John D., Khori Newlander, Andrew A. White, Ashley K. Lemke, and Lars E. Anderson. 2013. "Early Paleoindian Big-Game Hunting in North America: Provisioning or Politics?" *Quaternary International* 285:111–39. https://doi.org/10.1016/j.quaint.2010.10.027.

Speth, John D., and Susan L. Scott. 1989. "Horticulture and Large-Mammal Hunting: The Role of Resource Depletion and the Constraints of Time and

Labor." In *Farmers as Hunters*, ed. Susan Kent, 71–79. New York: Cambridge University Press.

Speth, John D., and Katherine A. Spielmann. 1983. "Energy Source, Protein Metabolism, and Hunter-Gatherer Subsistence Strategies." *Journal of Anthropological Archaeology* 2 (1): 1–31. https://doi.org/10.1016/0278-4165(83)90006-5.

Speth, John D., and Laura Staro. 2012. "Bison Hunting and the Emergence of Plains-Pueblo Interaction in Southeastern New Mexico: The View from Rocky Arroyo and Its Neighbors." *Artifact* 50:1–44.

Spielmann, Katherine A. 1983. "Late Prehistoric Exchange between the Southwest and Southern Plains." *Plains Anthropologist* 28 (102, Part 1): 257–72.

Spielmann, Katherine A. 2002. "Feasting, Craft Specialization, and the Ritual Mode of Production in Small-Scale Societies." *American Anthropologist* 104 (1): 195–207. https://doi.org/10.1525/aa.2002.104.1.195.

Spiess, Arthur E., and Deborah B. Wilson. 1989. "Paleoindian Lithic Distribution in the New England-Maritimes Region." In *Eastern Paleoindian Lithic Resource Use*, ed. Christopher J. Ellis and Jonathan C. Lothrop, 75–97. Boulder, CO: Westview Press.

Stafford, Michael D., George C. Frison, Dennis Stanford, and George Zeimans. 2003. "Digging for the Color of Life: Paleoindian Red Ochre Mining at the Powars II Site, Platte County, Wyoming, U.S.A." *Geoarchaeology: An International Journal* 18 (1): 71–90. https://doi.org/10.1002/gea.10051.

Stanford, Craig B. 2001. "A Comparison of Social Meat-Foraging by Chimpanzees and Human Foragers." In *Meat-Eating and Human Evolution*, ed. Craig B. Stanford and Henry T. Bunn, 122–40. Oxford: Oxford University Press.

Starks, Zona Spray. 2011. "Drying and Fermenting in the Arctic: Dictating Women's Roles in Alaska's Inupiat Culture." In *Cured, Fermented, and Smoked Foods: Proceedings of the Oxford Symposium on Food and Cookery 2010*, ed. Helen Saberi, 302–11. Totnes, England: Prospect Books.

Steegmann, A. Theodore, ed. 1983. *Boreal Forest Adaptations: The Northern Algonkians*. New York: Plenum Press. https://doi.org/10.1007/978-1-4613-3649-5.

Stefansson, Vilhjalmur. 1944. *Arctic Manual*. New York: Macmillan.

Stefansson, Vilhjalmur. 1956. *The Fat of the Land: Enlarged edition of Not by Bread Alone*. New York: Macmillan.

Steguweit, Leif. 1999. "Die Recken von Schöningen: 400,000 Jahre mit dem Speer." *Mitteilungsblatt der Gesellschaft für Urgeschichte* 8:5–14.

Stenton, Douglas R. 1991a. "Caribou Population Dynamics and Thule Culture Adaptations on Southern Baffin Island, N.W.T." *Arctic Anthropology* 28 (2): 15–43.

Stenton, Douglas R. 1991b. "The Adaptive Significance of Caribou Winter Clothing for Arctic Hunter-Gatherers." *Inuit Studies* 15 (1): 3–28.

Storck, Peter L. 1997. *The Fisher Site: Archaeological, Geological and Paleobotanical Studies at an Early Paleo-Indian Site in Southern Ontario, Canada. Memoir 30*. Ann Arbor: University of Michigan, Museum of Anthropology.

Stout, Selatie E. 1921. "Training Soldiers for the Roman Legion." *Classical Journal* 16 (7): 423–31.

Taçon, Paul S. C. 1991. "The Power of Stone: Symbolic Aspects of Stone Use and Tool Development in Western Arnhem Land, Australia." *Antiquity* 65 (247): 192–207. https://doi.org/10.1017/S0003598X00079655.

Tankersley, Kenneth B. 1994. "The Effects of Stone and Technology on Fluted-Point Morphometry." *American Antiquity* 59 (3): 498–510. https://doi.org/10.2307/282462.

Tanner, Adrian. 1979. *Bringing Home Animals: Religious Ideology and Mode of Production of the Mistassini Cree Hunters*. New York: St. Martin's Press.

Thiébaut, Céline, Émilie Claud, Marianne Deschamps, Discamps Emmanuel, Marie-Cécile Soulier, Célimène Mussini, Sandrine Costamagno, William Rendu, Michel Brenet, David Colonge, et al. 2014. "Diversité des productions lithiques du Paléolithique Moyen Récent (OIS 4-OIS 3): Enquête sur le rôle des facteurs environnementaux, fonctionnels et culturels." In *Transitions, ruptures et continuité en préhistoire, Vol. 2: Paléolithique et mésolithique. Actes du XXVIIe Congrès Préhistorique de France, Bordeaux-Les Eyzies, 31 mai–5 juin 2010*, ed. Jacques Jaubert, Nathalie Fourment and Pascal Depaepe, 281–98. Paris: Société Préhistorique Française.

Thieme, Hartmut. 1997. "Lower Paleolithic Hunting Spears from Germany." *Nature* 385 (6619): 807–10. https://doi.org/10.1038/385807a0.

Thieme, Hartmut, and Stephan Veil. 1985. "Neue Untersuchungen zum Eemzeitlichen Elefanten-Jagdplatz Lehringen, Ldkr. Verden." (Neue Folge) *Die Kunde* 36:11–58.

Thomas, Julian. 1886. *Cannibals and Convicts: Notes of Personal Experiences in the Western Pacific*. London: Cassell.

Thompson, David. 1916. *David Thompson's Narrative of His Explorations in Western America, 1784–1812*. Ed. Joseph B. Tyrrell. Publications of the Champlain Society 12. Toronto, ON: Champlain Society.

Thoms, Alston V. 1977. "A Preliminary Projectile Point Typology for the Southern Portion of the Northern Rio Grande Region, New Mexico." MA thesis, Department of Anthropology, Texas Tech University, Lubbock, TX.

Todd, Lawrence C. 1987. "Analysis of Kill-Butchery Bonebeds and Interpretation of Paleoindian Hunting." In *The Evolution of Human Hunting*, ed. Matthew H. Nitecki and Doris V. Nitecki, 225–66. New York: Plenum Press. https://doi.org/10.1007/978-1-4684-8833-3_7.

Todd, Lawrence C., Jack L. Hofman, and C. Bertrand Schultz. 1990. "Seasonality of the Scottsbluff and Lipscomb Bison Bonebeds: Implications for Modeling Paleoindian Subsistence." *American Antiquity* 55 (4): 813–27. https://doi.org/10.2307/281252.

Tourtellot, Gair. 1978. "Getting What Comes Unnaturally: On the Energetics of Maya Trade." In *Papers on the Economy and Architecture of the Ancient Maya*, ed. Raymond V. Sidrys, 72–85. Monograph 8. Los Angeles: University of California–Los Angeles, Institute of Archaeology.

Turner, Lucien M. 1894. "Ethnology of the Ungava District, Hudson Bay Territory." In *Eleventh Annual Report of the Bureau of Ethnology to the Secretary of the Smithsonian Institution, 1889–1890*, 167–350. Washington, DC: Government Printing Office.

Turq, Alain, Jean-Philippe Faivre, Brad Gravina, and Laurence Bourguignon. 2017. "Building Models of Neanderthal Territories from Raw Material Transports in the Aquitaine Basin (Southwestern France)." *Quaternary International* 433 (Part B): 88–101.

Turq, Alain, Wil Roebroeks, Laurence Bourguignon, and Jean-Philippe Faivre. 2013. "The Fragmented Character of Middle Palaeolithic Stone Tool Technology." *Journal of Human Evolution* 65 (5): 641–55. https://doi.org/10.1016/j.jhevol.2013.07.014.

van Kolfschoten, Thijs. 2014. "The Palaeolithic Locality Schöningen (Germany): A Review of the Mammalian Record." *Quaternary International* 326–27:469–80. https://doi.org/10.1016/j.quaint.2013.11.006.

Verrey, Robert A. 1986. "Paleoindian Stone Tool Manufacture at the Thunderbird Site (44WR11)." PhD dissertation, Department of Anthropology, Catholic University of America, Washington, DC.

Vierra, Bradley J. 2013. "Archaic Foraging Technology and Land-Use in the Northern Rio Grande." In *From Mountain Top to Valley Bottom: Understanding Past Land Use in the Northern Rio Grande Valley, New Mexico*, ed. Bradley J. Vierra, 145–60. Salt Lake City: University of Utah Press.

Villa, Paola, and Michel Lenoir. 2006. "Hunting Weapons of the Middle Stone Age and the Middle Palaeolithic: Spear Points from Sibudu, Rose Cottage and Bouheben." *Southern African Humanities (Pietermaritzburg, South Africa)* 18 (1): 89–122.

Villa, Paola, and Sylvain Soriano. 2010. "Hunting Weapons of Neanderthals and Early Modern Humans in South Africa: Similarities and Differences." *Journal of Anthropological Research* 66 (1): 5–38. https://doi.org/10.3998/jar.0521004.0066.102.

Visser, Margaret. 1992. *The Rituals of Dinner: The Origins, Evolution, Eccentricities, and Meaning of Table Manners*. New York: HarperCollins.

Wachowich, Nancy. 2014. "Stitching Lives: A Family History of Making Caribou Skin Clothing in the Canadian Arctic." In *Making and Growing: Anthropological Studies of Organisms and Artefacts*, ed. Elizabeth Hallam and Tim Ingold, 127–46. Burlington, VT: Ashgate.

Waguespack, Nicole M., Todd A. Shrivel, Allen Decoyer, Alice Allow, Adam Savage, Jamie Hyndman, and Dan Tapster. 2009. "Making a Point: Wood- Versus Stone-Tipped Projectiles." *Antiquity* 83 (321): 786–800. https://doi.org/10.1017/S000 3598X00098999.

Walker, Christopher S., and Steven E. Churchill. 2014. "Territory Size in *Canis lupus*: Implications for Neandertal Mobility." In *Reconstructing Mobility: Environmental, Behavioral, and Morphological Determinants*, ed. Kristina J. Carlson and Damien Marche, 209–26. New York: Springer. https://doi.org/10.1007/978-1-4899 -7460-0_12.

Warriss, Paul D. 2000. *Meat Science: An Introductory Text*. New York: CABI Publishing.

Weedman, Kathryn J. 2005. "Gender and Stone Tools: An Ethnographic Study of the Kenos and Game Hide workers of Southern Ethiopia." In *Gender and Hide Production*, ed. Lisa Frink and Kathryn Weedman, 175–96. Walnut Creek, CA: AltaMira Press.

Weedman Arthur, Kathryn J. 2010. "Feminine Knowledge and Skill Reconsidered: Women and Flaked Stone Tools." *American Anthropologist* 112 (2): 228–43. https://doi.org/10.1111/j.1548-1433.2010.01222.x.

Weltfish, Gene. 1977. *The Lost Universe: Pawnee Life and Culture*. Lincoln: University of Nebraska Press.

Wendorf, Fred. 1968. "Site 117: A Nubian Final Palaeolithic Graveyard Near Jebel Sahaba, Sudan." In *The Prehistory of Nubia*, vol. 2, ed. Fred Wendorf, 954–95. Publications 5. Fort Burgwin, NM: Fort Burgwin Research Center; and Dallas: Southern Methodist University Press.

Wenzel, Stefan. 2002. "Leben im Wald—die Archäologie der Letzten Warmzeit vor 125000 Jahren." *Mitteilungen der Gesellschaft für Urgeschichte* 11:35–63.

Whallon, Robert E. 2006. "Social Networks and Information: Non-'Utilitarian' Mobility among Hunter-Gatherers." *Journal of Anthropological Archaeology* 25 (2): 259–70. https://doi.org/10.1016/j.jaa.2005.11.004.

Wheat, Joe Ben. 1972. *The Olsen-Chubbuck Site: A Paleo-Indian Bison Kill. American Antiquity 37(1, Part 2)*. *Memoir 26*. Washington, DC: Society for American Archaeology.

White, J. Peter. 1977. "Crude, Colourless and Unenterprising? Prehistorians and their Views on the Stone Age of Sunda and Sahul." In *Sunda and Sahul*, ed. Jim Allen, Jack Golson, and Rhys Jones, 13–30. New York: Academic Press.

White, Mark J. 2000. "The Clactonian Question: On the Interpretation of Core-and-Flake Assemblages in the British Lower Paleolithic." *Journal of World Prehistory* 14 (1): 1–63. https://doi.org/10.1023/A:1007874901792.

Wiessner, Polly. 1982. "Risk, Reciprocity and Social Influences on! Kung San Economics." In *Politics and History in Band Societies*, ed. Eleanor B. Leacock and Richard B. Lee, 61–84. Cambridge: Cambridge University Press.

Wiessner, Polly. 2002. "Hunting, Healing, and Hxaro Exchange: A Long-Term Perspective on! Kung (Ju/'hoansi) Large-Game Hunting." *Evolution and Human Behavior* 23 (6): 407–36. https://doi.org/10.1016/S1090-5138(02)00096-X.

Wilson, Gilbert L. 1914. *Goodbird the Indian: His Story*. New York: Fleming H. Revell.

Winterhalder, Bruce. 2001. "The Behavioural Ecology of Hunter Gatherers." In *Hunter-Gatherers: An Interdisciplinary Perspective*, ed. Catherine Panter-Brick, Robert H. Layton, and Peter Rowley-Conwy, 12–38. Biosocial Society Symposium Series 13. Cambridge: Cambridge University Press.

Wissler, Clark. 1920. *North American Indians of the Plains*. 2nd ed. Handbook Series 1. New York: American Museum of Natural History. https://doi.org/10.5962/bhl.title.68260.

Wobst, H. Martin. 1974. "Boundary Conditions for Paleolithic Social Systems: A Simulation Approach." *American Antiquity* 39 (2, Part 1): 147–78. https://doi.org/10.2307/279579.

Wood, Brian M., and Frank W. Marlowe. 2013. "Household and Kin Provisioning by Hadza Men." *Human Nature (Hawthorne, N.Y.)* 24 (3): 280–317. https://doi.org/10.1007/s12110-013-9173-0.

Wood, Brian M., and Frank W. Marlowe. 2014. "Toward a Reality-Based Understanding of Hadza Men's Work: A Response to Hawkes et al. (2014)." *Human Nature (Hawthorne, N.Y.)* 25 (4): 620–30. https://doi.org/10.1007/s12110-014-9218-z.

Wood, W. Raymond. 1974. "Northern Plains Village Cultures: Internal Stability and External Relationships." *Journal of Anthropological Research* 30 (1): 1–16. https://doi.org/10.1086/jar.30.1.3629916.

Woodburn, James. 1970. *Hunters and Gatherers: The Material Culture of the Nomadic Hadza*. London: British Museum.

Wrangham, Richard W., and Dale Peterson. 1996. *Demonic Males: Apes and the Origins of Human Violence*. Boston: Houghton Mifflin.

Wu, Xinzhi, and Yaming Cui. 2010. "On the Origin of Modern Humans in China." *Before Farming* 2010 (4): 1–6. https://doi.org/10.3828/bfarm.2010.4.6.

Xhauflair, Hermine, Alfred Pawlik, Claire Gaillard, Hubert Forestier, Timothy James Vitales, John Rey Callado, Danilo Tandang, Noel Amano, Dante Manipon, and Eusebio Dizon. 2016. "Characterisation of the Use-Wear Resulting from Bamboo

Working and its Importance to Address the Hypothesis of the Existence of a Bamboo Industry in Prehistoric Southeast Asia." *Quaternary International* 416:95–125. https://doi.org/10.1016/j.quaint.2015.11.007.

Yengoyan, Aram A. 1968. "Demography and Ecological Influences on Aboriginal Australian Marriage Sections." In *Man the Hunter*, ed. Richard B. Lee and Irven DeVore, 185–99. Chicago: Aldine.

Yengoyan, Aram A. 2004. "Anthropological History and the Study of Hunters and Gatherers: Cultural and Non-cultural." In *Hunter-Gatherers in History, Archaeology and Anthropology*, ed. Alan Barnard, 57–66. Oxford: Berg.

Zedeño, María Nieves. 2009. "Animating by Association: Index Objects and Relational Taxonomies." *Cambridge Archaeological Journal* 19 (3): 407–17. https://doi .org/10.1017/S0959774309000596.

Zedeño, Maria Nieves, Jesse A. M. Ballenger, and John R. Murray. 2014. "Landscape Engineering and Organizational Complexity among Late Prehistoric Bison Hunters of the Northwestern Plains." *Current Anthropology* 55 (1): 23–58. https://doi.org/10.1086/674535.

Zhang, Yue, Xing Gao, Shuwen Pei, Fuyou Chen, Dongwei Niu, Xin Xu, Shuangquan Zhang, and Huimin Wang. 2016. "The Bone Needles from Shuidonggou Locality 12 and Implications for Human Subsistence Behaviors in North China." *Quaternary International* 400:149–57. https://doi.org/10.1016/j.qu 285285 aint.2015.06.041.

Zilhão, João. 2010. "Neanderthals Are Us: Genes and Culture." *Radical Anthropology* 4:5–15.

Zilhão, João. 2015. "Lower and Middle Palaeolithic Mortuary Behaviours and the Origins of Ritual Burial." In *Death Rituals, Social Order and the Archaeology of Immortality in the Ancient World: "Death Shall Have No Dominion,"* ed. Colin Renfrew, Michael J. Boyd, and Iain Morley, 27–44. Cambridge: Cambridge University Press.

Zollikofer, Christoph P. E., Marcia S. Ponce de León, Bernard Vandermeersch, and François Lévêque. 2002. "Evidence for Interpersonal Violence in the St. Césaire Neanderthal." *Proceedings of the National Academy of Sciences of the United States of America* 99 (9): 6444–48. https://doi.org/10.1073/pnas.082111899.

Contributors

JANE BALME
Associate Professor, Archaeology, University of Western
Australia and Centre for Rock Art Research and
Management, Crawley, WA, Australia

LELAND C. BEMENT
Archaeologist, Oklahoma Archeological Survey,
University of Oklahoma, Norman, Oklahoma, USA

JONATHAN DRIVER
Vice-President, Academic and Provost, Archaeology,
Simon Fraser University, Burnaby, BC, Canada

KRISTEN CARLSON
Assistant Professor, Anthropology, Augustana University,
Sioux Falls, South Dakota, USA

ADAM C. GRAVES
Owner, GRAVitate, LLC, Grand Prairie, Texas, USA

DAVID MAXWELL
Lecturer, Archaeology, Simon Fraser University, Burnaby,
BC, Canada

ULLA ODGAARD
Researcher, National Museum of Denmark,
Copenhagen, Denmark

JOHN D. SPETH
    Professor Emeritus, Anthropology, University of Michigan, Ann Arbor, Michigan, USA

MARÍA NIEVES ZEDEÑO
    Professor, Anthropology, University of Arizona, Tucson, Arizona, USA

organization, 4, 5, 6, 8, 12, 17, 18, 19, 20, 23, 24, 27, 34, 44, 53, 54, 56, 57, 90, 136, 190, 230; geopolitical, 27; hunter-gatherer, 19; labor, 53, 57; of large-scale hunting, 4, 5, 6, 12, 54; logistical, 230; social, 12, 18, 136; technology, 190; territorial, 17, 20, 23, 27, 34

Palaeolithic: Final, 172; Lower, 167; Middle, 167; Upper, 167
Paleoindian, 12, 28, 123, 130, 131, 135, 139, 142, 146, 147, 148, 156, 161, 163, 164, 166, 168–81, 185–91, 201, 203, 204, 206, 210, 214, 217–19, 221–25, 227, 229–35
pemmican, 10, 25, 31, 32, 33, 182, 183, 197, 224, 226, 227
Pleistocene, 43, 55, 146, 164, 165, 166, 167, 168, 173, 185, 210, 211, 216
pounds, 4, 5, 7, 25, 137; impounding, 32. *See also* cliff; dunes; kites; lakes; river; snow drifts

reindeer, 10, 74, 80, 164, 202, 205, 211, 212, 213. *See also* caribou
rendezvous, 9, 223. *See also* aggregation(s); nucleation(s)
rites, 221
ritual(s), 4, 5, 7, 8, 12, 18, 20, 22, 27, 28, 30, 89, 115, 130, 131, 137, 168, 177, 179, 180, 181, 185, 205, 207, 221, 233; items of, 168, 233; knowledge, 27, 115; offerings, 177, 179; ritualistic, 20; ritualization, 30; spaces (wheels, effigies and vision quest sites), 30; spiritual, 131, 179, 180, 181, 186, 218
river, traps in, 163

scalar, 6, 8, 10

season(s), seasonal, seasonally, seasonality, 9, 10, 11, 32, 46, 47, 48, 56, 86, 89, 96–104, 107, 113, 114, 121, 122, 125, 127, 128, 129, 130, 132, 139, 143, 145, 146, 147, 186, 203, 205, 213, 234
snow drifts, traps in, 163
specialization/specialized/special, 8, 25, 28, 43, 56, 115, 137, 172, 173, 175, 181, 182, 185, 186, 187, 196, 202, 204, 205, 210, 216, 217, 229; nonspecialized, 42; special treatment of bones, 91; specialists, 186, 187, 229
surplus, 3, 4, 9, 10, 11, 25, 47, 137, 219, 227; alternative, 11; discovery of a beached whale, 10; sharing, 219; storing, 227. *See also* abundance(s); cache, meat cache
symbol(s), symbolic, symbolizes, 56, 81, 168, 173, 181, 184, 190, 210, 217, 218, 231, 232

taboo, 6
tallow, 71, 83, 200, 224. *See also* fat; grease; marrow
territory, 16–23, 25–27, 29, 31–34, 132, 165, 178, 186
trade, 21, 22, 25, 27, 33, 34, 54, 83, 115, 129, 130, 136, 170, 182, 183, 192, 196, 213, 216, 224, 227

wallabies, 50, 51, 54
warfare, 33, 165. *See also* conflict
waste, 64, 81, 84, 85, 86, 87, 88, 90, 91, 92, 188, 190, 223, 234
weir, 4, 47, 48, 51, 53, 54. *See also* fish, fishing
women, 4, 6, 44, 51, 64, 78, 79, 84, 186, 192, 193, 198–201, 206, 207, 208, 214, 215, 220, 233; Neanderthal women, 207; sewing, 214, 215; tool stone for, 186, 206
wife/wives, 183, 193, 197–200, 217, 233